Native Americans and the Environment

Native Americans and the Environment

Perspectives on the Ecological Indian

Edited and with an introduction by
Michael E. Harkin and David Rich Lewis

Foreword by Judith Antell
Preface by Brian Hosmer
Afterword by Shepard Krech III

UNIVERSITY OF NEBRASKA PRESS · LINCOLN AND LONDON

Chapter 5, "Rationality and Resource Use among Hunters," is based upon a previously published article by the same name in *Circumpolar Religion and Ecology: An Anthropology of the North*, ed. T. Irimoto and T. Yamada (Tokyo: University of Tokyo Press, 1994). ❡ Chapter 1, "*Beyond the Ecological Indian*," and Afterword © 2007 by Shepard Krech III; all else © 2007 by the Board of Regents of the University of Nebraska ❡ All rights reserved ❡ Manufactured in the United States of America ❡ ∞ ❡ Library of Congress Cataloging-in-Publication Data ❡ Native Americans and the environment : perspectives on the ecological Indian / edited and with an introduction by Michael E. Harkin and David Rich Lewis ; foreword by Judith Antell ; preface by Brian Hosmer ; afterword by Shepard Krech III.

p. cm.

Includes bibliographical references and index.

ISBN-13: 978-0-8032-7361-0 (pbk. : alk. paper)

ISBN-10: 0-8032-7361-4 (pbk. : alk. paper)

1. Indigenous peoples—Ecology—North America. 2. Indian philosophy—North America. 3. Philosophy of nature—North America. 4. Human-animal relationships—North America. I. Harkin, Michael Eugene, 1958– . II. Lewis, David Rich.

GF501.N37 2007

304.2089'97—dc22

2006020776

Set in Quadraat by Kim Essman. ❡ Designed by R. W. Boeche. ❡

Contents

Illustrations

Tables

Foreword

Judith Antell

When Michael Harkin, Brian Hosmer, and I discussed proposing the "Re-figuring the Ecological Indian" conference to the University of Wyoming's American Heritage Center for its tenth annual symposium (2002), we believed the topic of Native peoples and their relationships with the environment to be important for many reasons and deserving of serious consideration. Shepard Krech's recently published and controversial book, *The Ecological Indian: Myth and History*, contributed to the timeliness of the discussion, it seemed to us.

While these foundational thoughts for the "Re-figuring the Ecological Indian" conference were hardly provocative, action that followed, as plans for the conference evolved, proved to be. Specifically, Shepard Krech was invited to give a keynote address. I supported the address because I was interested in hearing his arguments and evidence presented before an audience that was in significant measure Native American. Also, I believed the question-and-answer session following his presentation would provide an opportunity for critical discussion, challenges to Krech's premises and positions, and a necessary opportunity for debate. I anticipated a "Krech Meets the Critics" encounter that would represent the best traditions of the academy. What I failed to anticipate was the interpretation by some that the conference's invitation to Krech was an endorsement of him and his writings. I should have known better, and when it happened I had no trouble understanding why. I wish my timing had been better and that I had thought ahead instead of understanding after.

Gratefully, tribal people from our campus community, from our region, and from across the United States and Canada did participate in the conference as presenters, moderators, panel discussants, and audience members. Also, Native persons honored us with prayer, song, and welcoming words. Members of the Blackfeet, Lakota, Comanche, Penobscot, Cree, Abenaki, Diné, Northern Arapaho, Eastern Shoshone, Mohawk, Ardoch Algonquin, Ranamuri, Anishinaabe, and Sac and Fox nations were participants in "Re-figuring the Ecological Indian." Donald L. Fixico, Charlotte Black Elk, Curly Bear Wagner, Raymond Pierotti, Darren J. Ranco, Burton Hutchinson, Wesley Martel, John Yellowplume, and James Trosper were some of the tribal people who played key roles in the gathering.

"Re-figuring the Ecological Indian" was shaped by the Native peoples who participated in the conference itself as well as the Native peoples whose lives in relation to the environment were the subject of consideration. All value associated with the conference is a tribute to them.

Laramie, Wyoming

Preface

Brian Hosmer

From where I now sit, fortified by distances of time and geography, "Re-figuring the Ecological Indian," the tenth annual (2002) symposium of the University of Wyoming's American Heritage Center (AHC), seems an inspired event, not the least because it initiated conversations that inspired this volume, so expertly organized by Michael E. Harkin and David Rich Lewis. Emerging, as such things do, out of opportunity (in this case the publication of a thought-provoking book by an eminent anthropologist), supported by AHC leadership (Rick Ewig and Michael Devine in particular), and driven by a fruitful partnership of academic departments and programs from Anthropology and American Indian Studies to American Studies and History, "Re-figuring" promised to draw significant scholarly attention to what heretofore had been an under-noticed and under-appreciated series of very fine symposia, hosted by one of the Gem City's true jewels.

Of course, any piece that begins with the disclaimer "From where I now sit" telegraphs something more than misty reminiscence of halcyon days. Yes, "Re-figuring" put the AHC and its annual symposium on the map. And certainly, when all was said and done, participants and audience members enjoyed many stimulating conversations, provoked and inspired by a truly fine collection of thoughtful papers (a few of which are reproduced in this collection). But we didn't always believe we'd get there, or at least I didn't.

The stimulus for this symposium, it is true, was the 1999 publication of Shepard Krech's *The Ecological Indian: Myth and History*. And in pitching the idea to AHC interim director Rick Ewig, our organizing committee (Michael Harkin; Judith Antell, director of American Indian Studies at the University of Wyoming [UW]; and myself, then a member of the UW History Department), always conceived of a prominent role for Krech, even though we never intended the symposium to be *about* that book, either in critique or defense. Rather, we hoped that the book offered an opportunity to highlight emerging scholarship on Natives and the environment—in the broadest sense.

We were, to put it mildly, unprepared for the reaction. And fortified by that particular variety of naïveté (cluelessness?) reserved for academicians, we resolved to ride out (ignore?) the gathering storm, even if "resolve" suggests a higher degree of steadfastness than we possessed. Call it inertia, absence of an alternate plan, or a "deer in the headlights" kind of resolve.

As Michael Harkin and David Lewis recount in the introduction to this volume, the events of September 11, 2001, caused us to reschedule the symposium for the spring of 2002. By that time, passions seem to have cooled, Shep Krech felt a little less like we had used his feet to step (jump?) into a hornet's nest, and, remarkably, most of our original presenters made the trip anyway. Donald Fixico led the revised cast of characters and, in typical fashion, found a way to gently prod us into considering the moral and ethical dimensions of what we had set into motion.

By that time, organizers and audience members were receptive to what Fixico had to say. Months of e-mail denunciations had, I think, caused us to examine our original motivations for staging this academic gathering, forcing us to take seriously the full range of genuine scholarly concern that this volume evoked. Yes, as academics engaged in American Indian Studies, we knew that this topic positively invited controversy. But did we fully appreciate just how its message would be received, translated, transmitted, and (particularly by conservative talk-radio personalities) twisted into supporting a set of political positions clearly at variance with the author's own? Speaking only for myself, not so much. To the extent that the symposium proved successful, all to the good. But success or not, organizing it was a sobering experience, and a lesson I took with me when I moved to the Newberry Library in 2002.

But what of the issues, raised in the course of that scholarly gathering, and then afterward—in this volume and elsewhere? I interpret my role as "preface writer" fairly narrowly, so I don't see this as space for extended commentary. But since scholars rarely abandon any stage prematurely, allow me to suggest that, amid (or because of) the swirling controversy, the symposium presented opportunity to reflect upon power and representation, science versus myth (and mythmaking), attention given (by scholars) to Native perspectives, and the construction, and reification, of measurable categories.

These kinds of musings take us in several directions. For one, does it really matter if Indians are or are not, were or were not, "ecologists," as we commonly understand that term? Isn't "ecology," as attached to the distant past and across cultures, so hopelessly anachronistic as to obscure rather than to illuminate? Although this question is better addressed by contributors to this volume, it is clear that if we consider the reaction to advance publicity for our 2002 symposium, it matters a great deal—and not simply for emotional reasons, or fears that challenging this "trope" of the ecological Indian somehow undermines Native self-image, the reality of Indian cultural distinctiveness, notions of sustainability versus the consequences of modern, technological society, or just deeply held ideas about Indians and the environment.

Rather, and in the realm of public discourse certainly, this question is consequential indeed. Consider the commonplace, though facile and inaccurate, linkages between Indians as "noble savages" and conventional understandings of tribal sovereignty. First of all, the notion of sovereign *tribes* is missing, and indeed replaced by suggestions that Indians—for biological and historical reasons—are, individually, recipients of "special rights." But that aside, consider the public discourse on the Kennewick Man controversy and notice how representations of Indians (as noble in their savagery), guilt over their treatment (historically and contemporarily), and "special rights" are linked. So, when a well-respected national news program ran a story on Kennewick Man in which it attempted to discover why "Indians" were so opposed to scientific examination of the skeletal remains, its "answer" was simple: Indians fear that, if it is determined (by science and hence unassailable) that Kennewick Man was not the (biological) ancestor of historic

Native groups, Indian people would, ipso facto, lose their right to operate CASINOS. The implication being, of course, that if Natives weren't "here first," then their "special rights" were built upon a fiction.

Now of course, we scholars might argue, with great vehemence, that the one has very little to do with the other, that gaming exists for reasons other than who was "here first." But certainly we also know that the public discourse (and sometimes the scholarly discourse too) also reflects, recapitulates, and perpetuates historical operations of power. And that historically, our understandings of Indian histories and cultural values are shaped and reshaped, often in the service of ends inimical to those of Native peoples and communities, and often in spite of the best efforts of scholars who seek to ameliorate the manifold consequences of colonialism by injecting reason, balance, and scholarly disinterestedness into the public discourse.

Obviously, tension exists between Native peoples and academics, and this troubled relationship is the subject of a number of quite trenchant critiques. And so, the controversy that nearly engulfed the "Re-figuring" symposium can be understood in the light of this discourse, which is of course in some measure about power—the power to define and describe "Indianness" in the here and now and in the past.

But to describe it thus may distract as much as illuminate. After all, this power to define and describe, as claimed by non-Indians, is often supported by appeals to "science," and in this connection it may be instructive to recall the intricately intertwined histories of natural science and ethnology. Jefferson, of course, fancied himself a natural scientist, an ethnologist, and an archaeologist, and scientists of his particular mind-set, then and later, sought to create taxonomies, ways to measure observed phenomena, and interpretive frameworks in order to understand the natural world, of which Native peoples were assumed to be a component. And in a way he illustrates a pattern, seemingly rooted in the past (though perhaps not so much), of linking these emerging fields of inquiry via the history and culture of the Native peoples of North America.

The parallel development of ethnology and natural science—as fields of inquiry—is well known, as are its implications, particularly where lines are not exactly parallel after all but intersecting. And while scholars long ago rejected the notion that Indian peoples are "natural men and women," or subjects for natural history museums to consider alongside exotic flora and fauna, the temptation to see Native peoples through the lens of natural science persists, particularly, it seems, in popular tracts, written by scholars, in which a central concern is environmental degradation. What does it mean, for scholarly inquiry and for Native communities, when we seek answers for present-day problems in the experiences of indigenous peoples? How do we make sense of scientific evidence that humanizes Native peoples by questioning the trope of the "noble savage"? What happens when this evidence seems to suggest that cultural values play less of a role in human interactions with their environments than technology, population density, or luck?

We are, in a sense, speaking past one another, finding different things in the past, positing relationships between present-day concerns and historical events—even when we say we are not. But all is not lost. The "Refiguring" symposium ended quite well indeed, and this volume is a testament to a willingness to listen, as much as talk.

Chicago, Illinois

Acknowledgments

Many people and organizations have helped make this book appear. To begin with are all those who made the Laramie conference possible: Rick Ewig and Sally Sutherland of the American Heritage Center, and planning committee members John Dorst, Bill Gribb, Brian Hosmer, Judith Antell (Anishinaabe), Veronica Gambler (Northern Arapaho), and Frieda Knobloch. Those who generously provided funding included the American Heritage Center, the Rentschler Fund, the School of Environment and Natural Resources, American Indian Studies, and the departments of anthropology and history at the University of Wyoming. We also wish to acknowledge the many participants in that conference whose work does not appear in the present volume but whose stimulating contributions suggested the importance and complexity of this topic.

At a later stage, the preparation of the book itself, we would like to thank Mark Greene, director of the American Heritage Center, for his continuing support, and the University of Nebraska Press's editorial staff and anonymous reader. Additionally, for her very important work in editing the manuscript, we would like to thank Alison Harkin, and for his help in getting the manuscript ready for press, Michael Page. Finally, thanks to the *Western Historical Quarterly* and to the Department of History, Utah State University, for support in the final editorial and production stages.

Introduction

Michael E. Harkin and David Rich Lewis

This is not a book conceived primarily to assess Shepard Krech's *The Ecological Indian: Myth and History* (1999), but it is inevitable that it deals with Krech's book and its remarkable reception: remarkable for the penetration into the general media of an academic book, and remarkable for the strength of feeling associated with both positive and negative readings of it. That this event—the book's publication and reception—is a cultural event rather than merely an academic one is evident by the amount and intensity of discussion it fostered, in academic seminars and on talk radio at the end of the 1990s. That this epoch is now over has been brought home to us repeatedly: by the coming of the millennium and the contested presidential election, the stock market dot-com crash, and, of course, 9/11. Pointedly, the conference at the American Heritage Center at the University of Wyoming upon which the present volume is partly based was originally scheduled for that tragic week in September, and was postponed until the following spring.

So, if this is not exactly a contemporaneous assessment of the controversy over *The Ecological Indian*, it has the benefit of distance and perspective. Of course, many of the same issues and themes persist in the present, and the problematic that Krech explored has stimulated further scholarship (e.g., Hunn et al. 2004). However, a new set of issues having to do with cultural difference has taken priority for the foreseeable future. So rather than ask, "What is it about the ecological Indian critique that so sparked controversy?," we must ask "What was it?"

Like most motivating symbols, and all symbols in the political arena, the ecological Indian was eminently ambiguous (see Kertzer 1988, 57–76; Ortner 1973). On one level, of course, all populations and cultures are "ecological" in the rigorous sense of the term; that is, they necessarily have recurring, structured relations with the natural world. We might call this Ecological$_1$. On a second level we must address the concept of sustainability. While most Native American cultures demonstrated gross-level sustainability— the ability to persist in the same environment over millennia, although not necessarily at the same population level (e.g., the Mayas and the Anasazi-Pueblos, who suffered population declines in the wake of ecological and/or climatic changes)—the record with regard to particular species and even entire adaptations (e.g., terrestrial vs. maritime, faunal vs. plant) is not so clear. Thus, the precontact extirpation of game species such as elk in the intermontane West and seals in California seem clearly to be linked to human activity and resulted in a change in adaptive focus (see Kay and Simmons 2002). We will label the sustainability criterion Ecological$_2$. A third sense of the term is located at the level of discourse, where "ecological" refers to political support for sustainability, conservation, and a host of issues specific to industrial society, such as global warming, pollution controls, recycling, alternative fuels. We will label this Ecological$_3$. This is the most problematic sense, as it refers to an ideological matrix specific to industrial and post-industrial societies and thus is not relevant or appropriate to most of the Native American cases, from Paleoindians to the reservation period (see Nadasdy 1999, 2005). It is problematic in a second sense as well, insofar as it is essentially a utopian discourse, one with no actual referent. Environmentalism, as this ideology is more commonly called, meets many of the criteria of a religious movement, including the weekly ritual of recycling cans and newspapers (see Hitt 2003). Although it acts in the world, as a religious discourse it envisions an alternative, otherworldly reality. In sum, we agree with Paul Nadasdy's recent position that environmentalism is a complex and contradictory continuum that is in most ways more problematic than the ecological practices of indigenous peoples; our tripartite model should not, however, be confused with his (Nadasdy 2005).

Krech consciously chooses to operate on all three levels. Moreover, it is clear that he envisioned a book that would address the three levels in a somewhat ambiguous manner. As one prominent critic of Krech's told me, the use of the somewhat outdated term "ecological" to refer to what would, today, more commonly be called "environmental" or "conservationist" is a deliberate attempt to conflate the separate issues. This choice is, from our perspective, not a question of intentionally misleading the reader but one of glossing over, for rhetorical purposes, the significant differences among the three senses of the term "ecological"—of using a problematic term, already deeply embedded and conflated in rhetorical usage, as popular shorthand for the entire debate. A similar deconstruction could be performed on the problematic term "Indian," long discredited as an ethnonym, although still employed by many of both European and aboriginal descent. The use of both words suggests to us that the title is to be read, at least in part, ironically.

Irony can indeed be seen as the master trope of the book. The author is talking about a set of beliefs and practices that can only be loosely connected to an ideology of "ecology" as held by diverse, disparate groups of people over ten millennia, who cannot seriously be called by a single name, and certainly not one that invokes an entirely different place and people. Ethnographic irony is, of course, an established tradition, going back at least to Boas (see Hymes 1999; Krupat 1990). Irony and satire have, similarly, been adopted as rhetorical strategies by many Native Americans themselves, for example, Alexander Posey writing as Fus Fixico (see Littlefield and Petty 1993). The source of irony is the disjuncture between expectations outsiders hold of Native Americans, drawn from a standard cultural repertoire that has remained remarkably stable over the course of American history, and the reality—encountered on or off the reservation—of change, and Indians as modern peoples with deep traditions navigating present realities and needs.

This gap between expectations and reality can cut in different ways. As Philip J. Deloria (1998), Robert F. Berkhofer Jr. (1979), Sherry L. Smith (2000), and others have shown, images of Indians are organized around several foci, including primitivism (which can have both positive and negative aspects), savagery, violence, childlike naïveté, wisdom, and vanishing. Most relevant to our purposes is of course the notion of Indians living in harmony with nature. This has a long pedigree and, although superficially a wholly positive quality, especially in the contemporary setting, it is related to an ideology equating Indians with nature itself: a form of the terra nullius argument that provided the basic justification for conquest of Indian lands—that is, lands that were not "improved" were ripe for the taking (Lewis 1994, 7–12; Hagan 1980). Taken to the extreme, equating Indians with nature has the potential to deny Indians their history, their humanity, and even their modernity (Lewis 1995; Warren 2002).

Thus to argue, as Krech does, that Native Americans have acted in ways directly violating this stereotype of ecological primitivism is a welcome corrective to much of the stereotyping that has occurred around this issue. When these stereotypes come into conflict with contradictory evidence, the reaction can be violent, as seen in cases such as the Makah whale hunt (Bowechop, 2004; Erikson 2002, 205–12; Nadasdy 2005) and the nuclear waste controversy among the Skull Valley Goshutes of Utah (Lewis, this volume; Ishiyama 2003), usually to the detriment of embattled Native communities. However, debunking is at best a limited goal for a scholarly project, especially given the broad and necessarily superficial level at which it is possible to address this question. If one begins with the assumption that Indians lived in complete harmony with their environment, when it is not only possible but easy to find counterexamples, the blaze that results when this straw man is ignited generates, as the cliché goes, heat but no light.

What are we to make of that heat, the reaction from many (although certainly not all) Indian scholars and activists? Krech was shocked by the vehemence of the response (see Krech, this volume). Although the criticism of Krech at the Laramie conference was fairly muted, we do not believe this would have been true had the conference been held when originally scheduled. Vine Deloria Jr. had issued a call via H-Amindian and other internet discussion groups to attend the conference in protest. Ultimately, he did not make the two-hour drive from Boulder, Colorado, but the degree of vehemence in his call and in some other internet messages surprised the organizers, as Judith Antell attests in her foreword. Certainly, much of the impetus can be seen in the thesis of Deloria's book *Red Earth, White Lies: Native Americans and the Myth of Scientific Fact* (1995), which is that Native people had developed an aboriginal scientific tradition superior to that of Western science and that many of the theories of the latter, including planetary creation, peopling of the Western Hemisphere, and, significantly, the aboriginal overkill hypothesis were, in a word, "lies." Thus, Deloria's objection to Krech is twofold. First, the specific theory Krech embraces with respect to Pleistocene extinctions, a version of Paul Martin's aboriginal overkill hypothesis (1967), directly contradicts Deloria's own stated position. Second, Krech's status as an outsider, a non-Indian, makes it inappropriate in the first place to address questions relating to the presumed ancestors of Native Americans. Thus, Krech was merely a particularly egregious species of the genus "Anthro."

In fact, Deloria's response was predictable and even necessary. One could argue that it was the precise counter-equivalent of the way right-wing commentators embraced Krech's book, using it selectively to criticize Native Americans on sovereignty issues. Environmentalism and "Indians" are hot-button topics to both constituencies, and both entered the fray with gusto. It is also safe to say that neither side read the book particularly thoroughly or carefully—complex constructions disappeared in the search for simple statements and media sound bites.

Despite its status as artifact of the ideological battles of the late 1990s, *The Ecological Indian* raises serious issues of interest to scholars in several areas. This volume is organized around themes suggested by Krech's book: the overkill hypothesis, traditional ecological knowledge, contemporary resource management, representations of Indians and nature, and, finally, the controversy itself, approached from the vantage point of seven years of scholarly hindsight. The present volume attempts to extend, in several directions, the themes Krech laid out in *The Ecological Indian* (with the realization that those themes often appeared elsewhere first). As editors we take no general stand on that book, nor do most of the authors, even as they look at their own fields and research in the light of Krech's general arguments. We do, however, find the issues that it raises to be valuable and worthy of continued exploration.

The thinking behind this book emerged from a conference organized by Michael Harkin, Judith Antell (Anishinaabe), and Brian Hosmer in 2001 and which convened in 2002. Sponsored by the American Heritage Center and the University of Wyoming, "Re-figuring the Ecological Indian" brought together prominent scholars, Indian and non-Indian, from a range of disciplines to consider the issues raised by Krech. The present volume is not a proceedings of that conference, since fewer than half of the chapters (Krech, Ranco, Braun, and Lewis) were presented there. Rather, it is an extension of the conversation begun in Laramie, an exploration, elaboration, and critique of the major themes raised by Krech's work. The present authors are mostly anthropologists by training and ethnohistorians by approach; they are also non-Indian with several exceptions.

Part 1, "Shepard Krech and His Critics," opens this collection with three chapters that explicitly address The Ecological Indian as artifact, research, and political tract. Chapter 1 belongs to Shepard Krech III, professor of anthropology and director of the Haffenreffer Museum of Anthropology at Brown University. In "Beyond The Ecological Indian," Krech assesses the critical response to his thesis and research. Krech has been praised for his nuanced arguments and complex rendering of a subject too often oversimplified, even mythologized. On the other hand, he and his book have been called racist and politically incorrect, easily co-opted by those seeking to dismantle Native American lands, rights, and sovereignty; he has been assailed for his omissions, including his use of historical documents and the lack of Native oral testimony; and he has been critiqued for his vision of the state of contemporary Indian environmentalism. Krech's response here is measured, accepting yet complicating both praise and critiques with the recognition that indigenous experiences are far from monolithic, far from the essentialized image and its pervasive force in a modern world. We also give Krech the last word in this volume, in an afterword, where he assesses the responses of his colleagues in this book and the significance of this exercise.

In the second chapter, Darren J. Ranco, assistant professor of Native American Studies and Environmental Studies at Dartmouth College and a member of the Penobscot Indian Nation, offers an explicit critique and "intellectual archaeology" of Krech's text. Ranco argues that, far from opening new fields of debate and research, Krech's work is fairly typical in its analysis of the ecological Indian for scholars arguing whether or not Indians have, or ever did have, an ecological awareness. By urging us to take the "scientific evidence" at face value and to leave the stereotype of the ecological Indian in the waste bin of colonial invention, Ranco argues that Krech tries to hide the contemporary political aspects of his findings.

Ranco explores what he calls Krech's "invention of tradition" analysis, examining the political implications of Krech's representation of Native Americans in the light of his own ethnographic fieldwork among the Penobscots, the environmental condition of Indian lands, and the complex symbolic and legal relationships that exist between Indian tribes and governments in the United States and Canada in the twenty-first century. Ranco argues that whatever "ecological legitimacy" Indian nations possess reinforces their semi-sovereign political standing and their very identity as Indians—their Ecological$_3$ position gives them a seat and a voice at the policy table. Krech's arguments fundamentally undercut that recognition and resulting power, perpetuating a kind of neocolonialism. The result, says Ranco, is not an academic argument but one that involves the political life or death of indigenous peoples.

In chapter 3, Harvey A. Feit, professor of anthropology at McMaster University, explores Krech's arguments that Northern Algonquian hunters in the eastern Canadian fur trade learned resource conservation techniques from Europeans. While agreeing that the simplistic myth of the ecological Indian should be rejected, Feit finds fundamental flaws in Krech's logic and use of evidence. Feit reinterprets historic documents and Native testimony in the light of the scientific findings of modern beaver biologists to assess the ecological understandings and conservation techniques of both Native hunters and European traders. In many cases he finds evidence that Native hunting practices were (in some cases counter-intuitively) less destructive to beaver populations than "conservation" techniques recommended by European traders who did not have that collective generational experience with beaver—that they were Ecological$_2$. By the twentieth century, the imposition of such Euro-American conservation practices became key tools in the "benevolent regulation" of Indians and their resources, resulting in resource co-management at best and Native dispossession at worst. Like Ranco, Feit argues that by consistently privileging European over Native knowledge and explanations, Krech's book contributes to that subordination and the creation of an oversimplified counter-stereotype with serious political ramifications.

Part 2, "(Over)hunting Large Game," explores issues of overkill suggested by Krech's synthesis. In chapter 4, Robert L. Kelly, professor of anthropology at the University of Wyoming, and Mary M. Prasciunas, a PhD student in anthropology at the University of Wyoming, explore both the theoretical and the practical in their article "Did the Ancestors of Native Americans Cause Animal Extinctions in Late-Pleistocene North America? And Does It Matter If They Did?" The role of humans in the extinction of some thirty-six genera of mammals at the end of the Pleistocene some ten thousand years ago has been hotly debated for the last fifty years. Recent archaeological finds, analyses of radiocarbon-dated animal bone assemblages, and computer simulations have led scholars to very different conclusions. Some make the case for a strong human hand (predation or human-introduced hypervirulent diseases) in the extinctions, others for climatic change as the primary culprit, and still others for some combination of factors. Kelly and Prasciunas review the current literature on Pleistocene extinctions in North America, finding that climate change still seems to have the most explanatory power. And even if Native Americans were the primary cause, that finding, according to the authors, would have little practical bearing on modern Indian land-use patterns and rights—on Ecological$_3$. Rather than arguing over whether one human group is or is not inherently conservationist, they argue for recognizing humans as integral parts of their environments and considering the conditions under which conservation behaviors become desirable and cannot be ignored—embracing Ecological$_1$ but not necessarily Ecological$_2$ in their analysis.

Chapter 5, by Ernest S. Burch Jr., research associate at the Arctic Studies Center, Smithsonian National Museum of Natural History, extends Krech's analytical questions to the hunters and fishers of the Arctic and subarctic. Burch focuses his attention on the cognitive aspects of Inuit subsistence strategies and their effects on the environment—the human side of human ecology. Taking difficult and fluctuating environmental conditions and prey species populations as an ecological constant, Burch compares how the Iñupiat of northern Alaska and the Caribou Inuit of the central Canadian subarctic organized their understandings of subsistence environments and resources, how they acted over time and space with intended and unintended consequences, and how European contact affected that cognitive relationship and therefore the behavioral outcomes of resource use. Burch defines human subsistence beliefs and actions on a continuum from predominantly rational to predominantly nonrational, with intended and unintended consequences. By differentiating episodes of overkill from patterns of overharvest, he evaluates the Native subsistence (and conservation) ethic in motion.

Ultimately, Burch argues that while Inuits saw no systematic connection between their hunting and the numbers of their prey species, some, maybe most, Inuits achieved an ecological harmony learned over multiple generational experiences with a place, making multiple mistakes (including near-extinctions) and ecological adjustments (Ecological$_2$) in the process. Nonrational factors such as group beliefs and taboos, with their arational and unintended long-term consequences, were probably more important than any rational conservation ethic or consciousness in maintaining that relative balance, especially on an abundant frontier. European contact tested that balance with new technologies and new market prey, precipitating changes in Native religious practices and subsistence strategies, resulting in widespread overharvesting. In that way, Burch argues, Indians were no wiser than anyone else; nor were they endowed with a more innate or substantial environmental conservation ethic. Better science, Burch points out, would recognize the complex, situation-specific nature of indigenous subsistence beliefs and behaviors rather than continue to debate the dichotomization of Indians as rational conservationists or rapacious overkillers that is part of Ecological$_3$.

Dan Flores, A. B. Hammond Professor of History at the University of Montana revisits essential environmental issues in the near-extinction of bison on the northern plains of the United States. Those issues came to the fore in the crisis over the Bozeman Trail, when Red Cloud charged the U.S. government with culpability for scattering and destroying the herds. The government responded by continuing its program of designating buffalo grounds for specific tribes. But as Lakota winter counts make clear, the bison decline predated the Bozeman and most white trails. Flores traces this decline to climatic changes as well as to Lakota expansion and market-induced competition for bison. When Lakota bands warred to seize Crow buffalo grounds in the 1870s, agreed-upon tribal hunting areas disintegrated in a free-for-all among Indians, Canadian Métis, and whites for the last pockets of animals. As Flores has demonstrated in earlier articles about the southern plains (Flores 1991), Indians were players in that complex web of environmental, cultural, and market forces contributing to the near-extinction of modern bison. Flores and Burch recount histories in which disparate groups of Indian hunters were neither dispassionate bystanders nor passive victims (see also West 1998; Ostler 1999; Hämäläinen 2003).

Following from Flores's historical analysis of bison and Indians in the northern plains, part 3, "Representations of Indians and Animals," pairs articles that look at how that Plains Indian–bison relationship is (or is not) being portrayed. In chapter 7, "Watch for Falling Bison," John Dorst, professor of American Studies at the University of Wyoming, marks the ways in which museum displays develop ecological discourses relevant to Krech's arguments in The Ecological Indian. Since natural history museums have been central institutions in representing and interpreting human-bison relations for a general audience, Dorst compares bison displays at the Milwaukee Public Museum as an example of older natural history productions to a newer

display in the Draper Museum of Natural History at the Buffalo Bill Historical Center in Cody, Wyoming. Both meet the need for compelling spectacle
and for an acceptable historical and ecological narrative, even as they dis-
seminate a reductive image of Native peoples. Interestingly, plains hunters
are completely absent in the newer Draper Museum exhibit, which offers little direct reference to historic Native peoples. In that way, argues Dorst, it
is similar to Krech's book—a clinical marshaling of historical and archaeological evidence without confronting the complexity of the ecological Indian as an iconic element of our modern cultural knowledge (Ecological$_3$).
If that iconography is "a flexible tool in the repertoire of popular discourse
. . . that has more to do with our own modern lifeways than with the world
of pre-modern indigenous peoples," Dorst argues (like Ranco), understanding the ecological Indian's contemporary ideological value is as important
as questioning its scientific accuracy.

Sebastian F. Braun, assistant professor of anthropology at the University
of North Dakota, takes us from museum displays to visions of and policy debates about the future of the Great Plains in "Ecological and Un-ecological
Indians: The (Non)portrayal of Plains Indians in the Buffalo Commons Literature." Braun critically examines the relationships among Indian, bison,
and land in what he sees as an emergent "buffalo commons literature," assessing how the old myths and histories are still evident in today's discussions of the past and future of the Great Plains. He then compares that envisioned relationship and usage to the realities of contemporary tribal buffalo
programs, particularly the Cheyenne River Sioux and the InterTribal Bison
Cooperative. Unlike Ranco, Braun argues that the image of the ecological
Indian is not being used by or for Native peoples in this debate; rather, Native cultures (and their Ecological$_3$ representations) are being used for their
"authenticity" value by others, as tools to reach political goals that, at times,
run counter to current Indian political, economic, and cultural interests.

Part 4, "Traditional Ecological Knowledge," explores the nature of indigenous ideological systems, their significance as resource management
tools, and the extent to which they demonstrate or complicate images of an
indigenous conservation ethic. In chapter 9, "Swallowing Wealth: North-

west Coast Beliefs and Ecological Practices," Michael E. Harkin, professor of anthropology at the University of Wyoming, points out that assessments of ecological behavior (or its opposite) are based upon philosophical, epistemological, and political assumptions that are themselves late-twentieth-century North American and European products—Ecological$_3$. Since the criteria used are not entirely consistent with the actual behavior of either historic or contemporary indigenous groups, we are right to be suspicious of ideological manipulations (as Krech warns) when the two do line up. But how did we get to the point of considering Indians as ecological paragons in the first place?

The answer, argues Harkin, seems to involve a systematic misunderstanding of indigenous economies and ideologies. Harkin explores Northwest Coast Kwakwaka'wakw belief systems that demonstrate regulatory functions, stress delicate balances and moderation, yet celebrate excessive consumption. At the core of their ecological model is the paradox of an unstable system based on reciprocity where, in fact, seasonal oscillations in human predation make reciprocal repayment of presumptive debts to animal prey impossible. Harkin argues that Northwest Coast patterns of subsistence have more in common with those "feast and famine" patterns of the subarctic and that, in the end, Northwest Coast societies cannot be said to have been either environmentalist or anti-environmentalist—that they were both Ecological$_1$ and Ecological$_2$. The paradox that peoples with well-developed understandings of ecological cycles and connections may also have no developed conservation ethic should surprise no one, least of all modern SUV-driving Americans.

Stephen J. Langdon, professor of anthropology at the University of Alaska, Anchorage, follows with an ethno-archaeological analysis of Northwest Coast cultures in chapter 10, "Sustaining a Relationship." Archaeological research demonstrates the existence of a variety of structures used by the Klawock and Hinyaa Tlingits for harvesting salmon over the past two thousand years. Langdon discusses the nature of these structures, patterns of change and innovation over the years, and the logic of the most recent patterns of salmon harvest in the light of Tlingit mythic stories and Tlingit conceptualization of their relationship with salmon. He finds a cultural explanation for a specific historic shift in the nature of their technology and system of harvesting salmon—the accumulation of knowledge grounded in empirical events, interpreted through the mythic character of Salmon Boy, generating a new "logic of engagement" between humans and salmon. That logic is not one of harvesting strategies or efficiency techniques, Langdon maintains, but of how humans should interact with and treat each other, and hence treat humans in salmon form. The result: principles and structures limiting harvests, ensuring escapement, and sustaining the Tlingit relationship with a valued relative. Langdon finds an integrated expression of social and environmental ethics (Ecological$_1$) in his case, whereas Harkin finds the paradoxical coexistence of ecological knowledge without an equivalent conservation ethic.

Part 5, "Contemporary Resource Management Issues," explores the modern dimensions of indigenous resource use, putting the historical image of the ecological Indian and an indigenous conservation ethic to the test in modern Ecological$_3$ circumstances. In chapter 11, Larry Nesper, assistant professor of anthropology at the University of Wisconsin at Madison, and James H. Schlender (Anishinaabe), former executive administrator of the Great Lakes Indian Fish and Wildlife Commission, address Great Lakes tribes and the politics of intertribal resource management.

In 1984 the Great Lakes Indian Fish and Wildlife Commission emerged in the wake of a Seventh Circuit Court of Appeals decision affirming the nineteenth-century treaty rights of Ojibwe signatory bands. The commission, comprising representatives from eleven tribal governments in Wisconsin, Minnesota, and Michigan, set out to protect these treaty rights in ceded territories and to promote cooperative resource management between tribes and state departments of natural resources. Nesper and Schlender explore the difficulties of such cooperative management and the commission's leadership role in synthesizing an evolving indigenous spirituality around resource harvests. Their article explores the politics and cultural dimensions of contemporary resource management issues, highlighting how Ojibwes appropriate and blend biological science and law with their cultural traditions—signs of the vitality and modernity of a people who live by and with other peoples, and who evolve yet endure as Ojibwes.

From the Great Lakes to the Great Basin, David Rich Lewis, professor of history at Utah State University, looks at the still-unfolding story of Skull Valley Goshutes and their proposal to store forty thousand metric tons of high-level radioactive waste on their tiny reservation, forty-five miles southwest of Salt Lake City, Utah. Surrounded by military bombing ranges, federal nerve agent storage and disposal facilities, and private hazardous waste sites, with little water and no other marketable natural resources, the reservation houses fewer than thirty band members. The development of such a waste facility would bring the tribe jobs and millions of dollars annually. Goshute tribal supporters see the issue as one of cultural survival and renewal, as their sovereign right to make economic choices about their lands and resource use. On the other hand, for Utah politicians, residents, and environmentalists the issue is about the lack of state control or fiscal benefit, the fear of two million people living downwind from a nuclear repository, and the paradoxical image of the ecological Indian versus the reality of Goshutes—and all tribes—as modern corporate entities. In Utah, an identity war rages beneath the environmental battle over nuclear waste and tribal sovereignty, one informed by Ecological$_3$ definitions of who Indians are and how they should behave.

In many ways, the larger issue facing modern Skull Valley Goshutes parallels the Ecological$_2$ choices all groups have had to make, in all ages, about subsistence, persistence, and how to use their environments to those ends. Lewis's article addresses the past and present realities affecting Goshute environmental and economic decision making; the unusual coalition of environmentalists and "wise use" advocates coming together to oppose Goshute plans; and the larger issues of economic and cultural sustainability, environmentalism, and sovereignty facing Indians at the beginning of the twenty-first century. Lewis points out that the Goshute case is a stark reminder that no stereotype is without consequence. Even a positive trope such as the ecological Indian is a double-edged sword that can be used against the moral authority, authenticity, identity, and sovereignty of modern Indian peoples.

No edited volume can aspire to the degree of cogency and coherence that a good single-authored work can evince. However, what is given away in unity is gained in diversity, even—at the risk of sounding arcane—what the great Soviet-era semiotician Mikhail Bakhtin called "heteroglossia," a hallmark of democratic discourse. We are proud of the fact that our authors bridge a number of gaps that are often chasms, between Indian and non-Indian scholars, between American and non-American ones, between prehistory and history, and between science and the humanities. We believe that in the case of the complex issues surrounding the intellectual and practical use of the ecological Indian, such diversity is not only a benefit but a necessity.

It is certainly not possible to arrive at either a total or universally acceptable reading of the ecological Indian critique and associated counter- and metacritiques, regardless of the number of authors. The value of any line of inquiry—and we would argue that the current one was not created *ex nihilo* by Krech but was implicit in previous critical literature—is the productivity principle: Does it lead to additional discussion of and insights into an important topic? We believe and hope that the evidence provided in the present volume suggests that it does.

References

Berkhofer, Robert F., Jr. 1979. *The white man's Indian: Images of the American Indian from Columbus to the present.* New York: Vintage.

Bowechop, Janine, 2004. Contemporary Makah whaling. In *Coming to shore: Northwest Coast ethnology, tradition, and visions,* ed. Marie Mauzé, Michael Harkin, and Sergei Kan, 407–19. Lincoln: University of Nebraska Press.

Deloria, Philip J. 1998. *Playing Indian.* New Haven: Yale University Press.

Deloria, Vine, Jr. 1995. *Red earth, white lies: Native Americans and the myth of scientific fact.* New York: Scribner.

Erikson, Patricia. 2002. *Voices of a thousand people: The Makah cultural and research center.* Lincoln: University of Nebraska Press.

Flores, Dan. 1991. Bison ecology and bison diplomacy: The southern plains from 1800–1850. *Journal of American History* 78 (2): 465–85.

Hagan, William T. 1980. Justifying the dispossession of the Indian: The land utilization argument. In *American Indian environments: Ecological issues in Native American history*, ed. Christopher Vecsey and Robert W. Venables, 65–80. Syracuse: Syracuse University Press.

Hämäläinen, Pekka. 2003. The rise and fall of Plains Indian horse cultures. *Journal of American History* 90 (3): 833–62.

Hitt, Jack. 2003. Gospel according to earth: Sown by science, a new eco-faith takes root. *Harper's*, July, 41–55.

Hunn, Eugene S., Darryll R. Johnson, Priscilla N. Russell, and Thomas F. Thornton. 2003. Huna Tlingit traditional environmental knowledge, conservation, and the management of a "wilderness" park. *Current Anthropology* 44 supplement: s79–s103.

Hymes, Dell. 1999. Boas on the threshold of ethnopoetics. In *Theorizing the Americanist tradition*, ed. Lisa Philips Valentine and Regna Darnell, 84–104. Toronto: University of Toronto Press.

Ishiyama, Noriko. 2003. Environmental justice and American Indian tribal sovereignty: Case study of a land-use conflict in Skull Valley, Utah. *Antipode* 35 (1): 119–39.

Kay, Charles E., and Randy T. Simmons, eds. 2002. *Wilderness and political ecology: Aboriginal influences and the original state of nature*. Salt Lake City: University of Utah Press.

Kertzer, David. 1988. *Ritual, politics, and power*. New Haven: Yale University Press.

Krech, Shepard, III. 1999. *The ecological Indian: Myth and history*. New York: Norton.

Krupat, Arnold. 1990. Irony in anthropology: The work of Franz Boas. In *Modernist anthropology: From fieldwork to text*, ed. Marc Maragno, 133–45. Princeton: Princeton University Press.

Lewis, David Rich. 1994. *Neither wolf nor dog: American Indians, environment, and agrarian change*. New York: Oxford University Press.

———. 1995. Native Americans and the environment: A survey of twentieth-century issues. *American Indian Quarterly* 19 (3): 423–50.

Littlefield, Daniel F., Jr. and Carol A. Petty, eds. 1993. *The Fus Fixico letters by Alexander Posey*. Lincoln: University of Nebraska Press.

Martin, Paul S. 1967. Prehistoric overkill. In *Pleistocene extinctions: The search for a cause*, ed. Paul S. Martin and Herbert E. Wright Jr., 75–120. New Haven: Yale University Press.

Nadasdy, Paul. 1999. The politics of TEK: Power and the "integration" of knowledge. *Arctic Anthropology* 36:1–18.

———. 2005. Transcending the debate over the ecologically noble Indian: Indigenous peoples and environmentalism. *Ethnohistory* 52:291–332.

Ortner, Sherry. 1973. On key symbols. *American Anthropologist* 75:1338–76.

Ostler, Jeffrey. 1999. "They regard their passing as Wakan": Interpreting western Sioux explanations for the bison's decline. *Western Historical Quarterly* 30 (Winter): 475–97.

Smith, Sherry L. 2000. *Reimagining Indians: Native Americans through Anglo eyes, 1880–1940*. New York: Oxford University Press, 2000.

Warren, Louis S. 2002. The nature of conquest: Indians, Americans, and environmental history. In *A companion to American Indian history*, ed. Philip J. Deloria and Neal Salisbury, 278–306. Malden MA: Blackwell.

West, Elliott. 1998. *The contested plains: Indians, goldseekers, and the rush to Colorado*. Lawrence: University Press of Kansas.

Native Americans and the Environment

Shepard Krech and His Critics

1. Beyond *The Ecological Indian*

Shepard Krech III

At the heart of *The Ecological Indian* is the question of the fit between a noble image of American Indians and American Indian behavior. Since the early 1970s, a cherished received wisdom has been that North American Indians were original ecologists and conservationists.[1] But were they in actions as well as in image and ideals? Images, of course, have specific intellectual and popular histories and can be measured against human behavior (the myth—as dogma or cherished theory—and history of the subtitle). So in *The Ecological Indian* the two are juxtaposed in chapters ranging from the Pleistocene to the present, image against evidence from the sciences, archaeology, ethnology, and history, embracing testimony from indigenous and non-indigenous people as well as written and oral accounts removed in space or time, always querying the extent to which behavior reflects or departs from image. Were American Indians ecologists? That is, did they think of the environment and its components in interrelating, systemic ways? Were Indians conservationists? Did they intentionally use wisely to maintain future availability of resources, avoid waste or despoliation, and the like?[2]

My most general conclusion is that the rhetoric implicit in the image of the Ecological Indian masks complex and differing realities. Specific conclusions on the fit between image and behavior with respect to ecology, conservation, and other topics were mixed. To begin with, there were probably no more than 4 to 7 million people in North America on the eve of the arrival of Europeans. In the 2000 census, 4.3 million people lived in Colorado and 7.1 million in Virginia (and only 500,000 in Wyoming). Imagine the population of Colorado or Virginia scattered to the continent's winds and you might begin to imagine how often you would encounter other human beings. Density varied from region to region, of course, but it was far less than today's or, for that matter, Europe's in the fifteenth, sixteenth, and seventeenth centuries. In other words, there might have been too few American Indians too thinly spread out to have had much of a lasting impact on lands and resources.

This does not make it less imperative to discern the abundance of resources, impact of technology, extent of acquisitive intentions, or precise environmental attitudes, understandings, and actions, where the data allow such assessments. One thing does seem certain time and again: indigenous people possessed extensive and precise knowledge of their environment. There should be no difficulty inferring that American Indian comprehension of relationships between living organisms and their organic and inorganic environments has always been ecological. The comprehension is systemic and relational, but it is also, of course, cultural, and we must grant people their own cultural definitions and metaphors. That is to say, ecology is at base ethnoecology. For example, certain Plains Indians thought that buffalo not yet returned as expected from seasonal migrations remained on the lake-bottom prairies to which they had gone—spaces real enough in their ecosystems even if not in a Western ecologist's ecosystem; spaces that would also render conservation problematic under rapidly changing circumstances on the nineteenth-century prairies and plains.

From the standpoint of ecological thought, then, the very title The Ecological Indian is perhaps ironic. But so far as conservation—the second important component of the image of the Ecological Indian—is concerned, the story is quite different when it comes to the fit between image and behavior. For one thing, where it exists, the belief in reincarnation undermines if not precludes conservation. For another matter, conservation seems often to have been insignificant until commodification-induced extirpations of beaver, buffalo, deer, and other animals and plants. I return to this thought later.

The Response
I intended for The Ecological Indian not to be the last word but to "rekindle debate" on the fit between an essentialized and durable image of American

Indians and American Indian behavior, as well as to "spawn detailed analyses of the myriad relationships between indigenous people and their environments in North America" (Krech 1999, 28).

The critical response has formed mainly in reviews and in internet and radio commentary, and going beyond the book means confronting the response. One problem stems from its scope: in the first two and one-half years after it was published, more than ninety reviews in eight languages appeared, and they continue to appear.[3] On the whole critics are overwhelmingly positive.[4] While the praise is flattering, it is the small minority that pillory the book who interest me; points of tensions are often far more revealing of culture, power, and the like. So dealing with the response is not just daunting because of size but dyspeptic because, on occasion, the opposition is bilious. Any engaged in research on matters with politics and identity at the core, who arrive at conclusions that cut against the grain, might regard mine as a cautionary tale.

The harshest and most unforgiving critics happen also to be either environmentalists or American Indians, although to pigeonhole either in this way is to give the mistaken impression that they represent the entire category to which they belong. As important is that both care deeply about Indian country, even if, ironically, they sometimes find themselves on opposite sides of the fence on contemporary environmental issues. I expected this criticism, as did others. Nicholas Lemann (1999, 101), best known today for his trenchant analyses of contemporary American politics, remarked in the *New Yorker* that I would "surely be accused of being anti-Indian and anti-environmentalist," but he did not anticipate the highly personal nature of those accusations.

Indeed, one unfriendly review in the progressive weekly *The Nation* linked me to animal rightists who disrupt Makah whaling on the Olympic Peninsula, and accused me of having an "insidious [subtext]: It seeks to absolve Europeans of blame and ultimately can be used to help fuel a backlash of anti-Native sentiment in this country." In an over-the-top allusion, the reviewer implied that I and other non-Indians were summoned by an especially malevolent Native American witch (Pennypacker 2000, 30–31). An even more poisonous pen wielded in *The Ecologist* argued that I was "at the forefront of [a] new conspiracy" to "discredit the American Indian as an ecological model." The book, whose "purpose" is "to prove that there was no ecological Indian," is considered "the worst among many egregious examples of the American professoriate serving the systems that are so efficiently destroying the earth." The reviewer concludes: "There is no doubt a special, and very hot, place for them in the hell that they are determined to reduce this world to" (Sale 2000, 52).

A polemical review in *Indian Country Today* charged that I was seeking "to win converts to the camp that wants to dismantle reservations, destroy sovereignty and ignore American Indian fishing and hunting rights"; it accused me of "painting a terrifying" picture of contemporary Indian country and of "raising the threat of ecological or worse yet, nuclear holocaust" as I "scare" readers "into the conclusion that American Indians must be stopped from controlling their own resources at all costs" (Porterfield 1999). Months later came an editorial that labeled me and the *New Yorker*'s Lemann as debunkers "driven either by a political doctrine of the imperial kind or simply by a lazy or political approach to science, the written record and the lived experience of many traditional practitioners" (*Indian Country Today* 2000). And another critic lumped me with "a whole set of people out there attacking Indians in the guise of ecological history," charging us collectively with blaming the victim and "cook[ing] the facts." In electronic mail he calls me "the worst kind of racist."[5] E-mail and the anonymous world of talk radio seem especially to bring out astringent personal attacks.[6]

In America the race card is sometimes played by those who wish to capture the moral high ground from those with whom they disagree. It is a strategic move that works when the fear of being branded racist preempts further discussion and, as Pierre van den Berghe and others have remarked, can serve as an effective restraint. I understand racism to be the belief, first, that race (a social construct) determines human capacity, and second, that "races" are inherently superior or inferior relative to each other.[7] Is it racist to problematize an essentialist category like the Ecological Indian? Or to argue that a belief in reincarnation fundamentally contradicts Western-style conservation? Others who take measure of the book in full awareness of the charge have written forcefully in print that they consider the charge baseless and a red herring, that *The Ecological Indian* is "certainly not an anti-Indian book" (White 2000, 49) or that "[n]othing could be more false" than the charge (Flores 2001, 177).

Co-optation

Yet as remarked before, I'd like to account for the bile. One reason, I suspect, lies in the perception that *The Ecological Indian* is politically incorrect—"outrageously politically incorrect," one reviewer said (Holdridge 1999, 40–41). One reviewer remarked that I was "asking for trouble" by cutting against the grain of "liberal thinkers" who had embraced Indians through time and across space as ecologists and conservationists (Black 1999). *The Ecological Indian* was seen as out of sync with political winds that blew steadily in the 1980 and 1990s. Some regarded the epilogue on the contemporary scene as potentially "incendiary"—to which I will return.[8]

A second reason arises from fear of or actual co-optation of *The Ecological Indian* by special interests. As *The Nation's* critic remarked, *The Ecological Indian* "neatly suit[s] the purposes of the 'wise use' movement, in which advocates of white entitlement are contesting indigenous peoples' sovereignty, especially with regard to control of their own resources and lands" (Pennypacker 2000, 30).

This critic was on to co-optation, which, I believe, forms an important context in accounting for some of the negative reception to the book. Almost immediately, people with libertarian, free-market, property rights, education reform, and anti-sovereignty agendas appropriated *The Ecological Indian* to their own ends.[9] At first glance, their assessments appeared modest. For instance, the Independence Institute, a free-market think tank, led a list of new recommended books with *The Ecological Indian*, remarking that "an anthropologist shows that contrary to the contemporary myth portraying American Indians as sublime ecologists at one with nature, they were pretty much like everyone else. Some conserved resources, some wasted them, and all sought to shape the natural world to their purposes." In similar fashion, the Arizona chapter news of an organization called People for the U.S.A.! quoted *The Ecological Indian* accurately on the use of fire by Native people as a management tool.

There reasonableness ended. The Independence Institute recommended *The Ecological Indian* in the same breath as works on Franklin Delano Roosevelt's flaws, failed social and welfare policies, intimidation by forces of political correctness, and taking personal responsibility for smoking—a grouping that appeared surreal the first time I saw it. People for the U.S.A.!, which advocates private property rights, public lands access, and the economic benefits of copper mining, and fights conservation easements conflicting with private property interests, coupled *The Ecological Indian*'s conclusion that Indian lands were not "pristine" to the vilification of incompetent federal government management of fires.[10]

Some sites co-opted the book by carrying reviews striking their fancy. LewRockwell.com, a self-proclaimed "anti-state, anti-war, pro-market news site," republished a review of *The Ecological Indian* from the *Edmonton Journal* that uses blunt language to refer to American Indians and their practices.[11] *Center-Right*, a weekly newsletter of centrist, conservative, and libertarian ideas, carried a review that originally appeared in the *Detroit News* in which the author, a senior fellow at the Hoover Institution and head of a political economy center in Bozeman, Montana, lauded *The Ecological Indian* for "systematically debunk[ing] popular myths—many of them promoted by politically motivated greens pushing draconian environmental measures—and instead brings reality to the history of American Indians." He argued that *The Ecological Indian* "builds a foundation upon which we might build more workable ways of allocating and conserving scarce resources" (Anderson 1999).[12] It is a short step from here to the wise-use and property rights movements active in recent times, not just in the West but throughout the country.

Education reformists also took note of *The Ecological Indian*'s thesis. For example, one Web site that carried an essay for those bothered by "the politicization of the K–12 classroom" and "the effort to recruit . . . children—to brainwash them—to take sides in the great policy and political wars of our time" approved of *The Ecological Indian* as a check against teachers whose students "learn about such things as primitive paragons of eco-wisdom— indigenous peoples, for example— 'living in harmony with nature'; or about the ecological Satans, development and industrialization; or of Earth poisoned in its air, water, and soil. But they do not learn much of the science needed for actual understanding." Apparently others are political but not the reformists. A second site included *The Ecological Indian* among books on cultural literacy, angry parents, and failing schools, considering it "the perfect antidote to the mindless drivel heard so often in schools today."[13]

An even more serious form of co-optation of which I am aware was by anti-sovereignty interests. The link between *The Ecological Indian* and sovereignty and treaty rights has been most sharply drawn in Canada, where, in 1999—in virtually the same month my book appeared—the Supreme Court granted Indians the right, based in treaties, to take animals and plants almost at will, and a fierce backlash erupted in the lobster-fishing and logging Maritimes, the elk-hunting West, and elsewhere. One reviewer remarked that the "political relevance" of *The Ecological Indian* was "First . . . [that] Canadian Indians should not be accorded the superior sanction of high-minded environmentalism in negotiations of land settlements and their claims to the right to take game and fish where and when they choose. It should also mean much more balance in responding to native demands and needs simply because discussion of them no longer should be burdened with the guilt piled on the whites for so devastating a noble people whose societies once lived—and might do so again—in perfect harmony with nature" (Fisher 2000, C4). A deep ecologist wrote that *The Ecological Indian*'s history "will help in bringing some understanding to resolve pressing ecological and social issues" stemming from the Supreme Court decision (Orton 1999).

None should be surprised that my personal politics have been questioned or that some have speculated that *The Ecological Indian* is politically motivated. Co-optation helps explain why. Yet it is not I but others who link *The Ecological Indian* to education reform, property rights, and sovereignty. These links are neither necessary nor logical. In fact, one conclusion in *The Ecological Indian* is that American Indians, unburdened by stereotype, freed from being

held to standards that neither they nor others have actually met, liberated
from being condemned for not acting as popular culture would have them
act, can actually draw on a self-conscious ideology of respect for all forms
of life to manage, or co-manage, resources on and under their lands.[14]

Omissions

Now for some specific criticisms—but with your indulgence, I prefer not
to dwell on those who take me to task for saying what I did not say,[15] or for
not having written the book that they would have written, with a single exception, which is the charge that I ignored the role of Europeans in environmental change in North America. As other readers recognize, the intent
of the book was not to rehash the well-known history of European contact
with indigenous people or the environmental history of the continent under European impact, and yet, despite this separate focus, mention was
still made several times of the unquestioned role of the newcomers in environmental change. The bottom line on this point is that my critics and I
occupy common ground; we agree that whatever the impact of Indians on
land and resources, it didn't hold a candle to the long-term impact of people of European descent.[16]

A more productive critique to address begins with the criticism that The
Ecological Indian "almost completely" ignores the role of institutions. An exception is the discussion of family hunting territories in the context of beaver management. One reader, with the Pacific drainage in mind, thought
that "property rights in land . . . encouraged agricultural productivity . . .
good stewardship . . . and salmon selective harvesting and spawning." This
is entirely reasonable as a set of hypotheses to test, and is in fact borne out
in family hunting territories when it comes to densely distributed resources
like beaver or muskrats that stay put and people who can be made to adhere
to the rules (a function, perhaps, of leaders with power not just authority).
For common-access resources the hypotheses are important to test (even
though in South America, where despite tenure some indigenous people
continue to stress short-term gains over long-term conservation, there is
no automatic link between property rights and conservation).[17]

Another type of criticism stems from *The Ecological Indian*'s deliberate brevity. Cases were selected for discussion in the book because they illustrate important aspects of the historically changing relationship between Indians and the environment: Pleistocene extinctions; the disappearance of the Hohokam; the use of fire; the size of the aboriginal population; hunting buffalo, deer, and beaver; and the contemporary scene. They have also been roundly debated, and were therefore grist for my mill—one as interested in placing others' narratives in the context of their day as with the raw data.

I meant for *The Ecological Indian* to be compact, not comprehensive, a model for fine-grained analysis by others on other animals and resources. And so the question of whether the analysis of the exploitation of resources other than the ones considered, like salmon, whales, caribou, shellfish, or plants, would have altered the conclusions is legitimate to ask. As one both skeptical and wary of generalization, I would be glad for enlightenment on this point.

One potential shortcoming concerns plants, to which *The Ecological Indian* gives short shrift except for discussions of fire and the disappearance of the desert-dwelling agricultural Hohokam (who might have delivered too much salty water to salty soil, thereby destroying their crops and the base of urban life). In retrospect I regret not having dedicated more space to plant ecology and conservation. I suspect that practices to propagate and protect occur most frequently with respect to plants, and that routines like recurrent disturbance through clearing and burning enhance biodiversity. Even if such enhancement was unintentional, a by-product of other ends, it would have been profitable to explore these and other processes in greater detail (Smith and Wishnie 2000).

Restraint, Reincarnation, and Conservation

The Ecological Indian also largely ignored fishing and hunting animals other than buffalo, deer, and beaver. Would the analysis of the hunt for seals, whales, caribou, or the harvest of shellfish, or fishing for salmon and other finfish alter the conclusions?

For people in the North, who were not discussed in great detail, the answer seems to be no. For example, the hunt for large animals like caribou and mountain sheep, with the aid of firearms, and of musk oxen without them, reveals an abandon on the part of Iñupiat and Caribou Inuit hunters (Burch 1994). The conclusion for them and other North American foragers would probably not differ markedly from the global assessment that restraint in harvest is rare among hunting and foraging people, who instead make choices that maximize efficiency or contain the prospect of high yields (Alvard 1998b; Smith and Wishnie 2000) until a certain point in history when for different reasons restraint and conservation begin to loom as significant new strategies for indigenous people.

In North America, the rarity of restraint, one can reasonably hypothesize, had as much to do with indubitably indigenous culture as with maximizing efficiency; specifically, with culturally defined respect idealizing the relationship between human hunters and their prey, and with reincarnation. Indians governed the hunt with respect: respect for their prey, which (or rather who), properly approached in thought and deed, gave him- or herself up for sustenance and use. Hunters showed respect by killing animals offering themselves up (and by obeying proscriptions, which in most instances seem to have had little to do with killing too many animals—until the animals themselves became so scarce that another rationale came to bear). Not to kill animals offering themselves could be tantamount to a lack of respect, to denying them the reciprocity they offered humans and the opportunity to be reborn to be killed another day. Reincarnation figured not just in cases examined in The Ecological Indian but far more broadly. For example, the Northwest Coast Gitksans ritually treat each year's first salmon (one resource not considered in The Ecological Indian) with great care. They construct an elaborate cultural context for salmon modeled on human sentience and human social life. Yet all that is required to renew salmon, they say, is to return their bones to the water (Gottesfeld 1994).

In similar fashion, the Iñupiat and Inuit believed that seals, belugas, caribou, musk oxen, and other animals existed "in essentially unlimited supply" and that no link existed between the size of their kill and the availability of prey (Burch 1994, 165). And the Yupiit also understood animals and birds as "infinitely renewable" and unaffected directly by human predation (Fienup-Riordan 1990). It is very difficult to reconcile such beliefs or the behavior based on them with Western-style conservation. It is not that respect gets in the way of the latter but that its content needs to become compatible with certain tenets of conservation biology.

As for conservation, there is a debate over how to define it and over its unwelcome fusion with sustainability, as a number of scholars have recently explored. Some consider actions conservationist even if conserving is an unintended consequence or epiphenomenon of, say, low population density, limited technology, low demand for commodities, or other variables (Hunn 1982). Conflating conservation with sustainability, epiphenomenal conservation unfortunately muddies the waters.

Central to another, far more common definition of conservation dating from the fifteenth century are both intentionality and behavior (OED Online). In this definition, conservation means wise use to maintain future availability, avoiding waste or despoliation, and the like. I agree with it fully. Motivation and performance are central to conservation: the conservationist intends to and does prevent waste, depletion, environmental destruction, and extinction. Conservation, as one scholar puts it, "is by design" (Hames 1987, 93). In this view, practices are conservationist not because they have sustainable consequences but if they meet intentionally formulated ends (Hames 1987, 1991; Alvard 1993, 1994; Smith and Wishnie 2000).

Since the late 1980s, foraging and evolutionary theorists have empirically tested definitions of conservation presuming intentionality in a range of contemporary Amazonian societies. They make conservation operational by definitions such as "enduring a cost in the present so that some benefit [e.g., sustainable harvests] will be realized in the future" (Alvard 1993, 358; see also Alvard 1994, 134; Alvard 1995, 1998a; Stearman 1994). I regret having been almost totally unaware of this research when I was writing *The Ecological Indian*, because it has resulted in a sea change in the discourse of conservation in Amazonia and would have provided a more global context for my conclusions on conservation and ecology.

In Amazonia as in North America, indigenous people possess formidable environmental knowledge that is ecological with the same caveat mentioned earlier. They use this knowledge to develop strategies for adapting to or managing nutrient-poor environments to support human populations. Yet those whose hunts have been closely monitored show no restraint in their pursuit of susceptible fish or animals accessible to all. In other words, they are opportunistic, not prudent, predators. Little concerned for harvest sustainability, resting depleted areas near villages, or stewarding still-bountiful areas, many people pursue prey, even those they know to be vulnerable because of low reproduction rates, to the point of depleting local populations. One group caused the local extinction of fruit trees by cutting them down—because only slaves climb trees, they said, to pick fruit, and they no longer had slaves, but they did have axes (Alvard 1993, 1994; Hames 1987, 1991; FitzGibbon 1998).

This research also shows that when Amazonian indigenous people have taken actions contradicting their image as Ecological Indians—an image both they and various outsiders have promoted—they have incurred the wrath of international conservationists and environmentalists (as the Kayapos did when they engineered gold mining and timber harvests on their lands rather than fulfilling the goals of the international conservation community) and risked action against their claims or hopes for sovereign control over their lands. This is one substantial hidden cost to behavior at variance with image. One scholar concludes that the irrefutable logic and sentiment to grant Native people sovereign control over their lands should not include as one element "that they will choose to conserve," even when they adopt environmental agendas in rapidly changing Amazonia (Alvard 1994, 148; see also Redford and Stearman 1993; Stearman 1994; Hames 1991; Vickers 1994).

Yet there must, I would argue, be room for optimism. For example, in today's Yukon-Kuskokwim Delta, formerly unrestrained Yupiit hunters have adopted a U.S. Fish and Wildlife Goose Management Plan providing information on both local and lower-forty-eight kills of migratory geese. These Yupiit have evolved a conservation scheme premised on their role as predator, not on the limitless renewability of their prey (Zavaleta 1999). No matter the fate of this plan, examples like this leave room for hope for co-management schemes.

Evidence: Whose History?

Another important issue concerns evidence. An early review of *The Ecological Indian* predicted that others would fault me for reliance on the documentary historical record (Lemann 1999). Because most documents have been written by non-indigenous people, this criticism lends itself readily to the racialization of discourse—to identity and ethnic politics—and can be symptomatic of deeper chasms like the ones separating scientists and Umatillas over nine-thousand-year-old Kennewick Man or dividing Darwinian evolutionists and today's intelligent-design creationists over the origins of human life (Momaday 1996). These are debates over what constitutes evidence (and truth). Is historical evidence arrived at through the mix of inductive and deductive methodology of hypothesis-testing science, which proves more often what could not have been rather than what beyond certainty must have been? Or is evidence contained in narratives of ancient revealed truths? Drawn sharply, the lines reveal uncompromising epistemologies.

The question of how much weight to give oral and documentary sources—at the heart of which is reliability and validity in historical sources—is extremely important. *The Ecological Indian* uses many forms of evidence: documentary and oral, primary and secondary, written by eyewitnesses to events or recorded long after the fact, penned by historians, anthropologists, explorers, archaeologists, educators, a range of ordinary and extraordinary folks of different ethnic backgrounds, including American Indians. Even though the book is unexceptional in methodology for a work of anthropological synthesis, I left myself open to criticism by failing to discuss historiography in detail, and I thank Kimberly TallBear (2000a, 2000b) for pointing this out in her trenchant critique of my and Winona LaDuke's works.

Indian voices, by necessity filtered at times through non-Indians (as Black Elk is through John Neihardt), figure at several points in *The Ecological Indian*. They are discussed critically, accepted here and dismissed there (Krech 1999, 22, 42–43, 67–68, 84, 118, 144–45, 149, 166–67, 170–71, 196,

199, 213–14, 228). Of course, temporally *The Ecological Indian* is mainly a historical work, and many agree that in North America the recovery of the distant past through oral history has been greatly complicated by epidemics that killed many and shattered cultural knowledge. I am skeptical about using oral history for comprehensive explanation of continental events thousands of years ago (cf. Deloria 1995) or even for such actions as hunting or burning behavior of one's ancestors two hundred or four hundred years ago, statements concerning which often strike me as vague, remaining at best hypotheses to be tested. But oral accounts of significant epitomizing events, climatic or geological events hundreds of years ago, the year without summer, the flood following the collapse of a glacier-dammed lake, or some other natural catastrophe are ripe for investigation in specific local history (Cruikshank 1981).

Absent foundation or multiple lines of evidence, I admit to clear preference for documentary evidence recorded at or near the time of the event in question. Yet I cannot imagine anyone doing this kind of work today who does not appreciate selectivity, happenstance, and duplicity in the archival record. If the documentary record is preferred over oral testimony it is not because it somehow lacks prejudice or is safe from subsequent manipulation in the archives, but because it is at least fixed at the moment written. Despite its shortcomings, it is at least immune from today's dialogues and presentisms, which inevitably infect the oral report.

Historians working on black American history are painfully aware of the shortcomings of the oral record; painfully because oral history in this instance, as in others, has the potential to capture the voices of the voiceless, the forgotten, and the neglected in history. Karen Fields, for example, regretfully but dispassionately concludes that her Charleston, South Carolina, grandmother's memory is "ideologically tainted" and "summoned in view of present political purposes" that differ from Fields's assumptions about what is structurally important in history and that guide her elicitations (Fields 1994, 93).

One problem recognized by all is the fallibility of memory. This is an old saw in history. Thucydides complained that different eyewitnesses came to different conclusions on events of the Peloponnesian War, complicating his task. Yet if memory fails it can also be reliable. In recent years Italian historians have conducted much promising work on memory and history regarding the World War II era. Under promising circumstances—a superb memory of events thirty or more years after they occurred, a limited, discrete role in history—a person can have remarkable recall of events he or she witnessed and participated in, memory stable through tellings years apart (Hoffman and Hoffman 1994).

Such a person's memory is reliable. But for it to be valid it must correspond to reports by other eyewitnesses to the same events or other primary source material, which is often difficult to come by. For this reason, perhaps, contemporary Italian historians such as Alessandro Portelli and Luisa Passerini emphasize subjectivity in oral history. For them, the departures from fact are more interesting than adherences to fact for what they reveal about culture or power. Portelli's research on the murder by Germans of 335 Italian citizens in Rome in 1944, after Italian partisans had killed 33 German soldiers, is apt. Today, according to Portelli, people say that the Germans delivered an ultimatum that they would shoot ten Italians for every German killed unless the partisans turned themselves in. The partisans did not, and today's collective memory blames them. In actuality—the evidence is in documents—the Germans sent out the retaliatory order instantly, and blame properly belongs with them. Today's collective memory is wrong, yet it fits today's era, which has witnessed great growth in neofascism (Stille 2001; Passerini 1998; Portelli 1998).

Yet this is not reason enough to reject oral history altogether. I argue instead for its consideration on a case-by-case basis, for judging it critically with other forms of evidence, and for letting it function, where possible, in a collaborative role with other forms of evidence (as in the analysis in *The Ecological Indian* of nineteenth-century fires in northwestern Montana, which drew on oral history, primary and secondary documents, and fire-scar data).

This conclusion is based not just on analyses in North America—including my own of a mission school diet (Krech 1978)—but on recent cases demonstrating creatively the potential of history that draws fully on oral testimony, recorded documents, and science—on multiple lines of evidence. The best-known example involves the relationship between Thomas Jefferson and his slave Sally Hemings, who, according to Jefferson descendants and most historians (but not Hemings descendants), lacked intimacy with each other. In 1999 a group of European molecular biologists and a U.S. pathologist announced that certain Y-chromosome DNA sequences in the two families matched. They asserted a genetic link between Jefferson and Hemings descendants, confirming that Thomas Jefferson was one of several candidates to have fathered one or more children with Sally Hemings. Other candidates were his brother Randolph and his brother's son, but most historians now conclude that Thomas himself fathered Sally Heming's fifth child, Eston. The genetic data, in other words, turned received historical wisdom on its head. The data also lend support to Hemings family histories recorded both orally and in writing, and they contradict Jefferson descendants claiming that if anyone in the Jefferson family fathered a child with Sally Hemings it was a son of Thomas Jefferson's sister Martha Carr, a claim that is contradicted by Y-chromosome data transmitted through male links (Marshall 1999).

A second example, less well known, concerns the Bantu-speaking Lembas of southern Africa, who practice circumcision and abhor pork as well as meat from piglike hippos, and have long asserted that they possess deep links to faraway Judea. Many non-Lembas have scoffed at the assertions—until recently, when geneticists discovered in Lemba priests a set of DNA sequences (a set of mutations at nine sites) on the Y chromosome distinctive of Jewish priests who are the descendants of Aaron. This not only signals Jewish ancestry but allows calculation of when they last shared common ancestry with other Jews, and it neatly supplies support for Lemba oral tradition (Wade 1999). These and other examples[18] show the advantage of triangulating different lines of evidence—and provide confirmation from scientific evidence for oral history (which should not be taken to mean that the last word is in).

Contemporary Environmentalism

My penultimate remarks concern the book's epilogue, which attempts to measure the fit of the image of the Ecological Indian with American Indian behavior in the final decades of the twentieth century. Some find it largely silent on what one reader called the "resurgence of native environmentalism." I agree. Although it was never entirely absent at any time in history, American Indian environmentalism—a concern for the state of the environment and for acting on that concern—did not emerge as a force until the late twentieth century. When it involved action, its evolution, like that of other environmental movements, has been rapid and its ultimate success is difficult to predict. Nevertheless, today environmentalism thrives in Indian country (Brosius 1999; Little 1999).

Presented with the opportunity, I would update the story of the contemporary environmental movement and discourse. This is also a potentially productive research area for students in Native studies or anthropology. One trend is the development or enhancement of tribal-based environmental management or resource protection departments "to provide environmental protection and public awareness on environmental issues" (Fallon Paiute-Shoshones), to protect and assess the impact of projects on plant and animal resources as well as air and water quality (Pueblos of Jemez), or to alert tribal members to the presence of toxins and preserve wetlands (St. Regis Mohawks). Various Iroquoian tribes have been especially active, not surprising given industry's heavy and destructive hand on the St. Lawrence and elsewhere (Krech 2001).[19]

A number of broad-based environmental efforts have also emerged in Indian country. They include meetings sponsored by outsiders to cement relations between Indians and environmentalists, push continental and even global environmental causes (keep nuclear waste off Indian lands, combat environmental injustice in mining, oil, and hydroelectric projects, etc.), and argue for co-management (with scientists) of lands and natural resources.[20]

Specific decisions on environmental issues in turn-of-the-twenty-first-century Indian country range as widely today as when I was writing The Ecological Indian. On the side of the protectionists, environmentalists, and biophiliacs are decisions by Indian people to close a landfill ahead of time; control paper mill smokestack pollution and improve air quality; enable gray wolf recovery; block a timber company from gaining access to a pristine watershed; manage buffalo leaving Yellowstone for hunting and consumption; get out of logging and restore logging-damaged salmon streams; forbid the shipment of plutonium across tribal lands; sue the Army Corps of Engineers for violating the Clean Water Act and harming salmon; apprehend and prosecute tribal members who waste salmon; protect wetlands against casino and business expansions; and restore a stretch of the Rio Grande by clearing invasive species and planting native species (Krech 2001).[21]

In contrast are actions that often anger conservationists and environmentalists: arrange an easement from the U.S. Forest Service for a thirty-mile road to eight thousand acres of harvestable timber in southeastern Alaska; deplete the Cook Inlet population of belugas in order to consume and sell muktuk; hunt gray whales; take lobsters without regard to season; log previously off-limits Crown lands; offer the reservation for nuclear waste; cut natural gas, oil, coal, and electricity deals (some with the promise of quick review and little regulation); advance plans for a dam for future water use for industrial, residential, and resort use; build a three-billion-dollar pipeline for the transport of natural gas from northern Canada and Alaska to southern markets; propose harvesting shellfish in Long Island Sound; vote for mega-hydroelectric projects; or argue to hunt without regard to protections for endangered species (Krech 2001).[22]

At the time I wrote The Ecological Indian it seemed to me that American Indians often cannot afford, or are not interested in, positions staked out by environmentalists. I do not consider this observation especially novel. To boot, they are sometimes slammed by non-Indians when their behavior clashes with the image of the Ecological Indian. How much has changed today? Like rural communities elsewhere, Indian country seems frequently divided over growth and economic development issues. Not uncommon is a tribal leadership in favor of economic development opposed by tribal members who consider land's sacrality as its most important quality and take up environmentalist positions consistent with the Ecological Indian. Yet for many, economic concerns trump green issues. People desire jobs and disposable income and at least some of the trappings of middle-class American life. Today, many American Indians are interested in casinos. This does not mean that they want to sacrifice their identity as Indians or sense of belonging to place.

Arctic National Wildlife Refuge: The Gwich'in and Iñupiat

The complexity of these issues is revealed in a case that is very much in the public eye: whether or not to drill for oil in the Arctic National Wildlife Refuge (ANWR), the second-largest wildlife refuge in the nation, an important site for nesting birds and some 150,000 caribou calving and grazing in summer, and the most important pristine space left in the United States. It is the key resource case in early-twenty-first-century America and one that I track closely because of ethnography among the Teetl'it Gwich'in ("people of the head of the waters") in the 1970s. The fight over ANWR has swept up two indigenous groups, the Gwich'in and, less visible at first, the Iñupiat, as well as a host of environmentalists, bureaus and divisions of the United States government, politicians of all stripes, and the American public.

The Alaskan Gwich'in are not totally averse to development but are against drilling the calving grounds in ANWR. For them, caribou represent a significant source of protein and lie at the core of their cultural and ethnic identity. In the 1990s they secured important allies in the Wilderness Society, the Natural Resources Defense Council, the Audubon Society, and other environmental and conservation organizations and mounted an effective campaign against drilling (Krech 1999).[23]

They also had the executive branch on their side, though this ended with the 2000 election. Since that time, and especially since 9/11, pressure to open ANWR has increased steadily and the Gwich'in and their allies in the conservation and environmental fields have waged a desperate fight to sway public—and senatorial—opinion. In August 2001 the House approved drilling in

ANWR. But in April 2002 the Senate saved the day. No one expects the pressure to go away, since opening ANWR is central to the Bush administration's energy policy and is now wrapped in the cloak of national security.

Environmentalists have placed at the center of this struggle the Gwich'in, as people who revere the land and the caribou, but they have tended to remain silent on the Iñupiat. For example, one op-ed on ANWR that appeared in the *New York Times* in late February 2001 made an explicit plea not to drill land that for the Gwich'in is sacred (Cronon 2001). Yet in the old days, the coastal plain, including ANWR and the most visible part of the calving ground, was Iñupiat far more than Gwich'in territory—and today it is within North Slope Borough (Iñupiat) boundaries. In the old days the Gwich'in, save for one band, avoided coastal calving grounds because they were not only distant but dangerously inhabited by hostile Iñupiat. Even if the Iñupiat tended to hang around the coast (mosquitoes inland are fierce and plague caribou and man) and define sea mammals as real food, they have a greater claim on coastal sections of ANWR than the Gwich'in. And while many Iñupiat are opposed to drilling in the ocean where it might affect seals and bowhead whales, and some are ambivalent about drilling land portions of ANWR, many have proclaimed that "oil is the future." They say that they do not want to and cannot return to the past; that they do not want to lose health, education, and other benefits from North Slope oil; and that they believe ANWR can be drilled safely and without consequence to adaptable caribou. In the past, other Native organizations in Alaska—the interior Doyon Corporation and the statewide Alaska Federation of Natives—have sided with them (Krech 1999, 2001).[24]

The naive appropriation of the Gwich'in as privileged consumers of caribou on sacred ground, and therefore as indigenous people who occupy the high moral ground, is a dangerous strategy that can backfire.[25] It is not that they should not be privileged, or that they occupy low not high ground, or that they lack legitimate interest in migratory caribou. None of this is at issue. Rather it is because the argument is vulnerable to Iñupiat claims that at best complicate and at worst neutralize or trump Gwich'in claims.[26] Thus in April 2002 the energy lobby sent Iñupiat to Washington to try to convince fence-sitting senators to vote for drilling and indigenous economic development (Rosenbaum 2002).

This case exposes the danger of using an image of uncorrupted indigenous nobility as a basis for environmental action. The appropriation of the Gwich'in is unfortunate if one favors keeping ANWR pristine and letting the caribou and birds go about their business in a landscape unmarred by industrial architecture, noise, or sound. For this particular case there is a need to convince more people to value remaining quiet, pristine places as well as to resist destroying what cannot, within several lifetimes, be made whole again, without first determining that there is no other option (a point not yet reached).

Anthropological Ethics and Indian Country

To conclude, I wrote *The Ecological Indian* to scrutinize the fit between an image and behavior. As Peter Brosius (1999) and others (e.g., Dove 1999) have written with insight in different contexts, one goal here was to interrogate an essentialized image. As they (and others) have argued, there is reason to be concerned with the dehumanization inherent in such images. The co-optations of which I speak here were not entirely unanticipated—we live in a political world, after all—and they bother me as much as they do others. I suspect that my experience is no different from that of others who have written books useful to people with quite different political leanings from those of the authors. I am concerned about the impact of analytical interventions on people to whom they pertain, but I wonder what can be done, aside from self-censorship, to prevent any person on any side of any political spectrum from selective engagement with one's work. This is the dilemma of "unmasking" categories like the Ecological Indian. Perhaps, in the end, if the myths are taken away, as one caller to a radio program pleaded with me not to do, then new categories should be offered to replace the essentialized one left on the dustheap (Brosius 1999; Baviskar 1999; Berglund 1999; Dove 1999).

In this light it is understandable, to me at least, why some Indian people would react against *The Ecological Indian*. An important question to ask is where this might leave me, an anthropologist who has done ethnography in North America, with regard to oft-asserted ethical responsibilities of anthropologists toward the people about whom we write, a question that in some quarters today takes on a particular sense of urgency (Little 2000).[27] What makes answering this question difficult is that *The Ecological Indian* is about Indian country as a whole, and Indian country is far from monolithic in its reaction.[28] Thus some American Indians consider *The Ecological Indian* "valuable" (Kipp 2000) or "generally thoughtful and thought-provoking" (Justice 2001). Another reacts strongly to "desperate incoherence" in the critical review in *The Nation* (Cloud 2000). Yet another takes strong issue with "ludicrous" accusations in an editorial in *Indian Country Today* and states unequivocally that in *The Ecological Indian* there is "one axe to grind: The evidence should be considered" (Tallbear 2000a). One critic concludes in a letter submitted for publication in *The Nation*, "My Choctaw ancestors smelted iron on the banks of the Peace River in Mississippi. Once when I was a child, a heavy axe head, stained with time, was placed in my hands. Its energy surged through me, every cold curve of it radiating a fierce intelligence. Now, there hasn't been an ironworks in human history that didn't exact a heavy toll on its environment. What do I possibly gain by wishing the work of my ancestors to be some remarkable exception? For those who can find strength and allies for the present struggle by candidly facing the past," this reader concludes, *The Ecological Indian* is "an important book" (Cloud 2000).

The fact that opinion is divided on many matters, including those related to the environment—whether it is best, for example, to promote biodiversity or relieve poverty—complicates simple calls for social or political accountability (e.g., Brosius 1999; Hvalkov 1999; Kottak 1999). Indian country is not now and never has been a monolithic place in which culture or power or historical experience or memory is distributed uniformly or shared equally. Those who think otherwise invent a fiction as great as the image of the Ecological Indian.

Notes

1. George A. Rentschler Distinguished Visiting Lecture, American Heritage Center, University of Wyoming, April 26, 2002.

2. A collateral question (discussed below): Were American Indians environmentalists? That is, did they show concern for the state of the environment and perhaps act on that concern?

3. The database for my remarks consists first of reviews of *The Ecological Indian*. As of April 2002, reviews and comments had appeared in (chronologically) *Kirkus Reviews, Boston Globe* (carried in *Seattle Post-Intelligence, Arizona Daily Star, Arizona Republic, Minneapolis Star Tribune*), *Publishers Weekly, Booklist, Library Journal, Washington Post, Wall Street Journal, Discover, Detroit News* (carried in *Glenwood Post, High Country News,* and *Reason Magazine*), *Chronicle of Higher Education, New Yorker, National Review Online, Slate.com/Egghead, Brown Alumni Monthly, Natural History, Yale Alumni Magazine, Indian Country Today, New York Times, The Reviewer, High Country News, Salt Lake Tribune, Tampa Tribune & Times, Terrain, The Independent, Literary Review, National Post, Der Spiegel, Le monde diplomatique, Metroland, Tucson Weekly, Choice, Heterodoxy, Anthropology News, Vancouver Sun* (carried in *Seattle Times*), *NRC Handelsblad, Toronto Sun* (carried in *Ottawa Sun, The Daily Gleaner*), *New Republic, Groton Quarterly, Nation, New York Press, Science, L'actualité, The Report, American Archaeology, The Futurist, P.M. Peter Moosleitners interessantes Magazin, O estadao de S. Paulo, The Ecologist, Soundings, Environmental History, Indigo, Chosun Ilbo, IIIRM Publications, Times Literary Supplement, Minnesota History, Le Monde, H-Amindian/H-Net Book Review, Skeptical Inquirer, Le Québécois Libre, Environmental Ethics, The Skeptic, Worldviews, Baltimore Sun, Time Out, Recherches amérindiennes au Québec, Smoky Mountain News, Canadian Historical Review, American Historical Review, Sedmd Generace, Journal of American History, Times Higher Education Supplement, Internationalist Socialist Review, Human Ecology Review, BC Studies, Montana, Northeastern Naturalist, Isle, Down to Earth, Science News, Scientific and Medical Network, L'histoire, Ciudad Virtual de Antropologia y Arqueologia* [Equipo NAyA], *New York Review of Books, Louisiana History, Ethics, Place and Environment, American Forests, American Studies Today Online.* In addition, critics on amazon.com and elsewhere on the web have weighed in, as have they in live and taped shows with NPR affiliates in Pasadena, Wisconsin, Maine, Urbana-Champaign, other radio stations in Seattle, Philadelphia, Los Angeles, Boulder, Des Moines, Vancouver, and on "Native America Calling," distributed to NPR and twenty-seven Native radio stations by satellite, and in lectures, seminars, and courses in departments and programs of environmental history and science, religious studies, American studies, English, and anthropology, history, etc.

4. Critics have used language like "honestly curious," "meticulous," "well-documented," "definitive," "masterful," "sweeping," "first-rate social science," "courageous," "tour-de-force," "scrupulously honest," "extraordinarily careful," "ground-breaking," "compelling," "stunning," "what good science should be."

5. This critic is the prominent Lakota lawyer, historian, and author Vine Deloria Jr., who joined the fray in September 1999 after being contacted by a reporter writing a feature on *The Ecological Indian* for the *Chronicle of Higher Education* (Sharlet 1999). In an e-mail trail, Deloria and others excoriate *The Ecological Indian* (although they never made clear why). Deloria admitted to "attack[ing] Krech's thesis every chance I have gotten." Haliwah, October 17, 1999, first_nations mail archive; Sonja Keohane, January 19, 2000, first_nations mail archive; Sharon Green, January 19, 2000, first_nations mail archive; David Rider, January 19, 2000, first_nations mail archive; Kristin Iden, January 19, 2000, containing Vine Deloria to Kristen Iden, January 19, 2000, first_nations mail archive; kolahq to aeissing, March 3, 2000, "ALERT from Prof. Vine Deloria Jr.," containing Mike

Wicks to [clipped], March 3, 2000; Mike Wicks to www.egroups.com/message/aim/6726 ("attacking . . ."); Cathi Wherry to protecting knowledge, February 8, 2001, containing Morgan Wood to American Indian Studies section. See also Tim Johnson (1999, 19), who leads a list of "critics in the academy" with The Ecological Indian and labels as "debunkers" me and others who "[question] the practical and historical realities of Indian environmental ethos" and considers conclusions rooted in Indian belief systems as "almost ideological."

6. A commentator on one internet list suggested that it is "white" for me to write as I do and for the New York Times reviewer (a non-Native anthropologist) to endorse The Ecological Indian. Sometimes charges are aimed scattershot at anything and anyone in the way: a feature writer for Der Spiegel, a documentary filmmaker in England, any reviewer who regards The Ecological Indian positively, or white people in general (Haliwah, first_nations mail archive, 10/17/1999; Wood Owl, first_nations mail archive, 10/17/1999).

7. Two critics on amazon.com also raise the race specter. E. N. Anderson suggests that I quote "at length and with apparent favor—a lot of racist 19th-century writers who" wrote that "Native Americans were bloodthirsty savages who killed wantonly." Another ("a reader") considers The Ecological Indian "welcomed by all those who wish to corroborate their mindset belief that the Native Americans were an inferior race who needed to be pushed aside by the superiority of Western culture." One standard definition of race is "a division of mankind possessing traits that are transmissible by descent and sufficient to characterize it as a distinct human type" and of racism is "a belief that race is the primary determinant of human traits and capacities and that racial differences produce an inherent superiority of a particular race" (Merriam-Webster's Collegiate Dictionary On-line). Van den Berghe (1996, 1054–55) defines racism as "a set of beliefs held by individuals about categorical superiority or inferiority of groups socially defined by physical characteristics" and argues that the charge of racism can act as "effective behavioral and verbal restraint."

8. The Editors of Lingua Franca (1999) labeled The Ecological Indian "the most controversial academic book of the season."

9. Constructive Citizen Participation (http://www.islandnet.com/fficonnor/inprint3.html, accessed March 2000) lists The Ecological Indian presumably, as they put it, to prevent and resolve public controversy, perhaps because I am said to have discovered "widespread romantic inaccuracies about Indians in the environmental movement and the aboriginal community."

10. See the Independence Institute's Great Books Page (i2i.org/book/htm); Linda Gorman, Independence Institute, "Dangerous Myths" (http://i2i.org/SuptDocs/OpEdArcv/Gorman/ 00May02. ecological_indian.htm, accessed July 2000); People for the U.S.A.! (http://www.pfw.org/index.html, accessed March 2000; www.pfw.org/arizona/1199tucsonnews.html, accessed August 2000).

11. Lew Rockwell.com (http://www.lewrockwell.com/orig/gunter1.html, accessed March 2000) carried the hard-hitting review, Lorne Gunter, "Ecological Indian Is a Myth: Neither Criminals nor Saints, Early Natives Were Simply Human," Edmonton Journal.

12. Anderson's review was reprinted in the Glenwood Post, High Country News, Center-Right, and as "Rational Natives," Reason Online (http://www.reasonmag. com/0003/bk.ta.rational.htm, accessed July 2000).

13. "Education: Notes from a Parent: A Reading List about Education" (http://www.mcs.net/ ffishs/ schools/read.html, accessed August 2000 ["antidote.."]); a footnote on indigenous people as paragons of deep ecological wisdom reprints a precis of The Ecological Indian (Paul Gross, "Politicizing Science Education," http://www. edexcellence.net/ library/gross.html, accessed August 2000).

14. Some critics consider these thoughts patronizing.

15. E. N. Anderson, on amazon.com, takes issue with the notion that the buffalo jump was common. Yet the jump was not simply one of several communal hunting techniques; it was one in which ecology and conservation come to the fore. The same critic labels my chapter on beaver hunting "extreme" because, he asserts, "most authorities agree that beaver were more or less conserved until the white trappers got into the act," especially in the Southwest. Yet I do not hold people of European descent blameless in the decimation of the beaver in the Southwest (even if that was not the point of the chapter on beaver hunting in eastern and central Canada).

16. Compare, for example, the unfounded assertions in Galts 1999.

17. Anderson 1999 raises the issue of property rights but, with other fish to fry, argues that "Conservation depends on whether the institutions get the incentives right" and that The Ecological Indian helps us gain "better understanding of how we might use property rights to ensure good resource stewardship." On territoriality see also Hames 1987, 1991.

18. Another case suggestively bears on the Noachian deluge: the discovery, five hundred feet beneath the surface of the Black Sea, of a former shoreline and abrupt transition from freshwater to saltwater mollusks, fitting the theory about a breach in the Bosporus some seventy-five hundred years ago and flooding along the shoreline of the sea amounting, perhaps, to one mile a day (Ballard 2001).

19. The cases discussed here and in the following paragraph are not just hopeful (for the implementation of an environmental agenda in Indian country) but ripe for analysis. They are discussed at greater length in Krech 2001.

20. Again for more details see Krech 2001. Many of these efforts are concerned with environmental justice and with combating mining, hydrocarbon, and waste storage in Indian country. Even though they tend to separate indigenous and "traditional" from nontraditional and modern, and although some reach toward combining traditional ways of knowing with Western science to promote better resource and ecosystem management, for the most part they avoid lapsing into hegemonic stereotypes—in contrast to LaDuke (1999), for example, whose useful work on environmentalism in Indian country is marred by an insistence on industrial and indigenous ways of thinking, on the latter as traditional (aboriginal) and legitimate and the former as technological and anti-spiritual and anti-Indian (for critique see TallBear 2000b; Krech 2001).

21. These cases are broad-based and involve the Cocopahs, Forest County Potawatomis (in agreement with the federal government and the state of Wisconsin), Nez Perces, Siska Nation, various Plains Indian tribes, Eyak Corporation (with a sustainable development group), Kahnawake Mohawks, Mississippi Choctaws (together with the Army Corps of Engineers), Santa Ana Pueblos, and others (Krech 2001, compiled from H-Net and LexisNexis, 1999–2001).

22. These concern Chugach Alaska Corporation, Makahs, Mi'kmaqs, Maliseet), Southern Utes of Colorado, Canadian Gwich'in, Fort Mohave Tribe, Siksika First Nation, Denes, Mohegans, Crees, and the National Chief of the Canadian Assembly of First Nations (Krech 2001, compiled from H-Net and LexisNexis, 1999–2001).

23. In the past, the Gwich'in invited Exxon and others to prospect for oil and gas on 1.7 million acres of land where caribou winter (Krech 2001).

24. Some Iñupiat argue that the Gwich'in gave up rights over territory outside their own when they chose years ago not to be part of the Alaska Native Claims Settlement Act.

25. Some Gwich'in, at least, evidently call this land *vadzaih googii vi dehk'it gwanlii* (Cronon, "Neither Barren Nor Remote", which literally means "caribou their young their place is there" or col-

loquially "that's the place for the caribou's young" (for discussion of this phrase, thanks to John Ritter 2001). Yet some now render this phrase in English as "the sacred land where life begins," an understandable if overtly political attempt to make resources sacred in order to place them off limits. As a strategy, however, oversacralization has a potential downside: when caught out, the argument loses force, and genuinely sacred sites become vulnerable (Krech 2001).

26. I fail to understand the argument that the use of modern technology—guns versus caribou surrounds and snares—somehow makes Indians less Indian and their interests less legitimate.

27. Today in anthropology this question is more urgent than ever, given charges levied against researchers among the South American Yanomamos, which when first voiced centered on genocide but have since focused on unethical callousness—charges complicated by personal animosity and sharp ideological differences within anthropology concerning the implications of postmodernism for science.

28. Deloria worried that "one or two Indians will break ranks" from inexperience or naïveté (kolahq to aeissing, e-mail, March 3, 2000).

References

Alvard, Michael S. 1993. Testing the "ecologically noble savage" hypothesis: Interspecific prey choice by Piro hunters of Amazonian Peru. *Human Ecology* 21:355–87.

———. 1994. Conservation by Native peoples: Prey choice in a depleted habitat. *Human Nature* 5 (2): 127–54.

———. 1995. Intraspecific prey choice by Amazonian hunters. *Current Anthropology* 36:789–818.

———. 1998a. Evolutionary ecology and resource conservation. *Evolutionary Anthropology* 7:62–74.

———. 1998b. Indigenous hunting in the neotropics: Conservation or optimal foraging? In *Behavioral ecology and conservation biology*, ed. Tim Caro, 474–500. New York: Oxford University Press.

Anderson, Terry L. 1999. Indians also wasted abundant resources. *Detroit News*, September 8, A9.

Ballard, Robert D. Deep black sea. *National Geographic* 199 (5): 52–70.

Baviskar, Amita. 1999. Comment. *Current Anthropology* 40:288–89.

Berglund, Eeva. 1999. Comment. *Current Anthropology* 40:289–90.

Black, Margaret. 1999. Native soil. *Metroland* [Albany NY], December 2–8.

Brosius, J. Peter. 1999. Analyses and interventions: Anthropological engagements with environmentalism [and CA commentary]. *Current Anthropology* 40:277–309.

Burch, Ernest S., Jr. 1994. Rationality and resource use among hunters. In *Circumpolar religion and ecology: An anthropology of the north*, ed. Takashi Irimoto and Takako Yamada, 163–85. Tokyo: University of Tokyo Press.

Cloud, John. 2000. E-mail to Shepard Krech III, February 14.

Cronon, William. 2001. Neither barren nor remote. *New York Times*, February 28, A19.

Cruikshank, Julie. 1981. Legend and landscape: Convergence of oral and scientific traditions in the Yukon Territory. *Arctic Anthropology* 18 (2): 67–93.

Deloria, Vine, Jr. 1995. *Red earth, white lies: Native Americans and the myth of scientific fact*. New York: Scribner.

Dove, Michael. 1999. Comment. *Current Anthropology* 40:290–91.

Editors of Lingua Franca. 1999. Bury my heart at a toxic waste dump. In *Barbie's Malibu dream knee: News from academe*. http://slate.msn.com/Egghead/99–09–21/Egghead.asp (accessed September 1999).

Fields, Karen E. 1994. What one cannot remember mistakenly. In *Memory and history: Essays on recalling and interpreting experience*, ed. Jaclyn Jeffrey and Glenace Edwall, 89–106. Lanham MD: University Press of America.

Fienup-Riordan, Ann. 1990. Original ecologists? The relationship between Yup'ik Eskimos and animals. In *Eskimo essays: Yup'ik lives and how we see them*, ed. Ann Fienup-Riordan, 167–91. New Brunswick: Rutgers University Press.

Fisher, Douglas. 2000. The myth of the ecological Indian. *Toronto Sun*, January 23, C4.

FitzGibbon, Clare D. 1998. The management of subsistence harvesting: Behavioral ecology of hunters and their mammalian prey. In *Behavioral ecology and conservation biology*, ed. Tim Caro, 449–73. New York: Oxford University Press.

Flores, Dan. 2001. Review of *The ecological Indian. Journal of American History* 88 (1): 177–78.

Galts, Chad. 1999. A trail of myths. *Brown Alumni Monthly* 100 (1): 20–21.

Gottesfeld, Leslie M. Johnson. 1994. Conservation, territory, and traditional beliefs: An analysis of Gitksan and Wet'suwet'en subsistence, northwest British Columbia, Canada. *Human Ecology* 22:443–65.

Hames, Raymond. 1987. Game conservation or efficient hunting? In *The question of the commons: The culture and ecology of communal resources*, ed. Bonnie McCay and James M. Acheson, 92–107. Tucson: University of Arizona Press.

——. 1991. Wildlife conservation in tribal societies. In *Biodiversity: Culture, conservation, and ecodevelopment*, ed. Margaret L. Oldfield and Janis B. Alcorn, 172–99. Boulder CO: Westview Press.

Hoffman, Alice M., and Howard S. Hoffman. 1994. Reliability and validity in oral history: The case for memory. In *Memory and history: Essays on recalling and interpreting experience*, ed. Jaclyn Jeffrey and Glenace Edwall, 107–35. Lanham MD: University Press of America.

Holdridge, Randall. 1999. Up in smoke: Shepard Krech debunks the notion of "The ecological Indian." *Tucson Weekly*, December 23–29, 40–41.

Hunn, Eugene S. 1982. Mobility as a factor limiting resource use in the Columbia Plateau of North America. In *Resource managers: North American and Australian hunter-gatherers*, ed. Nancy M. Williams and Eugene S. Hunn, 17–43. Boulder CO: Westview Press.

Hvalkov, Soren. 1999. Comment. *Current Anthropology* 40:294–95.

Indian Country Today. 2000. Elders' concern is a true sentiment. May 10.

Johnson, Tim. 1999. World out of balance: In prescient time Native prophecy meets scientific prediction. *Native Americas* 16 (3–4): 8–25.

Justice, Daniel. 2001. Review of *The ecological Indian. Isle* 8 (1): 244–46.

Kipp, Woody. 2000. Lessons from the Native Americans. *Verde Balance*. wysiwyg://41/http://www.verde.com/balance/daeoaac42959ff393c0e445a0a019b30.htm (accessed July 2000).

Kottak, Conrad P. 1999. The new ecological anthropology. *American Anthropologist* 101:23–35.

Krech, Shepard, III. 1978. Nutritional evaluation of a mission residential school diet: The accuracy of informant recall. *Human Organization* 37:186–90.

———. 1999. *The ecological Indian: Myth and history.* New York: Norton.

———. 2001. Natural resource issues in Indian country. Sawyer Seminar, Modern Times, Rural Places, Massachusetts Institute of Technology, Cambridge, November 16.

LaDuke, Winona. 1999. *All our relations: Native struggles for land and life.* Cambridge: South End Press.

Lemann, Nicholas. 1999. Buffaloed. *New Yorker*, September 13, 98–101.

Little, Paul E. 1999. Environments and environmentalisms in anthropological research: Facing a new millennium. *Annual Review of Anthropology* 28:253–84.

Marshall, Eliot. 1999. Which Jefferson was the father? *Science* 283:153–54.

Momaday, N. Scott. 1996. Disturbing the spirits. *New York Times*, November 2.

Orton, David. 1999. Pick of the week: The ecological Indian. *The Reviewer*, October 24, 1999. http://www.jaalmag.com/thereviewer/24101999p.htm (accessed November 1999).

Oxford English dictionary online [OED online]. 2002. [Entries for] Conservation, Conserve, Sustainable.

Passerini, Luisa. 1998. Work ideology and consensus under Italian fascism. In *The oral history reader*, ed. Robert Perks and Alistair Thomson, 53–62. London: Routledge.

Pennypacker, Mindy. 2000. The first environmentalists. *Nation*, February 7, 29–31.

Portelli, Alessandro. 1998. What makes oral history different. In *The oral history reader*, ed. Robert Perks and Alistair Thomson, 63–74. London: Routledge.

Porterfield, K. Marie. 1999. Krech's "Ecological Indian": Propaganda, pure and simple. *Indian Country Today*, October 11–18, C2.

Redford, Kent, and Allyn Maclean Stearman. 1993. Forest-dwelling Native Amazonians and the conservation of biodiversity: Interest in common or in collision? *Conservation Biology* 7 (2): 248–55.

Ritter, John. 2001. E-mail to Shepard Krech III, March 1.

Rosenbaum, David. 2002. As two sides push, Arctic oil plan seems doomed. *New York Times*, April 18, A21.

Sale, Kirkpatrick. 2000. Again, the savage Indian. *The Ecologist* 30 (4): 52.

Sharlet, Jeff. 1999. An anthropologist finds Indians lived in less-than-perfect harmony with nature. *Chronicle of Higher Education* 46 (3): A19–21.

Smith, Eric Alden, and Mark Wishnie. 2000. Conservation and subsistence in small-scale societies. *Annual Review of Anthropology* 29:493–524.

Stearman, Allyn MacLean. 1994. "Only slaves climb trees": Revisiting the myth of the ecologically noble savage in Amazonia. *Human Nature* 5:339–57.

Stille, Alexander. 2001. Prospecting for truth in the ore of memory. *New York Times*, March 10, A15, 17.

TallBear, Kimberly. 2000a. Shepard Krech's *The ecological Indian*: One Indian's perspective. IIIRM [International Institute for Indigenous Resource Management] Publications. http://www.iiirm.org/review/bkreview.htm (accessed September 2000).

———. 2000b. The straitjacket of identity and confusion of sovereignty in Winona LaDuke's *All our relations*. IIIRM [International Institute for Indigenous Resource Management] Publications. http://www.iiirm.org/review/bkreview.htm (accessed September 2000).

van den Berghe, Pierre L. 1996. Racism. In *Encyclopedia of cultural anthropology*, ed. David Levinson and Melvin Ember, 3:1054–57. New York: Henry Holt.

Vickers, William T. 1994. From opportunism to nascent conservation. *Human Nature* 5:307–37.

Wade, Nicholas. 1999. DNA backs a tribe's tradition of early descent from the Jews. *New York Times*, May 9, 1, 20.

White, Richard. 2000. Dead certainties. *New Republic*, January 24, 44, 46–49.

Zavaleta, Erika. 1999. The emergence of waterfowl conservation among Yup'ik hunters in the Yukon-Kuskokwim Delta, Alaska. *Human Ecology* 27:231–66.

2. The Ecological Indian and the Politics of Representation

Critiquing The Ecological Indian in the Age of Ecocide

Darren J. Ranco

While claiming to open new fields of debate and research, Shepard Krech's *The Ecological Indian* (1999) is fairly typical in its analysis of the ecological Indian among scholars who argue against the notion that Indians have, or ever did have, an ecological awareness. Like others who have emphasized historical and current environmental practices, Krech concludes that we should give up the idea of the "ecological Indian" and leave the stereotype in the waste bin of colonial invention. The disturbing aspects of Krech's book lie precisely in this seemingly benign sentiment. By urging us to take the "scientific evidence" at its face value, he has tried to hide (unwittingly perhaps) the political aspects of his "findings." When he does confront the cultural politics of his claim, he treats it as an element that is external to culture itself: "American Indians have taken on the Noble Indian/Ecological Indian stereotype, embedding it in their self-fashioning, just as other indigenous people around the world have done with similar primordial ecological and conservationist stereotypes [footnote]. Yet its relationship to native cultures and behavior is deeply problematic. The Noble Indian/Ecological Indian distorts culture" (Krech 1999, 27).

Unlike the authors whose studies he cites in his footnote (Lears 1985; Keesing 1989; Sahlins 1993), Krech does not recognize such identity claims and the context and resistance to them as an object for cultural analysis; rather he sees these identity claims as a disturbance of "real" cultural behaviors. By treating such claims, a priori, as residing outside the realm of cultural analysis, he has given up on the possibility for cultural anthropology in a complex world, sensitive to multiple and local claims of identity in a power play that includes the rest of the world.

Drawing upon my own ethnographic fieldwork with the Penobscot Indian Nation in Maine and the Environmental Protection Agency (EPA), I will try to explore the historical, sociological, and representational complexity that Krech overlooks. First, I will explore how Krech (at least in the introduction and the epilogue to his book) appears to pass judgment rather than to analyze the current state of Indian identity practices, in his arguments that those identity practices do not live up to the primarily colonial and outside expectations of Indians as conservationists. Second, by using sources Krech cites, I will show how his project falls into the trap left by the "invention of tradition" school that presumes unified, ahistorical cultural identities and erases the logical and ontological continuities involved in current identity practices by colonized peoples. Third, I will give the historical context, sometimes referred to as "ecocide," in which Indian ecological self-representations are presented: colonization has left many Indian environments in disarray because of United States policies of resource extraction. Fourth, I will use my own fieldwork to show the legal and material context for such self-representation, how ecological self-representation in these ways is one of the few avenues for justice, and why this strategy often fails. Finally, I will indicate how these issues are part of a larger power dynamic in which—in the (often jurisprudentially driven) moment of self-representation—Indians have to fight for their rights in a situation where outsiders are seen as experts and Indians are biased, greedy individuals looking for special rights. This power play is perpetuated by scholars like Krech, who, by claiming interest only in truth and no interest in justice, are understood as experts by courts of law around the world.

Fragmented Cultures, Ethics, and Politically Engaged Scholarship

Without the introduction and the epilogue, I believe The Ecological Indian is an overview of scholarship with little political or intellectual importance. Krech's explicit goal of "rekindling debate" about the accuracy of the ecological Indian stereotype (28) reflects a vague privilege that I rarely encounter personally as an indigenous scholar. Asking or assessing one culture to meet the standards of another culture's stereotypes of them seems a dubious project—one that counters any definition of cultural relativism in anthropology. The introduction and epilogue to *The Ecological Indian* portray Native American cultures as being in a state of disarray. Members of Native American cultures are represented as hapless fools who have been "duped" into using the image of the noble savage (Berkhofer 1978) to get a few scraps of the colonial pie. The epilogue also describes Native communities as mandating a variety of environmentally destructive activities; although this is true, the description lacks an analysis of the structural conditions of intense poverty and hundreds of years of colonization that precipitated these activities.

Krech's only mention of sovereignty, the primary political struggle of Native Americans in the contemporary era, is presented in a negative light, ecologically: "Yet native people have often favored the extraction of resources, storage of waste, and other development projects—even those with a serious potential environmental impact—if they can gain control over them" (219). He completely ignores the 146 tribes that have been delegated authority over at least one EPA program (USEPA 1998) in the past fifteen years.

These problems are not profound, considering the task of Krech's project, but the study's goal belies an attitude of many scholars doing work with (and I emphasize this "with," as opposed to "on") Native Americans that is profoundly disengaged from Native communities. A few summers ago at the Newberry Library, I engaged a very influential anthropologist of Native North America in a heated debate about his criticisms of Eastern Cherokees, who he believes have chosen casinos and money over their traditional culture. I asked him when he last spent time in that community since his fieldwork in the 1950s and 1960s. He said he hadn't spent much time there since then, and I told him that it seemed unethical for him to criticize them from the vantage point of his endowed chair at a major research university. It is not that non-Indians cannot pass judgment on Indians, but to do so in place of analysis is another matter altogether, especially when an ethical research paradigm in Native communities is one of engagement, not judgment. My response to such judgments in place of analysis is simply, "Come to Indian country, help us with our issues, engage us, debate us, but do it from and *with* our communities." *The Ecological Indian*, as a text deliberately critical of Native cultures and practices, is an affront to Indian political struggle not because it uses false or untrue data, but because it is so grievously disengaged from the contemporary issues of Indian communities. This echoes my disagreement at the Newberry Library: Krech does not offer his critiques of Native environmental struggles—especially in the epilogue—as an engaged observer, but only as a casual, and distant, critic. Thus, we have to understand *The Ecological Indian* as part of a larger context of research ethics and who defines the "real" or "authentic" Indians.

The Invention of Tradition and the Politics of Representation

The most profound critique I have found of Krech's project comes from within his text and not from within the politics of distance and disaffection that inform and surround it. As mentioned earlier, in his footnote on page 27, Krech cites three sources (Lears, Keesing, and Sahlins) to back up his argument that Native Americans, like many other indigenous groups across the globe, have sought to "take on" the image of the ecological Indian to further their political goals. Marshall Sahlins's article (the very one cited by Krech to support his thesis) offers a particularly insightful critique of Krech's project to show how a dominant culture's stereotypes of a subordinate culture are inaccurate attempts to liberate it from oppression. Unfortunately, as Sahlins points out, this project may be as damaging as it is helpful. Thus, I am offering something of an archaeology of Krech's project from within his text—so as not to be accused of holding him to standards he has not set.

While a popular analysis of history has come from the "invention of tradition" thesis offered by Hobsbawm and Ranger in their 1983 edited volume of the same name, Sahlins suggests that not all inventions are rooted in the same authority of production. He puts forward the idea that "reified notions of cultural differences, as indexed by distinctive customs and traditions, can and have existed apart from any European presence" (1993, 4). By assuming that indigenous people have the ability and cultural traditions to understand difference, Sahlins sees the identity mechanisms operating in "taking on" cultural arguments, such as the ecological Indian, as a way to combat colonizers' hegemonic impositions. This practice of "culturism," Sahlins insists, must be understood as "the people's attempt to control their relationships with the dominant society, including control of the technical and political means that up to now have been used to victimize them. The empire strikes back" (4).

Sahlins even ironically argues that "Western intellectuals" [and I think it is safe to place Krech in this category] "have been too often disposed to write off the meanings as trivial, on grounds that the claims to cultural continuity are spurious" (4). These intellectuals, Sahlins argues correctly, often believe that calling these arguments "invented traditions" is helpful to the people doing the invention because all traditions are invented, but in fact, it "has the effect of erasing the logical and ontological continuities involved in the different ways that societies interpret and respond to the imperialist conjuncture" (4).

Sahlins also critiques the so-called experts in their upending the ability of "others" to make a political call for otherness in a world of unequal power. The "invention of tradition" crowd, according to Sahlins, has made the cultural movements of indigenous people seem as though they were "developed out of the colonial experience: an ethnic distinctiveness perceived from the vantage, if not also to the advantage, of the culture-of-dominance" (4). Sahlins says that those intellectuals who understand the world as a contingent set of practices, incoherent cultures, and shifting subjectivities (whom he labels "postmodernists") and those who understand the world as a connected, colonized set of economic and cultural practices (whom he labels "world systematists") are equally to blame for this denial, a priori, of historical continuity: "Yet all these tristes tropes of Western hegemony and local anarchy, of the contrast between a powerful World System and people's cultural incoherence, do they not mimic on an academic plane the same imperialism they would despise? As an attack on the cultural integrity and historical agency of the peripheral peoples, they do in theory what imperialism attempts in practice" (7).

Precisely what Sahlins wants from scholars is more historical awareness, not just of the problems in making and writing about history and tradition, but of the locally embedded meanings and identity practices of peoples. For example, he cites the Fijian *kerekere* and the Hawaiian *hula* as practices that other scholars see as "invented" traditions, functioning only to keep some semblance of an ethnic identity in a colonial order that has nothing to do with the traditional practices of these people. In opposition to this view, Sahlins points out that the current emphasis on *kerekere* is a uniquely Fijian identity practice. It may be both a current and a historical comment on the fact that white men initially refused to partake in the ceremony; this self-ishness, both as a historical fact and as a contemporary problem, is a Fijian mode of identity maintenance, which cannot be fully understood from a vantage point in the colonizers' history. Moreover, the Hawaiian *hula* tradition was purposely split into two forms in the nineteenth century—one for tourists and the other practiced self-consciously as a part of Hawaiian traditional culture, for country schools developed to resist "outside" innovations (Sahlins 1993, 11). For Sahlins, "local accents" such as these are not spurious inventions but "positional values whose differential relations to other categories of the indigenous scheme constitute logics of the possible effects of intrusive 'forces'" (13). To Sahlins, these practices allow us to understand "how the disciplines of the colonial state are culturally sabotaged" (13).

Thus, where Krech sees the notion of the ecological Indian as an intervention in understanding "true" cultural practices, Sahlins wants us to ask more questions of Indians to determine the veracity and actual content of these practices. It does not take a rocket scientist (or a political theorist) to understand that the idea of the ecological Indian fits well in the context of European and U.S. colonial practices, all of which have been designed to take and exploit the resources of Native American peoples. So, if social scientists want to know why Indians talk about land and assume the role of ecologists or conservationists, they have to understand that we see ourselves this way because of what we have witnessed others do. It is unclear, however, whether Krech is interested in an analysis of what Indians have to say and why they are saying it in any particular context, because he places culturist statements about the environment outside of cultural analysis itself, and moves it into the realm of cultural judgment.

"Ecocide," Colonization, and the Ethnographic Present

Having shown the potential theoretical downfalls of dismissing (and judging) the ecological Indian, I will now try to provide some of the sociological and historical context for indigenous claims of the ecological Indian. In their 1995 book, *The Ecocide of Native America: Environmental Destruction of Indian Lands and Peoples*, Donald Grinde and Bruce Johansen outline a number of situations defining what they consider an ecocide in North America—a series of colonial practices that have produced disastrous ecological effects on Indian lands. These effects have rendered the maintenance of land-based Indian cultures exceedingly difficult.

The term "ecocide" first made its way into the academy in a critical way in 1970, with the publication of Barry Weisberg's *Ecocide in Indochina: The Ecology of War*. Following Weisberg and Ward Churchill's *Struggle for the Land: Indigenous Resistance to Genocide, Ecocide, and Expropriation in Contemporary North America* (Churchill 1993), Grinde and Johansen implied, but did not theorize, that state policy has had a profound impact on American Indian environments and has been a large part of the colonial and assimilatory process. I trace this genealogy so that we can understand what is at stake for those of us who are actively engaged in trying to protect and clean up Indian environments—the very existence of Indian communities themselves.

While "ecocide" is a potentially controversial term, the basic premise is not that radical in the serious scholarship of Native America. In 1983, William Cronon published his seminal work, *Changes in the Land: Indians, Colonists, and the Ecology of New England*. Like those who claim ecocide, Cronon traces the impact of English colonial and economic practices on the ecology of New England and shows how this made maintaining their land-based cultures exceedingly difficult for Indians. Colonial impositions are by no means ignored in the last half of *The Ecological Indian*, which focuses on various aspects of hunting and trade. However, the emphasis on the continual material and cultural impacts of colonial practices is absent from Krech's introduction and epilogue overviews of the use and abuse of the ecological Indian. Without the foreground of the colonial scene, any analysis of Native Americans' contemporary land use seems dubious.

Krech's avoidance of the continued effects of colonization on current and past land practices is most apparent in the epilogue. Krech reiterates the purpose of his project—"to determine the extent to which Indians were ecologists and conservationists" (1999, 212). He gives specificity to the claim, raised in the introduction, that certain Indians have taken on the ecological Indian role as part of their self-definition. He also begins to specify certain Indians' "disingenuous" uses of this role. In fact, Krech measures Indians' contemporary behaviors against the "invented" image of the ecological Indian—the very technique of presumption Sahlins warns against. The Indian authors Krech cites as helping to "enforce" (213) the image of the ecological Indian—Chief Dan George, Ed McGaa, and Sun Bear—are all popular with non-Indian, leftist environmentalists, but they have somewhat less legitimacy among members of Native communities (213–14). While I do not wish to question anyone's commitment to political praxis, I do think these contemporary "enforcers" of the ecological Indian have distinctly different projects than the other Indians to whom Krech specifically refers—Vine Deloria Jr., Dennis Martinez, and Winona LaDuke—all of whom are engaged in distinctly critical projects attempting to decolonize and reclaim Indian lands and communities. Suggesting who profits from elaborations of the ecological Indian stereotype and who may or may not use it in political struggle belies more critical analytical problems in Krech's assessment of contemporary Indian land practices and uses of the ecological Indian image—the avoidance of historical and contemporary colonial arrangements, as well as the specific social contexts of utterance.

Using this "living" aspect of the ecological Indian embodied by these specific Indians, Krech gives examples of Native people who have, in recent years, "acted in ways befitting their image as respectful stewards of the earth and its resources" (1999, 214) and those Native people who have "favored the extraction of resources, storage of waste, and other development projects—even those with a serious potential environmental impact" (219). In all, the examples he gives are supposed to leave us with a balanced account—there are as many examples of the positive ecological Indian as there are negative examples of Indians destroying the environment. There are even examples of "split" Indian communities with individuals who want economic development at any cost and those who want to preserve the environment in ways consistent with the ecological Indian (215). The point is the same as it was in the introduction—the complicated world of Indian ecological behavior defies the stereotype of the ecological Indian and dehumanizes Indians. Krech's answer to this dilemma is to humanize Indians and make them seem as ecologically complicated as "we" are: "In Indian country as in the larger society, conservation is often sacrificed for economic security" (227).

While I appreciate these attempts at humanizing Indians and showing the complicated worlds they inhabit, Krech's lack of appreciation for the historical and contemporary aspects of colonization within Indian communities shows a troubling avoidance of power relationships. First, Krech portrays Indians as having somehow exacted control over the ecological Indian stereotype, a precontact, colonial (see Berkhofer 1978) intervention: "Indians themselves have set expectations for their behavior consistent with, and helping to enforce, the image of the Ecological Indian thriving in public culture" (1999, 213). This seems particularly disingenuous, given the weakness of such "culturalisms" (a theme I will take up later) in a situation where colonization has had profound impacts on Indian lands and resources and on Indians' ability to maintain land-based cultures. The fact that Indians now control about 2.3 percent of the land base they controlled some five hundred years ago is somehow not a mitigating factor in understanding contemporary Indian land practices (Frantz 1999, 39). In addition, the fact that the United States has pursued colonization by removing Indians from their lands (removal), fragmenting reservation lands through land reform (allotment), and forcing Indians into land practices of

Euro-American origin (allotment again) seemingly has no place in Krech's attempt to understand contemporary Indian land practices. Moreover, Indian community decisions that Krech believes do not fit the ecological Indian stereotype were made in the context of tribal governments originally brought into being as neocolonial arrangements to extract resources from retained Indian lands (Indian reorganization).

Many of Krech's examples of the "negative" ecological Indian category pertain to contemporary tribal governments' resource-extraction policies (1999, 219–20). It should be painfully obvious to anyone with an understanding of American Indian policy that the United States has targeted Indian lands, which they own "in trust" for Indian communities, for resource extraction in the past hundred years (see Fixico 1998). Because of federal policy, nearly all uranium mining operations occur on Indian lands, with Indians, many of whom have suffered long-term health effects, serving as the workforce (Eichstaedt 1994). One particular anti-environmental actor that Krech describes is the Crow Nation, which have maintained and tried to expand coal-stripping operations in the past twenty years. The Crow Reservation, originally 39 million acres, now encompasses only 2.2 million acres (Ambler 1990). With such a diminishment of land, it only makes sense that the Crow Indians have had to change their means of production. Moreover, official policy on Indian lands and resource development was best stated by Commissioner of Indian Affairs Cato Sells in 1914: "[I]t is an economic and social crime to permit thousands of acres of fertile land belonging to the Indians and capable of great industrial development to lie in unproductive idleness" (Ambler 1990, 37; also cited in Tsosie 1996, 301). With this as an explicit policy, the Indian Reorganization Act (1934), intended to promote self-government consistent with tribal sovereignty, created "tribal councils organized largely to 'rubberstamp' the BIA's approval of mineral leasing on the reservation" (Tsosie 1996, 301). With such decisions on tribal resources often originating and terminating in the Bureau of Indian Affairs, leases were signed for up to ninety years for mineral extractions at a fraction of market value (Fixico 1998, 147–48, 172–80). With the beginning of "self-determination" in the 1970s, "Indian nations could only hope to control the damage by renegotiating lease terms that practically gave away their mineral resources and by seeking remediation for environmental degradation" (Tsosie 1996, 302). Without foregrounding colonial policies, any interpretation—including the one in Krech's epilogue—of Indians' current land-use practices is inadequate at best, and unfair and divisive at worst.

Ecological Legitimacy, the Politics of Recognition, and the Ecological Indian

I agree wholeheartedly with Sahlins that to understand contemporary plays to authentic identities negotiated in colonial contexts we must take those who "invent" identities more seriously. In my own work I have followed up and elaborated on Sahlins's ideas to understand the ways in which Penobscot bureaucrats use the ecological Indian stereotype as a strategic intervention to establish what Laura Pulido has termed "ecological legitimacy" (1998, 121). For Pulido, ecological legitimacy occurs when a subordinate group can be seen as a "valid environmental actor, when its commitment to preserving the environment is not regarded as suspect" (121). In the context of Native American issues in the United States, this legitimacy is critically intertwined with the politics of recognition (see Taylor 1994)—the ability of a particular group of Indians to be recognized by the federal government as a semi-sovereign government that is "deserving" of certain rights and protections.

This raises the question of why legitimacy and recognition are so important to Indian nations. The impact of pollution on reservation environments is profound, and tribal peoples and governments are rarely consulted or informed about the pollution (see Williams 1994). If the group is included as a sovereign, tribal issues are hardly ever seen as critical to the regulatory activity of the federal government, despite EPA legal mandates to the contrary. Thus, while the terms of recognition may be a legal mandate, the terms of legitimacy are a social fact that makes the legal mandate a reality in the EPA bureaucracy. These matters therefore are left to any institution in which Indians depend on others to determine if they are Indian or not.

For the Penobscot Indian Nation, as for many other Indian nations, ecological legitimacy and recognition are matters of life and death. The primary residential part of the Penobscot Indian Nation reservation, called Indian Island, is thirty-five miles downstream from the Lincoln Pulp and Paper (LP&P) bleached kraft mill, where high-quality paper is manufactured and bleached—and from where dioxin is directly discharged into the river. For decades, the Penobscot River has been contaminated with 2,3,7,8–tetrachlorodibenzo-p-dioxin, more commonly known as TCDD or dioxin (see Graham 1992). Dioxin, a volatile toxin, is formed as a by-product of various industrial processes that involve the mixing of chlorine and organic materials under conditions of heat and pressure, such as herbicide production, solid waste incineration, metal smelting, and paper bleaching (Lakind and Rifkin 1990; Webster 1990). LP&P's discharge pipes are the source of dioxin contamination in the Penobscot River, and the state of Maine has issued a fish-consumption advisory as a result of the dioxin levels in the Penobscot River below LP&P. The advisory warns people not to consume more than twelve eight-ounce portions a year of fish caught in the river's fifty-six-miles between LP&P and Penobscot Bay. Many traditional hunting and fishing areas, as well as many reservation islands, including Indian Island, lie downriver from the mill.

On January 23, 1997, in an attempt to combat this grim fact, the EPA issued the LP&P National Pollution Discharge Elimination System (NPDES) permit, which had at the time the most stringent dioxin limits ever imposed on a kraft paper mill in the United States (USEPA 1997). Despite these significant gains, the Penobscot Nation formally challenged the permit, because it would not adequately protect tribal fishermen or others using the river resources regularly (Ranco 2000). The Penobscots fought hard to be included in the drafting of this permit, and it is fairly clear that the stringent discharge limits set by EPA in the final draft reflect tribal political involvement, even though the final product did not protect Penobscots to the extent that the Nation wanted. By examining the ways in which Penobscot bureaucrats used the ecological Indian stereotype to ensure ecological legitimacy and recognition, we gain a better sense of the reality of contemporary engagements with state controls over Indian environments, and of what it means for a scholar like Krech to dismiss the uses of this stereotype as "distorting culture."

One key aspect of ecological legitimacy is knowledge. Are you a legitimate finder of fact in a particular environmental dispute? This aspect hits "traditional" Native and other cultural and racial minorities hardest, because their knowledge is not typically understood by outsiders, let alone legitimized in environmental disputes. Part of this lack of credibility involves the framing of such knowledge as impartial and unpalatable to Western science. For example, while I was home a couple of years ago, an elder of ours told me about how he comes to know the river:

> This location is perfect. I can see the water and the ice as it goes out in the spring, and the sun comes up over there in the morning and reflects the water and I sit at my table and watch the water. One day I was sitting there realizing that I see more now; all of a sudden it dawned on me that I just don't see the reflection of the top of the water like a mirror. I see inside the water. I see the fish and the molecular life, the food chain right up to the humans and the bears and the eagles. Understanding this interconnectedness promotes more responsibility for what you do and how you think.

In the context of an EPA decision-making process, such knowledge is difficult to legitimize. However, the ecological Indian can help legitimize, at least partially, the formulation of such knowledge.

For example, in a letter to the EPA, John Banks, director of the Natural Resources Department of the Penobscot Indian Nation, explains why the Nation should be involved in the permitting process of an upstream paper company: "As with other Indian tribes, the natural world is the foundation for the practice of Indian religion. From the spiritual standpoint, the Penobscot River is viewed as the lifeblood of the tribe, a living, breathing, creation sustaining all life, and any threats to the river's ecological health is a loss of the tribe's spiritual health, those being one in the same" (Banks 1992, A1–A2). This is, of course, the ecological Indian—the same one that

Krech says distorts culture. Such a statement could have come from the scholarship of Calvin Martin, Krech, or Vine Deloria. Instead, this is a discourse used by tribal and EPA bureaucrats. By using the stereotype of the ecological Indian—the universal notion that Indian religions contain an extra amount of spirituality—to legitimize the different attitudes of Penobscots toward the river, Banks is reminding the EPA, in a common language, what makes the tribe "different." This recognition of difference, Banks hoped, would appeal to the EPA, with its political and legal mandates, to include the Nation in the permit-writing process—and also legitimize Penobscot knowledge in that process. By showing these two types of speech acts, I also want to point out that the ecological Indian discourse is flexible enough to give Banks's mediation of local knowledge at least a partial space for articulation.

In the politics of recognition, such images and knowledge play a key role in issues of ecological legitimacy. Merely "mediating" or "translating" knowledge is not enough in these situations—Banks had to get the EPA to recognize the Penobscot Nation as a significant political player, consistent with the Nation's status as a federally recognized tribe. The fact that Indians have to use a stereotype rooted in colonial desires for this type of recognition is tragic, not only because these stereotypes are "misleading" but because they potentially fulfill the colonial fantasies of disappearance. In this logic, if you stop acting like "real Indians," your political authority (and your land) might just disappear, even though the settler state has tried to assimilate you. This logic is particularly salient in Australia and Canada, where current controversies about aboriginal title to land focus upon proving a continued "cultural presence," whatever the state means by that, despite years of assimilation policies (see Speck 1998).

This colonial logic of recognition functions in the same way in the United States. As James Clifford points out in his study of the struggle of Mashpee Indians to gain political recognition from the United States (Clifford 1988), achieving recognition of Indianness (and thus access to rights and resources) is extremely difficult. He points out what many of us have known for a long time: claiming and proving Indian identity in a court of law forces us into impossible narratives that require proof of continued existence not necessarily consistent with legal requirements. Clifford states that "groups negotiating their identity in contexts of domination and exchange persist, patch themselves together in ways different from a living organism" (1988, 338). The evidence in such situations is always "surviving pieces" that are found or not found through experts and documents (289). Taking this approach even further, Elizabeth Povinelli suggests that proving one's indigenous identity is an "inspection [that] always already constitutes indigenous persons as failures of indigeneity as such. And that is the point. In certain contexts of recognition, Aboriginal persons must produce a detailed account of the content of their traditions and the force with which they identify with them" (2002, 39). The difficulties of proving this maintenance, this perfect complementarity, make culturalisms like the ecological Indian such weak legal arguments and make it easy for anthropologists like Krech to point to them as myth and criticize Indians for using them. The continued social antecedents to these myths, however, can be understood only in the context of indigenous actors appealing to settler nation-states to preserve their rights and lands. To this end, Krech's project says nothing—only that we, as Indians, fail to live up to an image imposed on us, and that somehow this is unconnected to the fact that our lands and rights continue to be polluted and disappear.

I suggest that the impossibilities of indigenous political recognition do not end once formal recognition is established. It is a primary social text in all interactions between indigenous citizens and settler nation-states. For example, the U.S. Supreme Court reasoned that because the Crow Nation could not prove that it had traditionally regulated duck hunting or fishing (there was only significant evidence of buffalo-hunting regulations), they could not regulate non-Indians who were hunting ducks or fishing on their reservation (*Montana v. United States*, 450 U.S. 544 [1981]). It is that simple, and in our search for justice Indians will continue to use these tools of recognition, however weak and mythical. In the social reality in which we live, using the ecological Indian as a strategy may or may not be conscious. What we as scholars must pay attention to, however, is the different ways in which these types of speech acts take place. I contend that Banks knows that EPA folks will recognize this, and I know that as a hunter and fisherman, he speaks about and knows our river in ways not contained in his letter to the EPA. Thus, to understand uses of such colonial interventions requires nuanced understandings of local ideals, intermediaries, and historical and sociological context—understandings sorely lacking in Krech's assessments of contemporary uses of the ecological Indian image.

Bias, the Invented Indian, and the Politics of Knowledge

The purpose of this chapter has not only been to examine the material and historical realities of Indians "using" the ecological Indian, or to point to the ways in which Sahlins says analyses like Krech's erase the "logical and ontological continuities" (1993, 4) of colonized peoples. As I pointed out at the beginning, such erasures occur in the context of a politics of knowledge, wherein distant expertise is normalized in deciding the fate of indigenous rights. Now that I have examined the material and historical contexts of claiming the ecological Indian, I would like to return to these issues in conclusion. As I pointed out earlier, the explicit purpose of Krech's book is "to rekindle debate on the fit between one of the most durable images of the American Indian and American Indian behavior" (Krech 1999, 28). For Krech, this urge to rekindle debate is scientific—he wants to take a "fresh look" (27) at the data and get rid of distorted, untrue images of the Indian. This project is not a new one for anthropologists working on Indian issues.

In 1990, James Clifton described the content of his edited volume The Invented Indian in similar ways: "This book is designed as an alternative to and a corrective for a standard narrative now so deeply embedded in the American consciousness that its origins and purposes, its authenticity and validity, are rarely questioned in public, then only with some hazard. Altogether, there is no political aim to the essays in this book. Jointly, we are advocates of one thing: clear thinking, reason, solid evidence, relevant theoretical ideas" (23). This is virtually the same purpose as that of The Ecological Indian—the intended "corrective" aspects of Clifton's volume are similar to Krech's claim of overcoming "distortion" of the ecological Indian (1999,

27). In Clifton's "exegesis," we are supposed to understand him as a scholar with an overwhelming interest in the truth, in a context where his "freedom of movement" is impeded by the "minefield" set by the "strategic positions" of certain Indians and their friends (1990, 21). Clifton and Krech share this proclaimed disinterested, "clear thinking" scholarship, which reveals critical aspects of the politics of recognition and ecological legitimacy.

As I hinted in the previous section, claims of "clear thought" or of overcoming "distortion" by experts at the moment of recognition are not without political valence. Courts of law are always about judgment, and experts like Krech and Clifton must make whatever analyses they might have into judgments in these instances, in which the stakes are not merely "political" but also material. As Clifford (1988) points out, the recognition of objectivity in courts of law is driven as much by narrative as by whatever data come to bear on the truth. Moreover, objectivity is defined by a certain kind of distance that is not equally available to all of us involved in the Indian game. In *The Cunning of Recognition* (2002), Elizabeth Povinelli describes the "general set of liberal ideals concerning the public sphere and civil society" (236) that define the terms of political recognition in modern democratic nation-states. In explicating these ideals, she uses two principles defined by Benjamin Lee: "The first is that all deliberations that affect the people should be accessible to public scrutiny. The second is . . . [that] the potential validity of what one argues stands in negative relation to one's self-interest; the more disinterested a position is, the more likely it is to be universally valid and rational" (1997, 342; also cited in Povinelli 2002, 236).

Krech and Clifton claim a distant, disinterested objectivity, and in the culture of liberal civil society this gives them authority over those of us who would be understood as having biased opinions because of our continued concern for Indian peoples. In the Mashpee case, the jury sided with Jean Guillemin and Francis Hutchins, relative newcomers to Indian affairs, over Jack Campisi and Vine Deloria, because the latter two had a track record of always fighting for Indians in their published work and personal behavior (Clifford 1988). Thus, the claim of disinterestedness is never outside the political sphere in which contemporary Indians find themselves—the ecological Indian and claims like it do not distort culture, as Krech contests. The use and abuse of the ecological Indian *is* culture—intimately a part of the culture of recognition and justice in which contemporary Indians exist. Claims of judgment in state scenes of recognition are not equally accessible to all—as a member of the Penobscot Indian Nation, I will never be the disinterested observer or social scientist that Krech and Clifton are, despite my years of "knowing" the Penobscot Indian community.

While my "self-interest" is exceedingly clear, it would be naive to think that anthropologists like Krech and Clifton have no interest in the outcome of Indian claims for recognition and justice. Defining such interest is somewhat difficult through the haze of objectivity, and the point of this chapter is not a personal attack. In his biting review of Clifton's edited volume, Vine Deloria identifies Clifton and his cohort as "determined to attack contemporary expressions of Indian-ness as fraudulent and invalid because modern Indians fall short of their expectations" (1998, 67) and do not meet their desires for authenticity and purity. Thus, by revisiting the politics of recognition, modern Indians do not deserve the continued expressions of their rights to reservation lands and resources—they fail the impossible test of indigeneity. Why would scholars such as Clifton, and by extrapolation, Krech, be so hostile to Indians' interests? For Deloria, it has to do with a "struggle for authority" (1998, 68) in which Indians are now starting to challenge the experts as we struggle to maintain our lands and cultures. By his own admission, Clifton, as a member of the Indian Claims Commission, had become increasingly frustrated by the claims of "born again" Indians seeking money in a purely political situation (Clifton 1990, 6). For Krech, who has worked with the Gwich'in, it might be that he does not want to pass judgment on either indigenous player in the decision to open up the Arctic National Wildlife Refuge (ANWR). The fact that the Iñupiat want to open ANWR to oil companies and that the Gwich'in do not may be a difficult personal situation for him. Unfortunately, we do not know how, or if, his attempts to liberate Indians from the ecological Indian have anything to do with this.

As it stands now, *The Ecological Indian* is firmly in the camp Sahlins identifies in his 1993 article—it "mimic[s] on an academic plane the same imperialism they [in this case, Krech] would despise" (7) by underplaying colonization and not fully examining or analyzing the often weak culturalisms of contemporary Indians rooted in claims for justice. By not connecting colonization to our understanding in situations such as the ANWR decision, Krech is not just passing judgment on Indians (as he does in identifying the "bad" Indians in his epilogue) without revealing his personal investment in such judgments; he is also, unwittingly, making it more difficult for us to understand contemporary Indians' complicated activities. Merely making "them" like "us"—as he does in his claim that "in Indian country as in the larger society, conservation is often sacrificed for economic security" (1999, 227)—is a pretense that colonization did not happen, that neocolonial arrangements do not continue to exist, and that reservation environments are not regularly targeted for detrimental environmental practices because of their unique semi-sovereign status.

References

Ambler, Marjane. 1990. *Breaking the iron bonds: Indian control of energy development.* Lawrence: University Press of Kansas.

Banks, John. 1992. *Benefits attributed to the Atlantic salmon.* Old Town ME: Penobscot Indian Nation.

Berkhofer, Robert F., Jr. 1978. *The white man's Indian: Images of the American Indian from Columbus to the present.* New York: Vintage.

Churchill, Ward. 1993. *Struggle for the land: Indigenous resistance to genocide, ecocide, and expropriation in contemporary North America.* Monroe ME: Common Courage Press.

Clifford, James. 1988. *The predicament of culture: Twentieth century ethnography, literature, and art.* Cambridge: Harvard University Press.

Clifton, James. 1990. Introduction: Memoir, exegesis. In *The invented Indian: Cultural fictions and governmental policies,* ed. James Clifton, 1–28. New Brunswick NJ: Transaction.

Cronon, William. 1983. *Changes in the land: Indians, colonists, and the ecology of New England.* New York: Hill and Wang.

Deloria, Vine, Jr. 1998. Comfortable fictions and the struggle for turf: An essay review of "The invented Indian: Cultural fictions and governmental policies." In *Natives and academics: Researching and writing about American Indians,* ed. Devon Mihesuah, 65–83. Lincoln: University of Nebraska Press.

Eichstaedt, Peter. 1994. *If you poison us: Uranium and Native Americans.* Santa Fe NM: Red Crane Books.

Fixico, Donald. 1998. *The invasion of Indian country in the twentieth century: American capitalism and tribal natural resources.* Niwot CO: University Press of Colorado.

Frantz, Klaus. 1999. *Indian reservations in the United States: Territory, sovereignty, and socioeconomic change.* Chicago: University of Chicago Press.

Graham, John D. 1994. The risk not reduced. *NYU Environmental Law Journal* 3:382–445.

Grinde, Donald A., and Bruce E. Johansen. 1995. *The ecocide of Native America: Environmental destruction of Indian lands and peoples.* Santa Fe NM: Clear Light.

Hobsbawm, Eric, and Terence Ranger, eds. 1983. *The invention of tradition.* New York: Cambridge University Press.

Keesing, Roger. 1989. Creating the past: Custom and identity in the contemporary Pacific. *Contemporary Pacific* 1:19–42.

Krech, Shepard, III. 1999. *The ecological Indian: Myth and history.* New York: Norton.

Lakind, Judy, and Erik Rifkin. 1990. Current method for setting dioxin limits in water requires re-examination. *Environmental Science Technology* 24 (7): 960–81.

Lears, T. J. Jackson. 1985. The concept of cultural hegemony: Problems and possibilities. *American Historical Review* 90:567–93.

Lee, Benjamin. 1997. *Talking heads: Language, metalanguage, and the semiotics of subjectivity.* Durham NC: Duke University Press.

Povinelli, Elizabeth. 2002. *The cunning of recognition: Indigenous alterities and the making of Australian multiculturalism.* Durham NC: Duke University Press.

Pulido, Laura. 1998. Ecological legitimacy and cultural essentialism: Hispano grazing in northern New Mexico. In *Chicano culture, ecology, politics: Subversive kin,* ed. Devon Peña, 121–40. Tucson: University of Arizona Press.

Ranco, Darren J. 2000. Environmental risk and politics in eastern Maine: The Penobscot Nation and the Environmental Protection Agency. PHD diss., Harvard University.

Sahlins, Marshall. 1993. Goodbye to tristes tropes: Ethnography in the context of modern world history. *Journal of Modern History* 65:1–25.

Speck, Dara Culhane. 1998. *The pleasure of the crown: Anthropology, law, and First Nations.* Burnaby BC: Talonbooks.

Taylor, Charles. 1994. The politics of recognition. In *Multiculturalism: Examining the politics of recognition,* ed. Amy Gutman, 25–73. Princeton: Princeton University Press.

Tsosie, Rebecca. 1996. Tribal environmental policy in an era of self-determination: The role of ethics, economics, and traditional ecological knowledge. *Vermont Law Review* 21:225–322.

USEPA. 1997. Joint public notice of the Lincoln Pulp and Paper Mill national discharge elimination system permit. Boston: Office of Ecosystem Protection, EPA–New England.

———. 1998. Treatment of tribes in the same manner as states/Program approval matrix. Washington DC: USEPA Office of Water.

Webster, Tom. 1990. Why dioxin and other halogenated aromatic hydrocarbons are bad news. *Journal of Pesticide Reform* 9 (4): 5–35.

Weisberg, Barry, ed. 1970. *Ecocide in Indochina: The ecology of war.* San Francisco: Canfield Press.

Williams, Robert A. 1994. Large binocular telescopes, red squirrel pitildndatas, and Apache sacred mountains: Decolonizing environmental law in a multicultural world. *West Virginia Law Review* 96:1133–1202.

3. Myths of the Ecological Whitemen

Histories, Science, and Rights in
North American–Native American Relations

Harvey A. Feit

In the final chapter of *The Ecological Indian: Myth and History* (1999), Shepard Krech sets out an argument about how the Northern Algonquian peoples came to be conservationists by learning from Europeans during the course of the commercial fur trade.[1] This argument synthesizes his review of the ethnohistories of beaver conservation in the subarctic and concludes his main argument for the volume as a whole. In this chapter I show how his argument and the policy conclusions he draws from it are significantly flawed.

I do agree with a careful critique of the popular idea that Native Americans were universally ecologists, or environmentalists or conservationists. These are often "mythic" statements, as Krech argues, that obscure the complexity and diversity of indigenous peoples' lives and of their uses of lands and resources. However, while rejecting the myth, we still need to carefully consider the ways in which specific Native American peoples have, or have not, under varying conditions, acted with respect and caring for lands, animals, and other peoples. I hope to give a better sense of some Native Americans' relationships to the environment, and also of relationships between Native Americans and North Americans.

Krech's choice of the ethnohistorical cases on which he based his fur-trade analyses, his selections from those cases of textual passages to quote, and his quick summaries of the available sources catch many of the highlights of the available literature on the northern fur trades. Furthermore, his ability to make this material accessible to nonspecialist readers is impressive.

His analyses in this chapter are based primarily on six important published ethnohistorical case studies, each of which, he notes, is specific to a particular area and time period (1999, 175–76). From this disparate and therefore fragmented set of records he attempts to synthesize a single historical account of Euro-Americans' conservation pedagogy for a vast continental expanse occupied by the Northern Algonquian peoples.[2] These peoples' lands stretched from Labrador to the Rocky Mountains, and the recorded fur trade covered three and a half centuries.[3]

Krech's analysis of this material is replete with surprising omissions, puzzling scholarly decisions, and problematic conclusions. In this chapter I therefore avoid examining Krech's choices of evidence or the diversity of the historical record in order to focus on the structure of the arguments Krech presents. I explore four central problems with his analyses.

First, Krech neglects to assess the effectiveness of fur traders' game-restoration policies or to consider whether the policies of nineteenth-century European fur traders could be considered conservation practices in a contemporary sense. Yet Krech argues that their policies were the primary means of restoring beaver populations and that they were the source of contemporary Northern Algonquian conservation practices.

Second, Krech's treatment of Northern Algonquians is equally problematic. He fails to consider whether the most widely acknowledged conservation practice used by Northern Algonquians during the nineteenth century, hunting territories, could have been learned from other Northern Algonquians, not mainly from fur traders. He also argues that Northern Algonquians' religious statements about human-animal relationships were demonstrably unrelated to "Western ecology" and to conserving game populations. But he omits to examine these statements in the light of the findings of biological research, which concur with some of the more enigmatic of them.

Third, having found fundamental problems with Krech's analyses of both fur traders and Northern Algonquians, I trace the changing understandings and intercultural communications between them by examining the process on a smaller scale. A case study of a mid-nineteenth-century Hudson's Bay Company (HBC) beaver-restocking experiment shows how HBC leadership initially misunderstood beaver conservation and ecology and how Northern Algonquians were involved in the HBC leadership's beginning to understand ideas of conservation and ecology.

Fourth, at the very end of his analyses Krech makes political and legal pronouncements about the rights that Native Americans can have today. He bases these policy arguments on the lack of conservation knowledge and practices among Northern Algonquians during the fur trade and on his conclusion that their present practices are derived from those of Euro-Americans. His policy arguments are misleading, both with respect to the present status of indigenous rights recognition and in relation to the lessons he draws from fur-trade histories about Euro-Americans' and Native Americans' respective authority to govern the land.

Before I examine each of these problems, I set out how Krech frames the arguments.

Overview of Krech's Main Argument

Krech asks how Northern Algonquians, by whom he means Anishinaabe (previously Ojibwas) and Cree-Innu peoples (previously Cree-Montagnais), came to generally conserve beavers and other wildlife populations. He first argues that the historical record is mixed on whether Northern Algonquians conserved beavers and other game, and he concludes from this that they did not do so widely or consistently and that they lacked developed concepts of conservation, environmental concern, or ecological ideas (1999, 206). In support of his arguments he cites ethnohistorical evidence of recurrent instances of depletion of beaver populations in the eastern subarctic by Northern Algonquian hunters as well as by non-Native trappers.[4] He also argues that the rituals and knowledge of the Northern Algonquians made conservation impossible (see below). There are several other threads to his argument about why historical Algonquians lacked these understandings and practices, but these are his key points.

Krech acknowledges that against his conclusion that historical Northern Algonquians did not systematically understand or practice conservation there is ample ethnographic evidence that twentieth-century Northern Algonquians "have shown an abiding concern for conservation, preventing waste, and managing hunting in family territories" (1999, 195). The main question he seeks to answer is how the assumed Northern Algonquian transition from having no, or minimal, thought of conservation to having widespread conservation concerns and practices came about (180–81, 206). His answer is that Northern Algonquians learned how to conserve game mainly from Euro-Americans (206).[5] He cites three key examples of Euro-American pedagogy.

Krech's earliest example of European advice on how to promote the recovery of beavers was given by the Jesuit priest Paul Le Jeune, who told Montagnais hunters in 1634 in the St. Lawrence Valley that each family should take "its own territory for hunting" and selectively trap only large male beavers (cited in Krech 1999, 182). On the question of whether this is the origin point or an important source of Northern Algonquian hunting territory practices, Krech varies his views. On one hand, hunting territories "surely had multiple beginnings" (180), but that Le Jeune made the recommendation he did "implies" it was a "novel" idea (182). Le Jeune's comments of 1634 are the only specific example Krech cites of a plan for game recovery by Europeans before the 1820s.[6]

Krech goes on to argue that the "watershed era for the development of conservation and family hunting territories" was from 1750 to 1830 and that there "were two important reasons for the change: the great decline in the numbers of beavers and other mammals, and the active promotion of conservation and territories," measures taken by the Hudson's Bay Company to increase beaver numbers (186). The former provided the context for the HBC promotion of hunting territories and "conservation" ideas that finally took hold among Northern Algonquians (Krech 1999, 204–6). Krech's final step is to add that in the 1930s the HBC, Quebec, and later the Ontario and Canadian governments established beaver preserves designed as conservation measures to restock beavers and instituted an explicitly pedagogical program that showed Crees how to conserve beavers (Krech 1999, 197; for a more detailed and different history of beaver reserves see Feit 2005).

Krech concludes: "Apparently, today's conservation ethic and practices were largely absent among Northern Algonquians until certain historical conditions emerged in the wake of the arrival of European outsiders mainly interested in controlling Indians economically and spiritually. Before the nineteenth century the conditions were local and nascent, as was the interest in conservation. During the nineteenth century they became widespread, as did the interest in conservation" (206). In this chapter I examine the key nineteenth-century examples of European-initiated "conservation" policies and pedagogy.

Krech sets out what he means by "conservation" in the first section of his book, where he defines his terms. Of ecology and ecologists he says: "When speaking of Native Americans as ecologists . . . we should mean that they have understood and thought about the environment and its interrelating components in systematic ways (even if the system, all increasingly agree, is more metaphor than hard and bounded reality). When we speak of them as environmentalists, we presumably mean showing concern for the state of the environment and perhaps acting on that concern" (24). He cites a definition of "conservationists" as those who act so as to "not waste or 'despoil, exhaust, or extinguish,'" and that they "with deliberation, leave the environment and resources like animal populations in a usable state for succeeding generations" (26; citing Jordan 1995).

Nineteenth-Century Fur Traders' "Recruitment" Policies as Pedagogy

Krech argues that when the 1821 amalgamation of the Hudson's Bay Company and the Northwest Company ended a long period of intense competition that had devastating impacts on beavers and other furbearer populations, HBC governor George Simpson tried to improve the fur trade under the new near-monopoly conditions. He reorganized the company, reduced and replaced staff, and took a firm hand in all matters. In addition to these initiatives, Krech writes, his "twin priorities were to 'nurse the country,' that is, not to hunt it and allow beavers and other depleted fur-bearing animals to 'recruit' or recover; and to encourage native people to develop hunting territories in which they could conserve beavers" (187). He instituted several major measures intended to nurse beavers: he sought to stop the killing of young beavers and summer beavers, he sought to restrict the availability of steel traps, and he tried to limit the total number of pelts purchased in particularly depleted regions (187). These policies were important because Simpson was in a position to press for them over the vast area where the HBC traded, although the implementation of the policies was uneven (194–95).

In order to evaluate the effects and effectiveness of HBC fur traders' policies, I will draw on the knowledge of both wildlife researchers and Native Americans. In the case of statements by Native Americans, I draw on my fieldwork among Waswanipi Crees.[7] Statements from wildlife researchers and Native American hunters are made from within different epistemologies and cosmologies, so that when I compare them I judge what it is plausible to treat as parallel or related knowledge statements.[8]

Selective Trapping Policies

One of Governor Simpson's policies was to instruct HBC traders to reduce purchases of young animals (Krech 1999, 187). Beavers do not generally leave the natal colony to go off to find a mate and possibly found a new colony until they are just short of two years of age, so a colony is typically composed of kits (born that year), yearlings (born the previous year), and a pair of mating beavers two or more years old. Simpson's policy was aimed at reducing harvests of kits (Innis 1962, 326; Bishop 1974, 124; Ray 1974, 199; Francis and Morantz 1983, 128). Not trapping kits would allow them to mature, thus increasing the average age and size of beavers harvested. This could therefore improve both average pelt values and subsistence food quantities from a given number of harvested beavers. Given the relatively inelastic demands of many Algonquian hunters for both trade goods (Krech 1999, 184) and game meat for subsistence, this policy could also have led to reduced beaver harvests, as the hunters' needs for trade value and subsistence could be met with fewer, larger animals. The HBC promoted this policy by encouragement and by periodically reducing tariffs paid for small pelts or refusing to purchase them at all. Thus they implemented the policy by actively using the levers of the trading process, not by intervening in Northern Algonquian trapping directly.

The policy implicitly assumed that Northern Algonquians knew how to generally avoid catching kits. Contemporary Waswanipi hunters speak about several ways to selectively trap beavers by age and size.[9] They say that the kits do not venture as far from the lodge as yearlings or adults and that by setting traps at sites distant from a lodge they can generally avoid trapping kits. They also say that when they catch beavers in a net or by hand in their burrows, they can release the younger and smaller animals. A published report advising on how to catch beavers alive in summer says the kits tire quickly when swimming, so much so that they are exhausted after a few dives and stay on the surface of the pond where they can be approached and picked up (Bailey 1922, 19).

Missionaries and fur traders have reported that techniques for locating and catching beavers by hand at burrows were known among Northern Algonquians throughout the fur-trade period from the seventeenth century on.[10] Therefore, when the HBC policy was introduced in the early nineteenth century, Northern Algonquians knew how to hunt beavers in ways that could selectively exclude kits from harvests, as the HBC policy implied.

Thus this HBC policy was a joint effort, because Northern Algonquian hunters had the knowledge of beaver behavior and of trapping techniques needed to implement the selective trapping strategy. As the missionary, trader, and ethnographic reports indicate, Europeans knew of this Algonquian knowledge. The successes of the trapping strategies the HBC promoted were thus partly attributable to the knowledge and skills the Northern Algonquian hunters brought to trapping and partly attributable to the advice and pricing pressures of the HBC traders. The Northern Algonquians were active participants in implementing these policies, a point that Krech does not acknowledge or specifically analyze.

From a fur trader's perspective, summer fur pelts, which are not as dense or as deeply colored as fall or winter pelts, are a commodity of significantly lower value, and deferring harvests from summer to fall or winter therefore increases the economic value of the pelts. When Governor Simpson instituted a policy of reducing prices or banning purchases of out-of-season pelts, he also spoke of it as a policy that would help beaver recovery.

Both wildlife biologists and Cree hunters today would agree that such a policy could have had a positive benefit. In his comprehensive review of beaver research, wildlife biologist Milan Novak says that because "kits depend on the adults and yearlings for survival, food acquisition, dam and lodge maintenance, and feedbed establishment during their first summer and winter, maintenance of the family group is important" (1987, 295). Contemporary Waswanipi Cree hunters say that delaying the harvest from summer to fall or winter can improve the survival of kits because the kits cannot build or repair the lodge, the dam, or the feedbed that must be prepared by the older beavers in order for the young to survive subarctic winters.

Policies to Limit Beaver Harvests

Fur traders and Northern Algonquian trappers generally agreed that steel traps made it easier to harvest more beavers. The HBC policy of reducing access to steel traps could have helped to reduce beaver harvests, but its precise effects varied among different trappers. Reducing the availability of steel traps would have curtailed highly mobile trappers who tried to trap out an area and then move to another the next season, as they depended on tending a large number of quickly set traps in order to trap both intensively and widely.

For more localized hunters who were oriented both to family subsistence drawn from diverse local wildlife harvests (including furbearers, big game, waterfowl, and fish) and to pelts they needed to acquire goods through trade, a reduction in the number of their steel traps left them still needing to catch sufficient beavers for subsistence or, alternatively, to increase harvests of other game. Simpson noted that this policy succeeded where other subsistence game was available, especially muskrats, but the policy did not succeed generally (Krech 1999, 188).

Another policy was to try to put a limit on the number of beaver pelts that fur-trading posts purchased in the areas controlled by the HBC. Where beavers were in short supply, the HBC tried to get traders to purchase pelts only up to a quota (Krech 1999, 187). This policy was applied intermittently at best, and local HBC traders were not themselves always consistent in pursuit of this policy, as it reduced the trading profits they had to report for the posts they managed. The HBC leadership was also inconsistent, as it did not reduce its purchases of beaver pelts in areas where there were still competing traders for fear that if the HBC bought fewer pelts, trappers would simply sell more pelts to those competitors (Francis and Morantz 1983, 130–31).

Indeed, the HBC not only maintained an unlimited willingness to buy beaver pelts in these areas but sometimes encouraged maximizing harvests (Krech 1999, 191; Francis and Morantz 1983, 129). It encouraged and sometimes actively supplied equipment to facilitate a trapping out of valuable furbearers, in hopes that smaller competing traders with less capital would be forced to withdraw from the areas, as they could not survive the ensuing periods of reduced trade. Simpson's long tenure as governor was marked by recurrent, systematic, and sometimes widespread campaigns to deplete the furbearers of those regions where there were competing fur traders or where the HBC's continuing access to the region was made uncertain by political circumstances (see Merk 1968; Innis 1962, 332; Francis and Morantz 1983, 129). These policies were destructive and wasteful of beavers and other furbearers, and they dramatically reduced their numbers on occasions.

Overall, Simpson's policies instituted to "recruit" beavers after 1821 were not judged to have had much success until the second half of the nineteenth century, although the reasons for this were multiple and varied by region (Krech 1999, 187–188). As we have seen, some of the HBC policies were effective; some were intermittently effective; some were effective with some groups of trappers and not others; some met both conservation and economic goals; and some were known to systematically deplete, not "recruit," game in order to benefit the HBC's economic interests. It is therefore not surprising that HBC policies did not have clear and repeatedly beneficial effects on beaver populations and that beaver recovery was slow and spotty, although HBC policies did help in some regions and probably "in general."

Overall, it is not clear what this inconsistent and partly contradictory set of policies would have taught to Northern Algonquian hunters about beaver recruitment.

Failing to Analyze Whether Fur Traders Were "Conservationists"
It is also not clear from this evaluation of HBC policies that the fur traders had what we could today call ecological knowledge of systemic environmental relationships, or environmentalist concerns, or consistent conservation practices, in the senses in which Krech has adopted these terms. That the HBC policies had mixed purposes and diverse effects is not surprising. Simpson did not use the term "conservation" for what he did; only Krech does. It is a fundamental analytical omission that Krech does not ask what nineteenth-century fur traders meant by "nurse the country" or "recruit" beavers or if their ideas fit twentieth-century definitions.

The concepts of conservation, environmentalism, and ecology developed over considerable time, and they were only well elaborated–and became part of a general European and North American awareness–during the latter decades of the nineteenth century, although they had earlier roots (see Marsh 1965; Hays 1969; MacKenzie 1988; Bramwell 1989; Grove 1995).[11] Modern game-hunting regulations and conservation tools were developed in the late nineteenth and early twentieth centuries in North America, although English roots reached back a millennium (McCandless 1985, chap. 1; Huntington 1992, chap. 2; Warren 1997). Wildlife management as a profession developed as part of the institutionalization of progressive conservationism in North American government policies in the early twentieth century (Worster 1977, chap. 13; Hays 1969; and see Leopold 1947 for the first scientific "textbook" on game management). Fully developed ideas of population biology and breeding populations of animals developed around the middle of the twentieth century (Worster 1977). Scientific knowledge of beaver population dynamics developed after the mid-twentieth century (see citations in Novak 1987).

Krech's failure to examine fur traders' policies in the light of the then-current historical understandings is hard to explain because his book is largely an analysis of ethnohistorical research, and he is aware of the growth of ecological, environmental, and conservation ideas and practices during these centuries. Krech actually notes the history of ecological, environmental, and conservationist ideas in European and American history in some detail in his introductory chapter (Krech 1999, 23–25). He cites, among others, George Perkins Marsh, whose *Man and Nature*, first published in 1864, was "one of the most critical early works for the development of both conservation and ecology"; Gifford Pinchot, an early-twentieth-century forester and government official, who is "widely regarded as the founder of contemporary conservationist policy in America"; John Muir, the contemporaneous "preservationist"; and many recent historical accounts of the period (see Krech 1999, 23–25, and notes 15–24 on pages 233–35).

Furthermore, as noted above, Krech carefully adopts explanatory definitions of what he means by "ecologists," "environmentalists," and "conservationists" (1999, 24–26), and he applies these definitions when judging whether nineteenth-century Northern Algonquians can be called by these terms (see below). But he does not analyze whether nineteenth-century European traders can be called by these terms; he simply labels their policies as conservation policies (186, 187, 190–94, 206, 207).

The above assessment of HBC policies indicates that these policies did not obviously conform to the definition of "conservation" given by Krech. They did not always avoid despoiling or exhausting game, nor did they consistently and "with deliberation, leave the environment and resources like animal populations in a usable state for succeeding generations," as Krech's definition of "conservation" requires (26; see below for a case study that explores some of what traders knew and did not know).

Krech's failure to locate European fur traders' policies in the history of environmental ideas and practices and his failure to evaluate whether their policies and practices conformed to his definition of "conservationist" undermine his claim that the fur traders were the sources of Northern Algonquians' current conservationist ideas and practices.

Ignoring Northern Algonquians' Pedagogy and Ideas

Consistent with his assumptions about nineteenth century fur traders, Krech argues that an expansion of the use of hunting territories by nineteenth-century Northern Algonquians was due primarily to the pedagogy of fur traders. He does not consider the importance of Northern Algonquians learning from other Northern Algonquians.

The HBC promoted the adoption of hunting territories by Northern Algonquians (Krech 1999, 187), and diverse commentators generally agree that such territories were potential means of aiding the growth of game populations. Having a recognized claim to use the same land year after year would allow hunters who left some beavers to reproduce to be more assured that the beavers would not be killed by other trappers in their absence.

But the HBC policies, begun in the 1820s, must be seen in the light of Northern Algonquians' use of hunting territories in several areas during the preceding decades. There are reports from fur traders that hunting territories were in use in the second half of the eighteenth century among Northern Algonquians on both the east and west coasts of James Bay (Krech 1999, 183). Some reports of hunting territories to the east of James Bay go back to the 1740s and occur repeatedly thereafter (Morantz 1983, 110–20).[12]

This is confirmed by what appears to be a survey that the HBC made about hunting territories around James Bay in about 1814–15 (Morantz 1986, 73–75). The surviving records from the London headquarters include general answers in the same numbered format from several post managers, confirming the existence of hunting territory systems that they vaguely described in similar terms. Toby Morantz notes that the similarity of the wording of the responses may indicate that the traders discussed their responses among themselves before sending them (1986, 73–75). However, Morantz and Krech differ over the implications of these documents for how and when hunting territories developed before 1821.[13] But the important point here is that both acknowledge that hunting territories were established among some Northern Algonquians for decades before the HBC initiated its policy in the 1820s.[14]

Thus Simpson's policies were promoting an existing practice, whatever its origin, and those Northern Algonquians who adopted or returned to hunting territory practices at the end of a disruptive period in the fur trade after 1821 could have learned of these techniques from other Northern Algonquians. Hunters would have periodically been in contact with other hunters who were using or who had previously used hunting territories, or they could have heard indirectly about those using hunting territories, and some might also have remembered or been told that their kinsmen had used such techniques in the past. Further, a commonsense view would suggest the importance of learning from other hunters. How else would new users learn to organize hunting in the territories, which typically would have been hundreds of square miles in size, so as to distribute the harvests of beavers among dozens and sometimes hundreds of colonies in ways that aided the recovery of beaver numbers? This could only be learned from other Northern Algonquian hunters or by experience. Fur-trade records do not indicate that the traders had detailed experience of organizing hunting by territories. Krech does not consider whether learning from other Northern Algonquian hunters was of central importance in the wider adoption of hunting territories.

Who Most Effectively Promoted Hunting Territories?

Despite HBC policies, the practice of using hunting territories did not spread smoothly or quickly after the reduction of the disruptive and intensely competitive fur trading in the 1820s. Simpson noted that the practice was only slowly taken up by Northern Algonquians even when they "may see ultimate benefit" (Krech 1999, 188). There were several reasons for this, some reported by the traders, others not considered.

Traders noted that where territories were not already in use, their practice required adjacent groups to agree not to trespass (Krech 1999, 193). Some Northern Algonquian groups did not readily adopt hunting territories, because they wanted mobility to pursue migratory subsistence game such as caribou (Krech 1999, 188). Furthermore, the continuing presence of smaller, independent traders and trappers, increased in numbers by the dismissal of many former HBC and Northwest Company employees during the period of consolidation, meant that itinerant trappers continued to disrupt local trappers' efforts to leave some beavers to reproduce.

The effectiveness of HBC policies was also limited by cultural misunderstandings. HBC traders had a different and incorrect idea of the social groups, or "families," that used hunting territories. Morantz analyzes social organization of the Crees on the east coast of James Bay in the nineteenth century from the data in the HBC trading post records, and she notes the lack of systematic analysis of Northern Algonquian social groups in the fur traders' reports (1983, 61). While many of the traders' detailed reports of who stayed with whom "indicate that extended families were the norm . . . the HBC traders persisted in listing the composition of nuclear families" (89). They thus conceptualized Crees as living in nuclear families, although the records of groups visiting the post indicate that extended families were the norm. Furthermore, Morantz shows that the composition of these extended family groups was frequently altered from year to year (90–93).

Thus hunting territories, where they were adopted by Northern Algonquians, were likely used by fluid extended families. The traders' vision of hunting territories was different, and it may have been too rigid, seeking to promote the use of hunting territories by small, relatively fixed nuclear kin groups. Simpson described his efforts as trying "to confine the natives throughout the country now by families to separate and distinct hunting grounds" (qtd. in Krech 1999, 187–88). This may indicate why fur traders' advice was not as effective as they hoped in encouraging the adoption of hunting territory practices.

Thus the use of hunting territories was a Northern Algonquian practice that most hunters probably learned from other hunters and which the HBC sought to encourage but with only partial success. Krech reaches a different and less plausible conclusion, without considering Northern Algonquians as pedagogues, that the use of hunting territories became more widespread mainly as a result of HBC promotion. The weight of evidence is that HBC policies encouraged and aided a Northern Algonquian practice.

Were Northern Algonquian Ideas Unrelated to "Western Game Management"?
Krech's argument that fur traders were responsible for the widespread development of beaver conservation during the nineteenth century rests in part on the assertion that the idea of conservation—specifically leaving some animals to reproduce for the future—was unknown to Northern Algonquians. Krech claims that Northern Algonquian ideas and beliefs contradict the idea of a relationship between current hunting practices and future game abundance or harvests.

Krech notes that there "is abundant evidence" that many of the Northern Algonquians' beliefs which "existed from the sixteenth up to the twentieth century" were inconsistent with conservation, albeit that they were not unchanging (1999, 204). These included ideas that animals have souls; that humans and animals have social and emotional relationships with each other; that animals know what is said about them and how their remains are treated; that there are rules for the treatment of bones and animal remains; and that animals are reincarnated (201–4). Krech shows that these ideas and practices were often not accompanied by what Europeans of the time thought was behavior that helped game abundance, and he concludes by generalizing that "what is striking about the taboos . . . is that they apparently had nothing to do with waste and the conservation of animal populations until recently" (204).

This last statement is not surprising. Nineteenth-century Northern Algonquians are no less likely to have used the ideas and practices of today's conservationists than the fur traders of the period were. But Krech goes on to argue that Northern Algonquians did not understand that there was a relationship between their hunting of animals and game numbers. He notes that at York Factory on the west coast of James Bay in the eighteenth century, Northern Algonquians told several HBC traders, in the context of caribou hunting, that "they could not kill too many" (204). This may have been the case with caribou at certain periods, given the limited numbers of hunters relative to the sometimes very large numbers of caribou in a herd at its peak, and given that caribou numbers vary over decades somewhat independently of harvest levels (see Berkes 1999, 97–99, for a recent review). But other Northern Algonquians made similar statements about the relationship of hunters and game more generally (Krech 1999, 204, citing Brightman 1993, 287–88).

From these puzzling reports of Northern Algonquian beliefs Krech mixes up a damning set of paraphrased statements and inferences, along with some conclusions:

> One can only speculate on the consequences of such beliefs for conservation. If caribou or other animals made themselves available to be killed no matter how many had been killed, then why stop killing them? . . . [Others have reported that] failure to kill animals who offered themselves to the hunter might have constituted an offense [to the animals]. If beavers disappeared from a region, the disappearance had nothing to do with hunting too many and everything to do with a deliberate or inadvertent taboo infraction. The reappearance of beavers was contingent not on adjusting how many animals one killed in the future but on exercising far greater care obeying the taboos. One reason to change tactics and, say, leave two beavers per lodge to produce the next generation, is if one started to doubt the wisdom of killing all beavers in the destructive synergy of competition and commodification (and if one was not starving). If a hunter could protect his ground from trespassers and poachers, then this new "rationality"–leaving a breeding core undisturbed–might influence how he managed beaver populations on his territory. (1999, 204–5)

Krech thus argues that the "rationality" of conservation practices had to be learned from fur traders because Northern Algonquians' statements about human-animal relationships that were exemplary of their beliefs, or "taboos," did not recognize the effects of their hunting on game numbers.

Krech's paradigmatic example of these statements, and the one he cites most often to demonstrate that Northern Algonquians lacked knowledge of how to increase game is, "Why would the York Factory Cree allege that 'the more they destroy the more plentiful they grow'?" (Krech 1999, 205, also at 186, 194, 204, quoting Andrew Graham's report of Northern Algonquians statements). Krech answers by noting that Northern Algonquians believe in animal reincarnation. But to ensure reincarnation, hunters had to follow "rules" or "taboos" that "Western ecologists would argue are unrelated to breeding success and conservation" (Krech 1999, 207). In Krech's argument this statement also indicates why conservation needed to be learned from the traders and other Euro-Americans (205, 207).

But the statements Krech quotes are both more and less puzzling than he makes them out to be. They are more puzzling because the York Factory Crees do not actually say that animals return in the same numbers: they say that the number of animals increases when they are hunted. This cannot be explained by reincarnation, as Krech infers, since there are more than the same numbers of animals available. The texts are less puzzling, however, because the statements Krech has singled out for paradigmatic treatment reveal the presence of just the kind of knowledge he thinks they deny; that is, they identify one of the relationships between how a hunter's harvests "might influence how he managed beaver populations on his territory" (Krech 1999, 205). Krech fails to consider what Northern Algonquians were saying in relation to what is known of beaver reproduction in twentieth-century biological research.

In his review of research on beavers, Novak reports that the fecundity of female beavers is density-dependent and that it consequently responds to trapping intensity. He reports that two studies found more kit beavers one or two years after trapping commenced at lodges, and another found that as the harvest rate increased during the course of a year, so did embryo counts of the breeding females during the same year, up to heavy harvests of about 70 percent, at which level they depressed embryo counts (Novak 1987, 286). Thus, trapping at a colony was associated with the breeding female's having an increased number of embryos formed and with an increase in the number of kits born, up to a reasonably high level of trapping intensity.

Novak points out that fecundity "thus can be manipulated by the manager" (1987, 286), the person who decides on the harvest level. Presumably, then, this relationship can be observed by a knowledgeable trapper as well as wildlife researchers, especially those who return to the same area repeatedly. A knowledgeable trapper, Northern Algonquian or Euro-Canadian, can also presumably "manipulate" fecundity under these conditions when deciding on harvest levels at beaver colonies.

Thus biologists find that with beavers, under wide conditions, harvesting can lead to increases in the numbers and the biological production of the game population. Furthermore, knowledge of these relationships, once observed or learned, can be used by managers or, I suggest, knowledgeable trappers to alter the condition of the game population and of the hunt.

Krech, like the traders before him, does not recognize that under some conditions the relationship between harvesting and game numbers is counter-intuitive: certain levels of harvesting of beavers do not reduce or deplete the population, but increase it. Thus Krech's argument that Northern Algonquians lacked an understanding of relationships between hunting and game numbers because they made counter-intuitive statements is wrong.

Is the same conclusion to be reached for all game and game hunting? As I understand the general biological evidence, no, although some conditions where harvesting game will increase their numbers are found with many other species. But these conditions are typically more restricted than in the case of beavers. A pattern where harvesting intensity has counter-intuitive effects can occur when certain biological populations are harvested after a period of non-use, or when harvesting goes from a very low level of use to more intensive harvesting. This might occur, for example, if a hunting territory were divided into sections each used every few years, as has been reported (see below).

Fikret Berkes, a human ecologist who did his doctorate in marine sciences and who has done research with contemporary James Bay Crees, has described what can happen when a lake that has not been fished or has been lightly fished starts to be harvested, even at low harvest rates. The fishing can result in removal of the old and large fish, but "the removal of such fish (and lowered competition for food) would result in higher survivorship, increased growth rates, and earlier maturation of the younger individuals of the same species" (1999, 119). This means that harvesting can increase fish numbers and total "biomass." Berkes goes on, "This phenomenon is known to scientists and managers as 'population compensatory responses' . . . and occurs with all living resources" (119). He claims that this "is the Western scientific counterpart of the Cree notion that continued proper use of resources is essential for sustainability" (119).

Northern Algonquians could readily have noted indicators of changes in fish or game abundance when harvesting or returning to the same area over time, as they do today (Feit 1987). Thus counter-intuitive relationships between harvests and game abundance might be observed under specific conditions for a wide variety of species.

Misrepresenting Northern Algonquians

Did Northern Algonquians understand that the relationship between harvest and game numbers was not always counter-intuitive? Recurrent reports of statements by Northern Algonquians demonstrate that they did. Despite denying that nineteenth-century Northern Algonquians understood such relationships, Krech cites statements in which they demonstrate their understanding that hunting could reduce game numbers. An example is trader Joseph Beioley's 1824 report of hunters at Rupert House. When asked not to kill summer beavers and to spare kit beavers in winter, the hunters said that this was "perfectly accordant with their own Ideas on the subject and their Desires of not impoverishing their Lands" (Krech 1999, 191; for a more extensive passage from this exchange see Francis and Morantz 1983, 129).

Krech's most extended example of a Northern Algonquian discussion of beaver depletion comes from the west coast of James Bay. In the 1790s, David Thompson, an HBC surveyor, reports that an old Western Woods Cree man, Krech summarizes, told him that declines in beavers were linked "to his tribesmen's desire for manufactured goods, to the lack of control over hunting, and to the attitude of a Cree creator" (1999, 189). The Cree is reported to have said that the "Great Spirit" was determined that beavers "are now all to be destroyed," and he recounted a story about beaver destruction in mythic times (Thompson qtd. in Krech 1999, 189). In his own time, he noted, God had given trespassing trappers castoreum, a natural scent and lure that is especially effective with steel traps, it being the "secret of the destruction." Thompson reports that the old man concluded, "We are now killing the Beaver without any labor, we are now rich, but [shall] soon be poor, for when the Beaver are destroyed we have nothing to depend on to purchase what we want for our families, strangers now run over our country with their iron traps, and we, and they will soon be poor" (189, brackets in Krech). Thompson reported that the prediction came true.

Krech comments as follows on the elder's statement without offering any explanation for his interpretation of it: "But predicated on an endless supply of beaver, this consumption could not last" (1999, 189). Krech misunderstands or misuses the old Cree hunter's reported statement; the hunter did not say there was an endless supply. His explanation was quite precise: the decline in beavers was occurring because of over-trapping, and the over-trapping was due to several things: his peoples' desire for trade goods, the presence of intruding trappers with a new technology, and the inability to control the trappers' actions. As Thompson said: "Every intelligent man saw the poverty that would follow the destruction of the Beaver, but there were no Chiefs to controul it; all ways perfect liberty and equality" (qtd. in Krech 1999, 189).

This is a story about a limited supply of beavers rather than of an endless supply or of failing to see the consequences of over-trapping. The Cree indicates why depletion is happening and, being a religious man, indicates that it must be the Great Spirit's will that this combination of events is happening, for the story of previous times indicates that it has happened before. This statement, despite its religious cosmology, demonstrates a clear and accurate prediction that present over-trapping will deplete the beaver population.

Thus, statements that Krech takes as exemplars of Northern Algonquians' general ignorance of conservation and of the relationship between present hunting and future game numbers are actually demonstrations of precisely this knowledge, sometimes in a counter-intuitive form.[15] Indeed, the frequency of fur traders' citations of these counter-intuitive statements by Northern Algonquians demonstrates the repeated failure of many fur traders, and later anthropologists and other North Americans and Europeans, to learn from Northern Algonquians.

Throughout these analyses, Krech demonstrates a systematic bias by treating the knowledge and skills of Northern Algonquians differently than European and North American knowledge and skills: he reports but then does not consider the significance of the statements of the Rupert House hunters supporting HBC policies; he misrepresents the statements of the elder Cree from the west coast of James Bay who recounted why beaver depletions were occurring; he fails to seriously examine Northern Algonquians' statements describing counter-intuitive effects of hunting on game numbers; and he pejoratively dismisses Northern Algonquians' religious perspectives on human-animal relationships (see Krech 199, 204–5). This can be compared to his unexamined assumption that the nineteenth-century fur traders were conservationists.

Learning about Game Conservation: A Case Study

Given the failures of Krech's analyses of both traders' and Northern Algonquians' knowledge and practices, is it possible to document what each might have learned from their long interaction? My view is that we cannot determine who taught conservation to whom over the course of the nineteenth century. The communicative interactions and the changes in understandings and values that such a question requires be examined are too subtle and complex to document in a general way from the fragmentary intercultural records of fur traders that Krech uses. Nevertheless, I think it is possible to examine especially well documented cases to find some partial answers.

Such a case is provided by one of the most frequently cited examples of HBC intentions to increase beaver numbers: the restocking of Charlton Island and a few other small islands in James Bay with beavers in the early to mid-nineteenth century. Starting in the 1830s, the HBC decided to restock the islands with the aim of running its own beaver "park" or "nursery." This has often been cited as an example of HBC conservation, but it is more an example of learning about conservation.

Governor Simpson reported in 1836 that he had talked to several "Gentlemen in this part of the Country" on the subject of establishing a nursery for beavers on Charlton Island, but he had not received a favorable response until R. Miles, the trader in charge of the Rupert House District, wrote him of the idea in 1836 (Brooks 1929, 14).[16] Simpson responded enthusiastically to the idea of "parking of Beaver," authorizing Miles to set up an "experiment" on Charlton Island (14). HBC documents noted that, because Charlton Island was some distance from shore, it would be "easy of protection from Indians" (16).

Henry Connolly, who worked for the HBC at the time, wrote about the events nearly three-quarters of a century later. His account gives a more local view of what happened after Miles took charge of the district "about 1835":

> One day the old coast Chief (who was always called the Governor) had a long talk with Mr. Miles. Among other matters, he spoke of the Charlton Island . . . . He said the island was about six or seven miles long and four or five broad, very level, well wooded and with many ponds, would make a fine preserve for Beaver, on which the Company should put the beaver to breed. Mr. Miles was very glad of this hint, and he told the old man he would see about it and he did not forget it, so at the meeting of the Governor and Council of the Southern department at Moose Factory in 1839 Mr. Miles proposed putting some beaver on the island which was agreed to by the Council, and orders were given to the gentlemen in charge of different districts to procure young beaver to be sent to Moose Fac-

> *tory to be given out to people to look after but some way or other*
> *they did not succeed. (Connolly n.d.)*

It is not clear from the available evidence whether Governor Simpson ever knew that the recommendation that restocking beavers on Charlton Island was feasible was made by the old coast chief at Rupert House.

Once he received approval for the old chief's idea, Miles struggled to get live beavers to restock the island. Simpson authorized catching young beavers in 1836 to be sent to Charlton in the spring of 1839, when he hoped to have "at least 100 pair" for restocking (Brooks 1929, 15). Miles wrote on February 1, 1839, that he had only acquired a second live beaver, also male (16). He noted that it initially was difficult to secure live beavers from many Indians because they "imagine the Beaver would leave their lands altogether were they to bring them here alive" (qtd. in Francis and Morantz 1983, 129). But by 1843 Simpson noted that a total of thirteen pairs had been relocated (Brooks 1929, 16, 19). Again, Connolly, gives us a more extended insight into what happened at Rupert House:

> *Where they succeeded was at Rupert's House where two old women*
> *took them [the beavers] in charge. They did not lose a single one. In*
> *the winter of 1839 two old men were sent to the island to hunt up*
> *any others but did not see any signs of them, only got three mar-*
> *tens and a few foxes. The old men drew a map of the island, of the*
> *creeks and ponds. Mr. Miles sent the map to England. Some time*
> *in June 1840 a boat was sent to Charlton Island, manned by some*
> *of the Company's men and Indians, taking four or five pairs of*
> *young beaver. A few days before the departure of the boat, the old*
> *Governor and another crossed over to the opposite side of the river*
> *to hunt, the tide being low. They perceived something lying on a*
> *lump. The younger man went to see what it was. It proved to be a*
> *large beaver asleep. When the man saw it to be beaver, ran up to*
> *it and caught it, but the beaver bit his hand, but would not let it*
> *go. When his companion reached him they secured him and pad-*
> *dled back to the post and brought it to the house. Mr. Miles was*

*very much pleased and gave the brave fellow a nice present. They
gave the beaver the name of old George in honor of the Governor.
Old George was sent to Charlton Island, where no doubt he helped
to increase and multiply his kind. (Connolly n.d.)*

Learning how to harvest the progeny of the beavers transported to the
island proved equally challenging for HBC men, although they again had
advice and help from Cree hunters. In 1843 Simpson noted that there were
fifteen beaver houses reported by Indians sent to the island to take stock,
although there was "no means of course of ascertaining the number in-
habiting these houses, and there may be other lodges as yet undiscovered"
(Brooks 1929, 19). By 1845 the first of the Indians asked to reside on the island as "keeper," Tom Pipes, reported that there were then at least forty
lodges, and Pipes and another Cree, Kataunawait, made a report in which
the lakes were referred to by letters or numbers for identification on the
maps (Brooks 1929, 20–22).

Joseph Gladman, a new trader at Rupert House, reported to Simpson that
after spending the winter of 1845–46 on Charlton the keepers "discovered
twenty new lodges." But despite finding additional colonies, they "retain
the opinion that the year olds did not make separate Lodges last summer,
but must in general be passing the Winter with the Parent Beaver, otherwise
they would have found more Lodges of ¾ Beaver [a measure of beaver pelt
size roughly equivalent to yearlings]" (Brooks 1929, 23). The report goes on
to suggest that the other explanation would be that some young were leaving the island, which the Indians thought possible from the tracks of beavers they saw along the seashore (23). In either case, the yearlings were not
establishing many new colonies.

Gladman added that the Indians "desire me to acquaint you that, in their
opinion, it is advisable to kill some of the old Beavers annually, to prevent
the Island being overstocked, or driving each other off, as they will be apt
to do, if they become too numerous" (Brooks 1929, 24). In 1847 the Indians
reported sixty-eight colonies and were "of the opinion that the land is now
well stocked . . . and that it is time to kill some of the Beaver to prevent them
becoming too numerous" (25–26). In 1848–49 they reported seventy lodges,

and that "in whatever direction they came upon Rivers or Lakes they were sure to see a lodge or Vestiges of Beaver (26). In 1849 they reported the island overstocked with beavers, and in 1850 they reported finding two dead beavers which they judged to have died trying to migrate off the island (27). The hunters' reports indicate that the beavers were at the limit of the island's ability to support their numbers, as they had warned since 1845–46, and they advised that it would be "advantageous if a few of the older Animals were killed" (27).

In May 1851, Simpson authorized Gladman "to draw 5000 Beaver Skins from the Island Preserves," of which there were three by this time, Charlton Island being the best established (Brooks 1929, 27). Gladman reported in March 1852 that the number of beaver pelts taken on Charlton Island "does not amount to one sixth of what was desired to be procured—The Indians give it as their opinion that there were not that number of beaver on the Island—as on taking a Lodge they seldom found the young ones of last spring except where there were only two old Beaver—but they often found several old and two year old Beaver in the same Lodge sometimes to the number of ten or twelve . . . and only a chance young one among them" (28). The Indians told Gladman that with so many older beavers in the lodges, young ones must have been killed or "perished during preceding seasons for want of water the Lodges being made in Lakes which would be entirely frozen to the bottom in winter—others have perished in the Sea when going on a quest of more favourable places of refuge" (28). Their comments indicate that overcrowding was already affecting the number of kits born and the number surviving. They also reported that their trapping effort left some beavers that were not harvested (28).

Neither Simpson nor Gladman initially understood what had happened. Simpson wrote that the number of beavers taken "has fallen very short of what we were led to expect last year from the highly colored reports made as to the number of beaver on the island, which, it was stated, were so numerous they were actually quitting it in quest of food in other places. To prevent a wholesale massacre in the preserve, the Council limited the hunts to 5000; I was, therefore, very much surprised to find that the total returns of

20 hunters employed all last Winter amounted to no more than 800 skins. You attribute this failure (for as compared with our expectations it may be so called) to sickness among the hunters, but I am disposed to believe that it is partially to be attributed to the fact that the beaver do not exist in the numbers represented to us" (Brooks 1929, 29).

Gladman replied that the Indians "one and all gave it as their candid opinion, that the Beaver were not so numerous upon the Island as the calculations would lead us to expect," but he went on to "regret that the information I received from the Indians regarding the Preserve has been deemed unsatisfactory, I however stated all which they told me" (29–30). Thus it was the calculations of beaver population growth made by the HBC that were too high.

How the calculations were made is unclear, and it is clouded by diverse accusations of blame. The HBC had Cree reports that there were more than seventy colonies in 1847, and as Samuel Hearne had reported in 1795, beavers had five or at most six young per year, so colonies would rarely exceed a dozen animals (1971). After the Crees reported in 1845 that it was time to harvest beavers and in 1848 that beavers were overstocked, the HBC leadership appears to have assumed that the growth in beaver colonies and numbers would continue during the several years that they delayed culling, even though Cree reports showed a rapid decline in the rate with which new beaver colonies were found, twenty in 1845–46, eight more in 1847, two more in 1848, although it may be that later reports have not survived in the records. The HBC appears to have assumed that beaver numbers could increase substantially because they were only limited by the abundance of food, and that food was abundant. But Cree reports stressed that the limited number of appropriate lake and stream sites was limiting the number of new colonies, and therefore the number of adults that were breeding.[17]

In 1856 Simpson himself concluded that "from what we can learn the number of beaver does not rapidly increase after attaining a certain point, which we may assume to be the maximum that the means of living and other local peculiarities, unknown to us, admit" (Brooks 1929, 31). If this statement is taken at face value, then this can be considered the moment at which the HBC leadership began to understand the complexity of beaver population dynamics.

Further, by attributing "the maximum" to the beavers' own "means of living and other local peculiarities," they also learned that they needed to know more about the dynamic interactions of animal populations in relation to environments. Thus, this may also be taken as the beginning, for the HBC leadership, of an awareness of ecological knowledge in the sense that Krech cites–thinking systematically about the environment and its components. These documents may therefore give us a rare glimpse into a decisive moment in the development of HBC learning about conservation.[18] This learning involved not only drawing lessons from the experience of HBC decisions about hunting that were implemented jointly with Northern Algonquians, but also having some help in understanding that experience from the commentaries provided by the Northern Algonquians, even if those commentaries were not yet fully understood by the HBC.

That the Charlton Island experiment provided the context in which the HBC leadership become aware of the complexity of game population dynamics and that these dynamics were related to environmental conditions puts into perspective what the HBC did not know when it implemented its measures to "recruit" beavers starting in the 1820s. It makes clear why Krech is in error to assume that these policies expressed contemporary ecological and conservation ideas.

In the decades after the initial Charlton Island experiment, Northern Algonquians appear to have had some direct influences on HBC practices. After the hunt of 1851–52 the HBC accepted the advice of the hunters not to trap the island again for a few years. Crees were reported in 1842 to be using rotational hunting in the Rupert House District: "They alternate years work different sections of their lands, leaving such to recruit two or even three years, or otherwise long ago their lands (particularly the Coast Indians whose Beaver grounds are so limited) would have been exhausted" (Krech 1999, 191; quoted here from Francis and Morantz 1983, 129). When the HBC recommended trapping on Charlton Island it did so every three or four years thereafter, with from 250 to 500 beavers commonly being taken in the hunts between 1853 and the 1870s (Brooks 1929, 31–38; Watt 1930a, 1–3). The HBC appears to have learned rotational trapping from the Northern Algonquians.

Thus there is no basis for Krech's ignoring the knowledge and active agency of Northern Algonquians in the processes leading to the recovery of beaver populations, or for his allowing only generally that it may have occurred, but only after the ideas and practices were learned from HBC traders (Krech 1999, 206). The process of developing practices that were forerunners of conservation programs was a mutual one. The evidence from this one particularly well documented case study shows that improvements in HBC policy and practices depended in important ways on Northern Algonquians' knowledge and experience. The Charlton Island case suggests that the general increase in beaver numbers across the region was primarily the result of the Northern Algonquians' efforts to reestablish beaver populations, aided by HBC efforts.

Interestingly, there is some evidence that this is how Cree hunters and some later HBC traders saw the process. James Watt, the HBC trader at Rupert House from the 1920s to the 1940s, found Cree hunters and retired HBC employees who had family stories of their parents' involvement in the Charlton Island beaver preserve, and oral traditions that a hunt there once caught more than eight hundred beavers, as well as stories of the succeeding decades (Watt 1930a, 3). Commenting in 1930 on an HBC London Committee letter of 1826, which took some of the early steps "to preserve the beaver," Watt said that after talking with elder Crees:

> So far as I have been able to learn from Indian traditions, the steps taken were to maintain the rights of an indian family to a specified hunting ground; the Indian then farmed his lands, when possible on a rotation system—leaving certain lakes and creeks unhunted for a term of years—until the beaver were sufficiently numerous to kill again.
>
> This was the general idea, but not always strictly adhered to. During the periodical scarcity of rabbits and other country food,

> *so many beaver were often killed for food as to seriously deplete*
> *the breeding stock.*
>
> *Even with this drawback the system worked sufficiently well*
> *for the company to ship from Ruperts House 4982 Beaver in 1893.*
> (Watt 1930b, 1)

This statement presents the HBC policies as helping Crees maintain their rights to their hunting territories, not creating them, and it reiterates that it was the Crees who practiced rotational use of hunting territories.

Thus Krech's analyses about how beavers recovered and how conservation developed is wrong, both because it denies the active and leading role of Native Americans and because it fails to recognize that the complex relationships between the Northern Algonquians and the fur traders were vital to the process.[19]

Krech's Policy Pronouncements:
Hidden Agendas and Misrepresented Choices

On the last pages of his final chapter, just preceding the epilogue, Krech offers his own political policy advice about the claims to lands and resources made by Northern Algonquians today: "over the last three decades the story of conservation has been inseparable from the all-embracing political and economic movement to control Northern Algonquian lands and energy" (1999, 198). He implies that it is Native Americans who have made the story of conservation a political one, not the rapid expansion of massive government and corporate resource exploitation projects into the North. Krech says that in the view of Crees and anthropologists who have "echoed" their rhetoric, myself included, "history legitimates the Cree authority, rather than provincial or federal authority, to manage natural resources" (199–200). Krech rejects Cree and Innu claims that they have "the right to decide resource and conservation issues" (207) and that "they, rather than the governmental or private interests, should be responsible for environmental management" (208).

Krech rejects these statements because Crees and other Native Americans "often base their claim on a natural right stemming from their relationship to the environment, which, in opposition to large-scale development projects, they present as balanced and harmonious" (207–8). In opposition to these claims, he asserts that he has shown that "the historical evidence is lacking for conservation until long after the arrival of Europeans, and it is quite equivocal and mixed for the family territorial system" (200). Thus Krech uses his ethnohistorical research as a means of deciding who has the most authoritative and legitimate claims to control and manage lands and resources in North America today, governments or Native Americans.

Krech does not mention these political policy goals in the introduction to his book or in the previous two hundred pages. I mention this not because I think it is wrong for scholars to address policy issues; scholars do need to address important national and international issues with their scholarship. But I think that when one of the goals of a scholarly book is to enter into political debate, the author has a responsibility to signal that intention to readers before they read the analyses.

Krech writes as if his political policy choices flow more or less directly from his historical research findings, but his policy pronouncements are embedded in complex legal, political, and historical issues that he either fails to address or misrepresents. He frames his policy pronouncements by adopting the self-image of a moderate. He writes that his rejection of Native Americans' authority over lands and resources does not mean, as some "might be tempted to argue," that Native Americans have no rights (208). Krech argues that Native Americans should be involved in the co-management of resources with governments, because "No one disputes that senior hunters have gained a detailed and sophisticated understanding (albeit cultural) of their surroundings and the animals" (209). He notes that co-management of natural resources is widespread today in the Canadian and Alaskan North (208).

But Krech does not make clear that co-management in the North is typically a government policy and that it does not fulfill widespread Native American visions or goals. Co-management, insofar as it is officially recognized today by governments in North America, is most commonly either a delegation of administrative authority given to Native American peoples by agencies of the government, or it is an advisory participation for Native American peoples in the institutions of the nation-state (although there are exceptions) (Spaeder and Feit 2005).

Thus co-management is not what most Cree and Innu peoples have sought, namely, decision-making authority based on recognition of their coexisting rights and governance, which exist independently of recognition by the governments of Canada or the United States. They are seeking more equal relationships based on their own authority to govern. Nevertheless, many Northern Algonquians also recognize that their authority must be exercised in the midst of, and in relationship with, governments, and their claim is not for exclusive governance (see Moses 2002 and Cree hunters' court testimonies cited in Richardson 1975; see Ashini 1995 for an Innu view; also see Scott 1988, Feit 2005, and Feit forthcoming).

Krech does not present these Northern Algonquian views. Instead, he misrepresents Northern Algonquians as arguing for completely exclusive rights, thus setting up a false choice between exclusive Native American management and exclusive government-mandated co-management. I understand that Northern Algonquians envision forms of dual self-determination with governments, not government-mandated co-management or their own exclusive governance.

Further, that Crees, Innus, and other Native Americans seek recognition of their rights does not derive fundamentally from a claim to be ecological Indians, or people who practiced twentieth-century forms of conservation before the twentieth century. It derives from their rights and their recognitions in law, from the histories of their relationships with European and other North American settlers and their descendants, and from their historical and current ways of caring for the land.

Krech does not mention that there are existing legal bases for indigenous rights. Indigenous rights are grounded in Native Americans' own legal systems, and they are also recognized by the courts and laws of the United States and Canada, by the Canadian constitution, and in international law and legal instruments. The extent and meaning of the rights and their recognitions are incompletely defined and highly contested (Morse 1985; Williams 1990; Anaya 1996; Alfred 1999; Harring 2002; Fixico 2002), but their existence is not in doubt in the United States or Canada, although this is not widely recognized in public debates. One of the strongest areas of agreed rights relates to basic indigenous rights to lands, wildlife, and their use (Hutchins, 2006). It is erroneous for Krech to write as if these indigenous rights can be dismissed today, as if the very existence of indigenous rights to lands and wildlife is completely open to question.

Further, Krech's policy conclusions present a choice between indigenous rights that are of autonomous origin from the nation-state, on the one hand, and nation-states' claims to sovereign supremacy, on the other. This framing of policy issues is the classic choice presented by Euro-American political systems rooted in nation-state sovereignty. But the ethnohistorical records Krech reviews do not support such a polarized choice, and they indicate that there are other possibilities that need consideration.

The fur trade described in the case studies Krech cites was based on establishing a variety of relationships between traders and Northern Algonquians, which both traders and hunters often saw as beneficial, even as they each contested the terms of trade and the obligations of relationships, and even as Europeans often accumulated excessive profits. The HBC generally preferred the Northern Algonquians to be on the land, controlling it against outsiders and using their social and tenure arrangements to organize the hunt and produce furs for the trade. The HBC did not attempt to take over the hunting activities on any large scale, and it did not attempt to take over the control of the land in practice. Its strategies were aimed at trying to maximize the Northern Algonquians' hunt for furbearers and to control as much of the trade as it could vis-à-vis its competitors. That is, Northern Algonquian authority and control of lands were generally crucial to the HBC's economic goals and profits and to its trying to reduce the access or survival of its competitors, and the HBC used and supported Northern Algonquian authority over the land rather than generally disrupting that authority.

Northern Algonquians, for their part, engaged in the trade for centuries mainly because they wanted to, and they often reshaped the trading relationships and practices dramatically to suit their visions. The histories of the fur trade thus include an enduring series of what ethnohistorians now often call "partnerships" (see Francis and Morantz 1983), although these also involved complex relations of power.

But the ethnohistories done to date are about trade and not about issues of governance authority, so there are only the most initial of results for this topic. European traders assumed that HBC governance authority prevailed because it derived from the company's being the royally chartered ruler of the James Bay and Hudson's Bay drainages from 1670 to 1869, when its lands were sold to Canada. Consistent with European ideas of the time, traders probably believed that Native American hunting societies had no organized forms of governance, a view that anthropological research has proven erroneous (Asch 1997; Tully 1995).

Thus there was also an effective Northern Algonquian occupation, tenure, and authority in forms appropriate to a hunting society. The record of the fur trade contains some imprecise reports of Northern Algonquian assertions of their authority. In the 1820s Rupert House Crees were reported to be "tenacious of their Property in their Lands and are not pleased when other Indians encroach on them" (qtd. in Krech 1999, 190). Such statements are difficult to interpret, because fur traders did not understand hunting territories or the "political" organization of territories or of hunting groups or bands.

The HBC also recognized Northern Algonquian authority, both implicitly and explicitly, because doing so was often valuable to its trade. Thus when the HBC leaders promoted Northern Algonquian use of hunting territories in order to help beaver recovery, they also understood that this could help to keep out itinerant trespassing trappers, many of whom who were less likely to be its customers. In promoting hunting territories, the HBC was promoting and implicitly recognizing both a form of Northern Algonquian land tenure and a form of Northern Algonquian authority over lands and wildlife. This was potentially significant for Northern Algonquians, whether the HBC understood the recognition or not.

Thus for long periods and over broad areas Euro-Americans and North-ern Algonquians coexisted without a consistent or effective repudiation of Northern Algonquian authority over lands and resources by the HBC or oth-ers. There were two coexisting claims to authority, both very different from that of a modern nation-state—a chartered trading company and hunting band societies—and a set of ad hoc accommodations, relationships, and sometimes partnerships that linked them.

For the twenty-first century I call this kind of relationship "messy co-governance rooted in coexistence," the unexpected conjuncture of Native American self-determination and Euro-American sovereignty (Feit 2005). This kind of relationship is not easy to "see" today because it does not con-form to the dominant assumptions of nation-state sovereignty. But it is not surprising that it developed during the fur-trade period in the Northern Al-gonquian region, because the HBC-mandated trading region was only nom-inally within a nation-state, although this changed over time. Such coexist-ing authority over the land was not equal; power shifted dramatically over time, and Euro-Canadians and Euro-Americans gained effective dominance, albeit only as recently as the 1970s in the eastern drainage of James Bay. But that dominance includes diverse recognitions of Native Americans' rights and authority, and Native American societies have survived, on the land, and have not been assimilated.

Thus the history of the fur trade does offer insights for policy choices today: it shows that the historical practices of authority and governance of both Euro-Americans and Native Americans coexisted. This does not fit into the choices offered by Krech. In his political conclusions there is no possi-bility of the coexistence of self-determining Native American peoples and nation-states. A key conclusion from the history of the fur trade is that the long and complex co-governance based on the coexistence of both Native American and nation-state authority should be recognized today.

Krech does not conscientiously attempt to use fur-trade history to con-sider what the policy choices or questions should be today. The Ecological Indian thus not only fails to present credible analyses of both nineteenth-century Euro-American fur traders and Native Americans, and of the politics of indigenous rights today, but it also disappoints and misleads readers about present circumstances and possibilities for North Americans and Native Americans.

Notes

1. Earlier versions of this chapter were given at the American Anthropological Association Annual Meeting, Chicago, November 19–23, 2003; and at the Canadian Ethnology Society Annual Meetings, London, Ontario, May 6–9, 2004. The funding for the research used in this article was provided by the Social Sciences and Humanities Research Council of Canada and the Arts Research Board of McMaster University. I received helpful advice and comments from Fikret Berkes, Mario Blaser, Monica Mulrennan, Douglas Nakashima, Matthew Ottereyes Sr., Richard Preston and Colin Scott. I also received help from Anne Morton and others at the Hudson's Bay Company Archives. I want to thank the Public Archives of Manitoba, Hudson's Bay Company Archives, and the National Archives of Canada for permissions to use their collections. I also want to thank the many hunters and elders among the Waswanipi Cree whose knowledge and experience I have drawn on in this article. The term "Whitemen," or more commonly "Whiteman," is used by contemporary James Bay Crees as a general designation for non-Natives.

2. I use the term *European* to refer to non-Natives during the period when many traders and missionaries were of European birth, including the British, or their local descendants. But I intend the term to include others born in North America and elsewhere as well. For the late nineteenth and twentieth centuries or for urban populations I use *North Americans* or *Americans* or *Canadians* for non-Natives, as is most appropriate to the context, and *Euro-American* to concisely encompass both periods. I intend the use of *Americans* or *Canadians* to be inclusive of people of the other country unless the context differentiates. Sometimes I use *Western*, as when I take up Krech's arguments about "Western" ideas or elsewhere where he has used the term, although I try to do so with caution, recognizing both the diversity of views it encompasses and the overly rigid separation it implies with non-Western ideas.

3. Krech's chapter focuses on the Northern Algonquians. When I want to use a term wider than *Northern Algonquians*, I will use *Native Americans*. In Canada the general term *First Nations* would apply today to the groups of Northern Algonquians that Krech discusses as well as to other "Indians" in Canada. Northern Algonquians lived on lands that are now part of both Canada and the United States. Given that *The Ecological Indian* was prepared and published through a U.S. publishing house, I have used the term *Native Americans*. However, the arguments I make in this chapter apply to both countries, and I sometimes use the word *indigenous* to recognize this, especially in legal contexts. I will use the term *Indians* when I am referring to European and North American ideas about Native Americans (see Berkhofer 1978).

4. The fur-trade records are replete with repeated game depletions, but these periods are typically followed by periods of game recovery. The sequences themselves can occur repeatedly in the same region only decades apart, suggesting that there are specific reasons for depletions at particular times. Since game recoveries were also recurrent in areas where Northern Algonquians continued to hunt, these too need analysis. Elsewhere I reanalyze the recurrent depletions and recovery of game and show that depletions are often related in the historical records to re-

ported periods of intrusions or trespass. Nevertheless, because "intrusions" and "trespass" and are imprecise terms in the records, it is not always possible to draw conclusions about who provoked particular depletions or why recoveries occurred (Feit forthcoming).

5. Related arguments have been made by a number of other scholars, including Ray (1975) and Brightman (1993).

6. Elsewhere I suggest that when the quotes from Le Jeune are read in their context it is apparent that Le Jeune was trying to sedentarize the Montagnais, and his primary goal was to make agriculture their primary means of subsistence, in order to more effectively convert them by getting them to reside at the mission sites. Game population recovery was a concession to the powerful fur traders in New France and a means of subsistence security in the context of the unreliable European farming practices in New France at the time. The territories Le Jeune refers to were therefore not to be residential lands of full-time hunters. Thus they were not what anthropologists have called hunting territories over the course of the last century (see Feit forthcoming).

7. I treat comments that have been made to me independently by several experienced Waswanipi Cree hunters as expert knowledge. When I consider statements by Cree experts I usually also seek out the views of wildlife management experts, and vice versa. I do this not to "verify" knowledge claims made by either but rather to "triangulate" understandings, because looking for second and sometimes third sources of information often adds to understandings of why things happen in a particular way or what their limits are. I did a total of a year of field research at Waswanipi in the James Bay region of northern Quebec between the falls of 1968 and of 1970, and summer or seasonal research each year from 1978 to 1987 and from 1997 to 1999. I was also a social science adviser to the James Bay Cree regional political organization from 1971 to 1978 and occasionally thereafter.

8. I typically express my conclusion as a statement about what "the beaver" do or as "what so-and-so says about the beaver," as the circumstance warrants. But I do not seek to make statements in the same form that either wildlife managers or Cree hunters would phrase their ideas—I express my understandings.

9. I use the term *hunting* to include trapping when I mean the wider pattern of Northern Algonquian living on the land and providing for both family subsistence and trade. I use *trapping* to refer specifically to the techniques used to capture furbearers or to trade-related hunting activities, depending on the context, whether conducted by Native Americans, Europeans, or North Americans. When I use *hunting* to refer to living on the land I use it to include the range of activities that were primarily the sphere of women in Northern Algonquian societies, often including small-game hunting and fishing and the butchering, specialized pelt processing, food preparation, and distribution of most game animal meat.

10. See Krech (1999, 182), seventeenth-century Jesuit reports in Thwaites (1897, 6:299, 301, 303), eighteenth-century HBC reports in Hearne (1971, 236–38), and reports that such techniques were widespread in the eighteenth and early nineteenth centuries in Lewis Henry Morgan's monograph on beavers (1986, 238–39). The eighteenth- and nineteenth-century reports do not indicate whether selective harvesting by age was being practiced at the burrows, but Paul Le Jeune's seventeenth-century account noted that Montagnais in the St. Lawrence Valley were not leaving live beavers at a colony.

11. Grove (1995) gives much earlier examples of environmentalism, environmental ideas, and land management, many in specifically colonial settings. Grove also indicates why they were not widely adopted and applied in Europe. Unfortunately, as yet we have little comparable re-

search for the non-tropical areas, and generally for the New World, although one such encounter is documented below.

12. Krech is reluctant to allow this well-documented 1740s east coast Cree use of hunting territories to be an example of a Northern Algonquian practice without European tutelage. He acknowledges this as one possibility, but he also argues that "perhaps" it is a result of practices arising from "fur traders concerned that destroyed commodities [furs] would erode their profits" (1999, 194–45), even though clear HBC policies were only established in the 1820s. Or perhaps, he suggests, "outsiders like Le Jeune," the Jesuit priest whose plans for the Montagnais he quotes from the 1630s, "had some sway over conservation attitudes" (194). Le Jeune spoke a hundred years earlier in another region (see note 6 and Feit [forthcoming] for a discussion of these arguments).

13. Morantz notes that only in the traders' reports of a decade later, in the 1820s, are there more precise descriptions of hunting territories (1986, 74–75). She suggests that one hypothesis is that the HBC traders did not understand the practices yet in 1814–15. Krech suggests that the later traders' reports were more accurate because the Northern Algonquians' practices themselves were emergent rather than well developed between the 1740s and the 1820s (1999, 190–91, 194). Morantz argues that given that there was only a decade between the 1814–15 reports and the more detailed ones, it is less likely that a rapid change in hunting territory practices developed than that the fur traders' understandings of the practices developed quickly (1986, 74–75).

14. See Feit 2004 for discussions of how hunting territories could have developed in the period before the arrival of Europeans.

15. Many of Krech's other inferences from Northern Algonquian statements, summarized in the passage quoted earlier from pages 204–5, are also oversimplified or erroneous. For example, I found that many Northern Algonquians believe that animals which present themselves to a hunter or which leave clear signs of their presence for a hunter should be killed. But this does not need to lead to over-hunting, as Krech suggests, because when hunters decide not to take more animals in an area they do not return to it again, sometimes for weeks or even several years. Thus they do not encounter animals or animal signs there anymore. Similarly, for Northern Algonquians there is no necessary contradiction between stopping the trapping at a beaver colony and thus leaving beavers alive whose signs a trapper has seen there. Many Cree hunters today think that the beavers that are not caught in the first week or two are signaling that they do not want to be caught, at least for the moment, and many trappers take their traps out and leave when this happens. Explaining animal declines by referring to causes other than hunting, such as violation of taboos, need not be surprising, since most northern mammals have highly variable population numbers that cannot be explained solely by hunting intensity. These variations are generally not well understood by wildlife researchers or by Crees. Thus having other explanations does not indicate that hunters are denying the effects their own hunting may be having. Stressing rituals of respect for animals can make sense in any society, not because it necessarily leads to immediate decisions on whether to harvest game at the time of the ritual, but because social groups are constantly faced with choices among conflicting needs and values. Highlighting the inherent value of animals through rituals can become part of the choices and debates over what is permissible and what is not morally acceptable in society, and it can also be a way of educating the young in these values and choices. We do not know if Northern Algonquian understandings and rituals worked this way in the seventeenth, eighteenth, and nineteenth centuries, as we generally lack sufficient material to interpret their ideas and practices of those periods in depth.

So we need to be cautious in our explanations of what such statements mean, because several explanations are possible.

16. I am indebted to Richard Preston for alerting me to some of the rich information about this HBC conservation initiative and for making available to me extracts from a manuscript written by Henry Connolly, who worked for the HBC in the 1830s in the district near Charlton Island. At the request of the HBC and in support of their claims to the island, Connolly swore an affidavit in 1903 or 1904, when he was retired, in which he affirmed that the HBC had placed beavers on Charlton Island (Connolly n.d.). His manuscript, which elaborates on this history, is being prepared for publication by Preston and James Morrison (see Preston 2004). My account is also based on a collection of forty-eight extracted references to HBC activities on the island drawn from Governor Simpson's and other HBC head office records prepared by J. Chadwick Brooks, the secretary of the HBC in 1929. These extracts extend from 1836 to 1871. Brooks prepared these as an affidavit in another HBC legal claim for title to Charlton Island (Brooks 1929). These sources are supplemented with information reported in a letter by James Watt, HBC postmaster at Rupert House in 1930, to his superior in support of his own proposal to reestablish a fur farm at the post. Watt's information is drawn from an old post journal he found from 1854–59 and from conversations this discovery provoked with local Cree hunters and retired HBC employees at Rupert House in 1930 (Watt 1930a).

17. To put the harvest quota of five thousand beavers into a broader perspective, I would note that the trade of the Rupert House post in the latter part of the nineteenth century was considered very good at nearly five thousand beaver pelts a year (Watt 1930b). It is difficult to estimate the size of the hinterland from which those pelts were drawn or the intensity of the hunt, but an approximation based late-twentieth-century maps of Rupert House Crees' hunting territories would be approximately 10,600 square miles. In the 1930s, HBC traders reported the area of Charlton Island as 115 square miles.

18. This was a decade before George Perkins Marsh's book, and several decades before the later-nineteenth-century conservation movement.

19. Krech's final example of European pedagogy occurs in the 1930s and 1940s when "the HBC, Quebec, and later, Ontario and the federal government joined forces to institute beaver preserves" and teach conservation to the Crees (1999, 197). In a detailed history of these well-documented events, I show that they involved complex forms of cooperation, independence, mutual aid, and effective co-governance among governments, traders, and Cree trappers (Feit 2005).

References

Alfred, Taiaike. 1999. *Peace, power, righteousness: An indigenous manifesto.* Toronto: Oxford University Press.

Anaya, S. J. 1996. *Indigenous peoples in international law.* New York: Oxford University Press.

Asch, Michael. 1997. *Aboriginal and treaty rights in Canada: Essays on law, equity, and respect for difference.* Vancouver: UBC Press.

Ashini, Daniel. 1995. The Innu struggle. In *On the land: Confronting the challenges of aboriginal self-determination in northern Quebec and Labrador,* ed. Bruce A. Hodgins and Kerry A. Cannon, 29–41. Toronto: Betelgeuse Books.

Bailey, Vernon. 1922. *Beaver habits, beaver control, and possibilities in beaver farming.* Bulletin 1087. Washington DC: U.S. Department of Agriculture.

Berkes, Fikret. 1999. *Sacred ecology: Traditional ecological knowledge and resource management.* Philadelphia: Taylor & Francis.

Berkhofer, Robert F., Jr. 1978. *The white man's Indian: Images of the American Indian from Columbus to the present.* New York: Knopf.

Bishop, Charles A. 1974. *The Northern Ojibwa and the fur trade.* Toronto: Holt, Rinehart and Winston of Canada.

Bramwell, Anna. 1989. *Ecology in the twentieth century.* New Haven: Yale University Press.

Brightman, Robert. 1993. *Grateful prey: Rock Cree human-animal relationships.* Berkeley: University of California Press.

Brooks, J. Chadwick. 1929. [Brooks to The Fur Trade Commissioner, June 28, 1929, and July 12, 1929–"Beaver Farms–Charlton Island"]. Provincial Archives of Manitoba, Hudson's Bay Company Archives, Unclassified, D.D. box 79A.

Connolly, Henry. n.d. Reminiscences of one of the last descendants of a bourgeois of the North West Company. Manuscript. National Archives of Canada, MG29, B15, vol. 61, folder 34.

Feit, Harvey A. 1987. Waswanipi Cree management of land and wildlife: Cree cultural ecology revisited. In *Native peoples: Native lands,* ed. Bruce Cox, 75–91. Ottawa: Carleton University Press.

———. 2004. Les territoires de chasse algonquiens avant leur "découverte"? Études et histoires sur les tenure, les incendies de forêt et la sociabilité de la chasse. *Recherches amérindiennes au Québec* 34 (3): 5–21.

———. 2005. Re-cognizing co-management as co-governance: Histories and visions of conservation at James Bay. *Anthropologica* 47 (2): 267–88.

———. Forthcoming. Objectivity, advocacy, and trust in Shepard Krech's *The ecological Indian.* In *Anthropology, First Nations, and law,* ed. Marc Pinkoski. Vancouver: UBC Press.

Fixico, Donald. 2002. Federal and state policies and American Indians. In *A companion to American Indian history,* ed. Philip J. Deloria and Neal Salisbury, 389–421. Malden MA: Blackwell.

Francis, Daniel, and Toby Morantz. 1983. *Partners in furs: A history of the fur trade in eastern James Bay, 1600–1870.* Montreal: McGill-Queen's University Press.

Grove, Richard H. 1995. *Green imperialism: Colonial expansion, tropical island edens, and the origins of environmentalism, 1600–1860.* Cambridge: Cambridge University Press.

Harring, Sydney L. 2002. Indian law, sovereignty, and state law: Native people and the law. In *A companion to American Indian history,* ed. Philip J. Deloria and Neal Salisbury, 441–59. Malden MA: Blackwell.

Hays, Samuel P. 1969 (1959). *Conservation and the gospel of efficiency: The progressive conservation movement, 1890–1920.* 1959. New York: Atheneum.

Hearne, Samuel. 1971. *A journey from . . . Hudson's Bay to the northern ocean . . . in the Years 1769, 1770, 1771, and 1772. 1795.* Edmonton: M. G. Hurtig.

Hutchins, Peter W. 2006. We are all here to stay: Managing lands and resources for cultural integrity and mutual advantage. Paper presented at the Congrès Annuel du Barreau du Québec, May 11–13, 2006, Montreal.

Huntington, Henry P. 1992. *Wildlife management and subsistence in Alaska.* Seattle: University of Washington Press.

Innis, Harold A. 1962. *The fur trade in Canada*. Rev. ed. 1930. Toronto: University of Toronto Press.

Jordan, Carl F. 1995. *Conservation: Replacing quantity with quality as a goal for global management*. New York: Wiley.

Krech, Shepard, III. 1999. *The ecological Indian: Myth and history*. New York: Norton.

Leopold, Aldo. 1947. *Game management*. 1933. New York: Scribner.

MacKenzie, John M. 1988. *The empire of nature: Hunting, conservation, and British imperialism*. Manchester: Manchester University Press.

Marsh, George Perkins. 1965. *Man and nature; Or, physical geography as modified by human action*. Ed. David Lowenthal. 1864. Cambridge: Harvard University Press.

McCandless, Robert G. 1985. *Yukon wildlife: A social history*. Edmonton: University of Alberta Press.

Merk, Frederick, ed. 1968. *Fur trade and empire: George Simpson's journal . . . 1824–25*. Rev. ed. Cambridge: Belknap Press of Harvard University.

Morantz, Toby. 1983. *An ethnohistorical study of eastern James Bay Cree social organization, 1700–1850*. Canadian Ethnology Service Paper no. 88. Ottawa: National Museums of Canada.

———. 1986. Historical perspectives on family hunting territories in eastern James Bay. *Anthropologica* ns 28 (1–2): 64–91.

Morgan, Lewis H. 1986. *The American beaver*. 1868. New York: Dover.

Morse, Bradford. 1985. *Aboriginal peoples and the law: Indian, Metis, and Inuit rights in Canada*. Ottawa: Carleton University Press.

Moses, Ted. 2002. A retrospective. In *I dream of yesterday and tomorrow*, ed. Michael Gnarowski, 22–48. Kemptville, Ontario: Golden Dog Press.

Novak, Milan. 1987. Beaver. In *Wild furbearer management and conservation in North America*, ed. Milan Novak et al., 282–312. Toronto: Ontario Ministry of Natural Resources.

Preston, Richard J. 2004. Henry Connolly's text and work. Unpublished paper given at the Centre for Rupert's Land Studies Colloquium, Kenora, Ontario, May 27–29, 2004.

Ray, Arthur J. 1974. *Indians in the fur trade: Their role as trappers, hunters, and middlemen in the lands southwest of Hudson Bay, 1660–1870*. Toronto: University of Toronto Press.

———. 1975. Some conservation schemes of the Hudson's Bay Company, 1821–50: An examination of the problems of resource management in the fur trade. *Journal of Historical Geography* 1 (1): 49–68.

Richardson, Boyce. 1975. *Strangers devour the land*. Toronto: Macmillan.

Scott, Colin H. 1988. Property, practice, and aboriginal rights among Quebec Cree hunters. In *Hunters and gatherers: Property, power, and ideology*, ed. Tim Ingold, David Riches, and James Woodburn, 35–51. New York: Berg Press.

Spaeder, Joseph, and Harvey A. Feit, eds. 2005. *Co-management and indigenous communities: Barriers and bridges to decentralized resource management*. Special issue of *Anthropologica* 47 (2): 147–288.

Thwaites, Reuben Gold, ed. 1896–1901. *The Jesuit relations and allied documents*. 73 vols. Burrows: Cleveland.

Tully, James. 1995. *Strange multiplicity: Constitutionalism in an age of diversity*. Cambridge: Cambridge University Press.

Warren, Louis S. 1997. *The hunter's game: Poachers and conservationists in twentieth-century America*. New Haven: Yale University Press.

Watt, James. 1930a. [J. S. C. Watt to V. W. West, April 24, 1930—"Old Records: Charlton Game Preserve"]. Provincial Archives of Manitoba, Hudson's Bay Company Archives, Unclassified, FTD, file 2-4-95, Buildings and Lands—Charlton Island, 1854–1930.

———. 1930b. [J. S. C. Watt to V. W. West, July 4, 1930–"Charlton Island: Beaver Farming"]. Provincial Archives of Manitoba, Hudson's Bay Company Archives, Unclassified, FTD, file 2-4-95, Buildings and Lands–Charlton Island, 1854–1930.

Williams, Robert A. 1990. *The American Indian in Western legal thought: The discourses of conquest.* New York: Oxford University Press.

Worster, Donald. 1977. *Nature's economy: A history of ecological ideas.* Cambridge: Cambridge University Press.

(Over)hunting Large Game

4. Did the Ancestors of Native Americans Cause Animal Extinctions in Late-Pleistocene North America?

And Does It Matter If They Did?

Robert L. Kelly and Mary M. Prasciunas

The relationship between the animal and human life of the New World has long been the subject of debate. As early as 1749 the French naturalist George-Louis Leclerc hypothesized that both humans—Native Americans—and the animals they fed upon had degenerated from their superior European forms because nature was less "active" and "energetic" on one side of the globe than on the other. In his *Notes on the State of Virginia* (1781), Thomas Jefferson responded to Leclerc in discussing the nature and origins of Native Americans, a subject that greatly intrigued him (and led him to undertake the first "scientific" excavation of an archaeological site in the United States). Jefferson admired the Native peoples of the New World and, unlike many of his contemporaries, believed them to be equal to Europeans in intellect. But he needed more substantive grounds on which to refute Leclerc.

One of the key elements of Leclerc's proposition was the claim that animals of the New World were smaller than those of Europe. Jefferson was aware of finds of the skeletal remains of mammoths, mastodons, and giant ground sloths in various places, such as Big Bone Lick, Kentucky. (And his interest is recognized through the scientific name for the giant ground sloth, *Megalonyx jefersoni*.) He once kept a mammoth skull in Monticello's front foyer, and while president he laid out mammoth bones in the White

House's East Room (dubbed the "Bone Room" by White House staff). Such large animals were proof that Leclerc's image of New World fauna, and hence his degeneration hypothesis, were incorrect.

The skeletal remains that decorated Monticello and the White House were undeniable evidence of a large fauna. But it was equally undeniable that there were no pachyderms tromping through Virginia's forests. Thus, one could have argued that mammoths and other large Pleistocene fauna were extinct precisely for the reason that Leclerc claimed. Whether this counterargument played a role in his thinking is unclear, but Jefferson believed that extinctions do not occur, that "such is the economy of nature, that in no instance can be produced her having permitted any race of her animals to become extinct." And so, when Jefferson sent Lewis and Clark west in 1803 he instructed them to keep an eye out for herds of mammoths on the Great Plains.

Unfortunately, they were ten thousand years too late.

Late-Pleistocene Extinctions

Scholars have debated the cause of late-Pleistocene extinctions since the early nineteenth century (Grayson 1984b; Martin and Steadman 1999). And with the unambiguous establishment, in the 1920s, of the presence of humans in late-Pleistocene North America, the role of Native Americans in the extinctions became central. The importance of understanding the cause of these extinctions is not purely academic. Martin (1990, 2002), for instance, argues that the wave of extinctions that began in the late Pleistocene is still occurring today and that the earth is in the midst of human-induced extinctions that will rival those of the late Cretaceous, when a meteor destroyed the earth's "Jurassic Park" fauna and gave rise to the dominance of mammals, including humans (see also Ward 1994). Many other ecologists unflinchingly use the late-Pleistocene extinctions as examples of what humans did in the past and what they are capable of doing in the future (e.g., Wilson 2002; Diamond 1992; Ward 2000). Martin and Burney (1999) even propose that we should reintroduce free-ranging elephant herds on North America's Great Plains so that the proboscidea can help reestablish stable ecological relationships there (see also Steadman 1989; Steadman and Olson 1985).

Of more immediate importance is the argument that if the ancestors of Native Americans caused the late-Pleistocene extinctions, then living Native Americans are not qualified to act as unchecked stewards of the environment.[1] On this basis, some argue that treaty-guaranteed fishing and hunting rights, such as those granted to the Chippewas in the nineteenth century, and that were contested in Minnesota and Wisconsin in the 1990s, should be repealed.

Leaving aside the politics, this chapter examines current thinking on the role of humans in late-Pleistocene extinctions. Explanations for extinctions are often polarized between two competing hypotheses: climatic change (Graham and Lundelius 1984; Guthrie 1984; Lundelius 1989) and human predation (Martin 1967, 1973, 1984; Martin and Steadman 1999). Recently, MacPhee and Marx (1997) have added an alternative that implicates the role of human-introduced hypervirulent diseases.

There are many variations on these general themes. Here we examine each hypothesis and the supporting arguments and criticisms. We focus on North America, where the archaeological and paleontological record is best known. We conclude that we simply do not know for certain, yet, what caused the late-Pleistocene extinctions, although the climate-change argument currently seems to have the most support. In addition, we conclude that *even if* Native Americans were the primary cause of the late-Pleistocene extinctions, that fact would have little bearing on the land-use rights of modern Native Americans.

Late-Pleistocene Extinctions: What Happened?

Because of a late-Pleistocene extinction event that was rapid, pervasive, and global, Lewis and Clark had to disappoint Jefferson. A period of alternating glacial and interglacial periods, the Pleistocene lasted from about 2 million to 10,000 years ago (Anderson 1984, 41). Most of the extinctions, however, occurred within its final few thousand years and were complete by 11,000–10,500 BP (Grayson 2001, 35; G. Haynes 2002a, 2002b; Holliday 2000b; Martin 1990; Martin and Burney 1999; Mead and Meltzer 1984; Meltzer and Mead 1985; Stuart 1991; all dates used here are in uncalibrated radiocarbon years before present [BP]; for a rough conversion to calendar years, add 2,000 to the radiocarbon years).

Table 4.1. Extinct late-Pleistocene North American mammals with date of latest appearance (adapted from Grayson 1991). Genera in boldface are the only genera unequivocally associated with kill sites (adapted from Grayson 1991 and Grayson and Meltzer 2002, 2003).

Order	Family	Genus	Common name	Youngest good date
Artiodactyla	Antilocapridae	Capromeryx	Diminutive pronghorn	None
		Tetrameryx	Shuler's pronghorn	None
		Stockoceros	Pronghorns	None
	Bovidae	Saiga	Saiga	None
		Euceratherium	Shrub ox	None
		Bootherium	Harlan's musk ox	None
	Camelidae	Camelops	Yesterday's camel	10,900 ± 750
		Hemiauchenia	Large-headed llama	None
		Palaeolama	Stout-legged llama	10,890 ± 130
	Cervidae	Cervalces	Elk-moose	None
		Navahoceros	Mountain deer	None
	Tayassuidae	Mylohyus	Long-nosed peccary	None
		Platygonus	Flat-headed peccary	None
Carnivora	Canidae	Cuon	Dhole	None
	Felidae	Homotherium	Scimitar cat	None
		Miracinonyx	American cheetah	None
		Smilodon	Sabertooth	11,130 ± 275
	Mustelidae	Brachyprotoma	Short-faced skunk	None
	Ursidae	Arctodus	Giant short-faced bear	None
		Tremarctos	Florida cave bear	None
Lagomorpha	Leporidae	Aztlanolagus	Aztlan rabbit	None
Perrisodactyla	Equidae	Equus	Horse	10,370 ± 350
	Tapiridae	Tapirus	Tapir	10,900 ± 450
Proboscidea	Elephantidae	Mammuthus	Mammoth	10,550 ± 350
	Mammutidae	Mammut	American mastodon	10,395 ± 110
Rodentia	Castoridae	Castoroides	Giant beaver	None
	Hydrochoeridae	Hydrochoerus	Holmes's capybara	None
		Neochoerus	Pinckney's capybara	None
Xenartha	Pampatheriidae	Holmesina	Northern pampathere	None
		Pampatherium	Southern pampathere	None
	Glyptodontidae	Glyptotherium	Simpson's glyptodont	None
	Megalonychidae	Megalonyx	Jefferson's ground sloth	12,190 ± 215
	Megatheriidae	Eremotherium	Rusconi's ground sloth	None
		Nothrotheriops	Shasta ground sloth	10,035 ± 250
	Mylodontidae	Glossotherium	Harlan's ground sloth	20,450 ± 460

Prior to the extinction event, more than one hundred genera of large mammals (> 44 kg) existed in North and South America (Martin 1984, 355; 1990, 188). Extinctions reduced this assemblage by more than two thirds (Martin and Szuter 1999, 37). In North America, thirty-five genera of mainly large mammals distributed across twenty-one families and seven orders became extinct near the terminal Pleistocene (Grayson 1991, 194; 2001, 35; Kurten and Anderson 1980; see table 4.1). This is more than the total number of mammals that became extinct throughout the past 4.8 million years, making the late Pleistocene witness to an extinction event unparalleled in the entire Cenozoic era (Martin 2002, 10; Martin and Steadman 1999). The event was not limited to North America: South and Central America lost forty-seven genera (Martin 2002, 18), and twenty-eight genera disappeared from Australia (Flannery and Roberts 1999). Large mammals were especially hard hit, but many species of birds, reptiles, and small mammals also disappeared. In addition, many species that managed to survive into the Holocene did so in far more restricted ranges than they enjoyed in the late Pleistocene (e.g., musk ox, which once lived as far south as Tennessee).

Late-Pleistocene extinctions are notable in that they were concentrated on megafauna and attendant parasites, predators, and commensals, to the exclusion of invertebrates, smaller fauna, and marine taxa. Martin suggests that this argues against a climatic (global) cause (Martin 1990, 189–92; 2002, 11; Martin and Steadman 1999, 17–18). Similarly, there were virtually no accompanying floral extinctions. Only one plant species in North America (a spruce, Picea critchfieldii) is known to have become extinct (Jackson and Weng 1999); Martin (2002, 9) suggests the possibility of human involvement, but paleoecologists attribute the loss of this spruce to climate change (Jackson and Weng 1999).

Something very drastic happened at the end of the Pleistocene. But what?

The Overkill Hypothesis

The overkill hypothesis argues that Clovis hunters were responsible for late-Pleistocene North American megafaunal extinctions. It also suggests a more general pattern of faunal extinction caused by human colonists throughout time and in many different parts of the world. An advocate of the overkill hypothesis for several decades, Paul Martin (1967, 1973, 1984, 1990, 2002; Martin and Steadman 1999; Mosimann and Martin 1975) proposed that big-game Clovis hunters from Siberia crossed into North America through an ice-free corridor between the Cordilleran and Laurentian ice sheets and moved quickly across the North American landscape, killing all large game before them in a "blitzkrieg" occupation. The Clovis Complex is the earliest accepted and well-dated North American cultural complex, dating to approximately 11,500–10,900 BP (Dixon 1999, 215; Fiedel 1999; Grayson 2001, 35; C. V. Haynes 1993; Taylor, Haynes, and Stuiver 1996). Clovis artifacts are the *only* stylistic artifact forms that appear in all forty-eight contiguous states, and they are associated with mammoth and mastodon remains in a few archaeological sites (Grayson 2001, 36; Grayson and Meltzer 2002; see Fiedel and Haynes 2004; Grayson and Meltzer 2004).

Although controversy exists as to the magnitude of Clovis dependence on meat and specialized big-game hunting, the association of distinctive Clovis fluted projectile points with mammoths and other large mammals does indicate that Clovis people did hunt mammoth at times (G. Haynes 2002a). Kelly and Todd (1988) argued that an Arctic adaptation to large-game hunting (but not exclusively of megafauna) in an unpopulated environment undergoing rapid environmental change explains the high mobility of Clovis populations. In this scenario, rapid late-Pleistocene environmental change (resulting in local extinctions) coupled with depletion due to hunting forced Clovis foragers to move to new territory frequently to maintain high return rates on hunting (Kelly 1996, 1999). But with no previous occupants to call upon for local landscape knowledge, Clovis hunters needed an adaptation that permitted the occupation of unknown terrain and that allowed them to eschew plant foods, the uses of which would have been unknown to Arctic foragers. Kelly and Todd argued that the same hunting adaptation would have been necessary to cross ecological boundaries without having to acquire new subsistence-related knowledge. Thus, a hunting adaptation both permitted and encouraged rapid movement. However, Kelly and Todd explicitly argued that such rapid movement could happen without a blitzkrieg of the faunal population.

A recent computer simulation suggests that, as is often true for colonizing animal populations, a highly mobile Clovis population could have had a substantial population growth rate (Surovell 2000). If so, then demographic pressure coupled with an adaptation that not only permitted but also required territorial mobility could have pushed colonists rapidly southward. Martin (1973) argues that such population densities would have quickly become sufficiently large to cause extinctions throughout the Americas by soon after 11,000 BP. This blitzkrieg could have been especially devastating because the megafauna had no experience with human hunters and thus were easily dispatched (Martin 1973, 1984, 2002; Mosimann and Martin 1975). In support of the blitzkrieg model are several computer simulations that can produce extinction purely as a product of human hunting (Alroy 2001; Holdaway and Jacomb 2000; Mithen 1997).

Why didn't all animals go extinct? Martin argues that the surviving species had characteristics that made them undesirable to human hunters. They were "cryptic or secretive in habits (moose, puma); erratic and unpredictable in movements (bison, caribou); sequestered in sparsely inhabited regions (polar bear, musk oxen); truculent or dangerous when approached (brown and polar bears); fleet of foot (pronghorn, gray wolf); denizens of rugged terrain (mountain goat, mountain sheep, jaguar); and in no case as promising a target for human hunters as the slow-moving ground sloths or as vulnerable to low levels of predation as the proboscidea" (Martin 2002, 17).

Evidence for Overkill

Foremost among the arguments in support of the overkill hypothesis are (1) the apparent chronological coincidence of megafaunal extinctions and the appearance of human hunters, (2) the observation that island fauna are frequently decimated by human colonization, and (3) arguments derived from ecological theory.

Chronology. The close chronological coincidence of late-Pleistocene megafaunal extinctions and the colonization of the New World was what initially generated the overkill hypothesis (Grayson 1991, 204–5). The latest occurrences of mammoths, for example, in North America are about 11,000 BP (Martin 1990, 195; Taylor, Haynes, and Stuiver 1996).[2] The paleontological record therefore points to a suspicious coincidence between the first arrival of humans and the disappearance of some megafauna (Martin 1967, 1990; Lyons, Smith, and Brown 2004; Surovell, Waguespack, and Brantingham 2005). For some, this coincidence strongly suggests a causal relationship.

The time-transgressive nature of late-Pleistocene extinctions has also been used to argue for human involvement and against a global cause of extinctions such as climatic change (Martin 1990, 188; Martin and Burney 1999, 60; Surovell, Waguespack, and Brantingham 2005). Although catastrophic extinctions did occur regionally, some researchers argue that extinctions were not synchronous but instead occurred only, and soon, after human colonization in the Americas, Australia, Madagascar, New Zealand, and the South Pacific (Martin 1990; Martin and Burney 1999, 61). While North American megafauna were extinct by 10,500 BP, large-mammal extinctions occurred in Australia as early as 50,000 BP (Miller et al. 1999), when that continent may have been first colonized by people. Indeed, the timing of the extinctions is quite suspicious (Lyons, Smith, and Brown 2004).

In contrast, overkill proponents point out that few large ungulate species have become extinct over the past forty thousand years in areas with longer histories of human occupation, such as Africa, Europe, and tropical Asia (Martin 1990, 188; Martin and Burney 1999, 61). Martin (2002, 24) argues that the success of large animals in these places is explained by a much longer history of human occupation on these continents, which allowed the fauna to develop a coevolutionary response to hominid predation. These animals evolved alongside ancient hominids; they never had to naively encounter sophisticated, fully armed hunters as did the fauna of the Americas, Australia, Madagascar, and the Pacific Islands. Megafaunal extinctions in Greater Australia (Australia, Tasmania, New Guinea, and New Zealand) appear to have occurred without associated environmental change, suggesting to overkill proponents that these regions provide independent tests of the model (Diamond, 1992; Martin 1967, 1984; Fiedel and Haynes 2004; Lyons, Smith, and Brown 2004).

Unfortunately, the empirical foundations of these arguments are not strong. In order for the chronological coincidence of Clovis and the extinctions to be significant, most if not all the extinctions would have to occur within the Clovis era, 11,500 to 10,900 BP. But this does not appear to be true. Of the thirty-five genera that became extinct at the end of the Pleistocene, radiocarbon dating can only show that fifteen survived past 12,000 BP (Grayson 1987, 1991, 2001; Grayson and Meltzer 2002; Meltzer and Mead 1985). Admittedly, though, the dating programs on all the involved species are not as thorough as one would like.

It is possible that humans were in the New World before, and perhaps long before, Clovis hunters. Recent data from South America, notably from the site of Monte Verde in southern Chile, suggest that humans were in South America by 12,500 BP. This might imply that people were in North America considerably before that date (if we accept the Bering land bridge as the entry point, and all evidence points to that as the case). If this is true, then pre-Clovis hunters might be responsible for the pre-12,000 BP extinctions.

However, there is no unequivocal evidence for a pre-Clovis human presence in interior North America, and Kelly (2003) argues that there is good reason to think that such evidence will never be found (though many competent archaeologists would disagree, e.g., Adovasio 2002). It is possible (though perhaps unlikely) that a pre-Clovis human migration moved along the west coast of North America and bypassed the North American interior, resulting in the populating of interior South America prior to North America. But even if this is true, Clovis hunters would still be the first occupants of interior North America—and the only humans potentially responsible for the extinctions there. Evidence of a pre-Clovis population elsewhere in the New World does not account for extinctions in interior North America prior to 12,000 BP.

Additionally, we would expect evidence that Clovis diet was biased toward large game. In recent years it has become popular to argue that Clovis hunters had a more generalized foraging adaptation (Dincauze 1993, 285; Dixon 1999, 250; Hudecek-Cuffe 1998; Meltzer 1993; Willig 1991, 93), relying upon a broad diet of fish, plants, and small animals such as turtles. However, this argument depends more on ethnographic analogy with modern foragers who know their environments intimately and whose movements are constrained by agricultural neighbors. Unfortunately, it is difficult to reconstruct Clovis diet from the currently known archaeological record, because our sample of sites is small and potentially biased toward large kill sites, and because small plant and animal remains do not always survive the ravages of time. Additionally, many Clovis sites were excavated decades ago when archaeologists did not have methods to recover what small faunal and botanical remains may have been present. One quantitative analysis of existing Clovis faunal assemblages shows a distinct bias toward large game animals, suggesting that Clovis hunters were big-game specialists (Waguespack and Surovell 2003). Yet another argues that when the various biases are taken into account, the evidence for big-game specialization disappears (Cannon and Meltzer 2004).

So, is there any *direct* evidence for big-game hunting? Distinctive fluted Clovis points turn up at only a few proboscidean sites in the New World (G. Haynes 1991, 197). Although thirteen of the thirty-five extinct genera occur in archaeological contexts, Grayson and Meltzer (Grayson 1991, 212; 2001, 37; Grayson and Meltzer 2002, 2003) note that only fourteen North American kill sites provide evidence that Clovis hunters targeted mammoths and mastodons. Because other fauna such as horses and camels are well represented in the paleontological record of the late Pleistocene, their lack of association with kill sites cannot be attributed to sample bias. In brief, we have no direct evidence that Clovis hunters took any megafauna other than mammoths and mastodons. For some, the handful of proboscidean kill sites is too few to indicate a heavy human reliance on mammoth hunting (e.g., Meltzer 1993; Dixon 1999, 216).

But Martin (1973, 1984; Martin and Steadman 1999) argues that extinctions occurred so rapidly that they would have left little evidence of hunting (rendering this version of the overkill hypothesis untestable). Short-term events often leave little to no trace archaeologically (e.g., despite knowledge of their route and intensive searches, archaeologists have a hard time finding evidence of the Lewis and Clark expedition). This explanation for the lack of evidence does not explain why only mammoth/mastodon kill sites have been unequivocally identified (Grayson 2001, 38).

Grayson and Meltzer's argument and Martin's counterargument are based on the assumption that fourteen is a "small" number. But Gary Haynes (1999, 13; 2002a, 2002b) argues that there are *fewer* elephant kill sites in all of Africa than in North America, despite Africa's having a larger landmass and tens of thousands of years of human hunting of elephants. In comparison, the Clovis record is rich in proboscidean kill sites. Surovell and Waguespack (2004) likewise show that the density of Clovis proboscidean kill sites is extraordinarily high, whether landmass, time, or a combination of the two is considered, compared to the Old World. Fourteen might actually be a large number.

What about the evidence from Europe and Australia? Contra Martin, extinctions and extirpations *did* occur in Europe at about the same time as those in North America. These included large game such as Irish elk, reindeer, mammoth, saiga, and the giant deer (Grayson and Meltzer 2003; see Fiedel and Haynes 2004; Grayson and Meltzer 2004). Since humans had hunted these animals for millennia, hunting probably played no direct and certainly no primary role in their extinctions.

Although the record of megafaunal extinctions in Greater Australia suggests that the timing of human colonization of the region coincides with extinctions (Brook and Bowman 2002, 14626; Flannery and Roberts 1999; Roberts et al. 2001; Thorne et al. 1999; Turney et al. 2001; Webb 1998; Wroe and Field 2001), the record is still not thoroughly dated. This is complicated by the fact that, as is true for the New World, there is no consensus on the timing of human colonization of Greater Australia, with estimates ranging from 43,000 BP (O'Connell and Allen 1998) to 71,500 BP (Brook and Bowman 2002). As in North America, there are few unambiguous associations between megafauna skeletal remains and evidence of human activity (Johnson 2002, 2221; Miller et al. 1999). Some conclude that there was a lengthy period of overlap between humans and Australian megafauna (Brook and Bowman 2002; Roberts et al. 2001), which would argue against the blitzkrieg model of overkill. To an extent, what happened in Australia

does not matter, for the North American case must be resolved independent of the Australian one.

Island Extinctions. Mass extinctions on many Pacific islands occurred only a
thousand to fifteen hundred years ago, coinciding with human colonization
(Martin 1990, 199). The paleontological records of many islands throughout the Pacific indicate that catastrophic extinctions did indeed accompany
human colonization (Martin 1990, 2002).

Olson and James (1982, 1984), for example, argue that Polynesians may
have quickly brought about the extinction of more than half the native species of the Hawaiian Islands through human predation, competition, predation by introduced non-native fauna, and landscape changes caused by
anthropogenic fires. Massive extinctions of land birds coincident with initial human colonization occurred on many oceanic islands (Grayson 2001,
29–30; Steadman 1995). A similar pattern of extinction and human colonization occurred on other islands, such as the West Indies (Steadman, Pregill, and Olson 1984), Madagascar (Burney 1997, 1999; Dewar 1997a, 1997b),
Corsica (Blondel and Vigne 1993; Vigne 1992; Vigne and Valladas 1996), and
other Mediterranean Islands (Alcover, Seguí, and Bover 1999). Some researchers use this evidence as analogs of Clovis hunting in North America.
Martin (1990, 196–98), in fact, argues against climatic change as a driving
force behind extinctions because no severe changes in island fauna occurred
during the late Pleistocene.

While Oceania provides evidence for the role of human colonization in
faunal extinctions, island faunas are particularly vulnerable to anthropogenic ecological changes, which often result in extinction (Grayson 2001;
Paulay 1994, 134; Simmons 1999; Steadman 1989, 178; Steadman et al. 1991,
126). Most islands were colonized not by hunter-gatherers but by horticulturalists whose lifeways (especially that of swidden horticulturalists) caused
rapid and pervasive changes to the indigenous vegetation, especially by the
burning and clearing of vegetation and by the introduction of non-native
species that competed with native fauna. With small populations, a lack of
defensive mechanisms, and, especially, no ready source of conspecifics to
replenish diminished populations, island faunas are more sensitive to ecological disruption than continental faunas (Steadman 1989, 178; Steadman

et al. 1991). Without guns, human predation has a different effect on island fauna than on continental fauna (with guns, obviously, Euro-Americans brought about the extinctions of some animals and drove others, such as bison, to the brink of extinction).

Because human colonization of North America occurred at the end of the last Ice Age, a time of enormous environmental change and human migration, it is difficult to isolate human involvement from environmental causes of extinction. But there is no evidence for significant human-induced vegetational change during Clovis times in North America (Grayson 2001, 42). Thus, it is inappropriate to use the documented fact of human-induced extinctions on islands as evidence that extinctions on continents were likewise caused by humans.

Ecology. Other arguments in favor of overkill explore the ecological relationships that existed among humans, megafauna, and the environment. Large herbivore feeding can actually increase an ecosystem's primary productivity (G. Haynes 2002a, 392). Therefore, mammoth and mastodon extinction could have had significant ripple effects on North American ecosystems (G. Haynes 2002a, 408–9). Owen-Smith (1987, 1999) argues that megafauna were "keystone" species that increased diversity and carrying capacity at the patch level through their feeding, trampling, and wallowing. The ecological dependence of smaller fauna on the proboscideans resulted in their extinction when humans hunted mammoths and mastodons to extinction (Owen-Smith 1999, 67).

For the keystone hypothesis to explain the extinction event, however, mammoths and mastodons must have been the first fauna to go extinct. But radiocarbon data do not support this chronology; in fact, they suggest that mammoths and mastodons were some of the last species to go (Grayson 2001, 38; see Table 1).

To discover the characteristics that made certain species more susceptible to extinction, Johnson (2002) compares the characteristics of late-Pleistocene species that disappeared in Australia, Eurasia, the Americas, and Madagascar to those species that survived. He concludes that mammal species with low reproductive rates were more likely to become extinct, although nocturnal and arboreal species that would have less contact with human hunters were more likely to survive. While his analysis does not support selective hunting of large-bodied species as the cause of extinction, and casts doubt on the blitzkrieg model, it does suggest that humans could have contributed to extinctions because even low-level hunting could severely affect species with low reproductive rates.

However, this explanation suggests that humans hunted animals to the point where the animals' numbers fell below a level of reproductive viability. This is difficult to square with what we know of foraging behavior. Ethnographic data show that foragers generally try to maintain as high a return rate as possible on their foraging efforts (Kelly 1995). For this reason, foragers abandon a habitat or drop an item from their diet when the benefits obtained from that habitat or item fall below the average return from harvesting other foods or searching other habitats. As resource density declines due to predation, foragers migrate or switch prey when the cost of foraging reaches a level that surpasses the cost of moving to a new territory, not when the animals became locally extinct (Kelly 1995, 80). Thus, Clovis (or any) hunters move before hunting a species to extinction, thus allowing a megafauna population to rebound (Webster and Webster 1984). Note that this is not because Clovis hunters wished to conserve their resource, but only to increase the return on their hunting efforts. (On islands, however, with limited places for hunters to go, this pattern could still result in extinction.)

Mithen (1997), however, argues that prey switching probably did not occur in the case of mammoth hunting *if* mammoth hunting was more of a prestige-oriented than a subsistence-oriented activity. The acquisition of ivory or vast amounts of meat could have conferred prestige on successful hunters (of course, we never will know if Clovis peoples considered proboscidean hunting prestigious or just "all in a day's work"). As mammoth populations diminished, there may have been an even greater demand for them. Mithen's computer simulation uses the sensitivity of mammoth populations to predation (due to long regeneration periods) to show that if mammoth hunting was intensive for even a short period, it may have been impossible for a population to recover.

Others argue that Clovis hunting of megafauna is compatible with optimal foraging theory (G. Haynes 1999; 2002a, 401–4; G. Haynes and Eiselt 1999). At the end of the Pleistocene, mammoths clustered into refugia due to environmental changes (G. Haynes 1999, 21; 2002a, 407). Instead of abandoning a patch when prey abundance fell, G. Haynes (2002a, 407) argues, Clovis hunters focused more heavily on megafauna hunting, choosing to forage in the remnant megafauna refugia where they knew megafauna would be concentrated and thus easier to locate. Concentrations of mammoths in restricted areas would yield greater return rates for human hunters exploiting these patches (G. Haynes 1999, 33; 2002a, 2002b; G. Haynes and Eiselt 1999, 83). Human hunting pressure could therefore have been responsible for late-Pleistocene extinctions of certain species—those with low reproductive rates who clustered in refugia during late-Pleistocene climatic change.

Thus, arguments derived from foraging theory can support or refute the overkill hypothesis. Although they help to guide thinking and models, they are not a substitute for the empirical record. But as noted above, that record's interpretation is equally controversial and can be used to support an interpretation of Clovis hunters as large-game specialists or generalists. At the moment, all we can say is that Clovis hunters definitely took some mammoths and mastodons, but we have no direct evidence for the hunting of any of the other large fauna that became extinct. Clovis hunters also took other resources—plants and small game—but we don't know if proboscideans were central or peripheral to diet. In sum, the jury is still out as to whether the archaeological record supports or refutes big-game specialization, and consequently on whether the record supports or refutes the overkill hypothesis.

The Hypervirulent Disease Hypothesis

An interesting alternative to the overkill model looks to humanly introduced disease as the culprit. MacPhee and Marx (1997) argue that the driving force behind late-Pleistocene extinctions was not hunting or ecological degradation but rather hypervirulent diseases (HVDs) introduced to the native fauna by humans and/or their dogs. Hypervirulent diseases would have resulted in massive extinctions that closely coincided with initial human colonization—but without evidence of predation.

MacPhee and Marx (1997) argue that the HVD hypothesis explains the differential survival of r- versus K-selected species. Young and old animals of large fauna with low reproductive rates (K-selected) would be especially susceptible to disease, resulting in smaller population sizes of large animals. In contrast, the life history characteristics of small-bodied fauna, such as higher reproductive rates that permit high degrees of mortality, would have protected these populations from disease-induced extinction (MacPhee and Marx 1997, 186). The HVD hypothesis also potentially explains the lack of abundant kill sites in the late-Pleistocene archaeological record of North America because the effects of human hunting would not have been severe; it is the mere presence of humans that matters in this explanation. Disease might also explain the fact that after initial human contact and significant faunal loss, the rate of extinction dropped abruptly and stayed low until recent times (MacPhee and Marx 1997).

The HVD model is an unlikely and, at present, inadequately tested explanation of extinctions (Alroy 1999; Burney 1999, 161; Owen-Smith 1999). Alroy (1999), for instance, argues that it fails to explain the intensity and body-size selectivity of late-Pleistocene extinctions. He also points out that mammals potentially carrying diseases immigrated into North America throughout the entire Cenozoic era without causing mass extinctions. By the time humans arrived in North America, fauna should have been exposed to many pathogens. Additionally, most mammalian diseases are restricted to a single order. There is no evidence of a deadly pandemic disease that is capable of spreading through populations of different orders such as would be required to explain the trans-taxonomic pattern of late-Pleistocene extinctions (Alroy 1999, 139). Lyons et al. (2004) point out that hypervirulent diseases are expected to attack animals of particular body size; thus, multiple diseases would be required to account for Pleistocene extinctions, and this seems unlikely.

The HVD hypothesis should be testable in that the pathogens responsible for mass extinction should be detectable in ancient DNA found in bones or tissues of extinct fauna. To date, researchers have not found any direct empirical evidence of HVD in extinct late-Pleistocene mammals. In sum, there is no good evidence to support the HVD hypothesis.

The Climatic-Change Hypothesis

The late Quaternary was a time of frequent climatic fluctuations during the transition from glacial to interglacial conditions, with an overall trend toward warming (Bond and Lotti 1995; Dansgaard et al. 1993; Grayson 1984a, 2001; Mayewski et al. 1993). During the full glacial, mean annual temperatures were as much as 5–7°C colder than modern temperatures. Around 14,500 BP, climatic warming began and glacial ice ablated (Wright 1993).

A cold pulse at the end of the Pleistocene known as the Younger Dryas (YD) briefly interrupted this warming trend. The YD was a Northern Hemisphere–driven cold event that reversed warm and wet conditions beginning at approximately 11,100/11,300 BP and ending around 10,000 BP (G. Haynes 2002a, 393). The climatic warming at the end of the YD cannot be the cause of the extinctions, as most extinctions were already complete by about 11,000 BP. Nor can the YD account for those extinctions that occurred before 12,000 BP. If anything, the *onset* of the YD might be responsible for the extinction of those animals that survived beyond 12,000 BP, and that would be odd because it would mean that species that survived for millennia in glacial conditions were done in by cold conditions.

Combining the overkill and climatic arguments, C. V. Haynes (1984, 1991) sees a period of desiccation and drought during the terminal Pleistocene throughout North America. This drought period appears to coincide with megafauna extinctions as well as the appearance of Clovis hunters. Haynes suggests that drought may have concentrated physiologically stressed megafaunal populations at water holes, making them easier prey for hunters (C. V. Haynes 1991, 447). However, Holliday (2000a) is unable to find evidence of this drought on the southern High Plains; instead, the evidence suggests that Clovis times were quite wet and that the succeeding Folsom times were characterized by periodic drought.

A common argument against climate change as a cause of extinction is that the fauna that became extinct at the end of the Pleistocene had survived some nine glacial/interglacial cycles over the past 700,000 years and must therefore have been able to adapt successfully to changing environmental conditions (Martin and Steadman 1999; Fiedel and Haynes 2004). However, terminal-Pleistocene climatic change may have been unlike past climatic changes in its form, rapidity, and intensity (Guthrie 1984, 291), especially during the YD.[3] For example, unlike any previous climatic warming, the terminal Pleistocene was followed by the Holocene (ca. 10,000 BP–present), a relatively warm and climatically stable period (Bond and Lotti 1995).

In fact, paleontological data point to environmental change at the end of the Pleistocene that was unlike any other climatic warming. Proponents of the overkill hypothesis tend to focus solely on the fate of large mammals, but the extinction of these fauna coincided with significant geographic reshuffling of many smaller species (FAUNMAP Working Group 1996; Grayson 1991, 214; 2001, 39; Stafford et al. 1999) and a fundamental reorganization of vegetation communities.

Many late-Pleistocene mammal communities have no modern analogs (FAUNMAP 1996, 1605; Graham and Lundelius 1984; Grayson 1991; Guthrie 1984; Lundelius 1989). Late-Pleistocene faunal assemblages show that many species lived cheek by jowl that are separated today by elevation or latitude (Grayson 1991, 215). The combinations of taxa present in the Pleistocene no longer exist, leading to the terms "disharmonious" (Graham and Lundelius 1984) or "intermingled" (Lundelius 1989) to describe them. For example, the yellow-cheeked vole today lives only in Alaska, and the western pack rat only in the western United States, but in the late Pleistocene both lived together in many localities including those outside their current ranges, such as Tennessee. Intermingled late-Pleistocene faunal assemblages are known from virtually all areas of the world that are represented by adequate data, including North America, Australia, southern Africa, and Eurasia (Graham and Lundelius 1984; see review in Guthrie 1984, 263–66; Lundelius 1989). These intermingled communities disappear at the same time that extinctions occur (Lundelius 1989, 415).

Frankly, we don't know if this correlation is significant. The terminal Pleistocene saw a reduction in arid grasslands and homogeneous vegetation communities and biomes, the latter marking a transition from a "plaid" to a latitudinal "band" plant distribution. Graham and Lundelius (1984) argue that geographic range restrictions coupled with decreasing plant community diversity may have contributed to extinction by increasing competition in choice locales, making it more difficult for megafauna to consume sufficient food for the winter (Grayson 1991, 216; Graham and Lundelius 1984; Guthrie 1984). Decreased diversity in local vegetation increased competition between large monogastrics (mastodons, mammoths, rhinos, large edantes, and horses) and ruminants (moose, deer, and bison) and reduced available nutrients for the former (Guthrie 1984, 284–85, 263). Thus, a reduction in range would have had a greater effect on megafauna than on smaller mammals, and once populations dropped below a critical demographic threshold, the species was doomed to local extinction.

Guthrie (1984) also suggests that the antiherbivory defense systems of many plants shifted to ones of increased toxins. Those mammals that were doomed to extinction were, for the most part, adapted to plants that were not allochemically well defended by having a tolerance for stems, which was then supplemented by other better-defended plant parts. Thus, animals could obtain adequate nutrition by mixing plant parts and diluting toxins. As plant diversity decreased, these mammals had to rely more heavily on allochemically defended plants. As a result, the mammals ingested more toxins than they could combat, resulting in reduced metabolic function, competitive abilities, and reproductive success. Thus, very complex and as yet poorly understood changes in vegetation communities (that have no modern analogs) could have brought about the late-Pleistocene extinctions.

Gary Haynes argues against the climate-change argument by pointing out that fossils of extinct large mammals from the late Pleistocene show no evidence of climate-induced stress in the form of poor health (2002a, 392; Fiedel and Haynes 2004). However, Guthrie (2003) has shown that late-Pleistocene horses in Alaska underwent a clear and rapid reduction in body size just prior to extinction. If this reduction in body size was a product of declining forage abundance and quality, then Guthrie's is the first demonstration of environmentally induced biological stress on a Pleistocene megafauna species.

We suspect that climate change is the most parsimonious and likely cause of late-Pleistocene extinctions in North America. Humans may have helped the process along in places, but it is likely that the result would have been the same even if human hunters were not present. The climatic-change hypothesis, however, is by no means proven and requires further testing.

Conclusion

Jefferson was wrong: extinctions do occur. In fact, 99 percent of all animal species that have ever existed on earth are extinct; death is an integral part of life. If the ancestors of Native Americans had never made it to the New World before Europeans arrived in the sixteenth century, would the French, British, and Spanish have brought back drawings of mammoths and mastodons instead of beavers and bison? Would Leclerc have changed his mind? Could Jefferson have stabled live pachyderms and ground sloths in the White House instead of just their skeletons? We *suspect* that the answer to these questions is no, because climate change is the most likely explanation for the extinction of North American megafauna. But we admit that we simply don't know the answer yet. It remains unknown whether human hunters, climatic change, or disease was the sole cause or whether they worked together.

Nonetheless, can we learn any lessons from what we do know of the events of ten thousand years ago? First, since the jury is still out on whether human hunting caused the extinctions, it is irresponsible for ecologists to point to the late-Pleistocene and Native American hunting practices as a warning of things to come if industrial society does not repent. For that lesson we need look no further than what almost happened to the American bison, and what did happen to the passenger pigeon.

And, therefore, it is also wrong to use Pleistocene extinctions as evidence that Native Americans are not capable of environmental stewardship. But what if we do discover incontrovertible evidence that the ancestors of Native Americans hunted mammoths and mastodons to extinction? In fact, it is already clear from island archaeology and paleontology and from cases such as the passenger pigeon and dodo bird that all peoples are capable of bringing about extinctions. And North American archaeological studies that focus on later time periods show that local extinctions or extreme depletions can result from long-term (hundreds of years) sustained human hunting (e.g., Broughton 2002; Hildebrant and Jones 2002). Native Americans did cause extirpations in many cases. Likewise, ethnographic studies of foraging peoples show that hunters aim to maximize the return rate from foraging regardless of the conservation consequences (e.g., Alvard 1993, 1994). Where hunters are geographically constrained, their efforts to maintain a high return from their hunting efforts will inevitably bring about extirpation and possibly extinction.

At the same time, we see explicit and effective efforts in many indigenous societies that aim to increase biodiversity and conserve resources (e.g., Minnis and Elisens 2000; Murray 2003). No one is naturally a conservationist, but everyone is capable of becoming one. Rather than argue about whether one human group is or is not inherently conservationist, it is better to understand the conditions under which conservation behaviors are prestigious and desirable, and when short-term needs relegate them to long-term luxuries that a society cannot afford (see, e.g., Zavaleta 1999).

Second, if the climatic-change argument is correct, then we see from the Pleistocene case that habitat degradation and geographic range restriction are major factors in the extinction process. This is commensurate with what we know of other instances of extinction, such as on islands. Climate change appears to have produced habitat degradation and range restriction in the late Pleistocene, but today such effects are often a result of human activities. Clearly, aiming for zero loss of habitat and range reduction must be an objective of development.

Third, this case study reminds us that humans are an integral part of the environment; they were in the late Pleistocene, and they are today. There has been no "natural" environment anywhere on earth for the last ten thousand years, if by "natural" we mean "no human presence." Even at relatively low population densities, humans can have large and long-standing effects on the environment. Sometimes these effects have produced environments that we now take to be natural and desirable. Through their use of fire, for example, Native North Americans probably produced the extensive oak forests of the eastern United States that we fight to maintain today; the same is probably true of the extensive eucalyptus forests in northern Australia. Humans are part of the environment. We change it, just as mammoths changed it by fertilizing it with their dung, tromping around bogs, and eating grass. Like mammoths and ground sloths, we could become extinct by environmental changes that are beyond our control—a meteor, perhaps—or we could become extinct through more subtle environmental changes that derive from our presence and behavior.

Unlike mammoths and ground sloths, however, we have a choice. And it is wiser to spend our time deciding what that choice will be (free-ranging elephants in Kansas?) and how we will attain it than to argue about whether one group of people is inherently better suited to make that choice than another. We would like to think that Thomas Jefferson, had he known what archaeologists and paleontologists know today, would come to the same conclusion.

Notes

1. The September 2002 judicial decision (upheld by the appeals court in February 2004) that the ninety-four-hundred-year-old Kennewick skeleton is not Native American might suggest to some that the earliest inhabitants of North America were not ancestral to modern Native Americans, making this statement irrelevant. Space does not permit us to present the argument here, so it will have to suffice to say that this judicial opinion is not coeval with a scientific one, and that arguing that Kennewick cannot be proven to be ancestral to Native American under federal law (Native American Graves Protection and Repatriation Act) does not mean that he was not Native American (see Kelly 2004).

2. There are a few "late" mammoths, e.g., the Fetterman mammoth in Wyoming, which dates to about 9000 BP (Byers 2002); these are outliers, and it is assumed that some unknown biochemical process has affected the radiocarbon dates.

3. However, the uniqueness of the late Pleistocene's climate change may be a function of the fact that we have a much more fine-grained and more intensively studied record than for the previous climatic changes.

References

Adovasio, J. M., with J. Page. 2002. *The first Americans: In pursuit of archaeology's greatest mystery.* New York: Random House.

Alcover, J. A., B. Seguí, and P. Bover. 1999. Extinctions and local disappearances of vertebrates in the western Mediterranean islands. In *Extinctions in near time: Causes, contexts, and consequences*, ed. R. D. E. MacPhee, 165–88. New York: Kluwer Academic/Plenum Publishers.

Alroy, J. 1999. Putting North America's end Pleistocene megafaunal extinction in context: Large-scale analyses of spatial patterns, extinction rates, and size distribution. In *Extinctions in near time: Causes, contexts, and consequences*, ed. R. D. E. MacPhee, 105–43. New York: Kluwer Academic/Plenum Publishers.

———. 2001. A multispecies overkill simulation of the end-Pleistocene megafaunal mass extinction. *Science* 292:1893–96.

Alvard, M. S. 1993. Testing the "ecologically noble savage" hypothesis: Interspecific prey choice by Piro hunters of Amazonian Peru. *Human Ecology* 21:355–87.

———. 1994. Conservation by Native peoples: Prey choice in a depleted habitat. *Human Nature* 5:127–54.

Anderson, E. 1984. Who's who in the Pleistocene: A mammalian bestiary. In *Quaternary extinctions: A prehistoric revolution*, ed. P. S. Martin and R. G. Klein, 40–89. Tucson: University of Arizona Press.

Blondel, J., and J. D. Vigne. 1993. Space, time, and man as determinants of diversity of birds and mammals in the Mediterranean region. In *Species diversity in ecological communities*, ed. R. E. Ricklefs and D. Schluter, 135–46. Chicago: University of Chicago Press.

Bond, G. C., and R. Lotti. 1995. Iceberg discharges into the North Atlantic on millennial time scales during the last glaciation. *Science* 267:1005–10.

Brook, B. W., and D. M. Bowman. 2002. Explaining the Pleistocene megafaunal extinctions: Models, chronologies, and assumptions. *Proceedings of the National Academy of Sciences* 99:14624–27.

Broughton, J. M. 2002. Pre-Columbian human impact on California vertebrates: Evidence from old bones and implications for wilderness policy. In *Wilderness and political ecology*, ed. Charles Kay and Randy Simmons, 44–71. Salt Lake City: University of Utah Press.

Burney, D. A. 1997. Tropical islands as paleoecological laboratories: Gauging the consequences of human arrival. *Human Ecology* 25:437–57.

———. 1999. Rates, patterns, and processes of landscape transformation and extinction in Madagascar. In *Extinctions in near time: Causes, contexts, and consequences*, ed. R. D. E. MacPhee, 145–64. New York: Kluwer Academic/Plenum Publishers.

Byers, D. 2002. Taphonomic analysis, associational integrity, and depositional history of the Fetterman mammoth, eastern Wyoming, U.S.A. *Geoarchaeology* 17:417–40.

Cannon, M. D., and D. J. Meltzer. 2004. Early Paleoindian foraging: Examining the faunal evidence for large mammal specialization and regional variability in prey choice. *Quaternary Science Reviews* 23:1955–87.

Dansgaard, W., S. J. Johnson, H. B. Clausen, D. Dahl-Jensen, N. S. Gundestrup, C. U. Hammer, C. S. Hridberg, J. P. Steffensen, A. E. Sveinbjornsdotir, J. Jouzel, and G. Bond 1993. Evidence for general instability of past climate from a 250–ky ice-core record. *Nature* 364:218–20.

Dewar, R. E. 1997a. Does it matter that Madagascar is an island? *Human Ecology* 25:481–89.

———. 1997b. Were people responsible for the extinction of Madagascar's subfossils, and how will we ever know? In *Natural change and human impact in Madagascar*, ed. S. M.

Goodman and B. D. Patterson, 364–77. Washington DC: Smithsonian Institution Press.

Diamond, J., 1992. *The third chimpanzee: The evolution and future of the human animal.* New York: Harper Collins.

Dincauze, D. F. 1993. Fluted points in the eastern forests. In *From Kostenki to Clovis: Upper Paleolithic–Paleo-Indian adaptations*, ed. O. Soffer and N. D. Praslov, 279–92. New York: Plenum Press.

Dixon, E. J. 1999. *Bones, boats, and bison: Archaeology and the first colonization of western North America.* Albuquerque: University of New Mexico Press.

FAUNMAP Working Group. 1996. Spatial response of mammals to late Quaternary environmental fluctuations. *Science* 272:1601–6.

Fiedel, S. J. 1999. Older than we thought: Implications of corrected dates for Paleoindians. *American Antiquity* 64:95–115.

Fiedel, S. J., and G. Haynes. 2004. A premature burial: Comments on Grayson and Meltzer's "Requiem for overkill." *Journal of Archaeological Science* 31:121–31.

Flannery, T. F., and R. G. Roberts. 1999. Late Quaternary extinctions in Australia: An overview. In *Extinctions in near time: Causes, contexts, and consequences*, ed. R. D. E. MacPhee, 239–55. New York: Kluwer Academic/Plenum Publishers.

Graham, R. W., and E. L. Lundelius Jr. 1984. Coevolutionary disequilibrium and Pleistocene extinctions. In *Quaternary extinctions: A prehistoric revolution*, ed. P. S. Martin and R. G. Klein, 211–22. Tucson: University of Arizona Press.

Grayson, D. K. 1984a. Explaining Pleistocene extinctions: Thoughts on the structure of a debate. In *Quaternary extinctions: A prehistoric revolution*, ed. P. S. Martin and R. G. Klein, 807–23. Tucson: University of Arizona Press.

———. 1984b. Nineteenth-century explanations of Pleistocene extinctions: A review and analysis. In *Quaternary extinctions: A prehistoric revolution*, ed. P. S. Martin and R. G. Klein, 5–39. Tucson: University of Arizona Press.

———. 1987. An analysis of the chronology of late Pleistocene mammalian extinctions in North America. *Quaternary Research* 28:281–89.

———. 1991. Late Pleistocene mammalian extinctions in North America: Taxonomy, chronology, and explanations. *Journal of World Prehistory* 5:193–231.

———. 2001. The archaeological record of human impacts on animal populations. *Journal of World Prehistory* 15:1–68.

Grayson, D. K., and D. J. Meltzer. 2002. The human colonization of North America, Clovis hunting and large mammal extinction. *Journal of World Prehistory* 16:313–59.

———. 2003. A requiem for North American overkill. *Journal of Archaeological Science* 30:1–9.

———. 2004. North American overkill continued? *Journal of Archaeological Science* 31:133–36.

Guthrie, R. D. 1984. Mosaics, allelochemics, and nutrients: An ecological theory of late Pleistocene megafaunal extinctions. In *Quaternary extinctions: A prehistoric revolution*, ed. P. S. Martin and R. G. Klein, 259–98. Tucson: University of Arizona Press.

———. 2003. Rapid body size decline in Alaskan Pleistocene horses before extinction. *Nature* 426:169–71.

Haynes, C. V., Jr., 1984. Stratigraphy and late Pleistocene extinction in the United States. In *Quaternary extinctions: A prehistoric revolution*, ed. P. S. Martin and R. G. Klein, 345–53. Tucson: University of Arizona Press.

———. 1991. Geoarchaeological and paleohydrological evidence for a Clovis-age drought in North America and its bearing on extinction. *Quaternary Research* 35:438–50.

———. 1993. Clovis-Folsom geochronology and climatic change. In *From Kostenki to Clovis: Upper Paleolithic–Paleo-Indian adaptations*, ed. O. Soffer and N. D. Praslov, 219–36. New York: Plenum Press.

Haynes, G. 1991. *Mammoths, mastodons, and elephants: Biology, behavior, and the fossil record.* New York: Cambridge University Press.

———. 1999. The role of mammoths in rapid Clovis dispersal. *Deisea* 6:9–38.

———. 2002a. The catastrophic extinction of North American mammoths and mastodonts. *World Archaeology* 33:391–416.

———. 2002b. *The early settlement of North America.* Cambridge: Cambridge University Press.

Haynes, G., and B. S. Eiselt. 1999. The power of Pleistocene hunter-gatherers: Forward and backward searching for evidence about mammoth extinction. In *Extinctions in near time: Causes, contexts, and consequences*, ed. R. D. E. MacPhee, 71–93. New York: Kluwer Academic/Plenum Publishers.

Hildebrant, W. R., and T. L. Jones. 2002. Depletion of prehistoric pinniped populations along the California and Oregon coasts: Were humans the cause? In *Wilderness and political ecology*, ed. Charles Kay and Randy Simmons, 44–71. Salt Lake City: University of Utah Press.

Holdaway, R. N., and C. Jacomb. 2000. Rapid extinction of the moas. *Science* 287:2250–54.

Holliday, V. T. 2000a. Folsom drought and episodic drying on the southern high plains from 10,900–10,200 14C yr BP. *Quaternary Research* 53:1–12.

———. 2000b. The evolution of Paleoindian geochronology and typology on the Great Plains. *Geoarchaeology* 15:227–90.

Hudecek-Cuffe, C. R. 1998. *Engendering northern plains Paleoindian archaeology.* Oxford: BAR International Series 699.

Jackson, S. T., and C. Weng. 1999. Late Quaternary extinction of a tree species in eastern North America. *Proceedings of the National Academy of Sciences* 96:13847–52.

Johnson, C. N. 2002. Determinants of loss of mammal species during the late Quaternary "megafaunal" extinctions: Life history and ecology but not body size. *Proceedings of the Royal Society, London* 269:2221–27.

Kelly, R. L. 1995. *The foraging spectrum: Diversity in hunter-gatherer lifeways.* Washington DC: Smithsonian Institution Press.

———. 1996. Ethnographic analogy and migration to the Western Hemisphere. In *Prehistoric dispersals of Mongoloid peoples*, ed. T. Akazawa and E. Szathmary, 228–40. Tokyo: Oxford University Press.

———. 1999. Hunter-gatherer foraging and colonization of the Western Hemisphere. *Anthropologie* 37 (1): 143–53.

———. 2003. Maybe we do know when people came to North America; and what does it mean if we do? *Quaternary International* 109–10:133–45.

———. 2004. Kennewick Man is Native American. *Society for American Archaeology Archaeological Record* 4 (5): 33–37.

Kelly, R. L., and L. C. Todd. 1988. Coming into the country: Early Paleoindian hunting and mobility. *American Antiquity* 53:231–44.

Kurten, B., and E. Anderson. 1980. *Pleistocene mammals of North America*. New York: Columbia University Press.

Lundelius, E. L., Jr., 1989. The implications of disharmonious assemblages for Pleistocene extinctions. *Journal of Archaeological Science* 16:407–17.

Lyons, S. K., F. A. Smith, and J. H. Brown. 2004. Of mice, mastodons, and men: Human-mediated extinctions on four continents. *Evolutionary Ecology Research* 6:339–58.

Lyons, S. K., F. A. Smith, P. J. Wagner, E. P. White, and J. H. Brown. 2004. Was a "hyperdisease" responsible for the late Pleistocene extinction? *Ecology Letters* 7:859–68.

MacPhee, R. D. E., and P. A. Marx. 1997. The 40,000 year plague: Humans, hyperdisease, and first contact extinctions. In *Natural change and human impact in Madagascar*, ed. S. M. Goodman and B. D. Patterson, 168–217. Washington DC: Smithsonian Institution Press.

Martin, P. S. 1967. Prehistoric overkill. In *Pleistocene extinctions: The search for a cause*, ed. P. S. Martin and H. E. Wright Jr., 75–120. New Haven: Yale University Press.

———. 1973. The discovery of America. *Science* 279:969–74.

———. 1984. Prehistoric overkill: The global model. In *Quaternary extinctions: A prehistoric revolution*, ed. P. S. Martin and R. G. Klein, 354–403. Tucson: University of Arizona Press.

———. 1990. 40,000 years of extinctions on the "planet of doom." *Palaeogeography, Palaeoclimatology, Palaeoecology (Global and Planetary Change Section)* 82:187–201.

———. 2002. Prehistoric extinctions: In the shadow of man. In *Wilderness and political ecology: Aboriginal influences and the original state of nature*, ed. C. E. Kay and R. T. Simmons, 1–27. Salt Lake City: University of Utah Press.

Martin, P. S., and D. A. Burney. 1999. Bring back the elephants. *Wild Earth* Spring:57–64.

Martin, P. S., and D. W. Steadman. 1999. Prehistoric extinctions on islands and continents. In *Extinctions in near time: Causes, contexts, and consequences*, ed. R. D. E. MacPhee, 17–52. New York: Kluwer Academic/Plenum Publishers.

Martin, P. S., and C. R. Szuter. 1999. War zones and game sinks in Lewis and Clark's west. *Conservation Biology* 13:36–45.

Mayewski, P. A., L. D. Meeker, S. Whitlow, M. S. Twickler, M. C. Morrison, R. B. Alley, P. Bloomfield, and K. Taylor. 1993. The atmosphere during the Younger Dryas. *Science* 261:195–97.

Mead, J. I., and D. J. Meltzer. 1984. North American late Quaternary extinctions and the radiocarbon record. In *Quaternary extinctions: A prehistoric revolution*, ed. P. S. Martin and R. G. Klein, 440–50. Tucson: University of Arizona Press.

Meltzer, D. J. 1993. Is there a Clovis adaptation? In *From Kostenki to Clovis: Upper Paleolithic–Paleo-Indian adaptations*, ed. O. Soffer and N. D. Praslov, 293–310. New York: Plenum.

Meltzer, D. J., and J. I. Mead. 1985. Dating late Pleistocene extinctions: Theoretical issues, analytical bias, and substantive results. In *Environments and extinctions: Man in late glacial North America*, ed. J. I. Mead and D. J. Meltzer, 145–73. Orono: Center for the Study of Early Man.

Miller, G. H., J. W. Magee, B. T. Johnson, M. L. Folgel, N. A. Spooner, N. T. McCulloch, and L. K. Nyliffe. 1999. Pleistocene extinction of *Genyornis newtoni*: Human impact on Australian megafauna. *Science* 238:205–8.

Minnis, P. E., and W. J. Elisens. 2000. *Biodiversity and native America*. Norman: University of Oklahoma Press.

Mithen, S. J. 1997. Simulating mammoth hunting and extinctions: Implications for North America. In *Time, process, and structured transformation in archaeology*, ed. S. V. Leeuw and J. McGlade, 176–215. London: Routledge.

Mosimann, J. E., and P. S. Martin. 1975. Simulating overkill by Paleoindians. *American Scientist* 63:304–13.

Murray, M. 2003. Overkill and sustainable use. *Science* 299: 1851–53.

O'Connell, J. F., and J. Allen. 1998. When did humans first arrive in Greater Australia and why is it important to know? *Evolutionary Anthropology* 6:132–46.

Olson, S. L., and H. F. James. 1982. Fossil birds from the Hawaiian Islands: Evidence for wholesale extinction by man before Western contact. *Science* 217:633–35.

———. 1984. The role of Polynesians in the extinction of the avifauna of the Hawaiian Islands. In *Quaternary extinctions: A prehistoric revolution*, ed. P. S. Martin and R. G. Klein, 768–80. Tucson: University of Arizona Press.

Owen-Smith, N. 1987. Pleistocene extinctions: the pivotal role of megaherbivores. *Paleobiology* 13:351–62.

———. 1999. The interaction of humans, megaherbivores, and habitats in the late Pleistocene extinction event. In *Extinctions in near time: Causes, contexts, and consequences*, ed. R. D. E. MacPhee, 57–69. New York: Kluwer Academic/Plenum Publishers.

Paulay, G. 1994. Biodiversity on oceanic islands: Its origin and extinction. *American Zoologist* 34:134–44.

Roberts, R. G., T. F. Flannery, L. K. Ayliffe, H. Yoshida, J. M. Olley, G. J. Prideaux, G. M. Laslett, A. Baynes, M. A. Smith, R. Jones, and B. L. Smith. 2001. New ages for the last Australian megafauna: Continent-wide extinction about 46,000 years ago. *Science* 292:1888–92.

Simmons, A. H. 1999. *Faunal extinction in an island society: Pygmy hippopotamus hunters of Cyprus*. New York: Kluwer Academic/Plenum Publishers.

Stafford, D. W., Jr., H. A. Semken, Jr., R. W. Graham, W. F. Klippel, A. Markova, N. G. Smirnov, and J. Southon. 1999. First accelerator 14C dates documenting contemporaneity of nonanalog species in late Pleistocene mammal communities. *Geology* 27:903–6.

Steadman, D. W. 1989. Extinction of birds in eastern Polynesia: A review of the record, and comparisons with other Pacific Island groups. *Journal of Archaeological Science* 16:177–205.

———. 1995. Prehistoric extinctions of Pacific Island birds: Biodiversity meets zooarchaeology. *Science* 267:1123–31.

Steadman, D. W., and S. L. Olson. 1985. Bird remains from an archaeological site on Henderson Island, South Pacific: Man-caused extinctions on an "uninhabited" island. *Proceedings of the National Academy of Science* 82:6191–95.

Steadman, D. W., G. K. Pregill, and S. L. Olson. 1984. Fossil vertebrates from Antigua, Lesser Antilles: Evidence for late Holocene human caused extinctions in the West Indies. *Proceedings of the National Academy of Sciences* 81:4448–51.

Steadman, D. W., T. W. Stafford Jr., D. J. Donahue, and A. J. T. Jull. 1991. Chronology of Holocene vertebrate extinction in the Galapagos Islands. *Quaternary Research* 36:126–33.

Stuart, A. J. 1991. Mammalian extinctions in the late Pleistocene of northern Eurasia and North America. *Biological Reviews* 66:453–62.

Surovell, T. A. 2000. Early Paleoindian women, children, mobility, and fertility. *American Antiquity* 65:493–508.

Surovell, T. A., and N. Waguespack. 2004. How many elephant kills are 14? Clovis mammoth kills in context. Paper presented at the 69th Annual Meeting of the Society for American Archaeology, Montreal.

Surovell, T. A., N. Waguespack, and P. J. Brantingham. 2005. Global archaeological evidence for proboscidean overkill. *Proceedings of the National Academy of Sciences* 102 (17): 6231–36.

Taylor, R. E., C. V. Haynes Jr., and M. Stuiver. 1996. Clovis and Folsom age estimates: Stratigraphic context and radiocarbon calibration. *Antiquity* 70:515–25.

Thorne, A., R. Grun, C. Mortimer, J. J. Spooner, M. McCulloch, L. Taylor, and D. Curnoe. 1999. Australia's oldest human remains: Age of the Lake Mungo 3 skeleton. *Journal of Human Evolution* 36:591–612.

Turney, C. S. M., M. I. Bird, L. K. Fifield, R. G. Roberts, M. Smith, C. E. Dortch, R. Grün, E. Lawson, L. K. Ayliffe, G. H. Miller, J. Dortch, and R. G. Cresswell. 2001. Early human occupation of Devil's Lair, southwestern Australia 50,000 years ago. *Quaternary Research* 55:3–13.

Vigne, J. D. 1992. Zooarchaeology and the biogeographical history of the mammals of Corsica and Sardinia since the last ice age. *Mammal Review* 22:87–96.

Vigne, J. D., and H. Valladas. 1996. Small mammal fossil assemblages as indicators of environmental change in northern Corsica during the last 2500 years. *Journal of Archaeological Science* 23:199–215.

Waguespack, N. M., and T. A. Surovell. 2003. Clovis hunting strategies, or how to make out on plentiful resources. *American Antiquity* 68:333–52.

Ward, P. D. 1994. *The end of evolution: On mass extinctions and the preservation of biodiversity.* New York: Bantam Books.

_____. 2000. *Rivers in time: The search for clues to Earth's mass extinctions.* New York: Columbia University Press.

Webb, R. E. 1998. Problems with radiometric "time": Dating the initial colonization of Sahul. *Radiocarbon* 40:749–58.

Webster, D., and G. Webster. 1984. Optimal hunting and Pleistocene extinction. *Human Ecology* 12:275–89.

Willig, J. A. 1991. Clovis technology and adaptation in far western North America: Regional pattern and environmental context. In *Clovis: Origins and adaptations,* ed. R. Bonnichsen and K. L. Turnmire, 91–118. Corvallis OR: Peopling of the Americas Publications.

Wilson, E. O. 2002. *The future of life.* New York: Vintage.

Wright, H. E. 1993. *Global climates since the last glacial maximum.* Minneapolis: University of Minnesota Press.

Wroe, S., and J. Field. 2001. Mystery of megafaunal extinctions remains. *Australian Science* 22:21–25.

Zavaleta, E. 1999. The emergence of waterfowl conservation among Yup'ik hunters in the Yukon-Kuskokwim delta, Alaska. *Human Ecology* 27:231–66.

5. Rationality and Resource Use among Hunters

Some Eskimo Examples

Ernest S. Burch Jr.

It is axiomatic among anthropologists and an article of faith among Natives that indigenous North Americans lived in harmony with their environments prior to European contact. To the extent that this proposition is correct, it suggests that Native American peoples used highly rational approaches to, and held remarkably long-term perspectives in, their relationships with their environments. Beneath the mysticism and rhetoric usually associated with assertions concerning these matters lie two sets of important empirical questions. First, did Native Americans really fit into their surroundings as perfectly as is generally believed, and if so, why? Second, did Native Americans' relationship to their surroundings deteriorate after contact with Europeans, and if so, why? These questions have been addressed in a number of recent publications (e.g., Hunn et al. 2003; Krech 1999; E. Smith and Wishnie 2000) but have not been answered to everyone's satisfaction. The purpose of the present chapter is to contribute to the discussion with an analysis of data from two Inuit Eskimo populations, the early contact Iñupiat of northern Alaska and the Caribou Inuit of the central Canadian subarctic.[1]

Before proceeding, I wish to comment on the general approach taken here. Human ecology is the study of the interactions between humans and their nonhuman environment; each side contributes input to and receives output from the other. A complete ecological study must deal with both sides of the equation. Most studies of northern ecology, however, focus primarily on the effect that the harsh environment has on people and on the human adaptations to that environment. It is known that, in the Arctic and subarctic, major fluctuations in the size of fish and game populations due to nonhuman factors could and did throw even the most well adjusted human populations out of harmony with their environments from time to time (Krupnik 1985). Thus, in an absolute sense, "ecological harmony" in northern regions was probably rare, and when it did occur it was short-lived (Krupnik 1993, 259–62).

In the present chapter I am concerned solely with the human side of the equation—the effect people have on their environment. From this point of view, the extent to which ecological harmony may be said to exist depends upon the ability of humans to take advantage of the resources of a given environment on a sustained-yield basis.

General Considerations

As its title suggests, this chapter analyzes Inuit subsistence strategy in terms of its cognitive aspects. Cognition, for present purposes, is defined as "knowledge or understanding of the situation or of phenomena in general" (Levy 1966, 217). Human action can be divided into several types based on its cognitive aspects (following Levy 1952, 242–45):[2]

1. *Rational action*: conscious action in which the objective and the subjective ends of action are identical and in which both means and ends are empirical.[3]

2. *Nonrational action*: all conscious action other than rational action.

3. *Irrational action*: nonrational action in which the objective and subjective ends of action are not identical, although both means and ends are empirical (e.g., ignorance and error).

4. *Arational action*: all nonrational action that is not irrational. (a) *Methodologically arational action*, in which the ends of the actor are empirical but the means are nonempirical, at least in part (e.g., magic). (b) *Ultimately arational action*, in which both the

ends and the means of the actor are at least in part nonempirical (e.g., religious action).

It is important to keep in mind the fact that the rational/nonrational distinction refers to the opposite poles of a continuum rather than to a dichotomy. Furthermore, while action can be entirely nonrational, such as when a person goes berserk and kills someone, it can never be wholly rational; ethical or aesthetic considerations and/or ignorance and error are always involved to some extent in what people do. Technically, therefore, acts should never be characterized as being either rational or nonrational but rather as being predominantly toward one pole or the other. The concept of "predominance" should be assumed in the use of those terms in this chapter, even though it is not always stated.

An important consideration in the analysis of the cognitive aspects of action is the time frame toward which the actors are oriented. Over the very long term, all acts are ultimately arational because, when pursued to their final justification, they rest on moral or aesthetic judgments. Over shorter time spans, however, most acts can be characterized as emphasizing one or a combination of the other types of knowledge.

Overkill versus Overharvest

It is useful to distinguish between "overkill" and "overharvest." *Overkill* is defined for present purposes as a harvest in excess of what people can process, promptly consume, or safely store, the balance being "wasted" (not put to any human use). *Overkill* refers to the outcome of a specific event and thus relates to a very brief time frame. *Overharvest*, in contrast, is defined as the extent to which harvesting in general exceeds the requirements for sustained yield, either of a particular species or of the entire array of species on which a particular human population depends. Thus defined, overharvest relates to the cumulative outcome of many events spread over a long period of time, certainly months, usually years.

Given these definitions, it is quite possible for overharvest to occur in the absence of overkill. Under the right conditions, people can exterminate one or more resource species without wasting anything. On the other hand, repeated instances of overkill of the members of a given prey population are very likely to result in overharvest, with negative consequences for the humans who depend on that population for their own survival. Conservation of a prey species as a general subsistence strategy consists of a deliberate effort to prevent overharvesting (E. Smith and Wishnie 2000, 501), but it manifests itself most obviously on a day-to-day basis in the minimization of the frequency and magnitude of overkills.

A successful conservation strategy requires both extensive geographic knowledge and a long-term perspective. However, Duerden and Kuhn (1998) note that traditional ecological knowledge was primarily local and secondarily regional. They could have added that almost all of the migratory species on which early contact northern people depended spend at least part of the year not only outside the district but outside the entire region of the people who depended on them. Thus, as Jochim (1976, 5) has pointed out, hunters generally operate in a context of "partial uncertainty" (i.e., ignorance), because "the exact consequences of various economic choices are not known, but at best are estimated from previous experience and new scouting information." Margolis (1977, 60) notes further that "there is a good deal of evidence that, under conditions of uncertainty human beings opt for schemes with superior short-term gains."

These considerations suggest that hunters are likely to exhibit a tendency toward a short-term orientation in their subsistence strategy. Ingold (1980, 71), indeed, says that it is essential for hunters to follow an opportunistic strategy of maximum kill even if they consume only a fraction of what is obtained. If that is so, hunters who have the means to engage in overkill will engage in overkill unless somehow constrained from doing so.

Constraints on overkill can be predominantly rational or nonrational or may involve some combination of the two. The obvious rational reason for preventing overkills is the threat that they might lead to overharvest. Such a policy requires that those involved recognize a clear-cut empirical relationship between the techniques used to harvest a given prey species and the size of the prey population to which they have access. However, as Ingold

(1980, 71) has observed, "The rationality of conservation is totally alien to a predatory subsistence economy, which rests on the fundamental premise that the herds are responsible for the existence of Man, rather than men—individually or collectively—for the perpetuation of the herds."

The Study Populations

Ingold's general assertion about conservation is exemplified by the two study populations. The basic worldviews of both the Alaskan Iñupiat and the Caribou Inuit held that animate resources existed in essentially unlimited supply. If there were not any caribou around, it was because they were somewhere else, not because their numbers had declined. Furthermore, their presence or absence in a given region was determined by spirits. From the Inuit point of view, the problem was not the size of fish or game populations but the extent to which spirits controlled access to the members of those populations. In general, Inuit failed to recognize any connection between the size of their harvest and the size of the fish and game populations on which they depended for survival.

The traditional Inuit perspective did not readily lend itself to a rational conservation strategy. However, as Freeman pointed out, one must distinguish between intent and consequence: "First, does this particular observed behavior or set of values or proscriptions in respect to animal-human interactions contribute to conservation or sustainable use of the resources? A second, and quite separate, question is: are the hunters consciously seeking these conservation objectives?" (1988, 10). In other words, is a "conservation effect" the result of a deliberate and rational harvest strategy (E. Smith and Wishnie 2000, 501, 505), or is it the fortuitous outcome of some other strategy (Hunn 1982, 36)? Several possibilities of a conservation effect resulting from predominantly nonrational acts do exist.

Irrational action, as defined above, involves ignorance and error. Ignorance and error could of course help keep fish or game harvests below what they otherwise might be, resulting in a conservation effect. However, they could also produce exactly the opposite outcome in the case of predators who were consciously attempting to conserve prey populations but who lacked the knowledge of how to go about it.

Irrationality probably was not much of a factor in early contact Inuit hunting and fishing tactics or technology. Inuit are generally considered to have been highly rational hunters (Binford 1978, 454). Their equipment was superbly adapted to the needs of the chase, and they were keen students of animal behavior and environmental conditions. In addition, their annual cycles of movement were neatly adjusted to anticipate those of their prey, and most of them exploited as diverse a resource base as their environment permitted. Of course, what we cannot know for certain because of the time gap is whether early contact Inuit used, say, a harpoon to capture sea mammals because it was the most effective weapon for the job, or because it was the weapon that their ancestors employed for the same purpose.

Where ignorance and error probably played the biggest role was in determining the location of the prey. This was of particular importance in all parts of the north with regard to caribou, the most migratory terrestrial animal in the world (Fancy et al. 1989). It was also a problem with regard to seals in those regions where breathing-hole hunting was practiced, although in the central Canadian Arctic a strategy was devised to deal with this problem (Damas 1969, 51). Otherwise, although many other northern species are migratory, the timing and direction of their movements are fairly regular and can be anticipated with reasonable accuracy by people familiar with the country. In most cases, the main difficulty is not in ascertaining where the animals are but in gaining access to them in the face of bad snow or ice conditions, high water levels, or stormy weather.

A final consideration is what happens when people move into territory that is new to them. Stefansson (1951, 62–63) commented at some length on the difficulty Inuit had in operating effectively in unoccupied country with which they were unfamiliar. This would have been a relatively short-term problem in most areas, however, because the prey species in the new region would have been nearly identical to those in their previous homeland, and both the strategy and tactics needed to harvest them would also have been very similar. Thus, the initial difficulties would have been resolved after a brief period of familiarization with the new country. In any event, fear of new places did not prevent their ancestors from expanding the whole way across the top of North America on at least two occasions.

Methodologically arational action, or magic, can also produce a conservation effect. Among Inuit, for example, taboos significantly constrained the pursuit, processing, and consumption of animal resources. At the same time, rituals of various kinds were practiced in efforts to improve the weather or to increase the accessibility of prey species. Magical songs and formulae were uttered at appropriate times before, during, and after the hunt, and amulets accompanied the hunter at all times. These activities could combine to reduce hunting success and hence produce a conservation effect.

The final possibility is for a conservation effect to be produced by ultimately arational action, or religion. Here there are two possibilities. The people involved could believe that conservation of prey populations is intrinsically good, or they could believe that there is such a thing as overkill and that it is intrinsically evil. Inuit are not known to have adhered to either view in early contact times.

The cognition involved in a given set of practices is not always what it seems to be. For example, Inuit generally consumed all usable parts of an animal, and they usually shared, redistributed, or stored for future consumption what they did not immediately require. These practices made the need to hunt less than it otherwise would have been and hence had something of a conservation effect. However, among caribou hunters there was one consistent exception to this rule: in late summer, when caribou were hunted primarily for their hides, it often happened that too many were taken for much of the meat to be consumed, processed, or stored (Jenness 1957, 70–71; Stefansson 1951, 80; Stoney 1900, 838). Unfortunately, we cannot now know the exact reasons why Inuit engaged in these practices. If they recognized the nutritional or conservational value of total consumption, then they were acting rationally. If they were total consumers because it was morally right not to waste anything, the action could be classified as ultimately arational. Again, if they consumed everything so as not to offend the animal's spirit, they were being methodologically arational.

It is instructive here to consider Stefansson's (1919, 451) observations on the presumably rational application of the heat-trap principle by Inuit:

> I have myself frequently said that the Eskimo applied the princi-
> ple of the greater weight of cold air towards keeping their houses
> warm. I am now clear they recognize no such principle, and that
> their using doors in the floor is as much a fashion with them as
> white bow ties are with us. I have been guilty of the same misuse
> of words in saying they have the dome principle in architecture.
> They do build domes, but they do not any more recognize a princi-
> ple in that than they do in trap doors. . . . I am convinced . . . that
> if any Eskimo does think a trap door keeps a house warmer than
> some other kind of door, the reason in his mind will be of the kind
> which makes him prefer a dried-up bumblebee to some other charm
> for warding off snow blindness.

The lesson to be learned from this is that we should be wary of assuming that a given set of activities is based on a particular understanding of the situation just because it resulted in a certain outcome. With humans it might be useful to distinguish between prudent predators, with a rational conservation strategy, and lucky predators, with a nonrational strategy that produces the same result.

The cognitive status of a given set of practices can also change over time. For example, if certain hunting practices were developed initially on the basis of their practical effectiveness but were still followed several generations later primarily because they were the traditional ways to hunt, what began as rational action has been transformed over time into arational action. A change from rational to some form of nonrational action is probably the more common sequence, but the reverse is also possible. For example, old British practices based on the view that "cleanliness is next to godliness" initially were probably ultimately arational, but they became rationalized after the "germ theory" of disease was propounded and people learned the empirical relationship between filth and sickness.

Case Studies

I would like to draw on the preceding discussion in an attempt to explain certain early contact changes in the hunting practices of two Inuit populations, the Iñupiat of northwestern Alaska and the Caribou Inuit of central subarctic Canada. Both peoples were descended from the bearers of the Thule culture. Thule spread across the northern periphery of North America from Alaska to (and including) Greenland between about AD 800 and 1400 (Dumond 1984, 77). By the time of the early contact period (roughly the eighteenth and nineteenth centuries in both regions) the two populations had developed a number of differences from their Thule ancestors, and they also differed from one another in various interesting respects.

The Northern Alaskan Iñupiat

The early contact (ca. 1775–1850) Iñupiat of northern Alaska lived in the original homeland of their Thule ancestors, and both their social systems and their patterns of interacting with their environment had apparently developed *in situ* from the Thule base.[4] In the early nineteenth century they numbered approximately eleven thousand and were organized in a number of autonomous social systems, or societies (Burch 1980, 1998; Ray 1967). The members of each society held dominion over a discrete estate, spoke a special subdialect of the common language, wore distinctive clothing, and adhered to an ideology of separateness from, and superiority to, neighboring peoples.

Relations between and among societies ranged from friendly to hostile, and a well-developed pattern of intersocietal relations involving both trade and warfare existed in the region (Burch 2005; Spencer 1959, 182). A similar pattern existed between the members of Iñupiaq societies and their Athapaskan-, Chukchi-, and Yup'ik-Eskimo-speaking neighbors in central and southwestern Alaska and eastern Siberia (D. Anderson 1974/75; Burch 1979a, 2005; Clark 1970, 1977; Clark and Clark 1976).

The ecology of the Iñupiat has been characterized (primarily by Spencer 1959) as involving a twofold division between those people who depended mainly on maritime resources (*ta_iu_miut*) and those who emphasized terrestrial resources (*nunamiut*). This is an unfortunate oversimplification of the actual situation. The differences in the environments of the several societies were much more subtle and diverse than the *ta_iu_miut/nunamiut* distinction would lead one to believe. It is more useful and accurate to conceive of Iñupiaq ecology as involving a different environment, and thus a different pattern of human environment relationships, for each society (Burch 1998, 307–8).

The precise territorial adaptations were supplemented by a finely tuned pattern of seasonal movements which required that some or all of the members of most societies venture into foreign territories for brief periods each year. These incursions were carried out in ways that did not conflict with the requirements of the owners of those territories.[5] In addition, Iñupiat had developed a complex intersocietal trade network in which resources were distributed far beyond the region in which they were originally produced (Burch 2005).

The seasonal fluctuations in resource abundance, distribution, and availability that are inherent in northern ecosystems were anticipated by the yearly cycles of movement of each society. Longer-term fluctuations were dealt with partly through a diversified resource base and partly through a pattern of alliances involving members of different societies in so-called trading partnerships (Burch 2005, 155–59; Spencer 1959, 167). The former provided some flexibility in the system, so that when one resource failed others could be drawn upon. The latter enabled families experiencing hardship in their home territory to find succor with partners in a neighboring one.

The general picture conveyed by the data is that in the early contact period the Iñupiat fit the stereotype of Native people living in ecological harmony. In other words, they were able to make efficient and full use of the resources provided by their environment without unduly taxing those resources. The fit was not perfect, of course, and at least one late-precontact case is known in which a society ceased to exist due to the extinction and dispersal of its members as a result of famine (Burch 1998, 369–72). Also, one resource species, the musk ox, was exterminated early in the early contact period (Campbell 1978, 200). Nevertheless, it is difficult to see how any people relying entirely on the resources found in northwestern Alaska could have improved on the basic Iñupiaq approach to subsistence. This is the first phenomenon requiring explanation.

In order to understand why the Iñupiat were so well adjusted to their environment, it is necessary to recall that the cultural, and probably the biological, ancestors of the early contact northern Alaskans had lived in the same general area for at least a millennium, and probably longer. They had had ample opportunity, through trial and error, to adjust to their environments. Similarly, the animal and fish species of the area also had plenty of time to adapt to the Iñupiat. The human adjustments included effective and presumably rational techniques for locating, pursuing, striking, killing, retrieving, butchering, and storing the fish and animals on which they relied for survival. However, they also included a complex array of ceremonial, ritual, and other magical practices. In some cases, people could not even live (or hunt or fish) in rich hunting or fishing areas because of their fears of nonempirical phenomena, such as ghosts of one kind or another (Burch 1971). And, there was always the problem of ignorance, which was greatest with respect to caribou migrations.

It appears that the Iñupiat attempted to develop, through both rational and nonrational means, ever more effective methods of coping with the harsh northern environment. In many cases (e.g., in hunting and fishing) they were faced with a problem, particularly where a substantial element of methodological arationality, or magic, was present. Even though the ends of the action were empirical, some aspects of the means were not. If conforming to certain taboos or practicing certain rituals failed to have the intended effect, people could not determine empirically whether or not the ritual or taboo (1) was followed or practiced correctly, (2) was the right one in the first place, or (3) had been the right one and was practiced correctly but was no longer sufficient for the intended purposes.

There seems to have been a strong tendency for shamans to adopt the last of the three interpretations in most cases. Thus, they added new taboos or rituals onto old ones rather than replacing them with something new. Over the centuries, this resulted in the accumulation of a tremendous number of restrictions on people's freedom of action in pursuing, killing, processing, and consuming fish and game. However satisfactory these customs may have been in helping the Iñupiat sustain their motivation to carry on in the face of adversity, they also interfered "seriously with the prosperity of the people" (Thornton 1931, 165) by keeping the subsistence process much less efficient than it otherwise would have been.

Just how conservation-minded the traditional Iñupiat were is difficult to say because of the time gap between then and now. However, a clue was provided by the Iñupiaq historian Simon Paneak (1971a, 2; 1971b, 9–10), who reported that one of the main causes of warfare between his ancestors and the (Athapaskan) Di'haįį Gwich'in was the belief among the latter that the Iñupiat frequently engaged in overkill. This suggests that either the Gwich'in recognized that there was a connection between the magnitude of a harvest and the size of the prey population, or that they had a moral objection to overkill, or both. By implication, the Iñupiat were not under either constraint.

On the other hand, according to other Iñupiaq elders I have interviewed, their ancestors did engage in some practices in which the relationship between the magnitude of the harvest and the size of the prey population was not only recognized but where the knowledge of that relationship served as a basis for action. For example, in the Selawik region, where extensive use was made of weirs in the outlets of small lakes, people deliberately pulled the traps for about half of each twenty-four-hour period so as not to exterminate the resident fish population. It should be noted that, because of the generally small size of many outlets in the Selawik area, it would have been quite possible to wipe out the fish population of many lakes through the use of weirs. Perhaps earlier people had done so from time to time and their unpleasant experience had subsequently led to the development of more a cautious strategy.

Many other practices were not explicitly undertaken with conservation of the prey as an objective, but had a conservation effect nevertheless. The Nuataa_miut, for example, engaged in a highly organized beluga hunt early each summer in which almost all of the active males in the society participated. However, instead of hunting every day while the belugas were running and killing as many as possible, they began with one massive hunt. The elder directing the hunt determined the point at which they had killed all they could handle. They were then prohibited by a series of taboos from doing any more beluga hunting until the harvest from the first kill had been entirely butchered, dried, and stored and the residue completely cleaned up and buried.[6] This could take as much as a week or ten days, during which numerous belugas went past without even being threatened. The Nuataa_miut followed the same procedure after a second hunt, and again after a third (if enough time remained to conduct one). Obviously, this strategy allowed many more belugas to escape than were killed. Whether or not the Nuataa_miut were aware of the conservation effect of their practices is unclear, but two things are certain. One is that the Iñupiat could have exterminated the beluga population over a few years if they had consistently taken as many animals as they were capable of killing. The second is that it was fear of offending the animals' spirits, not a deliberate conservation strategy, that restrained them from overkill.

My impression is that most apparent conservationist practices of the early contact Iñupiat were like the second example. The Iñupiat engaged in many practices that were nonrational in the short term because they resulted in harvests that were smaller than they otherwise might have been. These practices had the same consequences over the long term that a rational strategy would have had because they helped perpetuate the prey populations on which the people depended for their survival.

During the second half of the nineteenth century, ecological harmony in northwestern Alaska was destroyed. This was partly due to the depredations of Euro-American whalers, but partly also to the actions of the Iñupiat themselves. The Euro-Americans all but exterminated the whale and walrus populations on which many of the coastal people depended for a substantial part of their sustenance (Bockstoce 1980, 1986; Bockstoce and Botkin 1982, 1983). It was hunting by Iñupiat, however, that caused the decline of the Seward Peninsula, Nulato Hills, central Arctic, Teshekpuk, and western Arctic caribou herds (Aldrich 1889, 29; Leffingwell 1919, 62–63, 67; Murdoch 1892, 53; Nelson 1899, 119; Nelson and True 1887, 285; Stefansson 1951, 80, 380, 451; Wells and Kelly 1890, 26; Woolfe 1890). At least the first two of these herds became extinct in the process. Subsequently, Iñupiaq hunters shifted their attention to mountain sheep as an alternative source of meat, exterminating them in the Baird Mountains and significantly reducing their numbers in the De Long Mountains. The beaver populations in the Selawik and Kobuk valleys were wiped out, and the populations of other furbearers in several districts were significantly reduced. These declines in prey species occurred despite the fact that the human population was itself declining due to imported European diseases, which theoretically should have reduced the demand for country foods.

Repeated overkills soon resulted in overharvest, and eventually in widespread starvation and loss of human life. The traditional boundaries of societies broke down due to the death and dispersal of their members (Burch 1998, 320–27). Many of the survivors fled their homelands, primarily by moving north and northeast (R. Anderson 1951, 508; Jenness 1957, 164–65; Leffingwell 1919, 67; Stefansson 1951, 66–67; Wells and Kelly 1890, 9). In the process they came close to exterminating the mountain sheep in the central and eastern Brooks Range (Campbell 1978), and they significantly reduced the size of the Porcupine, central Arctic, and Teshekpuk caribou herds. They may, indeed, have nearly exterminated the central Arctic and Teshekpuk herds. These developments led to a further decline in the human population, which by 1900 had dropped to around forty-one hundred (U.S. Bureau of the Census 1900).

Here we are faced with the problem of explaining why a population with an apparent tradition of relatively safe, if not explicitly conservation-oriented, predation suddenly went on an apparent rampage. One possible reason is that Christianity destroyed their beliefs in the traditional system of taboos, rituals, and magical paraphernalia. However, the main decline in the caribou populations took place in the 1870s and 1880s, before missionaries arrived in the area, so Christianization could not have been a factor (Burch 1994). A second possible explanation is that increased hunting pressure was placed on the caribou population because the Americans had depleted the whale and walrus stocks. This certainly seems to be a reasonable supposition, and it may have been a factor. However, I know of no evidence showing this to be a major cause of the caribou decline. The coastal people who were affected by the drop in the whale and walrus populations had relied on those species for food, whereas they depended on caribou primarily for clothing. After the whale and walrus populations were reduced, fish, seals, and belugas were still available to harvest for food, but when the caribou disappeared they had no comparable alternative source of clothing.

I believe the evidence shows that the major cause of the decline in the caribou and mountain sheep populations was repeated overkill by Iñupiat using newly imported breech-loading rifles. I disagree on this point with my own earlier conclusions (Burch 1972, 356) and with those of Campbell (1978), Minc (1986), and Minc and Smith (1989). Previously, I had attributed the decline in caribou numbers to population dynamics intrinsic to the species. I still believe that caribou populations may undergo dramatic fluctuations in size regardless of human predation, but I no longer believe that this explanation suffices to explain the decline in question. It also does not explain the corresponding decline in other species.

Campbell (1978, 190, 195) agrees that the declines were caused by human overkill, but he claims that they were effected by means of traditional hunting techniques. I agree that substantial kills of caribou were made from time to time using traditional techniques, primarily during the hunt for hides in August and early September. But these were very local events; when a slaughter was taking place during an organized drive in one valley or on one lake, thousands of animals passed by unobserved, not to mention unmolested, in other localities. Additionally, while sheep are relatively easy to catch by the primary traditional technique of snaring, they are not easy to take in large numbers in that manner. Rifles may have been used in the Brooks Range to kill sheep even before they were used for caribou (Stoney 1900, 837–39).

Finally, Minc (1986, 57) and Minc and Smith (1989, 16) have attributed the decline in the caribou population to climatic deterioration. They do not discuss mountain sheep, but presumably that species could have been similarly affected by the same factors. Their formulations are elegant and convincing, but they unfortunately rest on a questionable database.

My own data, which have been significantly augmented since I wrote my 1972 article, show that the decline in the caribou population began in the Nulato Hills and on the Seward Peninsula in the early 1870s, about five years after breech-loading rifles first became available from Western traders on Norton Sound. The decline then spread north and northeast as whalers and shipborne traders made the new weapons readily available in other areas. The decline was not a smooth one, as depicted in my 1972 graph (Burch 1972, 357), but abrupt; most of it occurred between 1872 and 1882. The decline in mountain sheep began in the western Brooks Range in the mid-1880s, as refugees escaping famine to the south and west moved into the mountains in search of raw materials for food and clothing. The onslaught proceeded from west to east over the next two decades, as hunters cleaned out the animals in one district and moved on to the next.

The perfect correlation between the spread of breech-loading rifles on the one hand and the demise of the caribou and sheep populations on the other is difficult to explain on any basis other than cause and effect. This conclusion is supported by the observations of contemporary Western observers (cited above), who were unanimous in the view that the Iñupiat were wiping out the caribou populations with breech-loading rifles.

Breech-loading rifles gave the Iñupiat the means to engage in the overharvest of caribou and mountain sheep on a regional, as opposed to local, basis for the first time. It allowed them to employ their basically rational approach to hunting with a weapon that was technologically superior to anything they had ever possessed before. The combination was devastating to the caribou and sheep populations, and subsequently to the human population as well. If Westerners had not directly intervened in the situation, one may presume that, over time, either the human population would have become extinct or some sort of constraints on the use of the new technology would have emerged.

The extermination of beavers along the Kobuk and Selawik rivers seems to have happened before the advent of steel traps. This would suggest that, in contrast to the caribou decline, the advent of new technology was not a factor unless breech-loading rifles (instead of traps) came to be used for beaver hunting. Primarily, however, the beaver populations were negatively affected by the growth of the Western-centered fur trade during the nineteenth century. Traditionally, beavers had been taken for food rather than for their fur, and they were not particularly important in the Iñupiaq economy. It may be that the magical impediments that had grown up around many other types of predation simply had not developed with regard to beavers. In that case the Iñupiat would have been free from the outset to aggressively harvest a species that suddenly had increased dramatically in value.

The Caribou Inuit

The Caribou Inuit lived on or near the west coast of Hudson Bay, in the central Canadian subarctic.[7] The available evidence (Burch 1978) suggests that they originated as a consequence of a migration of people from the central Canadian Arctic coast in the seventeenth century. These immigrants absorbed or replaced a small earlier population of Inuit-speaking people. For most of the next century, the Caribou Inuit numbered perhaps 450 to 500 people and were organized in a single society whose range included both coastal and interior sectors. They utilized a diverse resource base that included a variety of sea mammals (including seals, belugas, walruses, and occasional bowhead whales), fish, and caribou.[8] At this time, sea mammals were apparently at least as important to them as caribou. Hudson's Bay Company personnel often could not get the Inuit to sell them blubber because they wanted to keep it for their own use.

In the late eighteenth or early nineteenth century, the population began to expand in both numbers and territory. Over the next century the Caribou Inuit spread out over the whole coast and most of the interior of what is now southern Kivalliq, Nunavut Territory (Burch 1979b, 192; 2004, 76–80; Csonka 1995, 107–47; J. Smith and Burch 1979, 83–85). The population grew to some fifteen hundred people, and by 1915 the original society had been replaced through a series of divisions by at least five, and probably six, successor societies. Geographic expansion was driven by population pressure but was greatly facilitated by the creation of a demographic vacuum in the interior in the late eighteenth century. This was caused by the depopulation of the region by its original Chipewyan Athapaskan inhabitants due to epidemics and territorial shifts related to the fur trade farther south (J. Smith 1976).

As the demographic expansion and societal proliferation occurred, the importance of sea mammals declined in the Inuit economy, while that of caribou and musk oxen rose. Eventually, caribou became overwhelmingly dominant as the source of raw materials for food and clothing (Birket-Smith 1929, 9, 88, 96, 137). Musk oxen were apparently harvested primarily as an emergency food when caribou were hard to come by; their hides were of little use to the Inuit. By the end of the nineteenth century, and probably some decades earlier, many of the descendants of the original Inuit population regarded seal meat and blubber as scarcely fit for human consumption. This change seems to have taken place entirely at the discretion of the people involved, and it occurred despite the fact that the activities of American whalers after 1860 (Ross 1975) seem to have had little or no impact on the seal and beluga populations of the region.

The inland expansion brought the Inuit into prime musk ox habitat. The Inuit had little or no use for musk ox robes, but as the economic shift proceeded, the relatively sedentary musk oxen were harvested for their meat when the highly migratory caribou were unavailable. The musk ox harvest suddenly increased after 1860, however, when the European demand for musk ox robes rose dramatically and when American whalers began competing with the Hudson's Bay Company for the Inuit trade. As a result, between 1860 and 1900 the number of musk oxen in the region dropped from some unknown but apparently large number (in the several thousands) to nearly zero (Burch 1977, 146–48).

In 1800 the numbers of caribou were roughly comparable in the two study regions, but musk oxen were much more abundant in the central Canadian subarctic than in northern Alaska. Beyond that, the environment of the Caribou Inuit was much poorer in resources than that of their counterparts in northwestern Alaska. It did not have anywhere near the diversity of species or the numbers of sea mammals, fish, or terrestrial mammals in general, and it had much less to offer in the way of vegetable products.

Even with this very important limitation, it appears that the Caribou Inuit failed to make use of all of the resources their country offered, at least after the economic shift away from marine resources began in the early nineteenth century. Even the people whose estates were along the coast made far less use of sea mammal products in the late 1800s than their ancestors had a century earlier, and much less than they themselves could have at the time. Both coastal and interior groups also used fish to a lesser extent than they could have.

The major questions relating to the Caribou Inuit case are as follows. First, why did they switch from a diversified economy, in which failure of one resource species could be offset by harvesting another, to a specialized economy overwhelmingly dependent on a single species, and a very unreliable one at that? Second, why did they exterminate the musk oxen of southern Kivalliq during the second half of the nineteenth century?

It is difficult to explain just why the narrow focus on terrestrial mammals developed, although certain things are known. First, as noted earlier, the Caribou Inuit of the early eighteenth century were probably recent immigrants to the region from the central Canadian Arctic coast, so they did not have hundreds of years of experience in the region to draw on. Second, it is evident from Hudson's Bay Company and other records that the Caribou Inuit population in the eighteenth century was small and that it was concentrated along the portion of the coast in which sea mammals were most abundant.

Some kind of trouble apparently developed early in the nineteenth century, and the original society split into two, referred to in the Hudson's Bay Company accounts as the "distant" and the "homeguard" "Esquimaux." Their estates were adjacent to one another along the coast. For some reason, the border between the two "daughter" societies was located precisely where the heartland of the original society had been. Thus, the richest area biologically had become marginal socially—a most unusual development for Inuit, if not for hunters in general. Social factors may have led to an early decline in the ability of the population to harvest sea mammals in their homeland, whatever their actual intentions may have been. It is known that they retained the knowledge of how to hunt sea mammals, however, since some of the "homeguards" were hired by the Hudson's Bay Company at Churchill to hunt belugas and seals almost every spring and summer until well into the twentieth century.

By the mid-nineteenth century the population had grown even more and had expanded into the interior of what is now southern Kivalliq. The inlanders were too far from the coast for anything but the most sporadic sea mammal hunting. They also did not trade systematically with their coastal relatives, which may explain why they did not use products derived from sea mammals. It does not, however, tell us why their relatives living near the coast also developed "an almost incredibly one-sided culture" focused on caribou (Birket-Smith 1929, 9).

Southern Kivalliq does have reasonably abundant fish resources, and the Caribou Inuit did do some fishing in spring with hook and line. They also fished more extensively in late summer, primarily with weirs, since the boulder-strewn rivers made seining extremely difficult. They set aside rather little for winter use, however, at least in part because they were so intent on hunting caribou during what would have been the most productive fishing season. In winter, when people needed them the most, southern Kivalliq fish are found only in ice-covered waters, primarily in lakes. Since their precise whereabouts are impossible to determine except through exhausting and time-consuming trial and error, the only effective way to harvest fish during the winter is with gill nets. The Caribou Inuit had known about gill nets since at least the mid-eighteenth century, when they had observed the crews of Hudson's Bay Company trading vessels using them for their own purposes. However, a taboo existed among the people forbidding the consumption of fish that had died while still in the water, as frequently happens in gill nets that are not tended every day. Their refusal to use gill nets meant that they had no effective means of exploiting the substantial populations of fish that inhabited the large lakes in their region.

The changes in Caribou Inuit food preferences remain almost as inexplicable today as they were in the early 1920s, when Knud Rasmussen (1930) and Kaj Birket-Smith (1929) wrote their authoritative accounts of Caribou

Inuit life. It may well be, as Frederica de Laguna (pers. comm., 1991) has suggested, that at some point shamans had forbidden the consumption of blubber for some reason. Another possibility is that the harvest, processing, or consumption of sea mammals may have become encumbered with so many taboos or other methodologically arational constraints as to make the hunting of sea mammals too onerous to be worth the effort. Or the change may have come about, as least in part, because of the easy accessibility of musk oxen. This leads us to the second major problem requiring explanation.

Superficially, it would appear that the "new technology hypothesis" used to explain overharvest in northern Alaska might also apply to the overharvest of musk oxen by the Caribou Inuit. However, this hypothesis does not account satisfactorily for all the evidence. It is true that the Caribou Inuit had firearms; indeed, they received them much earlier than their Alaskan counterparts had. Once they began to import firearms extensively, the Iñupiat received the most modern equipment available. Until the end of the nineteenth century, the Caribou Inuit received only muzzle loaders in trade, and they seem to have spent much of the year rusted or otherwise damaged into a state of uselessness. In addition, even when they did have firearms, the Caribou Inuit preferred traditional methods of hunting musk oxen. Traditional methods were also used in the major late-summer caribou hunts.

A more likely explanation lies in what might be called the "frontier hypothesis." According to this view, abundant resources may be available at little cost to the producer in areas that are habitable but uninhabited for some reason. Where this is so, "the failure to employ conservation techniques must be viewed as a rational choice" (Margolis 1977, 61). Why spend all of a frigid winter day walking around the country in a possibly fruitless search for caribou when one could go directly to a band of musk oxen and take what one wants? In the short term it was a very rational thing to do. Then, after the mid-nineteenth century, the market for musk ox hides increased dramatically, leading to an even greater harvest. Before about 1860, musk oxen were probably never killed for their hides; after 1860, hundreds of them were.

In 1919 the caribou population of southern Kivalliq crashed, apparently due to climatic causes, and several years of famine ensued (Csonka 1995, 155–61). Survivors of the first lean period tried to reach remnant musk ox populations on the western frontier, but they starved to death on the way. The newly arrived officers of the Royal Canadian Mounted Police begged the people to set gill nets, which they even offered to provide, but to no avail. Between about 1915 and 1925 the human population declined by about 70 percent. Two of the six societies of Caribou Inuit ceased to exist as autonomous systems, while the others barely managed to persist as viable units.[9] What had been rational in the short term proved disastrous in the end.

Conclusion

The first major question this chapter addressed is whether or not Native peoples of North America lived in ecological harmony prior to the arrival of Europeans. The answer suggested by the two study populations is that at least some—and, by extension, perhaps most—of them may have. Most of the hunting peoples among them probably were safe predators, making a living from a variety of fish and game species on a sustained-yield basis. However, to the extent that this was so, nonrational factors were probably at least as important as rational ones.

In cognitive terms, action that was methodologically arational from a short-term perspective produced an outcome that was rational from a long-term perspective (although that outcome was achieved by default rather than by intent). In this respect, the Inuit were probably similar not only to other hunters, such as the Naskapi (Moore 1957) or Rock Cree (Brightman 2002), but also to many small-scale agrarian peoples (Malinowski 1988; Rappaport 1988).

Lack of evidence from earlier periods makes it impossible to know how these situations developed. One can speculate that several generations of residence in a given area, and probably a number of resource crises, were required before a suitable ecological adjustment was made. From a long-term perspective, Inuit shamans may be said to have guessed correctly when they developed their system of taboos, rituals, and other methodologically arational practices. From a short-term viewpoint, however, these practices caused considerable hardship.

It is commonplace nowadays to attribute to Native Americans some special kind of wisdom with regard to their relationships with their environment, a wisdom supposedly not shared by people of non-Native ancestry. Examination of the two study populations in this chapter, however, dispels such a notion. Inuit—and, by extension, Native North Americans generally—were no wiser than anyone else. For example, the Alaskan Iñupiat exterminated the caribou and mountain sheep populations in the western part of their territory, an event that forced them to move to the northeast. Once they arrived at their destination, they did the same thing all over again. Similarly, the Caribou Inuit wiped out the musk oxen in their territory. Then, when the caribou crisis struck, people headed west to try to kill still more musk oxen instead of shifting their attention to sea mammals or fish, only to find that few musk oxen were left.

Deliberate conservation measures were practiced in some cases, as the example of the Selawik fishermen shows. One can speculate that the conditions required for deliberate conservation practices include a clear-cut empirical relationship between the techniques used to harvest a given prey species and the abundance of that species, combined with a high degree of control over the situation. However, these conditions rarely obtain, especially among hunters. A third condition may also be necessary—namely, a prey population that is large enough at the outset for people not to fear starvation as a result of any deliberate conservation practices.

The second major question addressed by this chapter is whether or not the relationship of Native Americans to their surroundings deteriorated after European contact, and if so, why? The evidence presented here suggests that it deteriorated significantly, for three major reasons. While these factors were maximized in this encounter, they are not necessarily restricted to it, so I will summarize them in more general terms.

The evidence suggests three situations in which a state of ecological harmony will probably be destroyed as a result of human action (cf. Murray 2003). One is when radically new subsistence technology is suddenly introduced to a region by invention or importation. A second is when a relatively un-important species suddenly acquires unprecedented value as a trade good. In both cases, it takes time for constraints to develop on the use of the new technology or the pursuit of the newly valuable species. In the interim, im-portant prey populations may be exterminated, with consequent impover-ishment or loss of human life. In the resulting crisis, the people may know *what* is wrong, even if they don't understand why, and may take steps to rem-edy the situation. These steps may be predominantly rational or nonrational in character. In either case, if they seem to work, they probably will be per-petuated. If they do not, the crisis may become a tragedy.

The third possibility was suggested by the evidence presented here but was not actually illustrated by it. This is the removal of a rational constraints on overkill through religious conversion. In fact, this did happen in north-western Alaska shortly after the time period with which we are concerned, when Christianity replaced the traditional system of beliefs about preda-tor-prey relations and its associated complex of rituals and taboos. Largely as a consequence, the beluga population that was so carefully nurtured by the Nuataa_miut is now a mere shadow of its former self.

Finally, the evidence reviewed here also suggests a situation in which eco-logical harmony may never appear in the first place. In this situation, hunt-ers inhabit what might be called an "affluent frontier." The qualifier is neces-sary because many, probably most, frontiers in human history have existed on the edges of barren wastelands, into which movement would obviously be disastrous. In contrast, an affluent frontier would be one on the edge of an area having substantial resources that could be readily exploited by im-migrants. Seduced by apparent abundance, uninhibited by human competi-tion, and unburdened by cognitive constraints (except, perhaps, short-lived ignorance of the new country), immigrants are easily led to the destruction of the very resources that attracted them in the first place. This conclusion is based primarily on the Caribou Inuit example, in which people expanded westward into prime musk ox habitat where year-round hunting pressure had never existed before. To a lesser extent it is confirmed by the Alaskan data as well. Once they had abandoned their traditional homelands due to the paucity of game there, the Iñupiat were essentially in a frontier situation in northeastern Alaska, which previously had lacked year-round human residents—and they quickly reduced the size of the caribou and sheep populations. On an affluent frontier, hunters apparently are no more restrained in their exploitation of abundant, readily acquired resources than are relatively modernized farmers (Margolis 1977).

Finally, I recommend that the polarizing debate over whether Native Americans were *either* rational conservationists *or* rapacious overkillers be dropped; it has become an ultimately arational debate rather than a scientific one. The evidence presented in this chapter, as in many other recent studies (see Murray 2003; E. Smith and Wishnie 2000, 493–94), shows early contact Native American hunters to have been ordinary human beings who engaged in behavior that involved cognitive orientations manifesting a complex mixture of rational and nonrational elements under a specific set of conditions. A nuanced understanding of the particular mix of cognitive orientations that guided specific peoples operating under specified conditions, without the wholesale categorization of the people involved as being either conservationists or savages, would make for better science. It would also help us achieve a greater understanding of social and ecological change and, in the contemporary world, might lead to more effective resource management.

Acknowledgments

I thank Frederica de Laguna, Harvey Feit, Ann Fienup-Riordan, Milton M. R. Freeman, Åke Hultkrantz, Charles Lucier, Robin Ridington, and Eric Alden Smith for comments on earlier drafts of this chapter.

Notes

This is a revised version of an article titled "Rationality and Resource Use among Hunters" and published in Circumpolar Religion and Ecology: An Anthropology of the North, ed. Takashi Irimoto and Takako Yamada (Tokyo: University of Tokyo Press, 1994), 163–85.

1. This chapter is based on both library and archival research and fieldwork. All material that is not otherwise documented derives from fieldwork.

2. Rationality is so highly institutionalized in modernized societies that the word *rational* often connotes "good" or "intelligent," whereas *nonrational* (or, more often, "irrational") connotes "bad" or "stupid." As used in the present chapter, these terms have absolutely no ethical implications, and they do not reflect on the intelligence of the people involved one way or another.

3. "Empirical" phenomena are those about which data may be apprehended directly through sensory perception (i.e., by one or more of the following: taste, touch, sight, smell, or hearing) or indirectly inferred by the use of instruments in which a sensory chain of connection is clear or presumed to be clear (Levy 1952, 241).

4. Fieldwork in northwestern Alaska was carried out on several occasions between 1960 and 1999. Support was provided over the years by the University of Alaska, Departments of Anthropology and Biological Sciences; the Canada Council; the U.S. National Park Service; the Minerals Management Service; NANA Regional Corporation; NANA Museum of the Arctic; the Alaska Department of Fish and Game, Division of Subsistence; the Alaska Historical Commission; University of Chicago, Department of Anthropology; the North Slope Borough Commission on History, Language and Culture; U.S. Geological Survey; and Kevin Waring Associates.

5. Students of aboriginal societies in Australia have found it useful to distinguish between the estate and the range of a given band (tribe, society, etc.). The former is the territory owned by the members of a given society, whereas the latter is the region actually used by the members of that society (Stanner 1965, 2–3). This distinction is equally useful in northwestern Alaska. The range of almost every Iñupiaq society was considerably greater than its estate.

6. Hunters were allowed to pursue other fish and game when they could not hunt belugas, but there was little else to hunt in the region at that season except migratory waterfowl.

7. Fieldwork in southern Keewatin was conducted by the author in the summer of 1968 and by Thomas C. Correll in 1969 and 1970. The Canada Council supported the fieldwork and some of the associated archival research. The reconstruction of the eighteenth- and nineteenth-century situations was based entirely on archival research conducted by the author.

8. This summary statement of the resource base of the eighteenth-century Caribou Inuit is based on the following sources: Bean (1755, fol. 31, 33), Ellis (1748, 147–48, 219–20, 229–32, 236, 239), Hearne (1795, 159–61, 339), Holt (1780, fol. 24), Hudson's Bay Company Archives (1774–1781, fol. 9, 81), Johnston (1764, fol. 16 d; 1765, fol. 24; 1766, fol. 23; 1769, fol. 41), Prince (1785, fol. 13), Robson (1752, 66), Stearns (1768, fol. 28), Swaine (1748, 1:94), Williams (1969, 214, 228, 236, 238, 241).

9. The Tahiuyarmiut and the Hauniqturmiut societies ceased to exist due to the famine of 1919–25.

References

Aldrich, Herbert L. 1889. *Arctic Alaska and Siberia, or, eight months with the Arctic whalemen.* Chicago: Rand McNally.

Anderson, Douglas D. 1974/75. Trade networks among the Selawik Eskimos, northwestern Alaska, during the late 19th and early 20th centuries. *Folk* 16–17:63–72.

Anderson, Rudolph M. 1951. Report on the natural history collections of the expedition. In Vilhjalmur Stefansson, *My life with the Eskimo*, 436–527. New York: MacMillan.

Bean, John. 1755. Journal of a voyage on board the "Churchill" sloop . . . . Hudson's Bay Company Archives, document B.42/a/44. Winnipeg, Manitoba.

Binford, Lewis R. 1978. Nunamiut ethnoarchaeology. New York: Academic Press.

Birket-Smith, Kaj. 1929. The Caribou Eskimos: Material and social life and their cultural position. Report of the Fifth Thule Expedition 1921–24, vol. 5, pts. 1 and 2. Copenhagen: Gyldendal Boghandel, Nordisk Forlag.

Bockstoce, John R. 1980. A preliminary estimate of the reduction of the western Arctic bowhead whale population by the pelagic whaling industry, 1848–1915. Marine Fisheries Review September–October:20–27.

———. 1986. Whales, ice and men: The history of whaling in the western Arctic. Seattle: University of Washington Press.

Bockstoce, John R., and Daniel B. Botkin. 1982. The harvest of Pacific walruses by the pelagic whaling industry, 1848 to 1914. Arctic and Alpine Research 14 (3): 183–88.

———. 1983. The historical status and reduction of the western Arctic bowhead whale (Balaena mysticetus) by the pelagic whaling industry, 1849–1914. Scientific reports of the International Whaling Commission, special issue no. 5:107–41.

Brightman, Robert. 2002. Grateful prey: Rock Cree human-animal relationships. Regina, Saskatchewan: University of Regina, Canadian Plains Research Center.

Burch, Ernest S., Jr. 1971. The nonempirical environment of the Arctic Alaskan Eskimos. Southwestern Journal of Anthropology 27 (2): 148–65.

———. 1972. The caribou/wild reindeer as a human resource. American Antiquity 37 (3): 339–68.

———. 1977. Muskox and man in the central Canadian subarctic, 1689–1974. Arctic 30 (3): 135–54.

———. 1978. Caribou Eskimo origins: An old problem reconsidered. Arctic Anthropology 15 (1): 1–35.

———. 1979a. Indians and Eskimos in north Alaska, 1816–1977: A study in changing ethnic relations. Arctic Anthropology 16 (2): 123–51.

———. 1979b. The Thule-historic Eskimo transition on the west coast of Hudson Bay. In Thule Eskimo culture: An archaeological retrospective, ed. Alan P. McCartney, 189–211. Archaeological Survey of Canada Paper no. 88. Ottawa: National Museum of Man.

———. 1980. Traditional Eskimo societies in northwest Alaska. Senri Ethnological Studies 4:253–304.

———. 1994. The Iñupiat and the Christianization of Arctic Alaska. Études/Inuit/Studies 18 (1–2): 81–108.

———. 1998. The Iñupiaq Eskimo nations of northwest Alaska. Fairbanks: University of Alaska Press.

———. 2004. The Caribou Inuit. In Native peoples: The Canadian experience, ed. R. Bruce Morrison and C. Roderick Wilson, 74–94. Don Mills, Ontario: Oxford University Press.

———. 2005. Alliance and conflict: The world system of the Iñupiaq Eskimos. Lincoln: University of Nebraska Press.

Campbell, John M. 1978. Aboriginal human overkill of game populations: Examples from interior north Alaska. In Archaeological essays in honor of Irving B. Rouse, ed. R. C. Dunnell and E. S. Hall Jr., 179–208. The Hague: Mouton.

Clark, Annette McFadyen. 1970. The Athabaskan-Eskimo interface. Canadian Archaeological Association Bulletin 2:13–23.

———. 1977. Trade at the cross roads. In Problems in the prehistory of the North American subarctic:

The Athapaskan question, ed. J. W. Helmer, S. Van Dyke and F. J. Kense, 130–34. Calgary: University of Calgary Archaeological Association.

Clark, Annette McFadyen, and Donald W. Clark. 1976. Koyukuk Indian-Kobuk Eskimo interaction. In *Contributions to anthropology: The interior peoples of northern Alaska,* ed. Edwin S. Hall Jr., 193–220. Ottawa: National Museum of Man. Archaeological survey of Canada paper no. 49.

Csonka, Yvon. 1995. *Les Ahiarmiut: A l'écart des Inuit Caribous.* Neuchâtel, Switzerland: Editions Victor Attinger.

Damas, David. 1969. Environment, history, and central Eskimo society. In *Contributions to anthropology: Ecological essays,* ed. David Damas, 40–64. Bulletin no. 230, Anthropological Series no. 86. Ottawa: National Museums of Canada.

Duerden, Frank, and Richard G. Kuhn. 1998. Scale, context, and application of traditional knowledge of the Canadian north. *Polar Record* 34 (188): 31–38.

Dumond, Don E. 1984. Prehistory: Summary. In *Handbook of North American Indians,* vol. 5, *Arctic,* ed. David Damas, 72–79. Washington DC: Smithsonian Institution.

Ellis, H. 1748. *A voyage to Hudson's Bay by the Dobbs Galley and California in the years 1746–1747.* London: H. Whitridge.

Fancy, S. G., L. F. Pank, K. R. Whitten, and W. L. Regelin. 1989. Seasonal movements of caribou in Alaska as determined by satellite. *Canadian Journal of Zoology* 67 (3): 644–50.

Freeman, Milton M. R. 1988. The significance of animals in the life of northern foraging peoples and its relevance today. In *International symposium on human-animal relationships in the north, February 23–25, 1988,* 5–12. Abashiri, Hokkaido, Japan.

Hearne, Samuel. 1795. *A journey from Prince of Wales's Fort in Hudson Bay to the Northern Ocean . . . in the years of 1769, 1770, 1771, 1772.* London: A. Strachan and T. Cadell.

Holt, George. 1780. Journal on board the sloop "Charlotte," by George Holt. Hudson's Bay Company Archives, document B.42/a/101. Winnipeg, Manitoba.

Hudson's Bay Company Archives. 1774–1781. Inward correspondence; Letters from Churchill to London, 1774–1791. Hudson's Bay Company Archives, document A.11/15. Winnipeg, Manitoba.

Hunn, Eugene S. 1982. Mobility as a factor limiting resource use in the Columbia Plateau of North America. In *Resource managers: North American and Australian hunter-gatherers,* ed. Nancy M. Williams and Eugene S. Hunn, 17–43. Boulder CO: Westview Press.

Hunn, Eugene S., Darryll R. Johnson, Priscilla N. Russell, and Thomas F. Thornton. 2003. Huna Tlingit traditional environmental knowledge, conservation, and the management of a "wilderness" park. *Current Anthropology* 44 (Supplement): S79–S103.

Ingold, Tim. 1980. *Hunters, pastoralists, and ranchers.* Cambridge: Cambridge University Press.

Jenness, Diamond. 1957. *Dawn in Arctic Alaska.* Minneapolis: University of Minnesota Press.

Jochim, Michael A. 1976. *Hunter-gatherer subsistence and settlement: A predictive model.* New York: Academic Press.

Johnston, Magnus. 1764. Journal of a voyage in the sloop "Churchill" from Churchill to the northward . . . Hudson's Bay Company Archives, document B.42/a/61. Winnipeg, Manitoba.

———. 1765. "Churchill" sloop journal for 1764–65, by Magnus Johnston, master. Hudson's Bay Company Archives, document B.42/a/63. Winnipeg, Manitoba.

———. 1766. Journal of the sloop "Churchill" on an expedition to the northern . . . 1766. Hudson's Bay Company Archives, document B.42/a/65. Winnipeg, Manitoba.

———. 1769. Journal on board the "Churchill" on an expedition to the northward. Hudson's Bay Company Archives, document B.42/a/75. Winnipeg, Manitoba.

Krech, Shepard, III. 1999. *The ecological Indian: Myth and history*. New York: Norton.

Krupnik, Igor I. 1985. Le Chasseur Traditionnel dans les Ecosystemes du Subarctique (l'Exemple des Esquimaux Asiatiques). *Inter-Nord* 17:105–10.

———. 1993. *Arctic adaptations: Native whalers and reindeer herders of northern Eurasia*. Expanded English edition. Hanover NH: University Press of New England.

Leffingwell, Ernest de Koven. 1919. The Canning River region, northern Alaska. U.S. Geological Survey, Professional Paper 109.

Levy, Marion J., Jr. 1952. *The structure of society*. Princeton NJ: Princeton University Press.

———. 1966. *Modernization and the structure of societies: A setting for international affairs*. Princeton NJ: Princeton University Press.

Malinowski, Bronislaw. 1988. Rational mastery by man of his surroundings. In *Anthropology for the nineties: Introductory readings*, ed. J. B. Cole, 404–11. New York: Free Press.

Margolis, M. 1977. Historical perspectives on frontier agriculture as an adaptive strategy. *American Ethnologist* 4 (1): 42–64.

Minc, L. D. 1986. Scarcity and survival: The role of oral tradition in mediating subsistence crises. *Journal of Anthropological Archaeology* 5 (1): 39–113.

Minc, L. D., and K. P. Smith. 1989. The spirit of survival: Cultural responses to resource variability in north Alaska. In *Bad year economics: Cultural responses to risk and uncertainty*, ed. P. Halstead and J. O'Shea, 8–39. Cambridge: Cambridge University Press.

Moore, O. K. 1957. Divination: A new perspective. *American Anthropologist* 59 (1): 69–74.

Murdoch, John. 1892. Ethnological results of the Point Barrow expedition. *Ninth annual report of the Bureau of American Ethnology, 1887–88*. Washington DC.

Murray, Martyn. 2003. Overkill and sustainable use. *Science* 299:1851–53.

Nelson, Edward W. 1899. The Eskimo about Bering Strait. *Eighteenth annual report of the Bureau of American Ethnology, 1896–97, pt. 1*. Washington DC.

Nelson, E. W., and F. W. True. 1887. Mammals of northern Alaska. In *Report upon natural history collections made in Alaska between the years 1877 and 1881*, ed. E. W. Nelson, 227–93. Washington DC: U.S. Army Signal Service.

Paneak, Simon. 1971a. Indian and Kobuk disputes: Hunting trips. Doris Duke Foundation Oral History Archive 314, tape 842. University of New Mexico, General Library, Albuquerque.

———. 1971b. Oral narratives. Doris Duke Foundation Oral History Archive 314, tape 842. University of New Mexico, General Library, Albuquerque.

Prince, Thomas. 1785. Journal of a voyage in the Churchill sloop. Hudson's Bay Company Archives, document B.42/a/105. Winnipeg, Manitoba.

Rappaport, Roy A. 1988. Ritual regulation of environmental relations among a New Guinea people. In *Anthropology for the nineties: Introductory readings*, ed. J. B. Cole, 384–403. New York: Free Press.

Rasmussen, Knud. 1930. *Observations on the intellectual culture of the Caribou Eskimos*. Report of the Fifth Thule Expedition, vol. 7, no. 3. Copenhagen: Gyldendal Boghandel, Nordisk Forlag.

Ray, Dorothy Jean. 1967. Land tenure and polity of the Bering Strait Eskimos. *Journal of the West* 6 (3): 371–94.

Robson, J. 1752. *An account of six years' residence in Hudson's Bay, from 1733 to 1736, and 1744 to 1747.* London: Payne & Bouquet.

Ross, W. Gillies. 1975. *Whaling and Eskimos: Hudson Bay, 1860–1915.* Publications in Ethnology no. 10. National Museum of Man, Ottawa.

Smith, Eric Alden, and Mark Wishnie. 2000. Conservation and subsistence in small-scale societies. *Annual Review of Anthropology* 29:493–524.

Smith, James G. E. 1976. Introduction: The historical and cultural position of the Chipewyan. *Arctic Anthropology* 8 (1): 1–5.

Smith, James G. E., and Ernest S. Burch, Jr. 1979. Chipewyan and Inuit in the central Canadian subarctic, 1613–1977. *Arctic Anthropology* 16 (2): 76–101.

Spencer, Robert F. 1959. *The north Alaskan Eskimo: A study in ecology and society.* Bureau of American Ethnology Bulletin 171. Washington DC: Smithsonian Institution.

Stanner, W. E. R. 1965. Aboriginal territorial organization: Estate, range, domain, and regime. *Oceania* 36 (1): 1–26.

Stearns, Joseph. 1768. Journal of a voyage in the sloop "Success" . . . on the Black Whale Fishery. Hudson's Bay Company Archives, document B.42/a/72. Winnipeg, Manitoba.

Stefansson, Vilhjalmur. 1919. Corrections and comments. *Anthropological papers of the American Museum of Natural History,* vol. 14, pt. 2, pp. 445–57.

———. 1951. *My life with the Eskimo.* New York: Macmillan.

Stoney, George M. 1900. Explorations in Alaska. *U.S. Naval Institute Proceedings* 91:533–84, 92:799–849.

[Swaine, Charles]. 1748. *An account of a voyage for the discovery of a northwest passage.* 2 vols. London: Jolliffe, Corbett, Clarke and Baldwin.

Thornton, Harrison Robertson. 1931. *Among the Eskimos of Wales, Alaska.* Baltimore: Johns Hopkins University Press.

U.S. Bureau of the Census. 1900. *Twelfth census of the United States, 1900.* Washington DC: National Archives. Microfilm no. 1828.

Wells, Roger, and John W. Kelly. 1890. English-Eskimo and Eskimo-English vocabularies, preceded by ethnographical memoranda concerning the Arctic Eskimos in Alaska and Siberia, by John W. Kelly. *Bureau of Education Circular* no. 2. Washington DC.

Williams, G., ed. 1969. Andrew Graham's observations on Hudson's Bay, 1767–91. *Hudson's Bay Record Society.* Vol. 27. London.

Woolfe, Henry D. 1890. Letter to Sheldon Jackson dated December 18, 1890. Published by Sheldon Jackson in Report on Educational Affairs in Alaska, in the *Report of the Commissioner of Education for 1892-93,* whole no. 218, vol. 2, 1726–27.

6. Wars over Buffalo

Stories versus Stories on the Northern Plains

Dan Flores

The historical events enfolding the Bozeman Trail and Red Cloud's War—
the only war against the U.S. military on the plains that Indians actually
won, it is often said—are rich with possibilities for understanding the role
of buffalo as a fulcrum in the history of the nineteenth-century plains. From
the perspective of environmental history the war was not actually a war over
a trail, or really a war to hold back U.S. military expansion on the northern
plains. Instead, like the Red River War on the southern plains, which the
Comanches, Kiowas, and Southern Cheyennes would wage the following
decade, Lakota and Cheyenne opposition to the Bozeman Trail ought to be
seen as a war to save the buffalo. In this instance, the buffalo herds to be
saved were largely those that the Western Lakota bands and the Cheyennes
had just wrestled from the Crows in a series of battles over the previous decades. The Bozeman Trail story, in other words, has an ecological dimension that significantly extends the context of this famous northern plains
event of a century and a half ago.

That context was at least partially visible then, and is apparent to us
now, primarily because of the frothy dialogue that took place during the
U.S. government's efforts to appease the Oglalas and other bands in discussions about the trail and its protecting forts during the 1860s. Military
commanders and representatives of the Peace Commission all talked to
the Indians, and the Indians talked back. Those discussions indicate that
at least as early as the 1860s, the Lakotas, Nakotas, and Cheyennes opposed

a trail through their newly won country primarily because they saw the arrival of the whites in the West as the reason why buffalo were becoming so hard to find. As historian Jeffrey Ostler has shown us in a splendid essay I build on here, for many northern plains people during the late nineteenth century, what Black Elk referred to as "the good"—his term for bison herds overspreading the country from horizon to horizon—was in jeopardy from the mere presence of white people in the West (Ostler 1999, 475–97; Neihardt 1971, 48–60). Western Lakota leaders told the U.S. treaty and peace commissioners who held council with them from 1865 to 1868 that buffalo were getting more difficult to find, that (according to leaders like Spotted Tail of the Brulés) the whites were to blame for this disturbing trend, and that constructing a road to bring even more whites across the headwaters of the Powder River buffalo range, which they had only recently seized from the Crows, would be disastrous for wildlife. Buffalo so disliked the smell of white people, Lakota band leaders insisted, that the mere appearance of whites in the West threatened environmental problems for the tribes.

That was the Indian version. Of course, the U.S. government had its own point of view. Opposing the Indian argument was another story of what was happening in the West, best articulated for Indian audiences by William Tecumseh Sherman, traveling with the special Peace Commission. Whites as the cause of wildlife depletion? That was not the case, Sherman argued, insisting that the white presence on the Bozeman Trail did not "disturb the buffalo, nor does it destroy the elk and antelope" (Ostler 1999, 485; *Papers* 51).

Of course, wars are always fought by people whose views about some crucial issue are at variance. And none of us needs to be told that groups tend to construct their own stories about why things happen, or happened, in the course of history. In our time no one—certainly no historian—should be so naive as to think that particular versions of history do not serve ideological ends. As often as not, history seems relevant to the present primarily because current politics require authentication by some historical example designed to silence the opposition. That is something of a drawback when your interest, as a student of the past, is to figure out how and why things happened. Naturally, all of us whose ancestors were involved in the West—

and mine have been involved for almost three centuries—are intrigued by how the history of the West gets explained. Particularly, the history of the interaction between humans and nature is a sensitive history, because decline seems so manifestly a part of it. One of the tasks of western environmental history has been to get buffalo, wolves, wild horses, and grasses back in the story. But the shorthand abstract of that wildlife narrative is that once there were millions of buffalo, wild horses, wolves, bears, and prairie dogs in the West; now there are few. What happened to many of these animals, and to the natural world of the Great Plains in the nineteenth century, implicates some of the events to which I will allude.

I will try to offer here a narrative synthesis, interpreted through the lens of environmental history and standing on the work of other scholars in various fields, of a third story—different from both Spotted Tail's and Sherman's—of how we might interpret history on the northern plains in the 1860s. This, then, is a modern historian's version of why the Bozeman Trail was such a line-in-the-sand event for western Sioux buffalo-hunting peoples. In the interpretive synthesis that follows, the Oglalas and related Teton bands of the Lakotas or western Sioux, like the other Indian peoples with whom they struggled for pockets of rich buffalo ground in the last century—and like the U.S. Army officers and peace commissioners and overlanders—were as subject to the dictates of human nature, and to the pull of their respective cultures, as we all are today, and as all humans ever have been. The Bozeman Trail story I tell here features people from all these groups who acted both nobly and selfishly, and many who indulged the human inclination to use up nature for short-term gain.[1] And these lessons, I would argue, are the same ones after all that so richly inform the stories that Shepard Krech's *The Ecological Indian: Myth and History* has offered up for our new understanding of Indian environmental history. I would join Krech in arguing that Indians have been a people without history for far too long now.

Looking back on the century that led up to the conflagration over the Bozeman Trail makes manifest that essential environmental issues were at the heart of the struggle for the northern plains in the mid-nineteenth century. Nineteenth-century Plains Indian history—and sources both Indian and white concur here—devolves to a great variety of Native American groups engaged in an almost unceasing struggle with one another for the great common resource that defined their lives as buffalo nations. As Richard White wrote in 1978, when the western Sioux peoples and the U.S. Army squared off after midcentury the confrontation was between the apparent winner of these intertribal struggles and an expansionist modern power utterly convinced of the inevitability of its mission to replace bison with civilization and its accoutrements (1978, 391–43). This is a story ripe with pathos, which is why it still grips us.

The reasons for the great Indian contest on the northern plains were evident to careful American observers in the West as early as the beginning of the nineteenth century. In the spring and summer of 1805, when Lewis and Clark poled and dragged their boats up the Missouri from the Mandan villages, they famously did not see a single Indian for more than five months. Their sole encounter with the plains Lakotas that year occurred far down the Missouri, south and east of the Mandans. What Lewis and Clark did see in that vast country up the river was a buffalo and wildlife paradise, an ecology that existed in good part because of Indian management principles the explorers noted but understood only vaguely.

At first the Americans were at a loss to explain the significant difference they found in wildlife populations between the Missouri and Columbia slopes of the Rockies. But after two and a half years in the West, on their return trip, William Clark penned this line of insight in his journal: "I have observed that in the country between the nations which are at war with each other the greatest numbers of wild animals are to be found" (Moulton 1993, 38). While their explanation for the game sink Lewis and Clark found west of the Rockies strikes me as debatable, Paul Martin and Christine Szuter have concluded that it was a Blackfeet-imposed neutral zone—what Martin and Szuter called a "war zone" and other scholars have referred to as "buffer zones" between tribes at war, in effect borderlands that no group occupied and regularly exploited—that accounted for the huge numbers of animals Lewis and Clark reported from the upper Missouri (Martin and Szuter 1999, 36–45; Hickerson 1965, 43–61).

While it was by no means the only such zone, in the nineteenth century this Great Upper Missouri Buffalo Buffer Zone was probably the largest one in the West. Contested by the Blackfeet, Mandan/Hidatsas, Arikaras, Assiniboines, Shoshones, and Crows, along with the Salish, Nez Perces, and other tribes from across the mountains, its irregular boundaries varied across the decades with the shifting fortunes of the tribes. But in the early nineteenth century this great zone of animals, over which only intrepid war parties dared roam, extended from Alberta to south of the Yellowstone, and from the Rockies nearly to the Sioux River, near present Vermilion, South Dakota. Other, smaller such zones existed across much of the plains, but this one seems to have been the main prize.

Establishing intertribal peace was one way to open up a buffer zone to hunting, but the tactic that produced the richest reward was a successfully prosecuted war, since it reserved the wildlife bounty for the winners alone. Among the most expansionist-minded plains tribes, in the 1820s it was the Pawnees who were prosecuting wars in contests for southern pieces of this zone. But as we know, a new power was emerging on the northern plains in the decades after Lewis and Clark. The Western Lakota peoples were beginning to make their push westward.

Who were these so-called Sioux? The Siouan language family is one of the mega-families on the continent, and among its groups are included a host of peoples—like the Mandans—who had become agriculturalists, and even some—the Crows—who were early buffalo hunters on the plains. But the groups whose identity is "Sioux" in American history were members of a woodland people whose march west earned them the name "western Sioux." All of them used the same name for their kinsmen, a word meaning "allies," but Santees pronounced the word "Dakota," Yanktons and Yanktonais "Nakota," and Tetons "Lakota" (Larson 1997; Price 1996).

It was Crees and Assiniboines who initially sent these Siouan peoples westward. Armed with guns from Canadian traders, in the 1670s they began pushing Siouan bands that were then primarily deer hunters and gatherers southward along the Minnesota River. Although whitetail deer were their traditional prey, these bands soon discovered that south of the Minnesota there were buffalo, an animal that early on seems to have lured the Yanktons and the Lakotas, including the Oglalas, onto the prairies.

In his final book, *Animals of the Soul*, religion scholar Joseph Epes Brown retrieved from several traditional Lakota elders whom he interviewed in the 1930s an echo of Lakota ecology as it evolved in its grassland form. The Lakotas perceived the world as a series of circles contained within ever-larger circles. Their society was highly competitive, for men especially, with war and the hunt the most democratic options for upward mobility. According to Brown, the Lakotas perceived the essential nature of individual animal species less through observation than through dreams or visions. There was a certain ranking of animals in Lakota taxonomy. To charismatic species—grizzlies, bison, eagles—they accorded their highest ranking, with bears ruling the underground, bison the surface, and eagles the air.

The Lakotas also saw a connection, involving energy flow, between animals that our scientific worldview would not think to link together. What they called *Umi* or *Yum* was the power of the whirlwind, an uncontained residue of the energy of the four winds, which only a small number of special animals—moths, dragonflies, spiders, bears, elk, and bison—possessed. The periodic disappearances of bison, for example, appeared to the Lakota to be associated with seasonal winds from the north and south. That bison did sometimes disappear confirmed their belief (and it was a general one across the plains) that bison had their origins underground. Management based on population counts, gender harvests, ecological relationships—on our modern principles of ecological science, in other words—seem to have been alien to them. When bison became difficult to find, the Lakotas and their kin engaged in buffalo-calling ceremonies to entice the animals to come near or to emerge from the ground (Brown 1992).

The Lakota division would eventually break into seven subtribes, which according to Catherine Price further divided into bands or *tiyospaye*, led by headmen called *itancans* and war leaders known as *blotahunkas*. Of the subtribes, the Oglalas and Brulés went to the prairie first. The others (the Mineconjous, Two Kettles, Sans Arcs, Hunkpapas, and Blackfeet Sioux) clung to their woodland homes into the late seventeenth century. But early on the Oglalas and Brulés began to acquire firearms at the Great Plains trade fairs, and soon they began to displace the agricultural Siouan peoples west of them (Larson 1997; Price 1996).

There was a motive and a pattern in the Lakota move ever westward. Confronting "the good," buffalo in the prairies, the Lakotas enjoyed growth and success. But there was a downside. Under strong hunting pressure, buffalo herds on the margins of the Great Plains disappeared fairly quickly, and soon the herds directly in the path of the Siouan push westward, along the Blue Earth River, were all but gone. Thus there commenced, even at the outset of the buffalo lifestyle on the plains, a need for Siouan bands to push even farther west in search of undiminished herds.

By 1760 the Lakotas had arrived at the Missouri and now confronted the Caddoan farmers there, Arikaras and Pawnees, perhaps twenty thousand of them. At the Missouri the Sioux encountered horses for the first time, supplied to the Caddoans by the Kiowas. Then smallpox, three epidemics of it among the Arikaras from 1772 to 1780, eliminated 80 percent of the Caddo opposition. It was in an effort to prevent American traders from supplying these reeling northern plains Caddoan farmers that the Tetons attempted to block Lewis and Clark's party from ascending the Missouri in 1804 (Larson 1997; Price 1996).

Brulé winter counts show that they suffered, too, from epidemics in 1779, 1780, and 1801. But these Lakotas continued to display a remarkable growth, from eighty-five hundred in 1805 to some twenty-five thousand by the 1850s. Horses and buffalo meat were unquestionably the keys to their demographic surge, although Richard White has argued that fairly widespread fur-trader vaccination of Siouan bands against smallpox offers another compelling explanation for their anomalous nineteenth-century population story. Whatever the exact combination of reasons, as Gary Anderson has recently argued for the Comanches on the southern plains (who, like the western Sioux, were never horticulturalists before becoming horse-mounted buffalo hunters) these Lakotas seem to have been engaging in a kind of ethnogenesis, re-creating themselves around new, richer possibilities than they had ever encountered (Howard 1976; White 1978; Anderson 1999).

Taking up former Arikara homelands in present South Dakota, and now mounted, the Lakotas continued their move westward up a pair of rivers, the Bad and the White, that would lead them eventually to the Badlands and the Black Hills. According to winter counts by American Horse and Cloud Shield (about the only kinds of documentation for these years), Standing Bull of the Oglalas discovered the Black Hills in 1775 or 1776 (Larson 1997). Here, however, Kiowas and Crows contested with the Blackfeet and other groups for the southern edges of the Great Upper Missouri Buffalo Buffer Zone. Lakotas entered this fray, driving the Kiowas out of the contest and sending them southward down the plains. Then, after allying themselves with the Cheyennes, they began to launch themselves against the Crows and access to the plum buffer zone prize in the West.

With the Kiowa retreat southward, new possibilities opened up there, too. About the time winter counts like John K. Bear's record a great Lakota/Cheyenne victory over the Crows—the year seems to have been 1822—other bands of Oglalas and Brulés had already pushed southward to the Platte (Howard 1976, 44–45). Most western Sioux bands by this time were being served in trade by the American Fur Company, whose traders, with the advent of steamboats on the Missouri by the 1830s, were turning from beavers to buffalo robes. On the Platte the Lakota bands would also establish trade relations with the Rocky Mountain Fur Company.

Buffalo robes had become a major hunting motive for Plains Indians at least as early as the 1820s, when river craft were shipping nearly 100,000 robes to New Orleans every year. As a direct result of steamboat capabilities in transporting bulky products, by the late 1830s the American Fur Company alone was sending 70,000 robes a year down the Missouri. By the 1840s the figures were in the range of 85,000–100,000 Indian-produced bison robes arriving in St. Louis annually. And the Hudson's Bay trade eventually nearly rivaled that farther south, reaching a zenith of 73,278 robes between 1841 and 1845. Either from competition or because the take was fading, from 1845 to 1853 the American Fur Company yearly average fell to about 30,850 (Burlingame 1929, 262–91).

At least one Hunkpapa headman, Little Bear, seems to have perceived this Lakota entry into the U.S. market economy during these years as a dangerous step. He began preaching the virtues of ending trade with the whites in the 1830s, and was still doing so in the 1850s. But Little Bear was the only Teton leader who seems to have felt so (Bray 1985, 39). Up and down the Great Plains the result of the market and the robe trade were the same: increased intertribal competition for every remaining pocket of buffalo in the West. Of all the causes of buffalo decline in the nineteenth century— and we now know that there were many—the global market's conversion of Indian hunters into market hunters was perhaps the most pernicious. Yet given the advantages of trade and trade contacts, few could resist its pull (Flores 2001).

By the 1840s the Lakotas had before them four prize buffalo grounds, some of them contested zones, others hunted chiefly by one tribe alone. They included the Forks of the Platte country, still mostly Pawnee hunting grounds; the Medicine Bow/Laramie Plains region; the Republican River (Kansas-Nebraska border); and the Yellowstone drainage, the southern (present Wyoming/Montana) streams of which were hunted by the Crows and the northern streams by the Blackfeet. The Lakotas began challenging for all these drainages in the years after the great smallpox epidemic of 1837, which swept away an estimated fifteen thousand Indians on the Missouri and left many of the enemies of the western Sioux decimated.

Richard Irving Dodge, that military writer of popular nineteenth-century books on the West, gained some firsthand ideas from his Indian contacts about how some of these contests in deep plains country transpired:

> A long-continued war between these tribes [the Lakotas, Pawnees, and Crows] taught at least mutual respect; and an immense area, embracing the Black Hills and the vast plains watered by the Niobrara and White Rivers became a debatable ground into which none but war parties ever penetrated. Hunted more or less by the surrounding tribes, immense numbers of buffalo took refuge in this debatable ground, where they were comparatively unmolested, re-

> *maining there summer and winter in security. When the Pawnees were finally overthrown and forced onto a reservation, the Sioux poured into this country, just suited to their tastes, and finding buffalo very plentiful, and a ready sale for their robes, made such a furious onslaught on the poor beasts, that in a few years, scarcely a buffalo could be found in all the wide area south of the Cheyenne and north and east of the North Platte. (1959, 130–31)*

Pushing into these new buffalo grounds in the 1840s, their numbers growing almost yearly, the western Siouan bands now confronted a riddle. Everywhere they looked, just beyond their reach there seemed to be great numbers of animals ripe for the taking. Yet inevitably, whenever they seized these new countries to the west, wildlife populations appeared to decrease not very many years after their arrival. It was a paradox that set them up inevitably to push on yet again (Kurz 1937, 25–45).

At the time the various divisions of these forestland Siouans had crossed the Missouri River and launched their destiny on the grassland seas of the Great Plains, flush times had held sway across the Great Bison Belt of North America. We now know that these halcyon times were partially a result of a hemispheric weather phenomenon called the Little Ice Age. According to a 1986 study in *Science*, the Little Ice Age climate favored c4 (warm season) grasses—buffalo grass and the grama grasses that bison especially favored—over c3 (cool season) grasses and woody vegetation (Neilson 1986). This is the climate regime, indeed, that helped create so large a biomass of buffalo out west that at the time Europeans were first appearing on the continent, the herds were spilling out of the Great Plains both eastward across the Mississippi and westward down the Snake—such a pressure of animals, evidently, that when virgin soil epidemics of Old World diseases decimated Indian populations and eased hunting pressure on bison, the expanding mass of buffalo squeezed like toothpaste into every nook-and-cranny prairie from Pennsylvania and Florida to Oregon and Idaho.

But the weather gods had some Coyote-like tricks to play on Great Plains history in the nineteenth century. For reasons that no one is quite yet sure about, the Little Ice Age's moister, grass-happy conditions began to dissipate during the first half of the century. Climatologist Harry Weakley's 1943 study, "A Tree Ring Record of Precipitation in Western Nebraska," shows specifically for the region into which the western Siouan speakers were moving a pattern that has by now become a classic climate interpretation for the nineteenth-century plains: a wet period from the turn of the century to 1821, gradually cycling toward less favorable conditions for grass and buffalo. The result was a series of spotty but serious droughts all over the plains in the 1840s, followed by one of the most serious dry pulses on record settling onto the plains from 1858 to 1866 (Weakley 1943; Schulman 1956, 85–89; Lawson 1974; Frits, Smith, and Holmes 1964; Coupland 1958).

What Weakley and a host of other climatologists have since documented were local manifestations of the end of the Little Ice Age in North America. The sheer scale of it all made this particular climatic downturn far worse on grass and animals than any merely localized drought, for unlike droughts since, it seems to have occurred simultaneously up and down the Great Plains. Two Texas scholars, in an exhaustive study of drought on the southern plains, used the June Palmer Drought Severity Index to conclude that between 1698 and 1980, the absolutely driest decade of record for the southern plains was neither the 1930s Dust Bowl nor the infamous 1950s, but the years from 1856 to 1864 (Stahle and Cleaveland 1988). The practical effect on buffalo, and by extension on people living off buffalo, was extraordinary and profound. Reid Bryson (1981) believes that these sudden and nearly unprecedented droughts of the 1850s and 1860s so dried up western grasslands that carrying capacity for buffalo may have been reduced by as much as 60 percent.

In any case, as with the Kiowa calendars, which began referring to shortages of buffalo farther south during the 1840s, western Sioux winter counts show that in 1842, 1843, and 1844 many western Sioux, even the Mandans and Hidatsas, set down as the most significant events for those years elaborate buffalo-calling ceremonies, an effort to lure bison once again to emerge from underground and overspread the plains (Howard 1976, 50).

In addition to the market, changing weather, competition from growing herds of Indian horses and wild mustangs for grass and water, and perhaps even the arrival of exotic bovine diseases on the overland trails, a source that began to eat away at buffalo on the northern plains was the Métis trade, which began in 1844 and funneled robes over the Red River route to St. Paul. Four carts blazed the Red River Trail that first year. Pembina became the Canadian base of the trail by 1854, at which time the trade had become voluminous enough that the northernmost Siouan bands clearly resented the Métis, and referred to them angrily during the councils held over the Bozeman Trail in the 1860s (Ostler 1999, 88).

But the 1840s and 1850s were the heyday, too, of the Oregon and Mormon trails, with fifty thousand white immigrants moving west up the Platte in 1849 alone. As had happened so many times before, large numbers of whites in the West meant disease for the Natives. But these decades were not just the cholera decades. As Elliott West has shown in his recent books on the central plains, Plains Indians were not simply being paranoid about the proximate effects of white overlanders. Spotted Tail and other Sioux spokesmen at the 1860s conferences *were* right. The white wagon trains—in Elliott West's phrase—were "great grass-gobbling machines" (West 1998, 233). And as Indians across the plains had already witnessed, many of the overlanders shot at everything in sight as a matter of course, frightening and disrupting what wildlife they failed to kill. In the early 1990s I hiked in to a Plains Indian petroglyph site that was about to disappear beneath a reservoir on the upper Brazos River to examine a historic Indian record of a white wagon train en route west. The "Wagon Train Site" documented a movable gun show, showing bullets spraying from the line of wagons in every direction. To Indian observers, the endless gunfire may have been the most memorable thing about an overland trek (Flores 1992).

Concerned, at least for traveling U.S. citizens, over these intertribal wars over buffalo grounds, the U.S. government developed a characteristic American idea in response. After midcentury, policy makers began to move toward the idea of what might be called "privatizing buffalo," assigning the tribes particular parcels of ground to hunt in exchange for safety for travelers on the trails. Annuities became the bait. The idea seems first to have emerged in the 1851 Horse Creek Conference, on the North Platte near Fort Laramie, but it was put into its most successful form by the treaties of Washington territorial governor Isaac Stevens. His agreements at Walla Walla, Hellgate, and with the Blackfeet at the mouth of the Judith River in 1855 guaranteed the rights of the mountain tribes (Salish, Kootenais, Nez Perces, Pend d'Oreilles, etc.) to continue to hunt buffalo east of the Continental Divide, even mapping out a zone for their hunt in the Missouri headwaters country of the Great Upper Missouri Buffalo Buffer Zone. At the Lame Bull Treaty this private buffalo pasture took the form of a common hunting ground from the Musselshell and Judith to the Three-Forks of the Missouri, set up for ninety-nine years. At the same time, the Lame Bull Treaty attempted to thwart the pressure being put on by the first waves of Sioux bands by proclaiming the Blackfeet at peace with the Sans Arcs and at least one other Sioux band. The treaties did not allow their signatories actually to settle in the region. The mountain tribes' pasture worked so well that one of its features, through the 1860s and 1870s, was army escorts accompanying the tribes across the mountains to "go to buffalo" (Farr 2003, 18–21; Kappler 1904, 737–38; Fahey 1974, 101).

The government tried something akin to this in the region of the Bozeman Trail in the decade prior to Red Cloud's War. It failed to work. The Sioux appearance on the northern plains was solidified by the 1851 Treaty of Fort Laramie. But that conference went on to affirm the status quo by leaving the southeastern reaches of the Great Upper Missouri Buffalo Buffer Zone in the hands of the Crows, stipulating a neutral zone between the Crows and the Sioux bands that was to run from the North Platte northeast along the divide between the Powder and Cheyenne rivers (the Belle Fourche drainage, in other words) that was to be a joint-use area for both.

Thus was opened to hunting one of the choicest portions of the northern plains, the region west of the Black Hills that warfare had kept free of exploitation until now. This was critical to the Miniconjous and Hunkpapas, whose hunting across the Badlands east of the Black Hills had by the 1850s resulted in a near extinction of buffalo there, reducing the bands to plant gathering and foraging, even to making peace, in 1846 or 1847, with the Arikaras in order to trade for corn (Howard 1976, 52). What the Crows got out of the arrangement was access to the traders on the North Platte.

In the nineteenth century the Crow country, as their descendants have often pointed out, seemed to be in exactly the right place for the Crows to reap a wildlife bounty. In effect it reached northward into the Great Upper Missouri Buffalo Buffer Zone of the lower Yellowstone River, from which the Crows had been largely excluded until the smallpox epidemic of 1837 reaped its whirlwind against the Blackfeet. Southward the Crow homeland extended from the Yellowstone into present Wyoming to the Laramie Fork on the North Platte, and included the Big Horn Mountains and the drainages of the Powder, Wind, and Big Horn rivers. Now, the Fort Laramie treaty had opened several of the drainages in the southern stretches to the western Sioux bands, whose total numbers by this point approached twenty-five thousand, compared to fewer than seven thousand Crows. For the Crows, and for the bison herds, the message was on the wall (Denig 1961, 139; Bray 1985, 35–38; McGinnis 1990, 62).

According to Kingsley Bray, for several years the Fort Laramie arrangement seems to have worked. But following the Grattan affair in August 1854, the Oglalas decided to draw farther away from the white trails. Much of the remaining country north of the Platte having been hunted out, the Oglalas looked to the joint-use Powder River country. An apparent Oglala council with the Crows in 1856 must have left the Oglalas and their allies dissatisfied—and so once again a war to get at buffalo grounds was the result. By 1861 or 1862, according to Cloud Shield's winter count, the Oglalas defeated a large Crow force under Little Rabbit. So it was that on the eve of John Bozeman's laying out his trail for miners to access the goldfields in Montana through this exact country, the Powder River drainage—home to a paradise of animals extending back at least to the time of Lewis and Clark—was finally the Lakotas' and their allies' to exploit. As they told their agent, they "liked this [Crow] country, here they could make plenty of robes and plenty of meat. Their country was wherever the buffalo ranged, here was plenty of buffalo. . . . It was their country and they had come to live in it" (Phillip

2005, 49). "We stole the hunting grounds of the Crows," a Cheyenne later boasted, "because they were the best" (Bray 1985, 38).

Alarmed at the idea of whites as competitors for buffalo and grass and furious at the overlanders' effect on the landscape and animals, as early as 1857, at the great summer council at Bear Butte when the western Sioux had decided to seize Crow buffalo grounds, the Teton bands apparently adopted a set of resolutions relating to the whites, too. They agreed among themselves that except for traders, all whites invading their lands west of the Missouri and north of the North Platte would be "whipped out," that they would allow no further overland trails in the region, and that they would accept no annuities accepted from the United States in any deal that abrogated those resolutions (Bray 1985, 42–43). When Red Cloud's Bad Faces band ran into James Sawyer's party, contracted out to the War Department to start construction on the Bozeman Trail, Red Cloud insisted that Sawyer halt his advance, since such a road would "disturb the buffalo" (Larson 1997, 86).

Who was right and who wrong in the stories that the Lakotas and the government proffered in the resulting negotiations? Obviously, Sherman's insistence that white trails had no effect on wildlife was bogus, a flimsy argument the Plains Indians were too experienced by now to fail to see through. And Red Cloud, Spotted Tail, and other Indian leaders by this time had become cognizant that the whites represented not just a local threat to buffalo but also a threat to a way of life based upon them. Even the special Peace Commission, which included several pro-Indian members, in its 1868 *Report* did not equivocate: "We do not contest the ever ready argument that civilization must not be arrested in its progress by a handful of savages. We earnestly desire speedy settlement of all our territories. None are more anxious than we to see the agricultural and mineral wealth developed by an individualistic, thrifty, and enlightened population. And we fully recognize the fact that the Indian must not stand in the way of this result" (Washburn 1973, 141).

On the other hand, Spotted Tail, Red Cloud, and others who argued at the negotiations, and elsewhere, that the whites were solely responsible for the fate of the buffalo in the 1860s were engaging in a bit of myopia them-

selves. While whites were a serious threat to buffalo, and white hide hunters unquestionably delivered the coup de grâce to the herds over the next
two decades, for the better part of a century the western Sioux themselves
had been executing a Pac-Man–like march westward, devouring one pocket
of buffalo after another. Honest individuals among them must have known
that very well. At the end of the 1860s that appetite had led them to the southern and eastern edges of the Great Upper Missouri Buffalo Buffer Zone, the
largest aggregate of buffalo on the Great Plains—and the last.

Note

1. Critical history makes obvious that our ancestors in the West—and that certainly includes
my own French/Spanish Louisiana forebears, who were traders to the Indians and mustangers on
the southern plains—interacted with their world through a maze of cultural, institutional, and
biological filters and were significantly involved in all these declines. In my case this has meant
saying in print that Pierre Bouet Lafitte, my great-grandfather four times removed, was implicated in the trade that removed wild horses from the West, and that the Utah practitioners of the
Mormonism in which I was raised made a mess of the Wasatch Front in the nineteenth century.
The aim of environmental history is not, in fact, to make particular individuals or groups look
bad but to explain what happened in the past with compassion both for the human actors and
for the natural world in hopes that we all can learn from the human story. I have to wonder at the
review by a prominent Native American scholar of an outstanding recent book on plains history,
which (because the work attempts to show that nineteenth-century Plains Indians were human,
hence fallible in their relationship with nature) charges its author with evincing an anti-Indian
position. See Deloria 1999.

References

Anderson, Gary. 1999. The Indian Southwest, 1580–1830: Ethnogenesis and reinvention. Norman:
    University of Oklahoma Press.
Bray, Kingsley. 1985. Lone Horn's peace: A new view of Sioux-Crow relations, 1851–1858. Ne-
    braska History 66:29–47.
Brown, Joseph Epes. 1992. Animals of the soul: Sacred animals of the Oglala Sioux. Rockport MA: El-
    ement Press.
Bryson, Reid. 1981. Chinook climates and plains peoples. Great Plains Quarterly Winter:12–13.
Burlingame, Merrill. 1929. The buffalo in trade and commerce. North Dakota Historical Quarterly
    3:262–91.
Coupland, Robert. 1958. The effects of fluctuations in weather upon the grasslands of the
    Great Plains. Botanical Review 24 (May).
Deloria, Vine, Jr. 1999. Review of The contested plains, by Elliott West. Western Historical Quarterly
    30:216–17.
Denig, Edwin Thompson. 1961. Five tribes of the upper Missouri. Ed. John Ewers. Norman: Univer-
    sity of Oklahoma Press.

Dodge, Richard. 1959. *The plains of the Great West and their inhabitants, being a description of the plains, &c. of the great North American desert.* New York: Archer House.

Fahey, John. 1974. *The Flathead Indians.* Norman: University of Oklahoma Press.

Farr, William. 2003. Going to buffalo: Indian hunting migrations across the Rocky Mountains. Part 1, Making meat and taking robes. *Montana, the Magazine of Western History* 53:2–21.

Flores, Dan. 1992. In search of Kokopelli: Vanishing rock art of the high plains. *Texas Parks and Wildlife Magazine* 50 (January): 28–35.

———. 2001. Bison ecology and bison diplomacy redux: Another look at the southern plains from 1800 to 1850. In *The natural West: Environmental history in the Great Plains and Rocky Mountains,* 50–70. Norman: University of Oklahoma Press.

Frits, H. C., D. G. Smith, and R. L. Holmes. 1964. *Tree ring evidence for climatic changes in western North America from 1500 AD to 1940 AD.* Tucson: Laboratory of Tree-Ring Research, University of Arizona Press.

Hickerson, Harold. 1965. The Virginia deer and intertribal buffer zones in the upper Mississippi Valley. In *Man, culture, and animals: The role of animals in human ecological adjustments,* ed. Anthony Leeds and Andrew Vayda, 43–61. Washington DC: American Association for the Advancement of Science.

Howard, James. 1976. Yanktonai ethnohistory and the John K. Bear winter count. *Plains Anthropologist* 21 (August): 28–52.

Kappler, Charles, ed. 1904. Treaty with the Blackfeet, 1855. *Indian affairs, laws, and treaties,* 2:735–41. Washington DC: Government Printing Office.

Kurz, Rudolph Friedrich. 1937. *Journal of Rudolph Friedrich Kurz: An account of his experiences among fur traders and American Indians on the Mississippi and upper Missouri rivers during the years 1846 to 1852.* Ed. J. N. B. Hewitt. Bureau of Ethnology Bulletin 115. Washington DC: Government Printing Office.

Larson, Robert. 1997. *Red Cloud: Warrior-statesman of the Lakota Sioux.* Norman: University of Oklahoma Press.

Lawson, Merlin. 1974. *The climate of the great American desert: Reconstructing the climate of western interior United States, 1800–1850.* Lincoln: University of Nebraska Press.

Martin, Paul, and Christine Szuter. 1999. War zones and game sinks in Lewis and Clark's West. *Conservation Biology* 13 (February): 36–45.

McGinnis, Anthony. 1990. *Counting coup and cutting horses: Intertribal warfare on the northern plains, 1738–1889.* Evergreen CO: Cordillera Press.

Moulton, Gary, ed. 1993. *Journals of the Lewis and Clark expedition.* Vol. 8. Lincoln: University of Nebraska Press.

Neihardt, John. 1971. The bison hunt. In *Black Elk speaks: Being the life story of a holy man of the Oglala Sioux,* 48–60. Lincoln: University of Nebraska Press, Bison Book edition.

Neilson, R. P. 1986. High resolution climatic analysis and Southwest biogeography. *Science* 232:27–34.

Ostler, Jeffrey. 1999. "They regard their passing as Wakan": Interpreting western Sioux explanations for the bison's decline. *Western Historical Quarterly* 30:475–97.

Papers relating to talks and councils held with the Indians in Dakota and Montana territories in the years 1866–1869. 1910. Washington DC: Government Printing Office.

Phillip, Gloria. 2005. The Nez Perce buffalo hunters and the broken Crow alliance. MA thesis in history, University of Montana.

Price, Catherine. 1996. The Oglala people, 1841–1879: A political history. Lincoln: University of Nebraska Press.

Schulman, Edmund. 1956. Dendroclimatic changes in semiarid America. Tucson: University of Arizona Press.

Stahle, David, and Malcolm Cleaveland. 1988. Texas drought history reconstructed and analyzed from 1698 to 1980. Journal of Climate 1:59–74.

Washburn, Wilcomb, ed. 1973. Indian Peace Commission report to President Andrew Johnson, January 7, 1868. In The American Indian and the United States: A documentary history. Vol. 1:134–63. New York: Random House.

Weakley, Harry. 1943. A tree ring record of precipitation in western Nebraska. Journal of Forestry 41:816–19.

West, Elliott. 1998. The contested plains: Indians, goldseekers, and the rush to Colorado. Lawrence: University Press of Kansas.

White, Richard. 1978. The winning of the West. Journal of American History 65:319–43.

Representations of Indians and Animals

7. Watch for Falling Bison

The Buffalo Hunt as Museum Trope and Ecological Allegory

John Dorst

Among the national icons we have minted from animate nature, the American bison yields pride of place only to the bald eagle. And even at that, the bison alone occupies the role of protagonist in a grand natural history narrative, perhaps the grandest in our national collection of master narratives. The disaster of the bison's sudden, all-but-complete eradication stands as the North American paradigm for heedless destruction of natural resources by human greed and arrogance. The bison's last-minute rescue and then modest recovery completes the ecological morality tale on a satisfyingly hopeful note, without which the bison's story would probably seem as Victorianly remote as that of the passenger pigeon.

It is, of course, another such icon that Shepard Krech undertakes to examine in *The Ecological Indian* (1999), but the bison as emblematic victim of ecological disaster and the Indian as emblematic good steward of natural resources are intimately bound together. In the natural history bison saga, the rapacious Euro-American stands forth especially vividly against the foil of the indigene as intuitive ecologist. It is not surprising, then, that Krech devotes a chapter to a case study of human/bison ecological relations. Just as the mounted, hunter-gatherer cultures of the nineteenth-century Plains Indians have provided the default image of indigenous peoples for the national popular culture, so the traditional bison hunt, the definitive mode of subsistence in these cultures, has become a standard image of pre-industrial, pre-capitalist ecological relations. As such, it serves as the binary counterpart to the wasteful, market-based exploitation that brought the bison to the brink of extinction. As in all his other chapters, Krech marshals ecological and historical data to complicate the familiar picture that dominates popular perception.

It is not my goal here to reassess Krech's data or his argument about buffalo ecology and the history of human exploitation of this animal. Krech's avowed goal in The Ecological Indian is to measure a popular icon against the documentary and archaeological record. My intention, rather, is to examine a bit more thoroughly some aspects of the popular perception itself. In particular, I want to consider the cultural construction of the *image* of human/bison relations in a context that has had considerable influence on our collective iconography. The natural history museum is one place where bison ecology and human/bison relations have frequently been represented and interpreted for a general audience. At the same time, these museums are sites of ecological exchange per se. As institutions of popular education, natural history museums participate in the production and dissemination of the icons, narratives, images, and binary constructions that constitute the unexamined conventions of a popular discourse. These institutions are both repositories of ecological information and themselves ecological niches where humans interact with nature in complexly adapted ways. By looking at the representation of traditional Native American bison hunting in this context—at two museums in particular, one old and one new—I hope to gain fresh perspective on the treatment of this subject in The Ecological Indian.

The symbolic importance of the bison in our national imagination goes hand in hand with its key role in the late-nineteenth-century emergence of both the modern natural history museum and the nascent ecological consciousness these institutions strove to instill in the general public. A signature moment in this history is the 1888 unveiling of William T. Hornaday's American Bison Group at the National Museum of Natural History in Washington DC. Hornaday both collected the specimens for this exhibit, on an

1886 expedition to Montana, Dakota, and Wyoming territories, and mounted them, using new, arts-based taxidermy techniques that revolutionized this craft and secured him a legitimate claim to the title "father of modern taxidermy." With this exhibit he also pioneered in the use of habitat elements to create scientifically accurate mini-environments that would provide the public a more holistic, ecologically informed view of wild nature (Wonders 1993, 120–23). Of course, all these innovations would become standard practice in the habitat dioramas we now take for granted as the definitive mode of natural history museum display.

Hornaday's motivation for creating his pathbreaking bison exhibit was his urgent concern that wild bison were about to disappear completely, depriving the American public of direct access to the most magnificent of North American quadrupeds. A scientifically informed and artistically rendered museum exhibit was at least one kind of preservation in the interest of public edification. Hornaday spoke with considerable authority on the matter of bison extinction. It was with great difficulty that he located the small groups from which he took his specimens, leading him later to bill his expedition as "the last bison hunt."[1] In 1887 he published a lengthy monograph, "The Extermination of the American Bison," in the Report of the U.S. National Museum (Hornaday 1889), in which he chronicles, along with the natural history and behavior of the species, the history of human interaction with bison, leading to the moment of their imminent extinction. Like his bison exhibit for natural history museology, this document is an important early contribution to the literature of scientifically grounded indictments of ecological degradation and advocacy for an informed conservation ethic.[2]

Unfortunately, Hornaday's progressive views on species preservation and the ecological understanding of nature were not matched by an enlightened understanding of the history and contemporary plight of Native peoples. His account of bison extermination is wholly lacking in the kind of holistic perspective he brings to bear in his natural history work. In this he was a man of his time rather than ahead of it, and the result was, from our perspective, a shocking insensitivity both to the cultural perspectives of tribal peoples and to the effects of pressures beyond their control. For example, Hornaday does not hesitate to criticize Indians for failing to show greater restraint in their own hunting practices as they watched the herds being driven farther and farther west by the pressures of settlement and eastern markets. "And now," he says, "as we read of the appalling slaughter, one can scarcely repress the feeling of grim satisfaction that arises when we also read that many of the ex-slaughterers are almost starving for the millions of pounds of fat and juicy meat they wasted a few years ago. Verily, the buffalo is in a great measure avenged already" (1889, 480–81). Or even more bluntly: "People who are so utterly senseless as to wantonly destroy their own source of food, as the Indians have done, certainly deserve to starve" (482).

Although he saves most of his ire for the massive and decisive Euro-American onslaught against the bison herds, Hornaday inventories a variety of traditional Indian hunting practices, simply adding them to the ledger of devastation alongside "still hunting" with large-caliber rifles,[3] the huge organized hunts devoted to filling market demands for hides, and the hunts to supply meat for transcontinental railroad workers (not to mention the "sport" hunting the railroads made possible). Among the traditional methods he describes are various forms of "impoundment," that is, trapping herds in enclosures where they can be easily killed; the "surround," or horse-mounted encirclement of large groups; winter hunting in deep snow where hunters use snowshoes to approach mired bison; and "decoying and driving," now more generally known as the buffalo jump. To the last of these I will return in moment.

In all these cases Hornaday draws on firsthand accounts by Euro-American observers (Meriwether Lewis and William Clark, George Catlin, Henry Dodge, etc.) who, for the most part, paint a picture of chaotic, merciless slaughter consistent with nineteenth-century notions of Indian savagery and irrationality. Given this perspective, it is no wonder Hornaday can only see what he considers evidence of uncivilized depravity. For example, he indicts the Sioux, "improvident savages" that they were, for an inability to recognize their own complicity in the decimation of the bison: "Naturally enough, they attributed their disappearance to the white man, who was therefore a robber, and a proper subject for the scalping-knife. Apparently it never occurred to the minds of the Sioux that they themselves were equally to blame," (1889, 490).

There is considerable irony in the fact that Hornaday could hold these views on American Indian cultures but also participate importantly in the creation of a modern institution, the natural history museum, which would become one of the primary—if flawed—vehicles for teaching the public to appreciate and admire such cultures. With the rise of cultural anthropology and its relativist ethos, at least the most blatant forms of social Darwinist racism were thoroughly discredited among the educated public. The development of the natural history museum in the twentieth and twenty-first centuries has been a story of increasing sensitivity to the complexities both of natural systems and of pre-industrial, pre-capitalist, and non-Western cultures.

It is nevertheless true that such institutions educate by presenting certain scenarios and icons, perpetuating through them a broadly shared conventional imagery and the ideology that goes along with it. Museums are of necessity highly selective in what they display and how they display it. I will turn now to how two natural history museums, one quite "classic" in its approach and the other "cutting edge," have chosen to present Indian/bison ecological interaction, as manifest in what have become mainstream images of Plains Indian subsistence hunting.

If it is not surprising that Krech includes a chapter on the buffalo in *The Ecological Indian*, it is also not surprising that that chapter begins at a site representative of one of the most dramatic scenes of encounter between humans and bison—a buffalo jump, specifically the Head-Smashed-In Buffalo Jump in Alberta, Canada. This is a useful excursion for the book's argument, since this site—a much-visited tourist attraction—has been interpreted in the standard binary terms Krech wants to undercut: "White people wasted and caused the extermination of the buffalo, whereas Indians were skillful, ecologically aware conservationists" (1999, 123).

Along with this generalizing comparison widely current in the popular imagination, there is a second binary worth noting. The cover of *The Ecological Indian* reproduces George Catlin's painting *Buffalo Chase with Bows* and *Lances*, a depiction of the pre-industrial, horse-mounted hunting on the open prairie that epitomizes the courage and skill of the plains hunter-warrior and contributes to his enshrinement in the national popular consciousness. The same painting is reproduced in Hornaday's polemical treatise to illustrate one further method of bison hunting—what he calls "running buffalo" (1889, 470). Panoramically depicted in the movie *Dances with Wolves* (1990), this is where the mounted hunter chases an individual animal and, at full gallop, brings it down at short range with arrow, lance, or small-caliber firearm.

Among his long litany of wanton slaughter, this is the only method to gain a measure of endorsement from Hornaday. Although only second to the still hunt in being "fatal to the race," and the approach most widely practiced, it is redeemed for him because it furnishes "sport of a superior kind—manly, exhilarating, and well spiced with danger" (1889, 470; see Krech 1999, 130). And of all the methods described, it is the only one in which the bison "had a fair show for his life, or partially so, at least" (471). Hornaday also admired the many skills, from horse training to dexterity with weapons, required for success. This mode of hunting inspired him with such admiration because it conformed closely to the ethos of elite Euro-American sport hunting and the rules of "fair chase" that were being codified at roughly the same time the bison population was dropping below the threshold of availability for either subsistence or sport.[4] The amenability of this hunting method to Euro-American standards of fair play and individual endeavor, along with its photogenic excitement, have contributed to its cultural selection as one of the premier popular icons of traditional subsistence practices.

In contrast to the heroically masculine and individualist hunt on horseback, there were, as Hornaday describes, the hunting methods that capitalized on the bison's herding and flight instincts to produce group kills. In his chapter on bison (and despite his book's cover illustration), Krech has more to say about these other subsistence strategies, with the buffalo jump given rhetorical prominence at the beginning of the discussion. Among the many methods of gathering and entrapment, the buffalo jump is easily the most dramatic and widely depicted. As Krech points out, this mode of hunting is generally presented in modern discourse as an embodiment of communal action, ingenuity, efficiency, and traditional knowledge about species behavior and landscape. Hornaday's vilification of "unsportsmanlike" group kills of all sorts has largely been displaced by this more positive image.

Despite such a revaluation, it does not seem too outrageous to suggest that the buffalo jump emerges as the dominant image of indigenous communal hunting, in part because it combines these positive associations with certain titillating violations of popular sensibilities. The indiscriminate nature of the kill and the cruelty, by modern standards, of purposely terrifying animals to produce crippling injuries are transgressions of "civilized" behavior. The ideas of communality, efficiency, and supposed absence of wastefulness serve to contain those associations that give the buffalo jump its charge of guilty pleasure as a fascinatingly gruesome embodiment of primitive subsistence. And like the mounted chase, the bison jump is notable, perhaps more so than the other communal methods, for its arresting visual drama. Hence it too has been culturally selected for elevation to emblematic status in our collective iconography of traditional Indian lifeways.

These two emblematic modes of bison hunting—the mounted chase and the stampeded herd falling over a precipice—are widely depicted, but for the sake of this discussion we might note their convenient juxtaposition in the setting of a very traditional natural history museum. The Milwaukee Public Museum (MPM) can serve as an example of "old style" practices in this museum genre. Founded in 1882, the MPM is a venerable example of the classic combination of natural history exhibitry with ethnographic displays of pre-industrial cultures from around the world. Sequences of diorama alcoves dominate its halls. In the Native American section we find Plains cultures represented in a life-size diorama that uses taxidermy, mannequins, habitat elements, and panoramic background painting to re-create the classic equestrian bison hunt.[5] In a plexiglass vitrine attached to the front of this large exhibit there is a miniature model of bison being stampeded over a cliff.

It is worth pointing out some of the details in these two displays, since they conveniently juxtapose many of the elements that have come to structure the popular representation of Native American bison hunting. The large diorama depicts two hunters riding at a gallop, one on each side of a group of stampeding *Bison bison*. In a three-dimensional replay of Catlin's painting, one hunter has just loosed an arrow into an adult male, while his companion is ready to thrust his spear into an adult female. The balanced composition, in which the two men attack inward from left and right margins of the herd, encompasses two hunting mini-dramas with somewhat different casts of characters. The hunter with the bow is frozen at a moment of serious peril, as the large bull seems about to gore his horse, a fact registered in the latter's raised head and wide-open mouth—markers of fear and pain. The iconography here highlights the scenario of heroic male antagonists locked in a struggle of uncertain outcome. In this form of hunting, success is anything but assured.

The hunter with the lance has already drawn blood on the cow and is about to thrust his weapon again. His reins fly loosely (one appears to have been broken) as his horse plunges at full gallop, and he uses both hands on the lance. Of particular interest is the presence of a yearling calf that, in its panicked flight, is cutting across the path of the beset cow, threatening to topple her disastrously. That we should take this to be her own offspring would conform both to actual bison behavior (a calf from one year stays with the mother until another is born) and to conventions of natural history display, namely, that the juvenile or infant animal "goes with" the female it is close to or touches.

Along with their compositional balance, these two mini-scenarios of the mounted bison hunt complement one another thematically as well. The action is frozen an instant after the use of the weapon in one case and just prior to it in the other. On one side the male animal strikes back at his attacker, while on the other the female seems about to receive a fatal blow and perhaps be tripped up by her own calf. While one can easily overread such displays, there do seem to be contrasted emotional tones in the two encounters of hunter and prey depicted, the one tending toward the heroic (and masculine), the other toward perhaps not the tragic, but at least shaded in the direction of pathos over the likely fate of a female (and mother).

One other element of this diorama should not be missed. In the background panorama painting we see that the three-dimensional animals in the foreground are only the vanguard of a large herd stretching into the distance across the plains. It goes without saying that these two hunters, themselves at great risk in their individual encounters with their quarry, cannot significantly diminish the bison population. The loss of the particular animals that seem in immediate danger here (a symbolic nuclear family perhaps?)[6] will not affect the larger ecology.

The miniature bison jump diorama tells a different natural history tale. Here the ingenuity of the hunting procedure, with its elaborate division of labor and coordination of communal effort, provides the explanatory (and justifying) background to the "shocking" visual drama of large animals tumbling from a precipice. The center of focus is an animal pair, in this case a bull and yearling calf, uncannily suspended in midair halfway down the cliff. Above them the rest of the herd is being prodded to the brink by men waving robes, while below them several animals have hit bottom and are being dispatched by bowmen positioned on overlooking ledges. To one side the human decoy, a man covered in a full bison robe with head attached, crouches just below the cliff brink, having completed his task of drawing the animals into the funnel that dooms them.

If one were to draw up a list of the unspoken rules that govern the "etiquette" of natural history display, it would surely include the dictum that exhibits not stray too far into the grotesque or gruesome, as defined by mainstream popular sensibilities. This being the case, it seems altogether natural that this miniature display should freeze the bison drive just at the beginning of its climax. The wholesale carnage described by contemporary observers of bison jumps is imminent but not yet realized in the model. Only a few animals have gone over the edge, and just three are dead or dying on the ground. How different our reaction would be if we were to see the whole herd stacked at the bottom of the cliff.

As already suggested, I believe the depiction of the bison jump is somewhat problematic for the general popular audience, and perhaps especially for adults concerned about how children will react to such displays. The accompanying label copy serves to cast this hunting practice in culturally "appropriate" terms.[7] The text, entitled "Bison Hunt Afoot," is worth quoting:

> *Before they had horses, villagers ventured onto the Plains on foot to hunt buffalo that supplied food, skins for tent covers, bedding, clothing, and bones and horns to make tools and utensils. In some places the people returned year after year where they had created "buffalo jumps," a corridor of rock piles funneling toward the edge of a cliff. A skilled and very brave man wearing a buffalo hide acted as a decoy, keeping a safe distance but gradually luring the curious buffalo toward the cliff. He dashed to safety as people hiding behind the rock piles jumped up waving hides and shouting to stampede the herd over the cliff. Women waited below, ready to begin skinning the animals and cutting the meat in strips to preserve by sun-drying.*

Beneath the surface of this soberly worded label we may discern several rhetorical moves to make the bison jump "safe" for popular consumption. First, it is presented as a method antecedent to the mounted hunt, and by implication inferior to it, abandoned when the horse became available. One might suggest that the seemingly more elaborate division of labor and relative safety of the hunters, along with the potentially greater yield, makes the buffalo jump (and other forms of communal hunting) at least as "evolved" as the method depicted in the diorama. But that runs counter to the popular perception of the equestrian Plains cultures as the epitome of traditional Indian lifeways.

Second, a heroic hunter is installed in the figure of the decoy, "a skilled and very brave man." The component of individual heroism helps bring communal hunting strategies within a familiar context for the modern popular audience, that is, the context of sport hunting as the unmarked category against which other hunting practices are tacitly evaluated. In this worldview, individual skill, perseverance, and courage are the qualities most associated with "acceptable" hunting. Finally, the label copy offers a list of the uses made of the bison by Plains Indians. Although not stated explicitly, the understood message is that the bison jump, while it might seem indiscriminate and brutal, is understandable in terms of the subsistence needs it met. This is, in other words, an indirect expression of the idea that in these traditional cultures nothing was wasted, there being a use for every part of the animal.

My larger point here is that these exhibits at the Milwaukee Public Museum provide a condensed illustration of how popular understandings of American Indian relations to the environment become both conventionalized and elaborated. In meeting the need both for compelling spectacle and for an "acceptable" historical and ecological narrative, displays such as these select and arrange elements that will connect with public expectations and fall within the limits of mainstream moral sensibilities. In doing so they provide a mechanism for disseminating the reductive image of Native peoples that Krech calls into question. At the same time, however, they reveal that this image is not so simple or static.

An important issue that Krech does not address in much depth in The Ecological Indian is why it should be that mainstream popular culture today embraces the icon so warmly.[8] Only by looking more closely at the structures, elaborations, and variations—that is, the full range of discourse that surrounds this popular image—will we gain better insight into this issue, which seems at least as important as demonstrating that the image is factually flawed. Museum representations of bison hunting provide just one small example of the many places one could go to explore what is actually a very complex discourse. As already implied, the MPM's elaboration of this theme offers a number of rhetorical subtleties worth considering for their ideological significance.

For example, the contrast between heroic individualism and communal cooperation reflected in the pairing of the two hunting strategies replays one of the most abiding themes in America's national mythos. The moral conundrum of how to choose between what seem like equally desirable but also inherently incompatible sets of values has been replayed in many forms and using many symbolic systems since the founding of the republic. That the individualism-versus-communalism dilemma is allegorically present in the MPM's exhibitry should not be surprising. It simply demonstrates yet again how the themes and iconography of popular culture—in this case, the iconography of Indian/bison ecology—provide vehicles through which the culture constantly revisits its abiding concerns. That the two forms of hunting are presented as reflecting a kind of cultural evolution, a hierarchy underscored by the physical dominance of the "higher" form over its supposed precursor, seems to be a subtle argument about how the individualist/communalist dilemma in the larger culture should be decided.

But perhaps that is not the only ideological message encoded in the MPM's bison-hunting display. The mounted hunters are indisputably representative of a heroic male ideal. The violence definitive of their iconic identity is depicted as no threat to the bison population as a whole, but the exhibit chooses to construct their heroic individualism as an assault on the elements of, symbolically speaking, a bison "family."[9] In doing so, what seems to be the overall choice in favor of the individualist ethos is called into question by the implied threat of those values to the putative foundation of social existence (as conceived by the mainstream audience). Through these discursive processes the bison-hunting ensemble at the MPM reenacts the endless project of popular culture—to give the appearance of resolving cultural dilemmas while simultaneously reactivating them.

However we wish to read this museum "text" about bison hunting, I believe that its construction of Indian/bison ecological relations, while feeding off the popular perceptions critiqued in The Ecological Indian, cannot be divorced from a consideration of the larger cultural context that ultimately motivates it. At this level the historical, ethnographic, or ecological accuracy of such exhibits is of less concern than their meanings as cultural texts in the society that produces them. And it is from this perspective that I will consider in conclusion a much more recent museum exhibit that also takes the bison hunt—specifically the bison jump—as its theme. I offer it as a comparative example and to demonstrate how this theme can serve a variety of larger ideological purposes when deployed in the context of public natural history discourse.

In June 2002 the Draper Museum of Natural History opened at the Buffalo Bill Historical Center in Cody, Wyoming. It is one of five units that explore regionally and historically appropriate themes. Not a "comprehensive" natural history museum like the MPM, which depicts ecosystems and cultures from around the world, the Draper takes as its focus the Greater Yellowstone Ecosystem, and especially the human encounter with this nationally significant environment. Unlike more traditional institutions, it is not organized into separate floors, galleries, rooms, and exhibit alcoves. Rather, it offers a continuously spiraling pathway meant to evoke a walk through the biomes one finds in the surrounding region, from high alpine rock down to short grass prairie. And in another departure from traditional arrangements, the exhibit spaces are not completely closed off from one another, so that one gets views from one thematic area into another, and even across the well-like volume of the museum as a whole. Semi-transparent scrims, re-created habitat elements, and partial walls, among other devices, provide the organizing syntax, without disrupting the smooth flow of the visitor's movement along the descending pathway.

Habitat scenes representing the various ecological zones make use of familiar museum techniques (taxidermy specimens, botanical and geological re-creations of environments, explanatory labeling), but newer, more high-tech elements are integrated as well. Small monitors showing brief animal documentaries, multi-screen programs on relevant topics (such as forest fires), piped-in nature sounds, and even subtly dispersed smells at appropriate places (such as the faint pine aroma around a display about forest succession) are some of the newer museological devices. These all mix together to make the Draper both a more fluid and open, and at the same time a more informationally and sensorily dense, natural history experience than the more traditional MPM.

What makes the Draper relevant to the present discussion is that its single most dramatic exhibit, extending from top to bottom down one whole wall of the museum, is a larger-than-life-size (1¼ scale) bronze of bison tumbling over a cliff toward the bottom level of the gallery. In keeping with the overall style of display, according to which the visitor is inserted as much as possible right into (re-created) nature, one can stand and look straight up at the three immense bison frozen in mid-tumble. The drama of the scene is made even more intense by a bank of large windows at the top of the wall against which the somewhat abstractly depicted animals are silhouetted. This is the only place where outside light comes into the museum. The bison jump tableau dominates the whole space, being visible from almost any point along the visitor pathway. That it is purposely so out of scale with everything else, both literally in its physical dimensions and figuratively in its heightened drama, gives it a special symbolic import that invites closer consideration.

For one thing, the centrality of this display in a brand-new museum goes some way toward confirming that the bison jump has achieved iconic status in mainstream culture. One might say it "stands in" for the whole array of pre-industrial subsistence methods once practiced by the indigenous peoples of this region. The details of its rhetoric, as with the MPM bison-hunting exhibits, reveal an interesting discourse that plays throughout the interpretive program of the museum.

Although the displays are quite different in style and interpretive approach, the Draper's bison jump has at least one element in common with the diorama miniature at the MPM. Here is the text from one of its interpretive panels:

> Native Americans hunted bison for thousands of years, developing ingenious methods of bringing down these powerful and dangerous beasts. One very effective technique was the bison jump. A successful hunt required great knowledge of bison and the landscape. Piles of stones placed in two long lines helped guide stampeding bison toward the edge of the cliff. Young men began a hunt by imitating sounds made by a lost bison calf, which drew the bison herd into position. Other members of the hunting party would then circle behind and scare the herd, stampeding it toward the cliff edge.

Depth in time, ingenuity, extensive practical knowledge, and cooperative action are the components that help create a positive tone for this display. Also, that the Plains peoples had many uses for the bison is explained in another panel. The close parallel to the MPM label copy supports a reading of the iconic bison hunt as a trope for "primitive subsistence" in general. It serves well as an emblematic position holder for a generalized popular concept of primitivism in that it combines a visually dramatic image of "barbaric" behavior with the redeeming associations of communal effort, cleverness, efficiency, and a deep understanding of animals and the landscape. In the MPM's American Indian gallery we see this trope juxtaposed to its logical binary counterpart, the (implicitly) more morally and technically evolved equestrian hunting strategy that conforms to mainstream notions of fair play and an ethos of bold individual endeavor. Interestingly, in the Draper Museum the horse-mounted Plains hunter is completely absent. In fact, there is very little direct reference to Native peoples at all, especially in the historical era.[10] There is, however, another activity to which the bison jump is implicitly contrasted. When museum visitors reach the lowest level of the spiral path and approach the bison jump wall, they find that the ultimate destination of the immense, bronze animals suspended overhead is the open pit of a modern archaeological dig. Layers of exposed bison bones project from the precisely dug walls of the excavation, and the paraphernalia of modern anthropological science are laid out as if in use.

A number of striking dislocations are in play here, making this bison jump ensemble an arrestingly incongruous and rather postmodern climax to the Draper's otherwise "realist" presentation of natural history. Both space and time are warped, the former by the larger-than-life bison about to "land" in a human-scaled archaeological dig, the latter by the morphing of premodern subsistence practices into the science that, centuries later, studies their residue. The human actors, both hunter and archaeologist, are entirely absent, with only the results of their respective labors to suggest their existence.

The contrast between two bison-hunting strategies at the MPM is absent here. Instead we have a contrast between "primitive," implicitly prehistoric subsistence technology and the modern scientific technology designed to understand those ancient practices. The latter is presented entirely realistically, with actual tools of the trade (even a hat) scattered around the site and accurate reproductions of the archaeological evidence projecting from convincingly re-created soil. The three falling bison, however, though they tumble down a realistic sandstone cliff, are cast in bronze. Fused together in one chaotic mass, they can only be read as a piece of sculpture, and indeed they are the work of a prominent wildlife artist.[11] This leaking of art into natural history display is particularly interesting.

Among other things, this presentation aestheticizes the practice of driving bison over a cliff. This is not the representation of "real" bison falling, as in the miniature diorama, but a romanticized, visually arresting image of such an event. This helps to locate the practice in the remote, imagined past of primitive cultures—a past figured architecturally by the bright light and blue sky one sees through the high windows. With the ethnographic reality of premodern subsistence safely transformed through art into a bronzed and bloodless monument to an imaginary past existing somewhere "outside," the four-square reality of modern scientific inquiry becomes the ultimate destination of the museum's prescribed pathway. The exhibit overall is about how scientists gather the quantifiable evidence through which we can appropriately "know" primitive subsistence practices, and in this it is of a piece with the rest of the museum's discourse.

Throughout the gallery, one encounters—in addition to representations of habitats and other natural history images—a running commentary on the practices and research questions of concern to modern scholars and scientists. Some of these research issues are also placed in the context of high-profile public policy issues, such as forest fire suppression and wolf reintroduction. The rhetorical red thread that runs through the whole museum is the idea of complexity itself, usually couched in terms of either/or debates about ecological issues and policies. For example, the exhibit on forest fire sets out the opposing views on whether active suppression is a wise ecological strategy. The labels and exhibits are careful not to take sides in such debates, presenting them rather as complex, open questions that, presumably, visitors will have to study further and decide about for themselves.[12]

As the place one ends up after spiraling down through biomes and ecological debates, the bison-jump excavation exhibit can be read as the culminating allegorical expression of the idea that precise science (grids and measuring devices are prominently displayed in the dig) yields the truth about ecological relations. And Plains Indian subsistence, abstracted to an artistic rendering of one highly dramatic form of bison hunting, serves as the allegorical representative of those relations. It works well as an image of "Ur-ecology"—a "before time" of interaction between humans and the environment. The design logic is impeccable. The monumental falling bison give mythic expression, visible throughout the museum, to the idea that humans have always been participants in ecological systems. And placing the excavation beneath them, on the bottom-most level of the gallery, locates modern science as the foundation upon which complex ecological understanding must be built.

In reading such meta-messages at two quite different natural history museums, one sees that the iconography of Indian bison hunting is a flexible tool in the repertoire of popular discourse. It can be activated in various ways to perform cultural work that has more to do with our own modern lifeways than with the world of premodern indigenous peoples. That this is so points us back one last time to Krech's *The Ecological Indian* for a quick look at its rhetorical procedures. One finds there a methodological strategy that, though eminently reasonable and judicious, has something in common with the mythos at work in the Draper.

It is probably inevitable in a scholarly study that sets out to "correct" popular misconceptions, or at least to complicate stock images and conventional ways of thinking, that an implicit opposition is established between what Krech sometimes refers to as "cultural knowledge" or "cultural definition" and scientific truth. He is nothing if not carefully clinical in his marshaling of historical and archaeological evidence. In the bison chapter, for example, he meticulously weighs his data to calculate the best possible estimates of population sizes, use requirements, and hunting yields, erring always on the side of conservatism. While other specialists might dispute his numbers, that he is an admirably careful scholar seems beyond dispute.

It does not diminish the value of this work to recognize, however, that in drawing together and interpreting a wide array of data to show the complexity of Indian/bison ecological relations, Krech largely leaves out of view the complexity of the ecological Indian icon itself as an element of our modern cultural knowledge. This is not unlike the Draper's dramatic aestheticizing of the bison jump in the interest of promoting modern science as the best way to know the ecological world. That the trope of the ecological Indian has been deployed in mainstream popular culture for all sorts of symbolic and ideological purposes—museum depictions of bison hunting being one small example—means that its contemporary discursive complexity deserves as much attention as the historical complexity of American Indian relations to the natural world. That the icon is so tenacious and widespread suggests that it has great cultural utility and resonance. Understanding the ecological Indian's contemporary value as an ideological resource seems to me just as important as questioning its scientific accuracy.

Notes

1. It is perhaps hard for us today to understand the logic that led Hornaday and his companions, after such difficulty in locating a few straggling remnants of the once vast herds, to kill every wild bison they encountered, twenty-five total, all in the interest of "preserving" the species in the form of museum display.

2. Hornaday went on in 1899 to become the first director of the New York Zoological Park (better known as the Bronx Zoo, and now the Wildlife Conservation Park). In this field, too, he made a significant mark, setting early national standards for live animal display (Kisling 2001, 163).

3. This was the method in which the hunter found a hiding spot from which he could kill large numbers of animals without putting the herd to flight. It was standard practice for individual or small-group professional hide hunters.

4. The Boone & Crockett Club, founded in 1887 by Theodore Roosevelt and George Bird Grinnell, undertook to establish and advocate a hunting code based on Euro-American notions of fair play. It took the individualized relationship between hunter and quarry as its standard and excoriated the practices of market hunting. It also disdained some hunting methods, such as driving game into deep snow or onto the ice, that were included in the hunting repertoire of some tribal peoples. The individual hunter on horseback perilously chasing after an individual bison conformed to the "manly" principles enshrined in the code. For the current rules of fair chase, see the dust jacket of Byers and Bettas 1999.

5. This exhibit was installed in 1966.

6. On the ideological underpinnings of natural history animal displays, see Haraway 1989, 26–58, and Wonders 1993, 223–25.

7. Although impressionistic, my direct observation of visitors at this museum suggests that

children are especially fascinated by the bison jump miniature—even more than by the physically dominant diorama of the mounted hunt—and their parents are frequently intent on providing culturally acceptable explanations for why these animals are being killed this way.

8. Krech's discussion (1999, 17–22) of how the ecological Indian fits into the centuries-old Euro-American discourse of Indian nobility is important, but it does not really get beneath the surface to explore how the icon operates in mainstream culture today.

9. Of course, at this level of analysis the fact that bison reproduction is not organized in "nuclear" families is largely beside the point.

10. I should add here that one of the five separate units at the Buffalo Bill Historical Center is the Plains Indian Museum, where the indigenous cultures of the region are explored in depth. Bison hunting per se is not given much attention there, but considerable attention is paid to the spiritual significance of the bison in these cultures.

11. The artist is T. D. Kelsey, and the sculpture is titled *Free Fall*.

12. This rhetorical "either/or-ism" is especially clear in the section that deals with wolf reintroduction. At one point visitors are invited to express their opinions on notepads. The comments are collected, and some of them have been tacked up in a wall display. There is precisely the same number of pro and anti sentiments.

References

Byers, C. Randall, and George A. Bettas, eds. 1999. *Records of North American big game*. 11th ed. Missoula MT: Boone and Crockett Club.

Dances with wolves. 1990. Directed by Kevin Costner. MGM, United Artists.

Haraway, Donna. 1989. Teddy bear patriarchy: Taxidermy in the Garden of Eden, New York City, 1908–36. In *Primate visions: Gender, race, and nature in the world of modern science*, 26–58. New York: Routledge.

Hornaday, William T. 1889 [1886]. The extermination of the American bison, with a sketch of its discovery and life history. *Report of the National Museum* [1889 rpt.], 1886–87:369–548.

Kisling, Vernon N., ed. 2001. *Zoo and aquarium history: Ancient animal collections to zoological gardens*. New York: CRC Press.

Krech, Shepard, III. 1999. *The ecological Indian: Myth and history*. New York: Norton.

Wonders, Karen. 1993. *Habitat dioramas: Illusions of wilderness in museums of natural history*. Figura Nova Series 25. Uppsala: Acta Universitatis Upsaliensis.

8. Ecological and Un-ecological Indians

The (Non)portrayal of Plains Indians
in the Buffalo Commons Literature

Sebastian F. Braun

A definition of others, or an essentialization, in general either paints a positive or a negative picture; but in either case, the picture painted is only a mirror reflection of the painter. In *The Ecological Indian: Myth and History*, Shepard Krech (1999) shows how this holds true for the ways in which diverse interest groups depict North American Indians and their relations to the environment.

While Krech looks at the relations of American Indians to buffalo from a primarily historical perspective, in this chapter I take a look at how myths and histories are still evident in today's discussions on the future of the Great Plains. For that purpose, I discuss some tendencies of how the buffalo commons debate, understood in a broad sense, sees Indian relations to buffalo.[1] I also look at recent historical revisions of the slaughter of the buffalo, which are backing up various viewpoints of the debate. Because buffalo historically were of significant cultural importance on the Great Plains and have become a symbol of contemporary relations to the environment, this reveals much about perspectives on the connection between Plains Indians and the environment in general.

Most plains reservations began to build small herds in the early 1970s, and the buffalo commons proposal (D. E. Popper and Popper 1987) and the subsequent social, ecological, and political debates have had little direct impact on tribes' decisions to bring back buffalo to their reservations. However, as the discussion helps to form the public opinion on buffalo, which in turn influences the political and legal landscapes, it has had and continues to have an indirect but nonetheless important impact on Plains Indians' tribal buffalo herds.

I use a variety of sources in my initial discussion and then draw from my fieldwork on Cheyenne River Sioux Reservation to give an example of contemporary relations between Indians and buffalo.[2] I begin with a look at three popular books: Ernest Callenbach's *Bring Back the Buffalo!* (1996), Richard Manning's *Grassland* (1995), and Andrew Isenberg's *The Destruction of the Bison* (2000).

Myth and History

The implicit motto of the buffalo, Callenbach says, "rings with a determination we remember well from our history: Live Free or Die!" (1996, 10). His argumentation is strongly based on the presentation of buffalo as "quintessentially American animals: stalwart, noble symbols of wildness, freedom, and self-sufficiency" (9) or as "a memorable symbol of fierce American pride in survival with freedom" (2).

Taking Turner's frontier thesis one step further, Callenbach does not even need Indians as marginal agents to form American values. The buffalo have become the anthropomorphic image of the noble savage: shaggy, wild, unpredictable, yet powerful enough to deserve respect, and naturally skilled in surviving. Implicit in this is a transformation of the ecological Indian to the ecological buffalo and finally, if they listen, the ecological American. Implicitly, at least, the buffalo are, and have always been, Americans; they have always lived the American ideal, and as such they have anticipated the American existence. Buffalo, then, are, if not mythical ancestors, at least mythical models.

Interestingly enough, Callenbach's view of the relation of buffalo with Americans is structurally not too different from Plains Indian perspectives on social relations between buffalo and mankind. Callenbach mentions that buffalo are seen as a model for Lakota culture (1996, 65), but in order to find a moral reason why Americans should protect them, he transforms the buffalo from a central symbol of Plains Indian culture to the symbolic representation of mythical American virtues. As the Plains Indians' experience would directly contradict these American virtues, this transformation can only be accomplished if the Indian symbolism is no longer valid. As Raymond Craib puts it, "Imperial history assigns meaning retrospectively and from without, rejecting context, locality, and specificity" (2000, 10). This is what happened, and happens, on the plains.

Manning, whose main argument is more historical than Callenbach's, much like Krech (1999, 29–43), starts his book at the beginning: with a look at the "blitzkrieg" theory of the prehistoric extinction of megafauna. He does not weigh the arguments too much, however; although he acknowledges that there might be some problems with the theory, he thinks that "even if overkill is not the sole factor at work in the wave of extinctions, it seems to be an idea we need just now. It is humbling. It is frightening in its implications for our ignorant application of power. It expands our notion of history" (1995, 60).

Manning uses the same notion of history—namely, that its primary purpose is to serve as a cautionary model for contemporary society—when he looks at the historical slaughter of the buffalo. He argues against Indian involvement in the near extinction, but astonishingly enough, culture had nothing to do with it. "Probably, we can leave rules, motive, ethic, and religion out of this argument. The bison and the plains tribes coexisted through the millennia simply because killing all the bison would have been an enormous effort and there was no reason to do so" (1995, 82). In view of his argumentation on the "blitzkrieg" theory, it is remarkable that Manning thinks that Plains Indians had no hand in the slaughter because "there was simply no point in doing so" (83). There were not enough people: "There were likely a hundred buffalo to every plains Indian. How big of a dent could the Indians make?" (82). How big of a dent, then, could the prehistoric cultures have made?

Plains Indian culture has to be left out of the equation, Manning says, because we cannot understand it. To do so, we "would have to account for motive and ethic wrapped deeply in a people who are willing to drag bison skulls attached to slits in their muscles by leather thongs. An answer would be somehow wrapped in the Sun Dance, and the understanding of this is lost to literate and literal Western minds" (1995, 81–82). Of course, the Sun Dance is not about dragging bison skulls, and Plains Indians, who are not more illiterate than Euro-Americans and have not been so for a long time, seem to understand the ceremony of the Sun Dance perfectly. In his effort to underline that we are too far removed from nature to understand a truly "ecological" culture, Manning goes beyond that and paints Indians as "primitive" in the true sense of the word: directly related to nature.

Isenberg, like Manning, takes the Native American experience as a cautionary model for his own society. Although he rests his case on historic Plains societies, arguing for their involvement in the slaughter of the buffalo, his message is very similar: "If the fate of the nomads offers a lesson to other societies that share those predicaments, it is to understand both the futility of riches and the fragility of nature" (2000, 122). Plains Indians are to blame just as much as the white hunters, Isenberg says, because "both Indians and Europeans had the opportunity to regulate commercial hunters and . . . declined to do so" (197). They have none but themselves to blame for their situation, or maybe an anonymous nature. "The poverty and misery that followed in the wake of the nomads' decimation of the herds," he says, "were unique to the ecological disaster that befell them" (122).

Isenberg points out that the sin of those painting ecological Indians is to fail to contextualize Indian and Euro-American relations to the buffalo (2000, 196, 197). Following his own agenda, however, he in turn does not contextualize relations between Indians and Euro-Americans, which makes him ignore any notions of distribution of power, and ultimately any notion of cultural difference. He acknowledges that "there were significant differences" between Indian and Euro-American societies, but says that they are "too obvious and lengthy to enumerate." In the final analysis, the differences are meaningless anyway, because they "must have seemed trivial to the bison" (197).

In order to make their differing arguments, Callenbach, Manning, and Isenberg draw on but ignore Plains Indian cultures. Imperial history, it seems, has reached its high point: by "rejecting context, locality and specificity," the Native peoples, by way of their cultures, have also been rejected and written off the page—and the land.

Land

Toward the end of Richard Wheeler's (1998) novel *The Buffalo Commons*, the private foundation that proposes and tries to create a buffalo commons runs into problems, because it cannot pay the taxes on the land. From the way the book is structured, there could be no question in my mind as to the solution to this problem. The foundation would turn the land over to Plains Indians, who would transform it into trust land, and the project would prosper. Even for a novel, that was a bit too naive an assumption. But that this solution is not even mentioned opened my eyes to the land aspect of the buffalo commons.

In the article that started the whole buffalo commons proposal, Deborah and Frank Popper say, "There may also be competing uses for the land. In South Dakota, several Sioux tribes are now bringing suit for 11,000 square miles, including much of the Black Hills. The federal government might settle these claims and other longstanding Plains Indian land claims by giving or selling the tribes chunks of the new commons" (1987, 18). The Poppers later revisit the idea in a much more general way: "Indian areas are the only parts of deep-rural Plains where populations are consistently growing. The Buffalo Commons, by contrast, amounts to an ongoing white agricultural pullback. . . . As a result, it could eventually lead to a settlement of long-standing Indian land claims" (1994, 97). Callenbach also acknowledges that, "From the Indian perspective," the land that, under the buffalo commons proposal, is not suitable for agriculture or ranching should be returned to the tribes, to restore the original reservations (1996, 82). As with the Poppers, however, this is a sideline in his argument for the establishment of a buffalo commons. In his response to a *Rocky Mountain News* editorial, Vine Deloria Jr. (1991) points out that the Poppers "could care less whether it is Indians or Neil Bush who lives on this land."

Frank Popper has become one of the board members of the so-called Million Acre Project, an attempt to realize the buffalo commons idea on a private-property basis, that has received endorsement from the Rosebud Reservation (NABJ 2001). But what this means is that Rosebud would convert itself into buffalo pasture, not that the future buffalo commons will be converted to tribal lands.

If the settlers are gone, why not give the land back? Once land gets turned into buffalo commons, why not at least give those lands that lie, for example, in the boundaries of the Great Sioux Reservation of 1868 back to the Lakotas? For various political and economic reasons, returning ranchland to the reservations is not a very popular proposal in local, state, or federal governments. Neither, to get back to Wheeler's novel, is it popular for environmental interest groups, who would, in the long run, lose their influence over the land. As Krech (1999, 219–26) shows, tribes, sometimes under economic and political pressure, do not always behave ecologically in the view of the interested beholders who forge the standards for such behavior. In their view, tribal ecological policies need some controls. Licht (1994, 34; 1997, 168) proposes a joint administration of a South Dakota Badlands buffalo reserve by the U.S. government and the Pine Ridge Reservation.

The argument of the buffalo commons is not one for a restoration of reservation sovereignty—not even ecological sovereignty over the fate of land and animals that indigenous peoples are connected to spiritually. The main argument of the buffalo commons is for the restoration of buffalo onto regions of the Great Plains whose post-conquest culture and society remains basically untouched. The proposal sometimes seems to be a continuation of George Catlin's vision of a national park where buffalo and Lakotas would live together, both adored in their wildness by benevolent tourists— "A nation's Park, containing man and beast, in all the wild and freshness of their nature's beauty!" (1989, 263).

Authenticity

Implicit in much of the logic of both positive and negative arguments about the ecological Indian and the buffalo commons is that if Western people speak with the voice of the land, they have become "indigenous" in the sense that they have now become the real stewards of the land. And as its stewards, they claim its ownership.

It is this relation to the quest for authenticity, and with it political agendas, that gives the debate about ecological Indians its contemporary impact. As can be seen by responses to Krech's book, this is not just an academic discussion. Rather, the academic debate was appropriated long ago by interest groups that use it to pursue political power. In turn, the public debate introduces the division between ecological and non-ecological Indians into the academic debate. In other words, while Krech (1999) writes about "myth and history," and I think "history" here stands for something like academic truth, his audience, just like Callenbach, Manning, and Isenberg, is mostly interested in mythical history and reads him like that. "Truth," as Paul Veyne says, "is the thin layer of gregarious self-satisfaction that separates us from the will to power" (1988, 128).

Anne Matthews describes how ranchers quote Black Elk to evoke their own connection to the land against the buffalo commons (1992, 52). After having lived on the land for five generations, ranchers on the plains have built their own connection with the land, a connection, however, that is not taken as authentic by the people who now arrive from the outside and want to tell them how they should treat the land. The ranchers who see themselves as stewards of Black Elk's land actually might feel much the same connection as Ruth Rudner, who asks herself, more or less rhetorically, if that is actually possible: "Sometimes I wonder if my longing for buffalo is not a longing for spirituality, a connection literally embedded in the earth from whence the buffalo came. Then I have to wonder if this is what the ranchers feel—a deep connection to their land—when they perceive threats to their way of life. Are they talking about a connection with the land? If that is true, how can they not support the Indian connection to the land and all it includes?" (2000, 77). The question at hand obviously regards what "the Indian connection to the land" is and what it includes. If the more fundamental question, whether there is anything like "the Indian"—or "the rancher," for that matter—is left aside for now, this is a debate about interpretation:

Who has the right to interpret another culture and thence gain authenticity for one's case?

By virtue of their connection to the land, many people on the plains see themselves in the role of defenders of the land, and of the values of the land, against the government. Not only Sagebrush Rebels contended that the farmers and ranchers of the Great Plains are the "New Indians" (Limerick 1987, 47, 48, 158). In a society that equates authenticity with historic age, it is only normal that both sides to the argument try to use the earliest historic records to provide themselves with authenticity. What is at least ironic, of course, is that the people they are forced to use as their mythical ancestors are the very same people their real ancestors drove off the land, and the very same people to whose real descendants they deny access to the land they thus claim. The identification with Indians comes from a perception of being treated unfairly (Wagoner 2002, 53), but this does not necessarily mean that the "New Indians" will treat Indians more fairly. In the political debates these arguments are used for, Indian nations have been almost invisible, not so much acknowledged as replaced by the "New Indians." As William Carlos Williams says: "The land! don't you feel it? Doesn't it make you want to go out and lift dead Indians tenderly from their graves, to steal from them—as if it must be clinging to their corpses—some authenticity[?]" (1966, 74). Authenticity not only for land ownership but also for the ways people want to treat the land on the Great Plains seems to come increasingly from lifting supposed Indian symbolism from its supposed graves and turning it into American ideals.

The problem for both sides, then, is that the Plains Indian nations are alive here and now, and as such, if they chose or were allowed to have voices, they could intervene with that supposed authenticity. What is missing—and logically has to be missing—in the interpretation are the voices of those who are being interpreted. It is for this reason that we end up with absentee ecological Indians, even if the authors present Native voices; those do not speak for themselves, cannot be allowed to speak for themselves, but are a part of the legitimizing process, lending authenticity. What is missing are the Native people and people trying to listen to them; what is not missing are people trying to speak for them.

Divisions

Ecological (and un-ecological) Indians or their values, as professed by whites, abound in the buffalo commons literature. "Western peoples," Callenbach writes, consider themselves to be apart from nature and display "biophobia" (1996, 145, 146); non-Western peoples by implication consider themselves to be a part of nature and are "ecological." I have already shown Manning's attempt to divide the non-literal minds of Natives from literal minds of the "West" (1995, 82). Wheeler uses a fictive Northern Cheyenne character, fittingly named John Trouble, to show the impact the buffalo commons proposal supposedly has on Plains Indians. He is a cattle rancher, and the appearance of wolves strikes something in him, maybe an innate ecological factor, that makes him long to know more about his people's traditions. In his last scene, apparently unable to reconcile his urges for a traditional connection to nature with his longing for modern commodities, "Trouble left the Keeper of the Hat and drove through a mysterious night, his soul more unsettled than ever" (Wheeler 1998, 387).

Much of the buffalo commons literature seems to make this fundamental division: Indians, because they are "ecological," are for buffalo; Euro-Americans, because they are technologically contaminated, are for cattle. I actually read Krech (1999) as an attempt to show how this division is not only useless but also senseless. This pertains to both white and Indian approaches to buffalo ranching.

While one of the main goals of buffalo commons supporters is to restore the plains ecosystem (Licht 1994, 1997; Callenbach 1996), this was not a main goal of the original plans to build a "buffalo industry." In fact, restoration was "a concept specifically opposed" by many arguing for a return of the buffalo for economic reasons (Scott 1998, 362). Almost from its beginning, the buffalo industry has been split into two camps with different management philosophies. There are those ranchers who try to keep their buffalo as "wild" as possible, and there are those who treat them as they are used to treating cattle. Often, the difference is reduced to the commercial product, as in "grassfed" versus "feedlot" meat, but it extends to questions of weaning, vaccines, electrical prods, and dehorning.

Tribal Approaches

At their inception, most tribal buffalo projects did not want to be a part of the commercial buffalo "industry." Buffalo herds were seen as a way to restore both cultural and ecological environments (Fox, Knowles, and Mitchell 1998, 220). Many tribes saw buffalo programs as a way to restore not only the ecosystem but also, in a holistic understanding of the concept, aspects of the traditional culture, from respect and responsibility to health issues. Revenues from tourism and meat sales were part of the expectations, but the projects were not primarily economic in their goals. One of the goals was certainly the building of a sustainable tribal economy based on buffalo products, but production of meat for export was largely a secondary concern. Buffalo were to be treated with respect, and they were seen as traditional teachers, used, for example, in addiction therapy. This approach put the tribal buffalo operations in some contrast to the industry as a whole (DuBray 1993).

As Manning briefly shows, however, ideological differences cut through any cultural and supposed "racial" boundaries, and for various reasons not all Indian people are in favor of returning buffalo to their reservations (1995, 243). More than a century of direct and indirect replacement of the values of Native cultures with the values of the dominant society did not go by without impact on reservations. The cattle culture has replaced the buffalo culture on all reservations on the Great Plains (see Iverson 1994), and outside cattle (i.e., cattle owned by off-reservation interests but grazing on leased reservation lands) have become one of the main avenues of income. "Many Indians have no respect for cattle and believe eating them makes you weak," says Callenbach (1996, 74). This might have been true at the beginning of the reservation period; today, however, many Lakota tell me that they prefer beef over buffalo meat, because buffalo is too lean and they like the fattier beef.

While many cattle ranchers—both on- and off-reservation—initially saw the buffalo herds as an exotic experiment, now that the buffalo projects on many reservations are outgrowing their initial pastures they have begun to compete for land and income. Many Indian ranchers see the buffalo as uneconomical animals that prevent the land from being leased to outside cattle, and they oppose the buffalo projects directly and indirectly. Tribal buffalo herds are also proving that their approaches are economically and culturally viable, and they attract the interest of political leaders. On reservations with tribal administrations that are more "progressive," buffalo programs that emphasize more traditional values and work for self-sufficiency and cultural revival are seen as a hindrance to achieving the full economic potential of the reservation. Fred DuBray, founder of Pte Hca Ka on Cheyenne River and co-founder of the InterTribal Bison Cooperative, sees the buffalo operations as a way to "heal that conflict" between traditional and progressive people (qtd. in Porterfield 1995). Having buffalo seems to be one point on which both can agree. Conflicts arise, however, over the directions of buffalo operations.

Buffalo Directions

On Cheyenne River, Pte Hca Ka was conceptualized as a nonprofit project. Its goal was to work for all the people and for the buffalo and to avoid becoming entangled in tribal politics. Buffalo management, as several people told me, was to leave buffalo alone as much as possible in order to keep them wild. Only in their wild state could they recover and live their own culture and, in the process help the Lakotas recover their place in the cosmos. A utilitarian management would have contradicted the goal to treat buffalo with respect, as relatives and teachers.

Over the years it became clear that Pte Hca Ka needed more rangeland for its expanding herd, and in 1999, with the help of a philanthropist, the corporation bought fee land from a grazing corporation. This land, besides providing grazing for the buffalo, was to be turned into a tribal park and research center. From the beginning, however, the land caught the attention of cattle ranchers, some of whom lobbied the tribal council to take hold of it and make it available for leasing to outside cattle. Although the overgrazed land was rested for a few years to restore its ecological value, pressure mounted to lease it out in order to create profits. The land and future park also attracted interest from some council members, perhaps because, as some people said, they wanted to take political credit for it. The tribal administration told Pte Hca Ka not to apply for outside grants or rely on the help of philanthropists, but to run the operation as a self-sufficient business. This proved to be impossible, mostly because the corporation had had to go into debt to acquire the land. It became clear that the land could not be paid off and that, without the help of the tribe, the project would have to declare bankruptcy.

The perceptions of the corporation had changed over time. Many people, perhaps not realizing that the program was still growing, felt it was time for Pte Hca Ka to provide more money and jobs for the tribe. In the beginning, all the communities had been given one buffalo per year for ceremonies or feasts. When some communities, preferring beef over buffalo, tried to get the cash value of the buffalo instead, this system was changed to one in which Pte Hca Ka gave money to the tribe for distribution to the communities. The original intent then became forgotten, and some members of the tribe, interested more in economic than cultural returns, began to ask for higher profits from the buffalo operation.

Finally, in the fall of 2001, the tribal administration took direct control of Pte Hca Ka and closed it down. There were allegations of ineffective management; however, nobody from the tribe had come out and spoken to the people running the buffalo operation prior to deciding to close it down. Everybody wanted to keep the newly acquired land, but the tribe had no monies allocated to pay for it. Thus the sale of some or all of the buffalo was considered to pay off the debt, but the buffalo market was too low. Somebody had to care of the buffalo, and in the spring of 2002 the tribe reopened the program, now under the tribal Game, Fish and Parks Department and almost entirely focusing on its development as a business. While the operation had previously been a model for the ecologically and culturally correct treatment of buffalo, it now modeled itself on the ranches that are focusing on the economic success of the meat market.

This also means that the traditional ecological knowledge of the buffalo and the grasslands has largely been replaced with the ecological knowledge of the cattle culture and the professional knowledge of biologists and economists. The buffalo are kept primarily as a business venture, including tourism and hunting. As Howard Harrod says, "In both these instances the living animals and their 'wild' contexts are portrayed through a cultural symbolism that renders animals as cultural artifacts, useful for human aesthetic or recreational needs. Such animals become 'stock' to be managed within the parks" (2000, xxiii).

Ecological Indians

The events at Pte Hca Ka are not unique. Other buffalo projects are facing similar pressures from their tribal administrations to deliver profits (e.g., Kozlowicz 2001). Such pressures are understandable if one takes into account the dire economic situations of plains reservations. All sides involved genuinely want to help their reservations, which are, after all, really not ecological refuges but places where people need to live with dignity (McCool 2000). "People can be influenced," Bateson says, "of course, by economic theories or by economic fallacies—or by hunger—but they cannot possibly be influenced by 'economics.' 'Economics' is a class of explanations, not itself an explanation of anything" (1958, 281). The same goes for "ecology," especially in cases where people are, indeed, influenced by hunger, poverty, oppression, and a number of other concrete phenomena. This, however, does not mean that the differences of opinion do not exist and that there is not a definite distribution of power that favors some over others.

I would like to emphasize that I am not saying that the new management of Pte Hca Ka is less ecological than the old one. In fact, former director Fred DuBray told me that he sees what happened as a necessary cycle; while it was important to stress cultural connections, now that the herd has reached about twenty-five hundred animals it is equally important to focus on business development. I have used the story of Pte Hca Ka to make the point that labels such as "ecological" cannot be used as absolutes, because they are always relative to the concrete phenomena people have to live in.

And what could be more ecological than taking the total environment into account? In the end, what perhaps makes many American Indians ecological, along with many other societies that have not become alienated from their environment, is that they still know that living means to compromise, and that absolutes will not get people anywhere.

In a *Chicago Tribune* article on Pte Hca Ka (Graham 2002), Stephen Torbit, director of the National Wildlife Federation's Rocky Mountain Natural Resource Center, says that Indians are "the only group that over all these years has remembered these are animals that should be respected, and allowed to roam wild and free." Contrast this with the much more realistic opinion of Roger Lawrence, then Pte Hca Ka herd manager, in the same article: "Many of the tribe's members farm cattle and will accept the buffalo only if they're enclosed by barbed wire fences and kept away from the range land where the cattle feed."

Cultural absolutes do not only influence outsiders' views on reservation culture when it comes to buffalo. In 2001 the International Society for the Protection of Mustangs and Burros (ISPMB) brought wild horses to Cheyenne River, to give them a refuge on the buffalo pasture and future Sioux National Park. Much as proponents of the buffalo commons use the traditional relationship between Plains Indians and buffalo, though perhaps with less justification, the ISPMB tries to make the case that wild horses are an essential part of traditional Lakota culture. In an interview on the *Native America Calling* radio program on November 1, 2001, ISPMB director Karen Sussman talked about the need to restore this "wonderful nobility" and the "oneness . . . of a Native American on a horse." Dennis Rousseau, director of the tribal Game, Fish and Parks Department, on the other hand, made the point that the horses have always been present on the reservation, where they are used on ranches. In fact, Cheyenne River is known all over the West for its cowboys and rodeo riders. Horses play a huge part in the culture, but quite a few people told me that a wild horse is a waste: it needs to be trained. Reality is always a bit more complex than the romanticized notions we have of how others should behave and think.

Many Plains Indians do feel a closeness to buffalo; many do not. I happen to agree with the people who work for buffalo programs as holistic restoration projects, not primarily economic enterprises, because I think the path to healing and sovereignty has to follow cultural appropriateness and self-sufficiency. I also understand, however, that reservations are in dire need of an influx of resources. If we depict Native societies as unified on this and other matters and do not try to understand different viewpoints, we strip them—and ourselves—of an important aspect of their complex reality. In fact, we strip them of their humanity. Depicting Native peoples as ecological Indians freezes them in an invented ethnographic present that has passed long ago.

Conclusions

It is relevant and helpful to look at how cultures deal with their environments; I do not think it is relevant or helpful at all to classify cultures as ecological or non-ecological. One way, we create the expectation for Native peoples to be purely ecological even when they have to fight for economic survival. The other way, we are blaming them for putting economy before ecology when they are just following the dominant society's lead.

In the quest for empowerment and visibility, cultural differences between Plains Indians and Euro-Americans, especially those that are regarded as positive by the public, have to be emphasized. It is normal that a culture that has been oppressed by the very same society that is appropriating its values, ceremonies, and history needs an unassailable backrest from which it can try to regroup in order to save itself. Difference is one of the essential ingredients of identity, and the stronger the attacks on this identity, the stronger the rootedness of the identity, and the difference, needs to be. Presenting oneself as ecological can be a valid and useful strategy.

However, the strategy of the ecological Indian as used in most of the buffalo commons debates—and, I would argue, in most other places—is not one used by or for Native peoples. Using other cultures as models for one's own might work if these cultures are political equals or outside one's own sphere of domination, but contemporary America is not La Hontan's France.

Painted to be ecological or non-ecological, Native cultures are used as a tool to reach political goals that are often directed squarely against their interests. Native cultures are only needed to provide moral authenticity, and it is an authenticity that, as Krech (1999) shows, has been reinterpreted according to the needs and wants of the dominant and often colonial society.

Notes

Thanks to Raymond J. DeMallie, Candice Lowe, and Ann Reed for their kind editorial suggestions. All mistakes are mine.

1. The buffalo commons debate stems from the proposal of the same name by Deborah and Frank Popper (1987). They argued for a return of the plains from mostly irrigated agriculture and cattle ranching to an unfenced commons area featuring wild buffalo herds. While the proposal did not call for the abandonment of all settlements, but envisioned opportunities for ecotourism and wind energy, local people on the plains did not appreciate what they perceived as a condemnation of their lifestyle and their future. Reality over the past fifteen years has shown that plains communities are adapting to the Poppers' predictions, which have come true to a large extent, especially in rural areas. Communities are not always reacting as the Poppers had envisioned them to do, however.

2. I wish to thank the people on Cheyenne River for their hospitality and friendship, the Swiss National Fund for Science for funding my fieldwork, and the David C. Skomp Foundation for predissertation grants.

References

Bateson, Gregory. 1958. *Naven*. Stanford: Stanford University Press.

Callenbach, Ernest. 1996. *Bring back the buffalo! A sustainable future for America's Great Plains*. Berkeley: University of California Press.

Catlin, George. 1989. *North American Indians*. Ed. Peter Mathiessen. New York: Penguin.

Craib, Raymond B. 2000. Cartography and power in the conquest and creation of New Spain. *Latin American Research Review* 35 (1): 7–36.

Deloria, Vine, Jr. 1991. "Buffalo commons" misunderstood. *Rocky Mountain News*, May 4.

DuBray, Fred. 1993. Ethno-ecological considerations in bison management. In *Proceedings of the North American Public Bison Herds Symposium, July 27–29, 1993, Lacrosse WI*, ed. R. E. Walker, 392–98. Custer SD: Custer State Park Press.

Fox, Mike, Craig J. Knowles, and Carl D. Mitchell. 1998. Bison management by the Gros Ventre and Assiniboine tribes. Fort Belknap Indian Reservation, Montana. In *International symposium on bison ecology and management in North America*, ed. L. Irby and J. Knight, 214–20. Bozeman: Montana State University.

Graham, Judith. 2002. For tribes, bringing back buffalo a labor of love. *Chicago Tribune*, November 3.

Harrod, Howard L. 2000. *The animals came dancing: Native American sacred ecology and animal kinship*. Tucson: University of Arizona Press.

Isenberg, Andrew C. 2000. *The destruction of the bison*. Cambridge: Cambridge University Press.

Iverson, Peter. 1994. *When Indians became cowboys: Native peoples and cattle ranching in the American West*. Norman: University of Oklahoma Press.

Kozlowicz, John. 2001. Bison to stay: Legislators reconsider shutting down Muscoda farm. *Hocak Worak*, July 10.

Krech, Shepard, III. 1999. *The ecological Indian: Myth and history*. New York: Norton.

Licht, Daniel S. 1994. The Great Plains: America's best chance for ecosystem restoration, part 2. *Wild Earth* Fall:31–35.

———. 1997. *Ecology and economics of the Great Plains*. Lincoln: University of Nebraska Press.

Limerick, Patricia N. 1987. *The legacy of conquest: The unbroken past of the American West*. New York: Norton.

Manning, Richard. 1995. *Grassland: The history, biology, politics, and promise of the American prairie*. New York: Penguin.

McCool, Daniel. 2000. Indian reservations: Environmental refuge or homelands? *High Country News* 32 (7): 10.

Matthews, Anne. 1992. *Where the buffalo roam: The storm over the revolutionary plan to restore America's Great Plains*. New York: Grove Weidenfeld.

NABJ. 2001. Tribe endorses effort to bring back buffalo. *North American Bison Journal*, September, 19.

Popper, Deborah E., and Frank J. Popper. 1987. The Great Plains: From dust to dust. *Planning*, December, 12–18.

Popper, Frank J., and Deborah E. Popper. 1994. Great Plains: Checkered past, hopeful future. *Forum for Applied Research and Public Policy* 9 (4): 89–100.

Porterfield, K. Marie. 1995. Bison herds thrive as tribes build heritage. *Indian Country Today*, November 9.

Rocky Mountain News. 1991. "Buffalo commons": Romantic fantasy from the east. April 18.

Rudner, Ruth. 2000. *A chorus of buffalo: Reflections on wildlife politics and an American icon*. Short Hills NJ: Burford Books.

Scott, Robert B. 1998. Wild bison restoration: The suitability of Montana's Big Open. In *International symposium on bison ecology and management in North America*, ed. L. Irby and J. Knight, 360–73. Bozeman: Montana State University.

Veyne, Paul. 1988. *Did the Greeks believe in their myths? An essay on constitutive imagination*. Chicago: University of Chicago Press.

Wagoner, Paula L. 2002. *"They treated us just like Indians": The worlds of Bennett County, South Dakota*. Lincoln: University of Nebraska Press.

Wheeler, Richard S. 1998. *The buffalo commons*. New York: Forge.

Williams, Carlos William. 1966. *In the American grain*. London: MacGibbon & Kee.

Traditional Ecological Knowledge

9. Swallowing Wealth

Northwest Coast Beliefs
and Ecological Practices

Michael E. Harkin

Shepard Krech's book *The Ecological Indian: Myth and History* (1999) created a stir in American academic and cultural circles. Its thesis—that North American Indians had, at various points in the past and in various places, despoiled the environment, driven game species to extinction, and generally made a mess of things, which was ameliorated only by their small numbers—was designed to create controversy, as indeed it did. By countering the hegemonic and "politically correct" notion of American Indians as environmental stewards, Krech's book was a rare scholarly work to be reviewed and discussed widely in the mass media. This phenomenon must be read against the backdrop of late-1990s American political ideology, for it is there—rather than in its substantive contribution to scholarly debates—that the book's real significance lies.

One of the few political issues during the second Clinton administration upon which there was general consensus, at least among the class of people who expressed opinion on public matters, was environmentalism. The paradigm of "paternalism," as Gisli Palsson (1996) calls it, dominated discussion in both major political parties. Nature must be "protected," primarily from an inherently "polluting" civilization, of which the protectors were themselves fully participating, if conflicted, members. The paradox of the dual role played by most high-consuming environmentalists is epitomized by the major consumer trend of the late 1990s: the increasing popularity of the suv, designed precisely to give access of a direct and damaging sort to national forests, parks, wilderness areas, and the like. The desire to obtain such access was reflected in endless media advertisements. Although most owners, at least in the eastern United States, rarely if ever used such vehicles for these purposes, in parts of the West owners of suvs and other all-terrain vehicles (snowmobiles, motorcycles, and four-wheel ATVs) did significant damage to fragile ecosystems by opening new roads in the wilderness, helping to spread invasive species, flattening shoots of delicate alpine flora, and disrupting wildlife breeding and feeding patterns. However, these people, far from identifying themselves with a counter-environmentalist subculture, professed a love for nature and stressed a Muirian communing with nature as the goal of such excursions. Many advertisements in this period reflected, accurately, the paradoxical desire to experience nature unmediated but within the framework of a high-producing and high-consuming lifestyle, on weekends and holidays. Whether or not suvs were used for these purposes, their high fuel consumption and poor emission controls meant they represented a large environmental burden even when used solely to commute in the "suburban" landscape of middle-class America.

This can all be read as a particularly poignant contradiction in the social formation of postmodern capitalism, where "lifestyle" choices become so central to identity and are fueled by such a high level of prosperity that ecological paradox can be experienced at the level of the individual rather than, as in modernism, the system. That is, no longer are factories (mostly empty, in any case, or so "high tech" that whatever pollution they do produce is effectively exported to third-world production plants, as with microchips, or to areas well hidden from the middle-class gaze) the main culprit in environmental degradation; rather, it is the consumer who wishes to "consume," among other things, a pristine natural ecosystem.

Against such a backdrop, the controversy over the "ecological Indian" can be read as a proxy for the paradox of postmodern consumerist society and its attendant guilt feelings. The ecological Indian represents an inversion of modern society in both moral and aesthetic terms, the most recent entry in the long history of Rousseau's "natural man" and Dryden's "noble savage" (which themselves played upon the imagery of churchmen such as Savonarola and Las Casas). Such a symbolic vehicle allows one to posit the existence of a species of humanity that is not at war with nature, and thus the possibility to escape the ecological degradation of contemporary society. (The notion that "we can learn from them" and thereby improve ourselves has a long pedigree in both religious and secular writing and practice.) By contrast, Krech's notion of the non-ecological Indian is openly threatening, not only because it overturns this comfortable utopia (much more comfortable than technological utopias that lead out of ecological crisis into something much more frightening) but also because it suggests that individuals or very small groups of people are capable of effecting irreversible damage on the environment simply by exercising apparently rational choice. To the SUV-driving, new-computer-purchasing public that also supports environmental political positions, this is the real nightmare.

Optimal foraging theory posits a utilitarian motivation and calculus to hunter-gatherer decisions when considered in aggregate (Ingold 1996). Individual decisions may constitute an effective maximizing strategy in terms of energy expenditure and return. Thus, an effective and efficient strategy of resource procurement is adaptively superior and becomes the cultural norm. However, one of several contradictions in such a model is that individually maximizing practices taken together may contribute to a "tragedy of the commons" rather than to a sustainable mode of subsistence (Hardin 1968; McKay and Acheson 1987). Thus, subarctic hunters might follow an "interstitial" tracking pattern and so maximize their take, but in doing so they might contribute to the long-term depletion of game species populations (Ingold 1996; Winterhalder 1981). Many, perhaps most, biologists working in this area assume such aboriginal overkill to be the case (Diamond 1997; Kay 1998).[1]

By the same token, cost-benefit calculations might have persuaded many Americans to purchase SUVs. According to some analyses, these vehicles are safer for their drivers and passengers but geometrically more dangerous to traditional cars with whom they collide. Taken together with the passive environmental load of such vehicles, they represent the apotheosis of "tragedy of the commons" decision making.

"Ecological Indians" have been widely assumed, by the public as well as many non-biologist scholars, to forego such rational calculus in favor of a mystical attachment to nature (see Martin 1978). Thus the inversion is complete; not merely at the level of behavior but at the level of cognition itself, Indians were thought to present a counterpoint to Western practical reason (Nadasdy 2005; see Sahlins 1976). This view is held with such vehemence that authors such as Diamond and Krech who question it are held to be "racist," despite their assertion of the anthropologically orthodox (and thus counter-racist) position of psychological universalism. That is, by attributing to them a more or less panhuman tendency to despoil Eden, these authors are denying a psychologically potent belief in Eden's persistence. Contemporary readers, much like Columbus, refuse to relinquish this equation of American Indians and a prelapsarian state of the world.

From the standpoint of ethnography rather than a priori philosophizing, neither American automobile purchases nor aboriginal hunters operate in a manner consistent with rational actor theory. Franco-American anthropologist Clotaire Rapaille, who himself helped in the design of a popular Chrysler vehicle, the PT Cruiser, suggests that buying decisions are based on largely unconscious symbolic factors with a high degree of psychological resonance, what he calls "archetypes." The design of the PT Cruiser and of SUVs generally expresses an external toughness and muscularity that has nothing to do with their crashworthiness (Gladwell 2004). They are a symbolic carapace against a world that most Americans see as increasingly hostile. Similarly, hunters base decisions on a variety of culturally and psychologically mediated factors. Indeed, among Athabaskan hunters in the Canadian subarctic, dreaming is a technique commonly used to determine where and for what animal one will hunt (Brody 1982). Thus hunting, like automobile buying, is a practical activity, but one that is permeated with culturally and personally variable desires ("dreams") and preferences.

On one level, the debate over the ecological Indian has revolved around empirical evidence, either of sound conservation practices or their opposite. Certainly, examples of both can be found. No serious scholar doubts the fact of the catastrophic reduction of subarctic beaver populations during the fur trade or the strong recent conflicts between aboriginal people and game conservation regimes (Brightman 1993, 244–302; Fineup-Riordan 1990; Krech 1981; Ray 1984). On the other hand, specific examples of environmental stewardship, such as the management of gull populations by the Huna Tlingits of Alaska, present cogent arguments for resource conservation (Hunn et al. 2003). What have tended to be at issue are more general statements of the character of North American Indian environmental practices (assuming there to be a single value for all of aboriginal North America) and, as a sort of stage-setting, the possible role of Native populations in the Pleistocene extinctions. The latter has been a rather old theme in American archaeology, first suggested by Paul Martin in 1967. The "overkill hypothesis" suggests that humans first arrived in North America shortly before the extinction of mammoths, mastodons, sloths, large bison, and other species that became extinct at the end of the Pleistocene, and that this was no coincidence. More recently, biologist Jared Diamond (1997) has suggested that it is a general tendency of all humans everywhere to extirpate attractive fauna in areas to which humans are new. Thus, only in Africa, where humans and large animals co-evolved, do these animals still survive. Charles Kay (1998) suggests that such aggression toward game animals persisted into the recent past and that populations of elk and deer were suppressed to such low levels as to have been an insignificant part of the environment of western North America prior to the decimation of the Native peoples themselves and the establishment of modern conservation regimes. Surrovell, Waguespack, and Brantingham (2005) have argued that temporal-spatial modeling of elephant and mammoth extinctions in the Pleistocene leaves little doubt that these resulted from human agency. On the other side, archaeologists such as Donald Grayson and David Meltzer (2002, 2003) have argued that climate change, not humans, was responsible for the Pleistocene extinctions, and that evidence of human predation, let alone extirpation, of megafauna is rare archaeologically.

Although this debate may be said to be empirical, it nonetheless operates at a high level of abstraction and crudeness (see Hornburg 1996, 58). Naturally, the Boasian impulse to examine different cultures on their own terms resists such generalizations. Certainly, we can posit at the gross level an opposition between sedentary and nomadic groups. Thus, conservation practices such as burning forests to create an optimal environment for deer in the eastern woodlands, where relatively sedentary and dense populations lived in towns, were common. On the other hand, in the western subarctic, with its very low human population density and high degree of human mobility, such practices were nonexistent. Moreover, overhunting was culturally supported. With several species of large fauna from which to choose, the temporary unavailability of one in a local area was less than catastrophic (Brightman 1993).

Moving beyond such gross-level distinctions, one must take into account specific groups and cultures. In particular, we must be aware of the "selections" made by a cultural order within a broader set of possibilities (Brightman 1993, 331; Sahlins 1976, 206). That is, given a hunter-gatherer technology set in a particular environment, say the subarctic, many formations are possible, including those that, as Brightman illustrates, are wasteful and even destructive of resources, or as Burch (this volume) suggests, needlessly avoids other resource species. Moreover, the assumptions of the ecological Indian paradigm—that is, ideas of paternalistic resource management combined with Levy-Bruhlian notions of mystical attachments to nature—are culturally specific discourses that will bear little resemblance to actual cultural orders of American Indian societies. Indeed, as Nadasdy has argued, conservationist discourse is both alien to ethnoecological models and powerful enough that it threatens to overwhelm them (1999, 2). Additionally, it is quite possible to question the underlying assumptions of the conservationist discourse, such as the very possibility of resource sustainability at anything above a minimal human population level and the effectiveness of scientific management, certainly if stretched out to an archaeological time frame.

If we avoid the Scylla of overgeneralization, we must avoid the Charybdis of overspecification as well. As Philippe Descola (1996) argues, it is not a question of infinite possible differences but rather of variations within a well-defined matrix. As a model of ethnoecologies he uses the example of kinship as a system of considerable but limited variation. To phrase this in Saussurean terms, we might say that such formulations are motivated rather than arbitrary. To push this further, as Beneveniste does with language, we might say that from a system-internal perspective, individual signs are motivated. That is, owing to its relation to other elements of a "cognized environment," the value of, for instance, Northwest Coast salmon is strongly determined (see Rappaport 1967).

Descola (1996) places most New World foragers in the category of "animism," by which he means that nonhuman species are treated as morally equivalent to humans and composing part of a universe of sentient beings, of which humans are only one element. Others may include deities or hypostatic forms of natural species. Modes of relation within this universe take on two main forms: reciprocity and predation. Reciprocity implies the need for a total balance in the exchange of substance between humans and nonhuman beings; predation describes the idea of an aggressive exploitation of such other-than-human beings as are useful. Descola examines ways in which these two forms interpenetrate and may constitute nested structures. Thus, elements of predation may be included within reciprocal systems, as humans employ methods to avoid strict equivalence (Descola 1996, 94).

This notion is worth pursuing further. Tim Ingold has applied a similar animistic model to circumpolar societies, in which, for these purposes, the Northwest Coast may be included.[2] In this worldview, individual beings, human or nonhuman, are nodes of energy that is constantly being exchanged between different life forms, which themselves are anything but stable: "The world of this 'animic' understanding is home to innumerable beings whose presence is manifested in this form or that, each engaged in the project of forging a life in the way peculiar to its kind. But in order to live, every such being must constantly draw upon the vitality of others. A complex network of reciprocal interdependence, based on the give and take of substance, care and vital force—the latter often envisioned as one or several kinds of spirit or soul—extends throughout the cosmos, linking human, animal, and all other forms of life" (Ingold 2000, 113). However, as I describe below in my discussion of the Kwakwa̱ka'wakw ecological model, humans never repay their debts to animals and thus never achieve genuine reciprocity. Rather, humans appear almost exclusively as predators rather than equal partners with animal species. This leads to an unstable system in which the lack of balance may lead to a change in mode, from the reciprocity that enables human survival, to predation, in which humans find themselves overmatched. Predation may be visited upon humans by spiritual entities acting as a proxy for victim species, thus reestablishing equilibrium. Moreover, the very instability of the system carries with it a permanent potentiality for changing modes. This "switching effect" makes the entire system unstable and paradoxical. This theme is illustrated nicely by a series of drawings by Inuit artist Davidialuk Alasuaq published in Ingold's book that depicts a hunter confronting what appears to be a caribou but then, upon being shot with an arrow, turns out to be a wolflike predator (2000, 117–22). This form of ecological peripeteia is visually represented, as Ingold states, in the Yup'ik *tunghak* masks, which open up to display a different animal and aspect than that represented on the outside. Similarly, the "transformation masks" of the Kwakwa̱ka'wakw and other Northwest Coast groups display multiple beings, almost always with a reversal of attitude toward humans.

Kwakwa̱ka'wakw Ethnoecology

An article by Judith Berman (2000) has synthesized quite elegantly the ethnoecological model of the Kwakwa̱ka'wakw. As an ideal type model it is an abstraction, but it seems to address some of the fundamental issues of Kwakwa̱ka'wakw ecology. In particular, Berman suggests that relations of both reciprocity and predation are contained within a system of seasonal oscillation. During the productive part of the year, roughly April to late November, the Kwakwa̱ka'wakw were focused on salmon, which were treated with "respect," a term still used widely. This respect derived from an original covenant in which Raven married a salmon and obtained salmon flesh from her, as a man in the patrilocal Kwakwaka'wakw society would obtain flesh from his wife in the form of children (2000, 68–69). Raven, however, is unable to complete the covenant, which entails returning the bones of salmon to the water. This river or ocean water is for the salmon "water of life," a shamanic substance that allows for the revival of the dead (see Furst 1989). Thus, in the long run nothing is lost; in fact, life substance is ultimately conserved in this system. This is perhaps the axiomatic point of Kwakwaka'wakw ecology, a second law of thermodynamics of the ecosystem.

This principle requires the consumers of salmon to treat those salmon with respect. This includes not only returning the bones to water but talking to salmon in a high-pitched voice, thought to be the register of the salmon themselves, before they are killed. These speeches are both an apology and an assurance that they will be reincarnated (Boas 1930, 1:201; Berman 2000, 60). On the collective level, runs of salmon—predictable and localized— are "greeted" at the beginning of the season by the First Salmon Ceremony (Amoss 1987; Boas 1921, 1318–19; Gunther 1926). This functions both to celebrate the return of the salmon runs, and thus the success of previous efforts at salmon preservation, and to assure the new run of salmon that they too will be treated with respect.

This season of plenty and respect, what the Kwakwaka'wakw call the *baxus*, contrasts with the sacred season, the *tsetsaiqa*. These two terms can be glossed as "human" and "shamans," respectively. During this dark time of the year, the world is said to be flipped over onto its back, like a plate: a useful model for the notion of switching between opposite states of the system. If the productive season is epitomized by the return of the salmon and their being greeted by the First Salmon Ceremony, the winter season is epitomized by the *hamatsa*, or cannibal dance (see Reid 1976). This dance, obtained from the Heiltsuk, dramatizes the anthropophagous spirit being Baxbakwalanusiwa, who preys upon humans. He captures initiates, who are said to be dead but are taken into the bush. They return during the height of the Winter Ceremonial, biting spectators and perhaps eating corpses, until they can be "tamed" and reintegrated into society, generally in time for the first salmon runs of the year. These two moments in the annual cycle—First Salmon Ceremony and the hamatsa—represent two modalities of relations between humans and the outside world: reciprocity and predation. Humans suffer a depletion of their life substance during the winter at the hands of Baxbakwalanusiwa as well as natural species (in their spiritual form) such as wolves and grizzlies. In effect, humans must pay for what they consume during the productive season. The symbolic identification of humans and salmon is represented by the wearing of red cedar bark; thus human initiates become red, succulent salmon flesh (Berman 2000, 91).

A common formulation is that for salmon, which live in villages and are organized just as humans, the seasons are reversed. Winter for humans is their summer, and vice versa. While they are being hunted, salmon experience something like what humans do in winter: individuals are "taken," only to return much later in a new guise. It is only through the intervention of shamans that this miraculous resurrection can occur. For salmon, humans take on this role, as indeed in some cases shamans were the ones to conduct First Salmon Ceremonies. This maintains putative equilibrium in the system as a whole. The flow of life substance is thus in some sense balanced.

As Berman points out, this natural reversal is not only seasonal but represents a reversion to the precultural state of the world: a world of darkness and predation (2000, 83–85). It is this world that more fully embodies the "animic" perspective. All bets are off; humans are as likely to be prey as predator. Humans thus play a mediating role in this system. However, this mediation does not redress the imbalance between humans and salmon; it only distributes reciprocity in Lévi-Straussian generalized exchange (Lévi-Strauss 1969). However, a further transformation effects what Berman calls "convection," a role reversal in which humans are capable of taking on the roles of both "downriver" (i.e., prey) and "upriver" (i.e., predator) species, and do so simultaneously. Humans take on the mantle (literally, in the form of a headdress) of salmon, in their spiritually potent form of Sisiutl. Often described as a "two-headed serpent," it is clearly associated with salmon rather than snakes. For instance, Sisiutl is said to be the "salmon of thunderbird." Moreover, it is really three-headed, not two-headed. A human head in the center suggests the key role of humans in effecting this transformation. The heads on either side represent both upriver and downriver predation (i.e., of the usual sort and its inversion). With this power humans are able to defeat the wolves in the Winter Ceremonial. Thus, the ur-predator is defeated by humans acting on behalf of prey species, not only salmon but also mink, whose original theft of the Winter Ceremonial from the wolves makes all this possible.

A Question of Balance

Metamorphosis is the central theme of the Winter Ceremonial. Transformation allows for the symbolic reversal of ecological vectors, as Berman correctly points out (2000, 91–93). However, one must question the degree to which this model represents balance, in the sense of reciprocity between humans and natural species, in general or in particular. Not even the generalized reciprocity of the originary situation, in which wolves prey on humans who prey on salmon, remains. Rather, the Winter Ceremonial allows humans to play a role of universal predator, in which they defeat both upriver and downriver species. Beyond this, humans are able to combine the roles of both predator and prey within the same moment. Thus, the hamatsa initiate is prey to the "real" Baxbakwalanusiwa and predator to non-initiates. On a more mundane level, potlatch hosts and guests similarly fill such simultaneous roles. From the materialist perspective, the host is essentially prey, as he is giving up actual salmon, which represents a considerable energetic investment on the part of his kin and residence group. However, on the symbolic level, he is in fact consuming his guests, whom he addresses as his "salmon" (Berman 2000, 192; Boas 1925, 152). Chiefs, the prototypical potlatch hosts, are capable of acting on both levels at once. The potlatch may be seen as a forum for such simultaneity, as the host is at once giving away literal food and wealth (salmon are often given the epithet "wealth") and devouring the guests as wealth.

What results from this model is a profoundly anthropocentric universe. Humans are the only species able to transform themselves at will and to operate simultaneously on the level of both praxis and of symbol. Moreover, humans have no true predators, having defeated wolves and being able to overcome the spiritual predation of Baxbakwalanusiwa, but they remain predators of other species, including those, such as mink and salmon, that have closely aligned themselves with human interests. Thus, what might at first glance appear to be a system based upon reciprocity relations turns out to be more fundamentally predatory. Perhaps more accurately, we might say that predation and reciprocity are simply different modalities of the same ecological and spiritual vectors, but that the reciprocity modality is marked and the predation modality unmarked.

Indeed, one modality can transform into its opposite instantaneously, and not merely with the change of seasons. Thus, in the potlatch the host and guest are both predator and prey. A Heiltsuk text closely related to the Kwakwaka'wakw text Berman sites connects the themes of transformation and paradoxical simultaneity to the origin of the shamanic ability to revive the dead and regenerate life more generally (Boas 1928, 27–33).[3] Real-Chief, who is a version of Raven, the culture hero, tries to make salmon out of alder wood. This does not work because he lacks a nose bone, so he goes to Owner-of-Salmon, who feeds him. Real-Chief steals the nose bone, but is caught. He then returns home and uses his water of life to revive a dead twin woman. The Heiltsuk considered twins to be reincarnations of salmon; thus a dead twin would be the same as a living salmon. Real-Chief marries her, and through her he is able to obtain salmon. This is achieved by the wife bathing in the water; the farther she goes into the water, the more salmon appear. At the same time, Real-Chief's hair grows long. Both salmon and hair reach a point of luxuriance that is impractical. The hair becomes entangled in the salmon that have been hung to dry. Real-Chief blames his wife, saying, "You tried to pull me, you who came from the ghosts." He tries to make amends, lying that he had actually expressed thanks for the abundant food. However, the wife is not fooled and repeats Real-Chief's words. Then she whistles, and the salmon begin to whistle. They all disappear, along with Real-Chief's hair.

This text sets forth the Heiltsuk version of the ecological matrix. Real-Chief, the great progenitor of the humanized world, with established oppositions and periodicity, sets out the terms of human material existence (see Berman 2000). In the first instance, he attempts to create salmon from whole cloth; this approach fails for want of a nose bone. Humans cannot make bones; bones are in essence the seed of life. Next, he tries to do what Raven does frequently: he steals the necessary object, as he steals the sun to create diurnal and seasonal cycles. This too fails; he is able to obtain a meal of salmon, but on his own he cannot ensure the continuation of salmon abundance. Finally, he settles on a strategy of alliance. Salmon and humans transform into each other in cycles of death and reincarnation. Marriage to a twin thus establishes a compact between salmon and humans. Real-Chief's hair grows long as a mark of his authority, as a chief who controls resources and feeds his people well. However, if humans fail to show adequate respect, as Real-Chief does, the salmon may disappear. This is a peripeteia as certainly as the transformation of prey into predator; the disappearance of the crucial food species would equally result in death. Whistling is the marker of the beginning of the sacred winter season and the coming of the Winter Ceremonial. In the text, it indicates a rapid change of state.

Moving beyond this surface reading, we can suppose that Real-Chief's relations with his affines are never on terribly solid ground in the first place. Marriage is, for the Kwakwaka'wakw and Heiltsuk, a form of wina (warfare). Mock battles occur prior to weddings, and the wedding ceremony itself entails a mock hunt. The hanging salmon may be equated with affinal potlatch guests (as in potlatch oratory), who leave quickly once they are offended. Potlatch guests who leave in this manner are at least potential enemies. Most warfare in the Wakashan-speaking region (including Heiltsuk, Haisla, Oowekeeno, Kwakwaka'wakw, and Nuu-Chah-Nulth) was between groups that also intermarried (see Boas 1928, 124–35; Swadesh 1948). Thus it is reasonable to assume that species such as salmon with whom humans mythically intermarried were only partial allies, and remained potential enemies. The requirements of potlatching with affines and dealing with salmon are homologous. As long as relations remain amicable, one is obligated to obtain the maximum benefit from the relation; this can take the form of either receiving or giving, depending upon perspective and intention. However, one must be aware that such a state of affairs can end at any moment. One must take full advantage of opportunities that present themselves.

This is a system based upon a generative paradox. In order to gain wealth/food from a species, humans must be in a state of reciprocity with that species. However, the actual exploitation of that wealth/food requires a predatory relation with the species, at least temporarily. Such a system cannot be self-regulating; rather, it is better characterized in terms of nonlinear dynamics, in particular catastrophe theory. As a small number of driving parameters (e.g., fish killing and consumption) change gradually, they can trigger a rapid shift from one state to an entirely different state. Such a "phase transition" may result in the disappearance of salmon altogether, as in the Heiltsuk text, or in the transformation of potlatch guests into enemies.

In fact, such an unstable system may represent ecological reality more closely than conventional schemata of ecosystem dynamics based on assumptions of homeostasis (see Jelinski 2005). "Tipping point" models have been applied to problems such as species extinction and climate change, both of which occur abruptly in the fossil and geological record. The traditional conservationist model of the environment is based on assumptions of a steady-state system in which human agency is an overwhelming factor. But if one views these matters from the perspective of geological—or even archaeological—time scales, both assumptions must be rejected. Ample evidence exists for such awareness on the part of Northwest Coast people, derived from their continuous habitation of their environment for ten millennia. Indeed, in 1986 I heard versions of Heiltsuk narratives of catastrophic floods that almost certainly referred to events at the beginning of the Holocene, during which sea levels rapidly rose (Josenhans et al. 1997; see McMillan and Hutchinson 2002). Such a deep knowledge of an environment and its history is conventionally equated with an ethic of conservationism. However, the two are not logically connected, and in many ways they may be opposed.

Ideology and Praxis

One implication of this analysis is an inability to make a simple connection between human behavior and the cognized environment. It is difficult to see how an ideology that warns of possible sudden catastrophe would actually be able to influence behavior in such a way as to avoid it. Unlike standard ecological ideologies based either on reciprocity or "paternalistic" protection, which could, at least in theory, lead to reduced taking of resources, such a "chaos" model of the environment does not seem to lead to any particular behavioral changes that would reduce the human environmental load. In fact, to the degree that it influences behavior, the influence is probably in the opposite direction.

However, a fair question that may be asked of any such formulations, either homeostatic or nonlinear, is, What effect do they have upon ecological praxis? The long functionalist genealogy deriving from Malinowski has taught anthropologists to look at such ideologies as minimally having material affects on the ecosystem and maximally constituting a homeostatic mechanism. As Rappaport describes for the Maring, the *kaiko* ceremonial cycle, in which large numbers of pigs are killed and boundary lines between groups relaid, has the effect of rebalancing levels of human and pig population relative to territory. Trigger mechanisms, particularly the complaints of those whose gardens have been trampled by neighbors' pigs, set the entire cycle into motion. The end result will be a reduction of such stressors and a period of optimal ecological functioning (see Biersack 1999).

It appears, from a North Americanist perspective at least, that such mechanisms and the material efficacy of eco-ritual practices more generally are very much the exception, not the rule. Surely, pigs are a unique case, as domesticates that can quickly revert to a feral state and compete directly with humans for many resources. The most important indigenous species in North America (salmon, bison, deer, caribou, etc.) have none of these characteristics. Human control over such species is not nearly as direct; humans cannot, at will, radically reduce population levels in a fell swoop. Such conservation practices as do exist are likely postcontact phenomena (Brightman 1993, 286–91; but see Feit, this volume). Nevertheless, it seems reasonable to hypothesize that ceremonies dealing explicitly with maintaining population levels of a key species and that, moreover, regulate the time and manner of their taking might have some direct impact on resource species population levels, and thus constitute a type of conservation regime.

Does the First Salmon Ceremony as practiced by Northwest Coast peoples from Oregon to Alaska fill this role? In order to do so, it would have had to (1) significantly delay the opening of a fishing "season," (2) hasten its closing, or (3) regulate the total number of fish that could be taken within a given time frame. The latter two were simply not the case. Seasons were in fact artificially delayed, but usually this delay was very brief. At the first sighting of the salmon, especially the early spring runs, when people were suffering hunger and even starving, the chief or a designated person would promptly hold the ceremony. Although examples in quasi-historical tales do exist of chiefs needlessly delaying the season's start, this appears to be a function of chiefly cruelty and despotism, leading to the chief's downfall. It is unlikely that chiefs would have frequently exercised this prerogative, as it would have opened the door to challenges to their legitimacy. On the whole, Northwest Coast chiefly authority was circumscribed to a large degree and could not survive such a test (Harkin 1996). As in the case of Real-Chief, chiefly prestige is closely linked with salmon availability.

Other aspects of salmon ceremonialism, such as care taken in the butchering of the fish and disposal of its bones, could potentially have led to lower levels of consumption, had they either slowed down the process or forced people to reckon with the putative moral equivalency of salmon and humans. However, there is no evidence that this occurred. On the contrary, excessive killing and consuming of salmon was culturally preferred. In the potlatch and other feasting contexts, guests were enjoined to eat to excess and even, in the Kwakwaka'wakw Grease Feast, to eat to the point of vomiting. Vomit is a pregnant cultural symbol of reversal and transformation, but it can be read as well on a literal level. Even at modern potlatches, much like at American Thanksgiving feasts, excessive consumption is encouraged.

Northwest Coast patterns of getting and consuming food have more in common with those of the subarctic than has been recognized. The "feast or famine" pattern of alternating excessive consumption and scarcity is characteristic of Northwest Coast seasonal variation (see Brightman 1993, 279–81). Late winter, after the bulk of dried salmon was consumed, people were often hungry, even to the point of famine, until the first run of salmon or oolichan arrived. Archaeologists Herbert Maschner and Kenneth Ames (1999) have argued that famine was a major cause of the warfare that is so prevalent in the archaeological record. One caveat with these data is that they pertain to the northern extremities of the Northwest Coast, where resources were less widely available and more "clumped" (Drucker 1983). Thus, control over a salmon stream could be a matter of life and death. However, stories of famine are frequent among more southerly peoples as well (Sobel and Bettles 2000). This is far from the picture of superabundance painted by Ruth Benedict and other symbolically oriented analysts of Northwest Coast culture (see Piddocke 1965).

In fact, we could argue more generally that in situations where food security is uncertain over the course of an annual cycle, cultures are more likely to develop an ethos of excessive consumption during periods of plenty. One aspect of this ideology is, as we have described above, the obligation to make the most of any opportunities that present themselves. As Brightman has argued for subarctic hunters, the obligation to take animals that offered themselves was primary; the ideology of conservation is a historic phenomenon, no doubt influenced in part by their experience of overkill during the fur trade (Brightman 1993, 284–85). On the Northwest Coast the evidence for conservation is no more compelling. In practical terms, presumed fish conservation techniques would have little or no effect on the problem of periodic food shortages: these were the result of usual annual and seasonal patterns of resource availability and, more exceptionally, climatic fluctuations related to sea water temperature and currents, not overkill. Moreover, the value of excessive consumption far outweighed any negative impact on fish stocks that may have occurred. The potlatch and associated feasts constituted the basis of chiefly power. Chiefly control of resources by ritual means was demonstrated by plenty, which provided a direct index of chiefly authority and legitimacy.

Far from representing an ethic of conservation, such an ideological complex may be seen to mystify certain ecological processes. Northwest Coast Natives were for the most part unaware, on the level of discourse, of the reproductive cycle of anadromous salmon, which spawned at streamheads, releasing fry to make the trip downstream and into the ocean. Only the upstream journey at the end of the life cycle was visible. Salmon were thus thought to come from a place of infinite wealth and to represent a steady supply of food, provided, of course, that the rituals were completed and the bones returned to water. In the subarctic, similar ideologies of mystical regeneration of animal stocks led directly to game depletion; the response to such depletion was not to conserve but rather to increase hunting (Brightman 1993, 289–91). We have no record of similar depletion of salmon stock, although this remains a possibility.

The lack of a developed ethic of conservation is no reason to deny Northwest Coast Natives an active role in managing their environment. In the Wakashan-speaking area some types of aquaculture were practiced, such as the capturing of herring roe on fir branches planted in shallow water. This demonstrates that, at least for herring, a practical knowledge of fish life cycles existed. Oral traditions claim that Salish-speaking peoples stocked some inland lakes with salmon, giving rise to the kokanee, a freshwater salmonid. Other stories suggest that Salish people helped salmon in their migrations when rockslides blocked their way (Turner 2005, 179). They also utilized fire to create favorable environments for plants such as camas and huckleberry (Turner 1999). However, management of the environment, either active or passive, is not evidence of a pervasive environmentalist ethic, certainly not one that would be consistent with modern environmentalist doctrine.

Conclusion

The danger of conducting such an analysis of ecological ideology is the desire to find a single, self-consistent system. While this is certainly possible, as Judith Berman has demonstrated, it is at best a partial picture of a society's representation of the environment. Even within the confines of explicitly ideological formulations of ecosystems, alternate readings are possible, as in the case of the Heiltsuk text analyzed in this chapter. Indeed, it would seem to be the case that ecological ideologies are particularly likely to be characterized by paradox. The existential fact that other living things must die so that humans can continue is a source of contradiction elaborated by many religions and ideologies. In such a context, the simultaneous holding of contradictory ideas constitutes the symbolic basis of the ideological system. The famous metaphorical elaborations of Northwest Coast people, where a dancer may be human and also a killer whale, a force of good and of evil, dead and alive, all at the same time, seems a particularly rich symbolic elaboration of this existential fact. Such a philosophy of the world cannot, and never could, provide a road map of resource management, as some authors have supposed (Martin 1978). Rather than a road map, they provide a poetics; rather than technology, the consolations of philosophy.

Conservationism is an ideology for the modern and postmodern era. Although it shares the same paradoxical quality of aboriginal environmental ideologies—the owner of the SUV must destroy nature in order to enjoy it, in a manner not unlike the fisher of salmon—the scale and technological power of modern society make it unique. To attempt to characterize premodern societies of whatever ethnic affiliation as either conservationist or anti-conservationist is fundamentally mistaken. The fact that aboriginal peoples held systematic ideologies loosely or strongly linked to ecological praxis is of interest and speaks to the first two meanings of "ecological" mentioned in the introduction, but not to the third.

Notes

1. Moreover, it is not at all clear that the maximizing or optimizing assumptions of optimal foraging theory hold true. Examples not only of overkill but also of species avoidance to the point of starvation must be considered (see Burch, this volume). Moreover, the method by which such practices become codified and transmitted in a mode analogous to the biological inheritance of traits is never revealed.

2. This is not to say that Northwest Coast cultures conform entirely to Ingold's model of animism, which he contrasts with totemism (Ingold 2000, 111–31). The essential distinction here is between a world already fully formed and thus in a sense inert, which is Ingold's idea of Australian aboriginal culture, and one that is always in the process of becoming. In Northwest Coast cultures both of these views are present, and they largely define the opposition between secular

and sacred seasons. Aesthetically, the division is between totemic art (the rather static, anatomical depiction of species) and masks and related paraphernalia. However, in Northwest Coast art each form contains within it the possibility of the other; through split representation and species hybridization, totemic art asserts the possibility of metamorphosis, while masks may "revert" to a static form (i.e., in the form of relief carvings on poles and other surfaces).

3. Versions of this story are common throughout the Northwest Coast. For the Tlingits it goes by name "Fog Woman" (Swanton 1909, 108).

References

Amoss, Pamela. 1987. The fish God gave us: The First Salmon Ceremony revived. *Arctic Anthropology* 24 (1): 56–66.

Berman, Judith. 2000. Red salmon and red cedar bark: Another look at the nineteenth-century Kwakwaka'wakw Winter Ceremonial. *BC Studies* special issue *Ethnographic Eyes* 125–26:53–98.

Biersack, Arletta. 1999. Introduction: From the "new ecology" to the new ecologies. *American Anthropologist* 101:5–18.

Boas, Franz. 1921. Ethnology of the Kwakiutl. *Thirty-fifth annual report of the Bureau of American Ethnology*, 43–1481. Washington DC: Government Printing Office.

––––––. 1925. *Contributions to the ethnology of the Kwakwaka'wakw*. Columbia University Contributions to Anthropology 3. New York: Columbia University Press.

––––––. 1928. *Bella Bella texts*. Columbia University Contributions to Anthropology 5. New York: Columbia University Press.

––––––. 1930. *The religion of the Kwakwaka'wakw Indians*. 2 pts. Columbia University Contributions to Anthropology 10. New York: Columbia University Press.

Brightman, Robert. 1993. *Grateful prey: Rock Cree human-animal relationships*. Berkeley: University of California Press.

Brody, Hugh. 1982. *Maps and dreams*. New York: Pantheon.

Descola, Philippe. 1996. Constructing natures: Symbolic ecology and social practice. In *Nature and society: Anthropological perspectives*, ed. Philippe Descola and Gisli Palsson, 82–102. New York: Routledge.

Diamond, Jared. 1997. *Guns, germs, and steel: The fates of human societies*. New York: Norton.

Drucker, Philip. 1983. Ecology and political organization on the Northwest Coast of North America. In *The development of political organization in Native North America*, ed. Elisabeth Tooker, 89–96. New York: J. J. Augustin.

Fineup-Riordan, Ann. 1990. Original ecologists? The relationship between Yup'ik Eskimos and animals. In *Eskimo essays: Yup'ik lives and how we see them*, 167–91. New Brunswick NJ: Rutgers University Press.

Furst, Peter. 1989. The water of life: Symbolism and natural history on the Northwest Coast. *Dialectical Anthropology* 14:95–115.

Gladwell, Malcolm. 2004. Big and bad: The false security of SUVs. *New Yorker*, 12 January, 28–33.

Grayson, Donald, and David Meltzer. 2002. Clovis hunting and large mammal extinction: A critical review of the evidence. *Journal of World* 16:313–60.

––––––. 2003. A requiem for North American overkill. *Journal of Archaeological Science* 30:585–94.

Gunther, Erna. 1926. Analysis of the First Salmon Ceremony. *American Anthropologist* 28 (4): 605–17.

Hardin, Garrett. 1968. The tragedy of the commons. *Science* 162:1243–48.

Harkin, Michael E. 1996. Carnival and authority: Heiltsuk schemata of power in ritual discourse. *Ethos* 24:281–313.

Hornburg, Alf. 1996. Ecology as semiotics: Outlines of a contextualist paradigm for human ecology. In *Nature and society: Anthropological perspectives*, ed. Philippe Descola and Gisli Palsson, 45–62. New York: Routledge.

Hunn, Eugene S., Darryll R. Johnson, Priscilla N. Russell, and Thomas F. Thornton. 2003. Huna Tlingit environmental knowledge, conservation, and the management of a "wilderness" park. *Current Anthropology* 44 (Supplement): S79–103.

Ingold, Tim. 1996. The optimal forager and the economic man. In *Nature and society: Anthropological perspectives*, ed. Philippe Descola and Gisli Palsson, 25–44. New York: Routledge.

———. 2000. *The perception of the environment: Essays in livelihood, dwelling, and skill*. New York: Routledge.

Jelinski, Dennis. 2005. There is no Mother Nature–There is no balance of nature: Culture, ecology, and conservation. *Human Ecology* 33:271–88.

Josenhans, Heiner, Daryl Fedje, Reinhard Pienitz, and John Southon. 1997. Early humans and rapidly changing Holocene sea levels in the Queen Charlotte Islands–Hecate Strait, British Columbia, Canada. *Science* 277:71–74.

Kay, Charles E. 1998. Are ecosystems structured from the top-down or bottom-up: A new look at an old debate. *Wildlife Society Bulletin* 26 (3): 484–99.

Krech, Shepard, III, ed. 1981. *Indians, animals, and the fur trade: A critique of "keepers of the game."* Athens: University of Georgia Press.

Lévi-Strauss, Claude. 1969. *Elementary structures of kinship*. Boston: Beacon.

Martin, Calvin. 1978. *Keepers of the game: Indian-animal relationships and the fur trade*. Berkeley: University of California Press.

Maschner, Herbert, and Kenneth M. Ames. 1999. *Peoples of the Northwest Coast: Their archaeology and prehistory*. London: Thames and Hudson.

McKay, Bonnie J., and James M. Acheson. 1987. *The question of the commons: The culture and ecology of communal resources*. Tucson: University of Arizona Press.

McMillan, Alan D., and Ian Hutchinson. 2002. When the mountain dwarfs danced: Aboriginal traditions of paleoseismic events along the Cascadia subduction zone of western North America. *Ethnohistory* 49:41–68.

Nadasdy, Paul. 1999. The politics of TEK: Power and the "integration" of knowledge. *Arctic Anthropology* 36 (1–2): 1–18.

———. 2005. Transcending the debate over the ecologically noble Indian: Indigenous peoples and environmentalism. *Ethnohistory* 52:291–332.

Palsson, Gisli. 1996. Human-environmental relations: Orientalism, paternalism, and communalism. In *Nature and society: Anthropological perspectives*, ed. Philippe Descola and Gisli Palsson, 63–81. New York: Routledge.

Piddocke, Stuart. 1965. The potlatch system of the southern Kwakwaka'wakw: A new perspective. *Southwestern Journal of Anthropology* 21 (3): 244–64.

Rappaport, Roy. 1967. *Pigs for the ancestors: Ritual in the ecology of a New Guinea people.* New Haven: Yale University Press.

Ray, Arthur. 1984. Periodic shortages, Native welfare, and the Hudson's Bay Company, 1670–1930. In *The Subarctic fur trade: Native social and economic adaptations,* ed. Shepard Krech III, 1–20. Toronto: University of Toronto Press.

Reid, Susan. 1976. The origins of the Tsetseqa in the Baxus: A study of Kwakwaka'wakw prayers, myths, and rituals. PhD diss., Department of Sociology and Anthropology, University of British Columbia.

Sahlins, Marshall. 1976. *Culture and practical reason.* Chicago: University of Chicago Press.

Sobel, Elizabeth, and Gordon Bettles. 2000. Winter hunger, winter myths: Subsistence risk and mythology among the Klamath and Modoc. *Journal of Anthropological Archaeology* 19:276–316.

Surrovell, Todd, Nicole Waguespack, and P. Jeffrey Brantingham. 2005. Global archaeological evidence for proboscidean overkill. *Proceedings of the National Academy of Sciences* 102:6231–36.

Swadesh, Morris. 1948. Motivations in Nootka warfare. *Southwestern Journal of Anthropology* 4 (1): 76–93.

Swanton, John. 1909. *Tlingit myths and texts.* Bureau of American Ethnology Bulletin 39. Washington DC: Government Printing Office.

Turner, Nancy. 1999. "Time to burn": Traditional use of fire to enhance resource production by aboriginal peoples in British Columbia. In *Indians, fire, and the land in the Pacific Northwest,* ed. Robert Boyd, 185–218. Corvallis: Oregon State University Press.

————. 2005. *The Earth's blanket: Traditional teachings for sustainable living.* Toronto: Douglas and McIntyre.

Winterhalder, Bruce. 1981. Optimal foraging strategies and hunter-gatherer research: Theories and models. In *Hunter-gatherer foraging strategies: Ethnographic and archaeological analyses,* ed. Bruce Winterhalder and E. A. Smith, 13–35. Chicago: University of Chicago Press.

10. Sustaining a Relationship

Inquiry into the Emergence of a Logic of
Engagement with Salmon among the Southern Tlingits

Stephen J. Langdon

Unpacking the complex interactions among concepts, technologies, behaviors, landscapes, climates, and ecosystems over the past twelve thousand years has recently become an important intersection for scholars from entirely different disciplinary and intellectual backgrounds. Erickson (2000) has claimed that there are four perspectives through which scholars view the relationship between humans and environment: the nature-centric perspective, the human adaptation perspective, the environmental determinism perspective, and the human-centric perspective. Research conducted from the human-centric perspective often utilizes the concept of "landscape" to advance at least a partially constructionist frame termed "historical ecology" for examining specific human-environment intersections and outcomes as they unfold through time (Balee 1998; Crumley 1994; Bender 1993; Lentz 2000). An extension of this approach is to investigate how human perceptions and cognitive constructions have been at work in these developments. Programmatic assertions about the need to explore how human actors consciously and unconsciously modified and created environmental surroundings for various purposes, while advancing a key insight, are extremely difficult to operationalize. Despite the problems in demonstrating how such a perspective can effectively be deployed, Tainter has argued that "historical research should be considered in policy decisions as routinely as are the findings of climatologists and biologists" (2000, 331).

Van der Leeuw and Redman (2002) have advanced the concept of "socio-natural studies" to position archaeological research, as a form of historical research, at the center of understanding long-term processes and impacts and to underscore the critical nature of previous human activity in constructing the contemporary environment. However, far too often the investigation and conceptualization of the "socio" portion of the formulation are given insufficient attention.

Such vantage points are particularly appealing to New World researchers for issues associated with post-agricultural change over the past three thousand years where evidences of intensification, development, and the intersection of climate, geomorphology, and human behavior can be attended to empirically. By contrast, in the recent past the hunting and gathering or foraging areas and periods have been assumed to follow one of the other three perspectives (no influence, benign influence, environmentally determined). As Hunn et al. (2004) have noted, however, the new received wisdom offered by conservation biologists and evolutionary anthropologists is that hunting and gathering or foraging forms of small-scale societies were rarely "pristine ecologists" but more typically were profligate destroyers with neither motive nor understanding through which to maintain or enhance their circumstances (Headland 1997; Kay 1994; Krech 1999; Smith and Wishnie 2000; Zavaleta 1999). There is little doubt that such bimodal, toggling vantage points from one extreme to another provide little in the way of understanding the dynamic relationships in which and through which human hunting, fishing, and gathering populations have existed in the New World or the manner in which indigenous Americans constructed and deployed understandings of their world.

Rarely in any of the recent research is the *longue durée* of New World population and environment considered in the light of the possibilities of the cumulation of knowledge and practice across time, through cycles and perhaps catastrophes of environmental variability; of the formulation of specific understandings in oral tradition; and of the intersection among understanding, concepts, technologies, practices, and the interactive dynamics among these components. Deloria (1995, 60) has been particularly vehement in his call for "Indian traditions [to] be taken seriously as valid bodies of knowledge" and for natural scientists to engage with indigenous North American oral tradition for insights into the environmental history of the continent. In archaeology his call has been heeded by Peter Whiteley (2002, 412), who has urged his fellow archaeologists to realize that "oral traditions contain a great deal of consistently reported information with strong internal standards of verifiability" and to use that information to construct new, truly interactive research questions. Ethnohistorian E. S. Burch (1992) provides an important discussion of the process by which he came to understand the accuracy and veracity of Iñupiaq and Gwich'in oral traditions in regard to their interaction in the Brooks Range of northern Alaska.

The linkage from oral history and tradition to mythic constructions and the *longue durée* is even more challenging. In a recent effort to conceptualize how humans perceive environmental conditions (continuity, change) and construct understandings of them, McIntosh, Tainter, and McIntosh (2000, 26) developed the concept of *symbolic reservoir*, defined as "the fluid repertoire of ideological, symbolic, metaphorical and mythical notions that gives all societies their dynamic consistency over time." Further, this reservoir comprises a "set of unconscious operating assumptions and generalized analytical procedures . . . employed by communities to develop shared perceptions" (26–27). Finally, the symbolic reservoir is organized into a *cultural schema* that is derived from the cosmological postulates of the symbolic reservoir of social memory, much of which is subliminal (27). This, they posit, is the foundation on which humans perceive and build their response to climatic and environmental change.

In the following discussion of the Hinyaa and Klawock Tlingit conceptualization and practice of their relationship with salmon, the mythic charter of relationship is examined as an instance of how the symbolic reservoir gives rise through the cultural schema to specific behaviors and interpretations. More critically, I will suggest that this schema provides the basis for a shift in nature of the technology and the system of harvesting salmon practiced by the Klawock and Hinyaa Tlingits that occurred in a specific historic period. As such, this shift constitutes a demonstration in the cumulation of knowledge grounded in the interpretation of empirical events through the mythic charter, thus generating a new logic of engagement with salmon.

Scenarios: Salmon and People on the
West Coast of the Prince of Wales Archipelago

The weeks preceding the annual return of salmon to the streams of the west coast of the Prince of Wales archipelago in southeastern Alaska in the 1750s was a time of much preparation and anticipation for the Hinyaa and Klawock Tlingits. At various sites, such at the mouth of the Klawock River, Little Salt Lake, and Deshuan, wooden-stake structures and rock wall alignments had been constructed for the taking of salmon. According to oral tradition, slaves were sent out to repair the wooden-stake weirs in the estuaries of the nearby streams by replacing stakes broken or washed away during the previous winter so the structures would be in working order for the return of the honored salmon (Edenso and Peratrovitch 1986). As the salmon arrival time neared, traps, which would be placed in openings in the stake-and-stone weir walls, were brought out from storage nearby and repaired as well; some Tlingits conceptualized these as "forts" for the visitors where the salmon could give themselves safely to those (people) they knew would care for them and ensure their opportunity to be reborn. When the first salmon (sockeye) arrived, all the clan or house members who owned the stream would be onsite wearing their regalia (woven blankets with totemic crests) to welcome back the salmon people, to sing and dance to demonstrate thanks and joy at their return. The clan or house leader (*sha da hune*) would open a trap and ceremoniously extract the first salmon, which would then be carefully cleaned and cooked, with all present eating a portion of the fish. The bones from the salmon were the carefully collected and returned to the water or burned in order to fulfill the ritual obligation called for by the mythic charter established in the Salmon Boy story, which required humans to allow salmon to return in the future (de Laguna 1972; Peck 1975; Swanton 1909).

Later, clan and house leaders would disperse to other locations, to streams and traps located on the islands to the west of Klawock and to Little Salt Lake, where they would await the arrival of pink and dog salmon in August and September. At these locations, semicircular rock walls constructed half-way in the intertidal zone would be watched with great expectation for the return of salmon. As the massive schools of fish streamed over the stone walls and past the excited people at high tide, the Tlingits would wait while all those that wished to ascended the streams to their spawning grounds to create their offspring. Then, as the tide ebbed and those salmon that did not ascend retreated from the stream mouth, some would be caught behind the stone walls as the tide continued out. These salmon, which, by not ascending when they could, chose to give themselves to the Tlingits, were taken by spear and leicester and were thanked and processed. I have termed this pattern "tidal pulse fishing" (see Langdon 2006 for an elaboration on its characteristics, logic, and practice).

While the description provided above concerns the behaviors described and recalled by elders concerning how their immediate ancestors thought about and behaved toward salmon, the long history of Tlingit occupation of the region, likely several thousand years, allows us to pose some intriguing questions. Among the questions that can be posed for the admittedly limited archaeological and oral historical evidence are the following: What are the premises, the logic of engagement as an element of the cultural schema, by which the Tlingits conceived of their relationship to the salmon? Through what symbolic repertoire did that logic of engagement call forth the behaviors described above? What strategies, techniques, and locations did these understandings lead the Klawock and Hinyaa Tlingits to employ in the capture and use of salmon? Is there evidence about how long this system might have been in place and if it differed from previous systems? Finally, what might have led to the appearance of the logic of engagement that was found when Europeans first entered these waters?

This chapter's first objective is to describe the premises and practices of the logic of engagement. In order to comprehend how it must be understood from the Tlingit perspective, one must dismiss ideas about harvesting strategies or efficiency-oriented techniques. Instead it must be seen as a set of specific ways of behaving toward another person, a person in another form. The logic of engagement with salmon is premised on the logic of engagement with humans: What is required of me in my behavior toward other humans to sustain a positive, fulfilling relationship? Eighty-two-year-old Tlingit elder James Osborne put it this way: "In order to understand how we treat salmon, you have to realize that we treat them like we would like to be treated" (pers. comm., 2003). This statement, still obtainable from a devoutly fundamentalist Christian, born again as an escape from alcoholism, speaks to the logic of engagement taught to him as a child by his "aunties" at Hoktaheen, "the wake of the little bird stream" on Yakobi Island west of Hoonah, as he participated with his gaff hook in the capture of salmon. It is a logic of relational sustainability (Langdon 2003): correct attitude, action, and ritual practice sustain the relationship between people and salmon, ensuring the return of the salmon people, who will give themselves to right-acting humans so that they too can reproduce.

Salmon Boy: The Tlingit Mythic Charter

What is the source of James Osborne's assertion that Tlingits must treat salmon as Tlingits wish to be treated? The source of that assertion is to be found in the Salmon Boy story he was taught as a child by his mother and aunts. This account, the Tlingit mythic charter for relating to salmon, was told to me over and over again by Tlingit elders in the summer of 2003 in response to the question, What were you taught as a child about salmon? It is central to the cultural schema of the Tlingits and, as will be discussed later, is a critical component of the patterning of the technology and practice of salmon utilization. The following summary is based on versions found in de Laguna (1972) and Peck (1975).

A young boy is hungry and asks his mother for some food. She directs him to the remaining small amount of dried fish. The piece he selects has mold on it, and he throws it down in disgust. His mother reprimands him for his behavior. He leaves the house, wearing a copper necklace, and goes down to the beach to check his bird snare. He slips and falls into the water but is saved from drowning by the salmon people, who take him to live with them in their village at the bottom of the ocean. There the boy sees that salmon are people, and the salmon chief teaches him many things about how to treat salmon. Finally, the salmon chief tells the salmon people to get in their canoes, as it is time to return to their streams. As they approach the stream, the chief tells Salmon Boy to stand up in the canoe to see where they are. He stands up, but in actuality, because he is a salmon, he jumps out of the water. He notices his parents on the bank at their fish camp. Salmon Boy proceeds up the estuary to where his mother is processing other salmon. She notices the beautiful fish presenting itself to her and tells her husband to come and catch it. So he spears Salmon Boy and hands him to his wife. She begins to cut the head off at the gills but then notices the copper necklace. In amazement, she recalls that this was what her son was wearing when he disappeared, and calls her husband. Then they ask a shaman what they should do. He tells them to lay the salmon on a plank and place it high up in the house overnight. They do this, and the next morning Salmon Boy comes down and greets his parents, who are astonished and overjoyed to see him. They ask what happened to him, and he tells them of his experiences and what he had been taught. He then teaches the other humans how to respect salmon and how to place all the bones in the fire so the salmon can be regenerated. In some versions the salmon bones are to be returned to the water. Salmon Boy goes on to become a powerful shaman.

From this mythic charter, Tlingits acquire a number of concepts about salmon: that they are persons like themselves, that they feel and make choices, that they attend to human action and communication, that they require respectful treatment, and that they will not return if they are not treated with respect. In addition, a specific ritual action (treating the bones) is required of humans to sustain the relationship. These concepts are in turn translated into a number of principles on how salmon should be treated. They are to be handled with care when caught and not thrown or tossed around. They are to be killed by striking a blow to the top of their head while the head is facing upstream toward the spawning grounds (to allow the spirit to ascend to the spawning bed with its fellow travelers). Tlingits are to take only what is needed and are to utilize all parts of the fish with no waste. Salmon are never to be spoken about badly, nor are they to be played with. Finally, in giving themselves to people, salmon provide the example for sharing with others.

As a mythic charter, the Salmon Boy story is part of the symbolic repertoire that in turn is a core component of the cultural schema that can be returned to for inquiry and guidance by Tlingits when conditions and perceptions of those conditions require contemplation about unexpected circumstances. Osborne gives us the fundamental template for interrogating the account: salmon wish to be treated like we wish to be treated. The question that follows directly from this is open-ended, namely, How do I wish to be treated? There can be many answers to that question, some of which are grounded in broad patterns of human activity and others that are linked to specific Tlingit cultural practices. The answers can then be put to use by developing technologies and practices founded on this logic of engagement.

How did the scenarios and intersections described above come to exist? The answer to that question must query the *longue durée* of Tlingit presence in southeastern Alaska and look to the complex interactions among myth, perception, technology, and practice.

Archaeological Overview

Archaeologists generally use three or four temporal divisions to organize the limited evidence for human occupation and cultural development in southeastern Alaska. There is substantial concurrence among researchers for the earliest periods of archaeological evidence occurring from 10,000 BCE to approximately 6000–5000 BCE. For purposes of this discussion, a useful starting point is the tripartite division proposed by Moss (1998, 92), consisting of an early period (10,000 BCE to 5000 BCE), a middle period (5000 BCE to 1500 BCE), and a late period (1500 BCE to contact).

Present evidence indicates that the earliest human occupants of southeastern Alaska arrived about 10,000 BCE and moved from north to south, either by land or sea (Ackerman 1968; Davis 1989, 1990). The oldest human remains presently known from Alaska, dated to 9730 BCE, were found in a karsitic cave at the northern end of Prince of Wales Island (Dixon et al. 1997; Heaton, Talbot, and Shields 1996). The early occupants had established a maritime adaptation by 8200 BCE, as demonstrated from the Chuck Lake site on Heceta Island, where evidence of long-distance trade in obsidian and utilization of marine fish such as cod, rockfish, and halibut are found (Ackerman et al. 1985).

The environment of the early period differed dramatically from that of more recent periods as sea levels first rose and then fell more than three hundred feet during the period, creating an unstable land-sea interface. As a result of this instability, there are no stratified sites in southeastern Alaska that span the entirety of the early period. Knud Fladmark (1975) has argued that sea-level stabilization occurred around 6000 BCE, allowing for the buildup of delta and beach deposits suitable for shellfish and creating stable spawning beds for salmon. Evidence indicates that shell midden sites begin to appear after 5000 BCE and increase through time (Maschner 1992). Another influential environmental change during the early period is the advance of the coniferous rain forest from the Puget Sound area north to southeastern Alaska, where by 7500 BCE the current floral assemblage appears to have been well established.

The middle period (5000–1500 BCE) is marked by a change in lithic technology as new tools appear designed for heavy and detailed woodworking. Remnant wooden stakes found in the estuarine muds of the southern part of southeastern Alaska demonstrate that by 4000 BCE the region's residents had begun to build intertidal weirs and traps for channeling and harvesting salmon. The number of these sites escalates and appears to peak between 500 BCE and 500 CE (Moss and Erlandson 1998). Large wood-plank houses characteristic of the contact period began to appear in the region around 500 BCE.

It is not clear who the early and middle-period residents of southeastern Alaska were. However, three lines of evidence suggest that Tlingits were present and were likely the region's primary residents from 3000 BCE to the present. First, historical linguistic evidence of a highly qualified nature presented by Krauss (1973) suggests that the Tlingit language grew out of the organic amalgamation of several languages and dialects that had separated individually from a Proto-Athabascan stock between 4000 BCE and 2000 BCE north and east of the Coast Range in what is now southern Yukon Territory. Subsequently, these dialectal forms were carried to the southeastern Alaska coast by different migrant streams whose encounters and interactions along southeastern Alaska led to the emergence of the Tlingit language with several dialectical variants.

Second, Tlingit oral traditions are rich in migration accounts. Movement into southeastern Alaska occurred at different times and through different routes. Coastal migration north from the region of the Nass and Skeena rivers, riverine migration from the east down the Stikine and Taku rivers (sometimes under glaciers), and overland migration from the north across icefields from the Copper River to Yakutat Bay are all represented in Tlingit oral traditions (de Laguna 1972; Olson 1967; Swanton 1909). A continuing stream of population movement characterizes these accounts (Hope 2000).

Third, continuity in artifact construction provides supporting evidence for Tlingit presence in the region over the past seven thousand years. In 1994 a spruce root basket remnant was discovered in the estuarine muds of the Thorne River on the east side of Prince of Wales Island; it dates to 4760 BCE (Fifield 1995). Expert analysis revealed that the style of construction "closely resembles the ethnographic Tlingit and Haida basketry" (Croes 2001, 151).

All three lines of evidence point to Tlingit presence over the last five thousand years, and certainly within the last two thousand years in the Alexander Archipelago region of southeastern Alaska.

The late period (1500 BCE to contact) is generally characterized as having strong similarity to the contact-period cultures identified in the accounts of eighteenth- and nineteenth-century explorers and traders. Winter village sites with multiple houses are more prevalent and are accompanied by fort sites and evidence of social stratification (Ames and Maschner 1999). Mass harvesting, processing, and storage of salmon is seen as the subsistence basis, supplemented by a wide array of other marine resources. Scholars disagree on the nature of cultural and environmental change during the late period, with Maschner (1997a) positing the introduction of an "Asiatic warfare complex" to account for the appearance of forts and increased violence, while Moss and Erlandson (1992) suggest that population increase and declines in resources resulting from to neoglacial conditions are primarily responsible. Of particular relevance to the argument presented below is the recent suggestion that an "ecosystem collapse" occurred in the North Pacific region around 1150 CE (Maschner, Finney, and Tews 2004). Given mass harvesting of salmon by Tlingits dating back nearly four thousand years, what evidence is there concerning possible changes in salmon-harvesting technologies, locations, and practice related to this period? The next section discusses evidence for Tlingit salmon-harvesting technologies from sites in southeastern Alaska, especially from the west coast of the Prince of Wales archipelago.

Intertidal Fish Traps in Southeastern Alaska

The intertidal remains of structures associated with prehistoric fishing activities are abundant in southeastern Alaska, particularly in the southern region from Angoon south. Two major material forms have been identified: structures composed of stones piled into walls creating alignments and features, and structures composed of wooden stakes driven into the intertidal substrate to create alignments and features. Intertidal stone structures are reported in the Ketchikan vicinity (Ackerman and Shaw 1981) and with great frequency for the west coast region of the Prince of Wales archipelago (Langdon, Reger, and Wooley 1986; Langdon, Reger, and Campbell 1995).

The remains of wooden-stake fishing structures from the intertidal areas of southeastern Alaska first appear around 4000 BCE, but most are found after 3500 BCE (Moss, Erlandson, and Stuckenrath 1990; Moss and Erlandson 1998). Between 2500 and 2000 BCE, however, it appears that quite substantial structures were being built consisting of many stakes driven into estuarine bottoms (Moss and Erlandson 1998). Enormous concentrations of stake remnants have been identified since 1990 at such locations Redfish Bay, Exchange Cove, 108 Creek, and Cosmos Cove on the northeast side of

Prince of Wales Island and at Staney Creek, Klawock River, and Little Salt
Lake on the west side of Prince of Wales Island. Moss and Erlandson (1998,
189) note that nearly 50 percent of the dates in southeastern Alaska fall between 2500 and 1500 BCE.

Remnants of the wooden-stake structures typically do not provide a clear
view of the scale or logic of the structures, or the time available for thorough
investigation is insufficient to provide detailed descriptions. Sketches of
the wooden-stake trap features discovered at Kanalku Bay and Walker Cove
near Angoon show long, linear alignments that presumably acted to funnel
salmon, but they do not show capture areas or precisely link the features to
specific streams (Moss 1989). Ream and Saleeby's (1987) sketches from Exchange Cove indicate wooden-stake linear alignments beginning near the
mouth of the stream and extending down the bay in the lower part of the
intertidal zone, also suggesting a funneling function. A similar linear patterning along a short stretch of Staney Creek on the west coast of Prince of
Wales Island has been reported (Terry Fifield, pers. comm.). In some cases
it appears that alignments were constructed perpendicular to stream flow
in the intertidal areas as well. While there are many other cases of intertidal wooden-stake features, the number of stakes is typically too few or
the patterning too jumbled to make a determination of the scale, form, and
logic of the structures that were there. Thus, while Maschner (1997b) reports eleven wooden-stake intertidal fish weir features in Tebenkof Bay on
Kuiu Island, he gives no information on the scale, form, position, or logic
of the structures. The seven dates reported for Tebenkof Bay range across
the period from 2800 to 300 BCE.

Little Salt Lake: A Profuse Patterning

In contrast to the cases discussed above, patterning of intertidal wooden-
stake features is considerably clearer at a site known as Little Salt Lake on
the west coast of Prince of Wales Island, where extensive research has been
conducted intermittently over nearly twenty years (Langdon, Reger, and
Campbell 1995). Approximately two miles north of the much larger and
more productive Klawock River is an embayment known locally as Little

Salt Lake. Streams drain into the Little Salt Lake basin from the northeast and southeast. Both have short lengths for in-stream salmonid spawning due to the proximity of rapidly rising landforms to the east of Little Salt Lake. The shorter stream will be referred to hereafter as North Stream and the longer one as Little Salt Lake Stream.

The two streams support pink, chum, and coho salmon. Surveys of the two streams for spawning populations since 1985 indicate that pink salmon are by far the most numerous species. It also appears that the bulk of the run returns in the first two weeks of September in most years. The maximum estimated spawning population for Little Salt Lake Stream was 55,000 pinks on September 6, 1986, while 15,000 pinks were estimated in North Stream on August 15, 1986. The lowest estimated spawning populations since 1985 are 1,200 for North Stream and 3,000 for Little Salt Lake Stream.

Little Salt Lake was discovered in 1986 as part of a broad regional survey of the west-central Prince of Wales archipelago shoreline for intertidal remains of fishing structures. Three subsequent seasons of fieldwork led to the identification of at least twenty-eight discrete features ranging in age from 2280 BCE to 310 BCE. Based on the identification of more than two thousand buried wooden stakes in one feature (Pavement I, discussed below), it is likely that more than ten thousand buried wooden stakes are found in Little Salt Lake.

As research on the stake patterns in Little Salt Lake continued, I developed a terminology to discuss and categorize the phenomena identified. The term *feature* is defined as a relatively discrete alignment of stakes and/ or stakes and stones that can be distinguished from other features. These appear to have integrity; that is, they were created and/or re-created consciously by humans with specific purposes in mind. A number of different types of features have been identified that will be described below.

Of the twenty-eight features identified to date in Little Salt Lake, some stand independently while others appear to interlock with each other. In addition, there are numerous additional cases of single, isolated stakes or of pairs or small groups of stakes that we are not willing to label as features due to the limited number of stakes or the lack of clear coherent design in

Table 10.1. Little Salt Lake fishing features: Type and frequency

Feature type	Frequency	Description	Function	Location
Pavements	3	Wide (1–3 m), dense linear wooden-stake concentrations	Barrier, lead impoundment	Middle intertidal, form or on ridges
Pairs aligned	3	Twin stakes, separated 5–10 cm. Pairs intermittently spaced, 1–3 m apart—some have flat stones (30 cm) abutting stakes where they enter mud	Brace	Lower intertidal, softest mud
Isolated stakes	4	Single stakes, no feature or alignment evident	Unknown	Upper intertidal
Linear alignments				
Concentrated	11	Narrow (< 15 cm) dense stake pattern, varying lengths	Barrier, lead	Upper and middle intertidal
Interspersed	7	Narrow (< 15 cm) sparse stake pattern, varying lengths	Brace	Upper and middle intertidal
Chevron	2	Narrow (< 15 cm) dense stake pattern, varying lengths	Barrier, lead	Upper and middle intertidal
Stone-stake alignments	2	Stone wall, 1–2 stones high and wide	Foundation	Middle intertidal

the pattern of distribution. Table 10.1 presents the typology, frequency, and apparent function of the features identified.

Pavements. A pavement is a feature consisting of densely packed stakes (circular wooden lengths) of different diameters arranged in a linear alignment usually somewhere between 1 to 1.5 meters in width and extending, in Little Salt Lake, from 70 to 100 meters in length. The pavement areas are approximately 2 meters in width. Some of the stakes protrude slightly (generally less than 5 centimeters) above the surface. Many more are either flush to the surface or buried slightly (several centimeters below the surface) beneath it. Three distinct pavement structures ranging in length from 70 to

100 meters have been identified in Little Salt Lake, and the characteristics of each are discussed below (see figure 10.1).

Pairs and piles. In the lowest-lying areas of the bay, extremely difficult to access due to the dangerous penetrability of the muddy silts that form the bottom, another feature type is found. In these areas are found pairs of buried stakes, comprising a unit separated by 5 to 20 centimeters. The distance from one pair to the next is typically between 1 to 3 meters before another similar pair is found. In addition to the stake pairs, in the lowest area in the western part of the bay the stakes are invariably accompanied by several 10- to 20-centimeter flat stones, which constitute the piles in the term for this feature.

Sequences of pair and pile units form a feature with an identifiable linear pattern. Two of these features form semicircular arcs, while several others are linear in design. It is inferred that the pairs provide a brace structure to support a lattice fence inserted between the stakes. The rock piles provide support for the stakes as well as possible stepping stones for those deploying the lattice fences.

Linear alignments. By far the most frequent feature types in Little Salt Lake are linear alignments of stakes. There are substantial differences, however, in how stakes were made and how they were patterned. In some alignments branches are still attached to the stakes, while in others branches have been detached. In some alignments stakes are closely packed together forming a relatively solid wall, while in other lines there is a notable spacing of 10 to 50 centimeters between individual stakes. The more densely concentrated alignments are considerably more frequent.

It is likely that these linear alignments represent different technologies. The regularly spaced stakes may be the foundations or supports for lattice wall structures that could be attached to the stakes and then taken down when fishing was completed. The tightly packed stakes, on the other hand, imply that they comprised a wall or funneling feature.

Stone structures. There are only two features in Little Salt Lake that use stone as part of the structure, and since they are not central to the argument of this chapter they will not be discussed further.

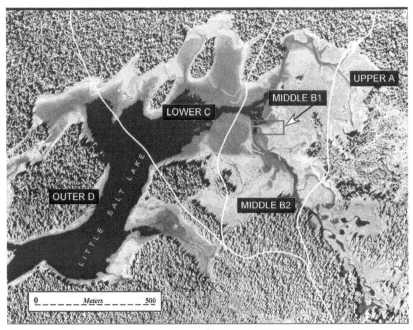

Figure 10.1. Intertidal zonation and wooden-stake fish trap features in Little Salt Lake, Prince of Wales Island, southeast Alaska.

Little Salt Lake Harvest Strategies: Location, Technology, Timing, and the Logic of Engagement

The drainage system, estuaries, intertidal zone, and subtidal components of Little Salt Lake can be divided into four sections, as illustrated in figure 10.2. The upper zone (A) consists of grass-covered wetlands at the upper extreme of the tidal range and is inundated during approximately 30 percent or less of the tidal range. Some of this area is reached by salt water only at the highest tides, while the lowest portion of the zone is reached by high water at least once a day on the highest tide of the day. The middle zone (B) is the intertidal and estuarine zone immediately below the upper zone. It is defined by permeable sands primarily in the intertidal beach area and gravels in the estuarine area. This zone is covered by salt water from 30 to 70 percent of the tidal range, and the predominant vegetation is yellow fucus, a seaweed whose abundance waxes and wanes from spring to winter. The lower zone (C) is the least-exposed intertidal area, being open to the atmosphere for less than 30 percent of the tidal range, with some portions

Table 10.2. Little Salt Lake fishing technologies: Location, strategy, age.

Location (Zone)	Technologies	Strategy	Dates
Upper (A)	Scattered, single wood stakes	Unknown	> 2000 BCE
Middle (B1)	Pavements, tight linear, spaced linear	Incoming entrapment, funneling	1400–1100 BCE
Middle (B2)	Pavements, spaced linear, pairs	Outgoing impoundment, blocking, funneling	1050–500 BCE
Lower (C)	Tight linear, spaced linear, pairs	Outgoing impoundment, blocking	< 1000 BCE
Outer (D)	Rocks, spaced linear, plank stake	Outgoing	350 BCE

only exposed on the extreme lowest tides of the year. The substrate of zone C consists of muds and silts with little or no vegetation.

The outer zone (D) is defined differently from the other three zones. It is the entrance zone to Little Salt Lake that falls outside the estuarine zone. It includes the complete range of tidal zones discussed above but lies outside of the estuarine zone of the two freshwater streams that drain into Little Salt Lake proper. An extremely small freshwater drainage enters the upper zone from the east.

Table 10.2 presents information on the distribution of wooden stakes, alignments, and features among these four zones. In the upper zone, only scattered individual wooden stakes have been identified to date. Three of the four stakes were located in the estuary of Little Salt Creek, one at the bottom of the zone and the other two toward the top of the zone. The fourth stake was located in the estuary of the North Stream. The two stakes dated from this zone both were dated to before 2000 BCE. It was not possible to discern how the stakes were being used as a technology in a harvest strategy.

In the middle zone we can identify a number of different technologies and at least two dramatically different strategies of harvesting. Perhaps the most impressive discrete feature in all of Little Salt Lake is the complex consisting of Pavement I and the wooden-stake features to which it is joined found in the middle zone and labeled B1 on figure 10.1. Pavement I and the two features associated with it form a sophisticated weir-and-trap

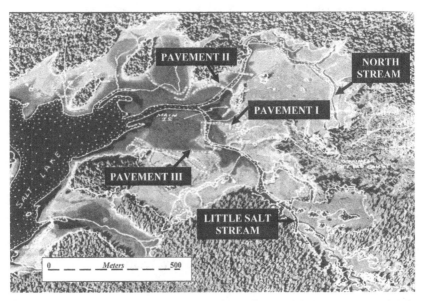

Figure 10.2. Major wooden-stake features (pavements) located in the intertidal zone of Little Salt Lake.

complex. The strategy of this complex is that the pavement which intersects and crosses the estuarine channel at the intersection of the two streams acts at a minimum as a weir to funnel the salmon, first to a triangular trap that probably consisted of one hundred to two hundred stakes with branches to hold fish and direct them toward probably a fully enclosed box or barrel trap that was seated between or attached to the stakes at the end of the triangular trap opposite the weir.

The strategy apparent in this complex is that the pavement with the stakes crossing the lower estuarine section of Little Salt Lake Stream will funnel salmon away from the stream channel as they proceed up the bay on the incoming tide. The salmon will be diverted and funneled into first the holding area and then into the box or barrel trap. Harvesting occurs on the incoming portion of the tide, and salmon are held without possibility of escape or retreat in the two holding areas. Salmon are not captured by this complex on the ebb tide when those that do not ascend the stream to spawn retreat back into the bay.

Three radiocarbon dates have been obtained from this complex. Two dates acquired from Pavement I, one from the inner and one from the outer edge, are 1380 and 1240 BCE, respectively; a stake in one of the triangular walls was dated to 1140 BCE. It is possible to infer that this complex was functioning over this period perhaps initially as a simple weir to be used for spearing salmon that neared the structure and later followed by the development of the trap features that allowed for more intensive harvesting and holding for processing.

The basic logic of engagement practiced at this complex of interlocking features is to take salmon on the incoming tide as they travel toward their spawning stream. The technology does not allow for trapped salmon to escape if they are not taken and processed or eaten.

The alignments and features in the other areas of the middle zone (B2) utilize some of the technologies found in B1 but also represent innovations as well. In this zone are found the two other pavements whose construction appears similar but whose positioning and strategic design indicate a quite different logic of engagement and strategy of harvest.

On the west side of the North Stream, beginning approximately 40 meters from the estuarine intersection of Little Salt Lake Stream and North Stream, is Pavement II. Like Pavement I, Pavement II is constructed as a dense concentration of buried stakes with and without branches. Pavement II begins just below the mean high-water mark in the upper tidal range near a point and creates a shallow arc before hooking to run parallel to the edge of the North Stream channel for about 7 meters. The arcing form of Pavement II creates an impoundment as a circular feature with an opening to the upstream side and a closed front on the downstream side. Unlike Pavement I, Pavement II has no other alignments or traps associated with it.

Around the point to the west of the end of Pavement II begins another arcing feature that extends from just below mean high water in a long, looping arc down into an extremely dangerous silty and quicksandy portion of the lower intertidal zone (C) before curving back up to the middle tidal range. The feature is composed of the interspersed paired stakes with the rock piles. Another similar feature is found west of this feature.

Moving further west in the embayment to an area between two islands, another type of feature is found. In this embayment, tight linear features of buried wooden stakes are found the middle and lower tidal zones. The two features of this design form shallow Vs or chevrons, with stakes extending down in lines from the upper tidal zone to the lower tidal zone. In both cases there is a gap at the apex of the chevron. It is likely that a slat basket-type trap was positioned in this location on both features to receive salmon funneled to it by the wings of the chevron weirs.

On the west side of Little Salt Lake, and on the west side of Little Salt Lake Stream in the upper tidal flats away from the estuarine portion of the stream, is Pavement III. This feature is constructed in a similar fashion to Pavements I and II but differs in that is a linear feature 1 meter in width extending approximately 70 meters from west to east tapering into interspersed single-stake alignments on either end. Unlike Pavement I, there are no traps appended to the pavement, nor are there any gaps in the alignment into which traps could be placed. Unlike Pavement II, it does not form an impoundment for holding fish on a receding tide; rather, it appears to both block salmon from moving into the extreme shallows of the southern portion of Little Salt Lake and/or act as a funneling platform for the use of spears as salmon move up and down the estuary.

Near the west end of the interior of Little Salt Lake and near the boundary with the outer zone (D), a tight alignment of stakes extends down from the point in an arc, hooking back in the middle tidal range. It too is open to the upstream side and closed on the down-bay side.

Throughout zone B2, the logic of engagement is quite distinct from that identified and discussed above in zone B1. Arcing structures, some approximating semicircular forms, with openings to the upland side are predominant. Neither Pavement II nor Pavement III crosses either Little Salt Lake Stream or North Stream in the estuarine zone. These impoundment structures work only on the ebb tide; that is, they are designed to capture salmon only when the tide is falling. The placement and structure of the impoundment allow salmon to freely pass by them on the incoming tide, to pass over them at and near high tide, and to be available for human harvesting only on the outgoing tide. This mass-harvesting strategy thus allows salmon to move unimpeded into the stream and travel to their spawning grounds. This pattern represents a radical reformulation of the logic of engagement that I have termed "tidal pulse fishing" (see Langdon 2006 for a fuller discussion).

In this area, three additional carbon dates have been taken from three distinct structures. Pavement II has been dated to 980 BCE, Pavement III to 540 BCE, and the paired stakes arc in the low tidal range composed of dangerous muds and silts immediately to the west of Pavement II has been dated to 1040 BCE. These dates are all more recent than Pavement I and its associated features discussed above.

In the outer zone (D), the zone of Little Salt Lake away from the estuaries of the two main streams, one structure had been identified consisting of a new form of stake—planks, and rocks serving as support. This structure also takes the form of the semicircular arc open to the upland side of a slough that could have been a small stream previously. It also would use the tidal pulse fishing logic of engagement and thus indicate the continuity of this approach through time. The plank stake from this structure has been dated to 350 BCE.

Little Salt Lake: Accounting for Innovation—Environment and Oral Tradition

What accounts for the innovations among the Klawock and Hinyaa Tlingits described above—the radical shift in the logic of engagement practiced in the utilization of salmon and the apparent timing of this innovation? Archaeological research conducted on nearby Kuiu Island by Maschner (1992, 1997b) provides a number of data points for consideration. Extraordinarily detailed and informative oral tradition given in 1934 by Klawock Ganaxadi leader John Darrow reported in Olson (1967) is of substantial relevance to these issues as well. A significant degree of intersection in the two data sets on some critical points offers insight into the questions at hand and also poses larger temporal and regional issues for the Gulf of Alaska ecosystem.

Maschner (1992, 1997b) conducted archaeological survey and excavation research throughout Tebenkof Bay, a major embayment on the west coast of Kuiu Island with strong environmental similarities to the Klawock region. Data from the Tebenkof Bay sites indicate that salmon were of little subsistence importance up until 1500 BCE, the end of the middle period (Maschner 1997b, 91). Over the next five hundred years, the importance of salmon increased dramatically, such that "after AD 1300, salmon contribute over 90% of the fish vertebrae remains by weight" (Maschner 1997b, 91). Thus there is a substantial shift in dependency from cod, herring, and halibut to salmon over this eight-hundred-year period.

With regard to the subsistence utilization of other species in Tebenkof Bay, Maschner (1997b, 91) states: "Perhaps the most startling finding in the temporal distribution is the nearly complete switch from a sea mammal based harvesting pattern to one based on terrestrial mammals, occurring after AD 1300. . . . This transition is primarily from harbor seal and sea otter to deer and canids." Maschner and Reedy-Maschner (Maschner 1997a, 1997b; Maschner and Reedy-Maschner 1998) eschew an environmental explanation for this shift and instead posit the introduction of the bow and arrow in the context of the "Asiatic warfare complex" as the causal mechanism. They suggest that open-water hunting of sea mammals and fishing for bottom fish became more dangerous due to the new militarism and that populations looked to increasing localization of resource use to minimize exposure. In their view, the subsistence strategy of salmon and deer seen after 1300 CE was a response to social and cultural factors and not environmental factors.

Maschner's (1997b) contentions about a dramatic and massive shift from marine mammal harvests to terrestrial mammal harvests before and after 900 BCE are disputed by Moss (pers. comm., June 13, 2005), who contends that the number of identified bones used as the basis for Maschner's claims are too few to be indicative of any pattern. Further, the number of bones reported could have come from a single individual in many cases and were not analyzed using a minimum number of individuals methodology. In addition, in Moss's view, the spotty and highly concentrated location of mammal bones in southeastern Alaskan middens limits the reliability of the data for trend analyses such as those offered by Maschner.

Elsewhere, however, Maschner, Finney, and Tews (2004) have suggested that the timing of 1150 CE is important around the Gulf of Alaska as a pivot point in ecosystem characteristics, increased salmon productivity, subsistence focus, and settlement patterns. This date corresponds remarkably well with the shift in the logic of engagement for salmon harvesting identified at Little Salt Lake.

John Darrow was the last Klawock Ganaxadi clan leader, and his detailed account of the founding and subsequent history of the people of Klawock, given in 1934, includes important information on the subsistence history of the community and region (Olson 1967). Darrow relates how the Ganaxadi and their Tekwedih in-laws came to the Klawock River by traveling over the mountains from the east side of Prince of Wales Island. He does not mention any other people residing in the Klawock River/Lagoon area at the time of their arrival. Subsequently the two clans built a number of houses and shared the resources of the lake, river, lagoon, and inlet. Gradually the Klawock Tlingit numbers increased and new houses were built down on the lagoon for the additional population. However, a catastrophe occurred—all of the sea mammals disappeared from the region and the population began to disperse to the outer islands and other areas. Moss (pers. comm.) points out that Darrow's observations on the disappearance of sea mammals from the vicinity of Klawock may be a localized phenomenon in response to greater human numbers and hunting activity in the Klawock area and not a regional pattern. It is likely that at this time Baker Island, a Pacific Ocean fronting island to the west of Klawock, became the home of the Dekiganaxadi, which means "Ganaxadi far out," a group that split off from the Klawock Ganaxadi. A totem pole found in the Klawock totem park and an oral tradition linked to the Dekiganaxadi village on Baker Island are presented in Garfield and Forrest (1961, 113–15).

Darrow also describes a subgroup of Ganaxadi occupying Little Salt Lake. He states, "all of them are dead now" (Olson 1934). His reference to the disappearance of the Little Salt Lake people likely refers to the impact of the two smallpox epidemics (1836 and 1862) that swept through the southern Tlingit region and caused massive population decline.

Finally, Darrow states that after the disappearance of the sea mammals, the Klawock people built a weir in the lagoon (Olson 1967, 104). This action presumably reflects the decision made by the Klawock Tlingits to increase their salmon take to replace the sea mammal food missing from their diet.

Bearing in mind Moss's concerns that presently reported mammalian data by Maschner are insufficient for trend analysis, comparison of the information from Darrow and Maschner offers interesting congruences and clarifications along with a key difference. Darrow describes the disappearance of sea mammals from the Klawock vicinity following a considerable period of occupation. Maschner's data indicate a near disappearance of sea mammal remains in the archaeological record after 1300 CE. This would appear to provide us with a date for this occurrence and give it at least a subregional signature. While Maschner attributes the shift to social and cultural factors, Darrow's account appears to indicate an ecological shift or collapse of some kind. Darrow reports that the weir was built following the collapse and thus provides a clarification to Maschner's account, as salmon intensification is a response to new environmental conditions. Darrow's account indicates dispersion and salmon intensification (with no mention of deer) as responses of the Klawock Tlingits to their new circumstances, while Maschner argues for localization and intensification as responses to increased danger. Darrow does not report any conflict associated with the dispersion, and in this regard there is a key difference between the changes asserted and inferable from oral tradition and those inferred from the archaeological record. Nevertheless, Tlingit structures termed nu (forts) are often used, as seen in the earlier discussion of temporality, as markers distinguishing the middle from the late periods. The beginning of the fort sites are dated by both Maschner (1997a; Maschner and Reedy-Maschner 1998; Ames and Maschner 1999) and Moss (1998; Moss and Erlandson 1992) to approximately 1500 BCE, predating the intensification of salmon use by five hundred years. Darrow's lack of mention of increased warfare and battles for territory during this time of resource alteration and adjustment would appear to indicate that no significant shift in the frequency, intensity, or technologies of warfare attended the changes that occurred at that time.

Whether or not shifts in mammal usage due to ecological or social and cultural factors occurred between 1150 BCE and 700 BCE, the number of fish-trap sites and the number of fish traps per site increased over this time span, and the orientation of virtually all identifiable trap structures shifted to tidal pulse fishing. The Maschner perspective suggests that intensification of salmon harvest was a response to likely human population increase and subsequent conflict. The Moss perspective suggests that the pattern of intensification of salmon harvest, if any, was a response to likely human population increase.

Additionally it is possible that both increased human population and intensification of salmon harvest may be related to increased salmon numbers. However, the shift of harvest orientation to tidal pulse fishing does not intuitively follow from increased salmon numbers unless all the increase resulted from intertidal spawning. This would appear to be highly unlikely.

Little Salt Lake in Context: Nearby Sites
on the West Coast of Prince of Wales Island

Little Salt Lake is a remarkable laboratory for investigating the intersections among people, technology, environment, resources, practice, and time. Additional information can be added from other sites on the west coast of the Prince of Wales archipelago to contextualize the picture obtained at Little Salt Lake.

The Klawock lake and river system is the largest salmon producer on Prince of Wales Island. Archaeological research indicates that humans were living on the river proper in the neighborhood of 6000 BCE. Research on the fishing structures of the Klawock River and lagoon have revealed two types of wooden-stake structures utilized for salmon harvest. In the lagoon area to the south of the estuary of the Klawock River, a place named Ganaxadi Real Bay, a series of semicircular grass arcs are found, inside some of which are found wooden stakes. The former wooden-stake structures have trapped sediments through the centuries, creating the contexts for intertidal grasses to establish themselves in semicircular forms. These forms have the same location and orientation as the ones in Little Salt Lake: they are open to the forest and therefore acted as impoundments to capture salmon on the ebb tides when they were functioning. As such, their function corresponds to the tidal pulse logic of engagement. The single wooden stake dated from this complex, interlocking set of structures gives an age of 1035 BCE.

In the estuary portion of the Klawock River proper a different technological design of buried wooden stakes is found. A set of grassy islands with V points toward the bay are found on the north side of the stream channel. These V-pointed grassy islands have been created by centuries of settled sediments. The wooden-stake structures here consist of tight linear alignments of stakes running parallel to the shore in the northern half of the channel with wings forming a forty-five-degree V shape. The points of the Vs are directed outward, down the channel away from the Klawock River. One exceptionally well preserved V structure consists of more than seven hundred buried wooden stakes tightly packed together, especially at the apex of the V. One stake from this Klawock estuary V structure has been dated to 735 BCE. These structures also are designed not to intercept salmon on their passage and ascent to the Klawock River but rather to impound salmon that retreat on the ebb tide back down the estuary toward the lagoon and inlet.

Both the Klawock lagoon semicircular wooden-stake arcs and the Klawock estuary V wooden-stake traps operate on the logic of engagement of tidal pulse fishing. The dates obtained from them indicate they fall after the revolution in technology identified at Little Salt Lake.

The beaches of Prince of Wales Island away from the major rivers and in the estuary zones of the small streams draining the islands west of Prince of Wales Island are geomorphologically different from those of main drainages of Prince of Wales Island proper. Rocky intertidal zones with stones and boulders are characteristic of these areas, and here the stones were used by the Tlingits to create intertidal semicircular traps and weirs (Langdon, Reger, and Wooley 1986; Langdon 1986, 2006). A wide range of alignments, features, composites, and complexes dots the intertidal landscape of these outer islands (Langdon, Reger, and Wooley 1986). These structures invariably operate on the same logic of engagement described above—tidal pulse fishing. Given Darrow's discussion of dispersion and the evidence of shift at Little Salt Lake, it is possible to suggest that Klawock Tlingit expansion into these outer islands was carried out with tidal pulse fishing technologies employed for salmon capture. The dispersion/expansion therefore occurred after the innovations documented at Little Salt Lake had been developed and in congruence with the oral tradition provided by John Darrow (Olson 1967). One wooden stake buried in a intertidal stone weir on the east coast of San Fernando Island has been dated to 1050 BCE (Moss and Erlandson 1998).

Moss and Erlandson (1998, 189) points out that while intertidal weir fishing sites in Alaska date back "nearly 4000 BP," "almost 50 percent of the dates cluster between 2500 and 1500 BP." The development of new technologies and strategies around 1100 BCE resulted in substantial reductions in the amount of wooden materials used and thereby likely reduced the size of the archaeologically identifiable signature. Thus, counterintuitively, the shift to pink and dog salmon, tidal pulse fishing, and lattice fence walls all contributed to intensification that left a less-identifiable archaeological signature than the preceding technological forms and practices.

Caveats and Considerations

Several caveats and considerations should be borne in mind concerning the materials presented thus far. The first is the issue of continuity and in situ development. The case above has assumed that the Klawock and Hinyaa Tlingits have occupied the Klawock River–Little Salt Lake area for fifteen hundred years and that the practices were replicated through oral tradition, instruction, and demonstration over this period. However, it is possible that the shift in technology could be the result of an immigrant group's arriving in the region at approximately 1100 BCE. Nothing in Darrow's account suggests such invasion, but Tlingit oral traditions include many accounts of separation, migration, and movement (Rabich Campbell 1989; Emmons 1991; Olson 1967). Darrow's own account of the settlement of Klawock specifies migration and travel from the east side of Prince of Wales Island to the west side via the Harris River (Olson 1967, 103).

In keeping with the suggestion that an immigrant group brought a new technique, it should be noted that intertidal stone fishing structures are numerous along the northern and central British Columbia coast. Thus the change in logic of engagement could be the result of a new group of people entering the region. One oral tradition concerning the migration of the Naasteidi clan into the region from the Nass River region indicates movement from the south but contains no information concerning fishing techniques.

A second consideration related to material utility concerns relative costs and impacts of technologies that might be factors in prompting change in fishing practices. The construction technique used in Pavement I consists of wooden stakes with branches driven in close proximity to each other, presumably with other branches woven in, to create the barrier or funneling wall. This is a permanent structure that persists in the intertidal structure throughout the year. In the spring it might need to be repaired based on flood or ice damage that occurred over the winter. The scale of the pavement structure requires a substantial initial labor investment that produces an essentially immobile factor of production. Should the stream course alter, the utility of the structure might decline to the point of unproductiveness. Related to this permanence is the fact that these structures create contexts for increased sedimentation and may themselves be factors in altering the course of the river (Langdon, Reger, and Wooley 1986; Putnam and Greiser 1993).

By contrast, the technologies of pairs and interspersed stake alignments appear to implicate the historically identified and ethnographically described lattice fence structures. Lattice fence structures could be placed between the pairs or attached to the interval stake alignments to create barriers or funnels. This type of weir wall would be impermanent in that the lattice fences can be taken down when the harvesting is completed and stored nearby for installation the next year. Hinyaa Tlingit elder Clara Peratrovitch terms these "fences" and states that her mother informed her that they would be "rolled up and stored for the winter" (pers. comm., 2003). Such a technique would require much less cost to drive new stakes in order to alter the pattern of funneling or blocking. Thus, lowered labor costs, reduced environmental impacts (which may have been stimulated by the mythic charter), and increased flexibility may also be implicated in the technological shift and the logic of engagement.

Additional considerations regarding material utility relate to biological aspects of pink and chum salmon behavior and ecology. Both species are found in a large number of streams, including very small ones. In addition, some segments of both species spawn intertidally. Furthermore, the nutritional quality (protein content) declines precipitously in the two species upon entering freshwater. Behaviorally, both species tend to school in shallow waters and wait for appropriate water conditions (temperature, quantity) prior to ascending, thus making them available to tidal pulse fishing through several tidal cycles.

Finally, evidence from Tebenkof Bay and Little Salt Lake indicate a peaking of activity around 1000 BCE followed by a subsequent decline of population beginning in Tebenkof Bay around 1300 CE (Maschner 1997b). At present no environmental or resource data demonstrate how the onset of the Little Ice Age might be implicated in this decline or whether local or regional sociopolitical events are in play. If a decline in salmonid production is related to the population dip, then it is quite possible that the ritual intensification based on the Salmon Boy myth may have occurred at this later period, leading to the ritual practices described and recalled by Tlingit elders. In this scenario, tidal pulse fishing continued but was buttressed by heightened ritual intensification and attention to the training of young people in appropriate behaviors several hundred years later (1400–1500 CE) than presented previously.

Myth, Innovation in Technology, and Practice Pragmatics: The Parameters of Relational Sustainability among the Klawock and Hinyaa Tlingits

It is time now to examine the relationships among the Salmon Boy mythic charter, the shift in the logic of engagement, and the practices of the Tlingit people on the return of salmon to their streams of origin and how they produce a cultural schema of relational sustainability (Langdon 2003). While it is not possible to state how long the Salmon Boy mythic charter has been present among the Tlingits, evidence from the Bering Straits region indicates that the religious and philosophical premises of the essential "personal" quality of entities and forces in the universe has been present for at least two thousand years in that part of the world. A similar time frame or an even earlier appearance for this constellation of religious and philosophical premises and the practices that flow from them is entirely plausible for the Tlingit region.

The profundity of James Osborne's admonishment is the touchstone for translating the Salmon Boy mythic charter into practices and behaviors. What is it that we as people value (and therefore what salmon people value), how do we wish to be treated, and most importantly, how should we treat others (especially salmon people) that we value? Two underlying principles in the mythic charter help flesh out answers to these questions.

First, salmon transit between their homes under the ocean and the streams where they give themselves to their human hosts. In so doing, they come and go—through time (they are present for short periods of time in summer and fall and gone for longer periods of time in winter and spring), through space (they are sometimes under the ocean and sometimes in the streams), and through existence (they exist where normal people can see them in this plane of existence as fish, and they exist where normal people cannot see them in another plane of existence as people). The upshot of these comings and goings is that human people must behave in a manner such that those sentient, attendant, and volitional salmon people will come back—will return so that human relationships with them can be sustained in order to ensure that both salmon and humans will be sustained and persist. If they are not respected and treated honorably, salmon may either not return or go elsewhere. The Salmon Boy myth provides some explicit directions on how humans are to behave, but its fundamental implicit principle must be returned to for reflection and examination to deepen the understanding and provide guidance on how humans should act.

The second critical point of the Salmon Boy myth is the necessity of the ritual act of burning all the salmon bones after the fish has been consumed. The pragmatics of this ritual act are that only by its completion will it be possible for the salmon to regenerate, become a person in its undersea village home, and subsequently return once again to the stream where it can give itself to worthy humans. Humans must carry out this ritual act to ensure the regeneration of the salmon people, and in the monumental significance of the act it becomes sacred.

The necessity of appropriate human behaviors to ensure the return and regeneration of salmon is a cultural schema that can be characterized as relational sustainability (Langdon 2003). The principles of "persons" standing in mutually reciprocal relations of giving and respectful treatment ensuring the continuous recycling of "persons" in human and salmon form through life and death are the cosmological foundation of this system.

The notion of shared "personness" provides a range of insights that humans can call on to examine for behavioral implications and for guidance in human action. Among Tlingits, the hit (house) is a primary physical and social unit providing identity and daily life in realities of production, distribution, consumption, and protection for a core group of people (Emmons 1991; Fair 2000). It is central as the locus of reproduction—biological in the forming of new lives, social in the positioning of new lives in the stream of lives that have come before (covered by the Tlingit concept shagoon), and cultural in the training of human minds and bodies to behave in appropriate ways. In Tlingit thought, the hit is also in some sense a fortress and a sanctorum that protects its members from social and physical vicissitudes (Fair 2000).

It is in this concatenation of dimensions of home that the foundation for the innovation of tidal pulse fishing can be found. As the marine mammal populations declined, Tlingit attention turned to the salmon as a replacement. In keeping with the guidance of long-standing cultural schema and guided by the Salmon Boy mythic charter, Tlingits carefully examined how they might further their relations with salmon so that this relationship would continue. Through empirical, biological observation, Tlingits determined that male and female salmon build "houses" in the gravels of the streams to which they seek to return. Here eggs are deposited by females and fertilized with milt by the males. The fertilized eggs are then buried and protected in their "houses." From those "houses" come their children in the spring, traveling outward as small fry to their ocean homes. As human persons, Tlingits require and value their homes at the center of their existence for daily life and reproduction. It therefore became a central understanding that salmon people must be allowed to travel to their streams and make homes in which their offspring will be protected.

This can be seen as a process of reflecting upon the mythic charter of Salmon Boy for insights into how shared "personness" can be translated into specific behaviors toward salmon. The mythic charter thus generates through reflection a logic of engagement that empirically results in the protection of salmon escapement. In addition to tidal pulse fishing, Tlingit elders report a number of empirical acts they learned from their elders to take to protect the in-stream homes of salmon, including harvesting ducks that stir up salmon nests to gain access to fertilized eggs, reducing the excess number of dolly varden that consume eggs and fry, and destroying of beaver dams that block passage to salmon homes (Langdon 2004, 2005).

While the empirical and biological are critical to survival and reproduction, other considerations are at least as important to existence. For Tlingits, each human person exists in an absolutely necessary web of relationships that combines elements from two sides—the clans of the mother and father and the moieties in which each clan is embedded. Clans are totemic corporate entities that utilize specific symbols to represent themselves; known as crests, artistic renderings of these symbols are commonly placed on blankets and other items that members of clans wear on ceremonial occasions. Objects known as *at.oow*, such as hats, blankets, tunics, and other items representing critical events in the heritage of the clan, are revered elements of the clan's collective existence. Ceremonial occasions at which critical social and cultural practices are conducted to maintain and reproduce the Tlingit order have at their core oratorical speechmaking, song and dance, and the presentation of *at.oow*. These celebrations and the artistic forms that accompany them are enormously valued by Tlingits as joyous exuberance and shared expression.

As these are valued and necessary in human existence, Tlingits determined through reflection grounded in the mythic charter that similar forms of behavior would be valued by salmon persons. Therefore, ceremonial institutions to welcome back salmon through song, dance, and regalia at the time of the reappearance of the salmon were developed and practiced, as described by Christine Edenso and Clara Peratrovitch (1986). Behaviors and objects cannot be perfunctorily performed and constructed among Tlingits; rather, they must draw upon the depths of expressiveness in voice, in body movement, and in the aesthetic representations that are presented to salmon when they return. This represents the highest level of "respect" that Tlingits can show to both valued and necessary other human beings and valued and necessary salmon beings.

One of the most compelling examples of the power and expression of these conceptualizations and practices can be seen in the wood carving depicting a salmon with a human person (Salmon Boy) embedded in the belly portion of the fish (see fig. 10.3). In the 1880s, U.S. Navy officer and ethnographer George Emmons collected a magnificently carved wooden object in the vicinity of Wrangell, Alaska. As beautiful and marvelously crafted as it is, it invites our wonder and astonishment. Yet this object was not found in a Tlingit house prominently placed for human daily viewing. Nor did it serve as a piece of regalia to be ceremoniously danced with or brought out for others to see and admire at significant and momentous occasions as *at.oow*. Instead, as William Holm (1987, 216) recounts, "This carved stake was fastened upright to the frame of a fish weir set near the mouth of a salmon spawning stream."

The object is a representation of the central principle of the Salmon Boy myth, that salmon are persons. Holm (1987, 216) suggests that "the fish trap stake probably reminded the approaching salmon that they were respected by the fisherman, who intended to treat them according to Salmon-Boy's instructions." But let us extend our interpretation of this object, let us go beyond mere didactic and mnemonic representation in order to understand a

Figure 10.3. Tlingit fish trap stake from Wrangell, Alaska. The trap stake is carved to represent the Tlingit Salmon Boy myth. It was attached to an intertidal fish trap so that it could be seen by a jumping salmon. Courtesy of the Burke Museum of Natural History and Culture, Catalog number 1390, trap stick, Tlingit/Stikine.

deeper and more nuanced meeting in the context of the mythic charter and "relational sustainability."

The location of the object is significant in that it was placed on the weir so that it would be seen by a *jumping* salmon. This placement is designed to interface with Salmon Boy's own account of being directed by the salmon chief to stand up and see where they were, but in his fish form, standing up was actually jumping out of the water. The stake trap could be seen by a jumping salmon but probably not by a swimming salmon.

And what would the jumping salmon see? What would be seen is a marvelous representation of the mythic charter and announcement of the trap owner's knowledge of and intent to abide by the requirements of that charter. But further, this is an object of great beauty and wonder, something that the salmon would appreciate in its own right as well as reflect upon the respect being demonstrated by the stake presenter through the exquisite quality of the carving. It is not a representation to "lure" or "attract" or even merely a "reminder." The effort and precision lavished on this carving surely makes it a *presentation*, a gift of beauty for salmon to behold, offered to salmon as a "person in other form" with whom the human person seeks to sustain a relationship. This offer of beauty and wonder to the salmon "persons in other form" is one of the multi-stranded engagements that compose the practice of "relational sustainability." It is a testimony to the power of the mythic charter to generate behaviors by human persons that respect salmon persons.

Conclusion

Over the *longue durée* of at least five thousand years of engagement, Tlingit populations in southeastern Alaska developed understandings and practices that allowed them to sustain their relationship with salmon people. Along the way concepts and technologies were developed, innovations were brought into practice, and rituals emphasizing respect were created and elaborated. About thirty-five hundred years ago, a labor-intensive technology of weirs and traps deployed in the estuaries diverted incoming salmon into harvest locations. These structures were the mainstays of salmon harvest for about two millennia. Between 1500 and 1000 BCE, a new logic, that of tidal pulse fishing, emerged that allowed salmon to proceed unhindered on the incoming tide so that those who wished could reach their homes and spawn. Only those that backed out on the ebb tide were caught by the new technologies. In addition, the cosmological principle of treating salmon "like we would like to be treated" was utilized as the foundation for guidance in the elaboration of complex ritual and artistic systems that treated salmon with the respect and honor that Tlingits held as the manner in which they wished to be treated. Relational sustainability as the logic of engagement was designed to ensure the return and continuity of relationships between salmon and humans and was constructed for mutual benefit.

Some would argue that the logics of material utility discussed above are sufficient to account for the appearance of tidal pulse fishing and lattice fence structures. Kew (1992) has provided an elegant sequence of technological development for Fraser River salmon built on a logic of engagement that is entirely material. Tidal pulse fishing likewise might be the most "efficient" technique for harvesting pink and dog salmon and therefore explainable by that logic alone. However, efficiency of harvest is hardly a satisfactory premise by which to explain tidal pulse fishing. The Euro-American capitalist canners and their fishermen who entered southeastern Alaska in the late nineteenth century operated on such material utilities. Driven by the directive of profit maximization at any and all cost, they treated salmon as mute, dumb organisms biblically given as available for exploitation by humankind. Neither animistic sentimentalities nor treatment of honor, respect, and prestations of beauty for salmon were forthcoming from these newcomers. The fishing techniques Euro-Americans deployed in southeastern Alaska between 1878 and 1900 nearly destroyed the salmon stocks of the region. In 1896 Commander Jefferson Moser traveled through the west coast of the Prince of Wales archipelago and noted that everywhere he stopped, Tlingit and Haida chiefs came out to tell him of the devastation being wreaked upon their salmon and their concerns for the survival of their people and villages (Moser 1899). The harvesting logic the Euro-American capitalists employed was to block the streams at mean high water and harvest all the salmon as they pressed against the net, logs, or chicken wire placed in their way as they fought to get to their homes. These profit-maximizing practices, based on material principles, resulted in wanton waste and destruction. Material utility in its capitalist guise was incapable of creating a sustainable relationship precisely because its logic was purely, starkly, and insanely material.

Reconfiguring understandings of indigenous North American populations' interactions with their environments is only beginning, but the possibilities and vistas are profound. Evidence from elsewhere in the Gulf of Alaska concerning the productivity of salmon populations utilized by Alutiiq populations indicates that over a period of eight hundred years, the Karluk River and lake system on Kodiak Island supported four to six million sockeye salmon annually, well above levels present over the previous twelve hundred years (Finney et al. 2002). This occurred when archaeological evidence indicates that human populations were at their prehistoric maximum (Jordan and Knecht 1988; Crowell, Steffian, and Pullar 2001). It is possible that the patterns of human engagement in the last thousand years before Euro-American penetration may have enhanced and/or optimized salmon abundance through conscious intervention. Such reevaluation would dramatically alter present understandings, and only future research will provide additional insight into these emerging perspectives.

The pragmatics of practice (technical, ritual, aesthetic) exhibited by the Klawock and Hinyaa Tlingits toward salmon strongly suggests a powerful intersection of concept, belief, and behavior according to an entirely different framework. Reflection upon and cognitive immersion in the mythic charter of Salmon Boy gave rise to the materially rational innovation of tidal pulse fishing and the mythically rational innovation of ritual intensification expressed through ceremonial elaboration, artistic representation, and the continuous replication of the Salmon Boy mythic charter through oral transmission to children.

References

Ackerman, Robert. 1968. Archaeology of the Glacier Bay region, southeastern Alaska. Washington State University, Laboratory of Anthropology, Report of Investigations. Pullman.

Ackerman, Robert, K. C. Reid, J. D. Gallison, and M. E. Roe. 1985. Archaeology of Heceta Island: A survey of 16 timber harvest units in the Tongass National Forest, southeastern Alaska. Washington State University, Center for Northwest Anthropology, Project Reports 3. Pullman.

Ackerman, Robert, and Robert Shaw. 1981. Beach-front boulder alignments in southeastern Alaska. In Megaliths to medicine wheels: Boulder structures in archaeology, ed. M. Wilson, K. L. Road, and K. J. Hardy, 269–77. Calgary, Alberta: University of Calgary Archaeological Association.

Ames, Kenneth, and Herbert Maschner. 1999. Peoples of the Northwest Coast: Their archaeology and prehistory. London: Thames and Hudson.

Balee, Edward, ed. 1998. *Advances in historical ecology*. New York: Columbia University Press.

Bender, Barbara, ed. 1993. *Landscape: Politics and perspectives*. Berg: Oxford.

Burch, E. S. 1991. From skeptic to believer: The making of an oral historian. *Alaska History* 6 (1): 1–16.

Croes, Dale. 2001. North coast prehistory: Reflections from Northwest Coast wet site research. In *Perspectives on northern Northwest Coast prehistory*, ed. J. Cybulski, 145–71. Archaeological Survey of Canada, Mercury Series Paper 160. Ottawa: Canadian Museum of Civilization.

Crowell, Aron, Amy Steffian, and Gordon Pullar, eds. 2001. *Looking both ways: Heritage and identity of the Alutiiq people*. Fairbanks: University of Alaska Press.

Crumley, Carole, ed. 1994. *Historical ecology*. Santa Fe: SAR Press.

Davis, Stanley, ed. 1989. *The Hidden Falls site, Baranof Island, Alaska*. Alaska Anthropological Association Monograph Series, no. 5. Anchorage: Alaska Anthropological Association

———. 1990. Prehistory of southeast Alaska. In *Handbook of North American Indians*. Vol. 7, *Northwest Coast*, ed. W. Suttles, 197–202. Washington DC: Smithsonian Institution.

de Laguna, Frederica. 1972. *Under Mt. St. Elias: The history and culture of the Yakutat Tlingit*. Smithsonian Contributions to Anthropology 7 (3 parts). Washington DC: Smithsonian Institution Press.

Deloria, Vine, Jr. 1995. *Red earth, white lies: Native Americans and the myth of scientific fact*. New York: Scribner.

Dixon, E. J., T. H. Heaton, T. E. Fifield, T. D. Hamilton, D. E. Putnam, and F. Grady. 1997. Late Quaternary regional geoarchaeology of southeast Alaska karst: A progress report. *Geoarchaeology* 12 (6): 689–712.

Edenso, Christine, and Clara Peratrovitch. 1986. Tape recording in Tlingit from Edenso translated by Peratrovitch. Transcript in possession of author.

Emmons, George. 1991. *The Tlingit Indians*. Seattle: University of Washington Press.

Erickson, Craig. 2000. The Lake Titicaca basin: A precolumbian built landscape. In *Imperfect balance: Landscape transformations in the Precolumbian Americas*, ed. D. Lentz, 311–56. New York: Columbia University Press.

Fair, Susan. 2000. Architecture of the northern Northwest Coast: Symbol and solidarity. In *Ceremony 2000: Restoring balance through culture*, ed. R. Worl and S. Fair, 115–22. Juneau: Sealaska Heritage Foundation.

Fifield, Terry. 1995. The Thorne River basket: Benefits through cooperation. Paper presented at "Hidden Dimensions: The Cultural Significance of Wetlands Archaeology" conference, University of British Columbia, Vancouver, May 1995.

Finney, Bruce, Irene Gregory-Eaves, Marianne S. V. Douglas, and John P. Smol. 2002. Fisheries productivity in the northeastern Pacific Ocean over the past 2200 years. *Nature* 416:729–33.

Fladmark, Knud. 1975. A paleoecological model for Northwest Coast prehistory. National Museum of Man Mercury Series, Archaeological Survey of Canada Paper no. 43. Ottawa: National Museums of Canada.

Garfield, Viola, and Linn Forrest. 1961. *The wolf and the raven*. Seattle: University of Washington Press.

Headland, Thomas. 1997. Revisionism in ecological anthropology. *Current Anthropology* 38 (4): 605–31.

Heaton, T. H., Talbot, S. L., and Shields, G. F. 1996. An Ice Age refugium for large mammals in the Alexander Archipelago, southeastern Alaska. *Quaternary Research* 46 (2): 186–92.

Holm, William. 1987. *Spirit and ancestor: A century of Northwest Coast Indian art at the Burke Museum.* Seattle: University of Washington Press.

Hope, Andrew III. 2000. On migrations. In *Will the time ever come? A Tlingit source book,* ed. A. Hope III and T. Thornton, 23–33. Fairbanks: Alaska Native Knowledge Network, University of Alaska.

Hunn, Eugene, Daryl Johnson, Priscilla Russell, and Thomas Thornton. 2003. Huna Tlingit traditional environmental knowledge, conservation, and the management of a "wilderness" park. *Current Anthropology* 44 S5:S79–S103.

Jordan, Richard, and Richard Knecht. 1988. Archaeological research on Western Kodiak Island, Alaska: The development of Koniag culture. In *The late prehistoric development of Alaska's native people,* ed. R. Shaw, R. Harritt, and D. Dumond, 225–306. Alaska Anthropological Association Monograph no. 4. Anchorage.

Kay, Charles. 1994. Aboriginal overkill: The role of Native Americans in structuring Western ecosystems. *Human Nature* 5:359–98.

Kew, Michael. 1992. Salmon availability, technology, and cultural adaptation in the Fraser River watershed. In *A complex culture of the British Columbia Plateau,* ed. B. Hayden, 177–221. Vancouver: University of British Columbia Press.

Krauss, Michael. 1973. Na-Dene. *Current Trends in Linguistics* 9:146–206.

Krech, Shepard, III. 1999. *The ecological Indian: Myth and history.* New York: Norton.

Langdon, Steve J. 1986. Traditional Tlingit stone fishing technologies. *Alaska Native News* 4 (3): 21–26.

———. 2003. Relational sustainability: Indigenous northern North American logic of engagement. Paper presented in the session "Conservation as Science Discourse and Practices of Control: Conflicts with Indigenous Peoples" at the 102nd annual meeting of the American Anthropological Association, Chicago, November 20.

———. 2004. Tlingit salmon concepts and practices: Implications for presence and productivity. Interim report on Hoonah and Klawock Tlingit traditional salmon ecological knowledge. Presented to Office of Subsistence Management, U.S. Fish and Wildlife Service, Juneau, Alaska.

———. 2005. Traditional knowledge and harvesting of salmon by *HUNA* and *HINYAA TLINGIT.* FIS report 02-104 (draft final). Anchorage: U.S. Department of Interior, Fish and Wildlife Service, Office of Subsistence Management.

———. 2006. Tidal pulse fishing: Selective traditional Tlingit salmon fishing techniques on the west coast of the Prince of Wales archipelago. In *Integrating local level ecological knowledge with natural resource management: Exploring the possibilities and the obstacles,* ed. C. Menzies. Lincoln: University of Nebraska Press.

Langdon, Steve J., Douglas Reger, and Neil Campbell. 1995. Pavements, pairs, pound, piles, and puzzles: Investigating the intertidal fishing structures in Little Salt Lake, Prince of Wales Island, southeast Alaska. Paper presented at "Hidden Dimensions: The Cultural Significance of Wetlands Archaeology" conference, University of British Columbia, Vancouver, May, 1995.

Langdon, Steve J., Douglas Reger, and Christopher Wooley. 1986. Using aerial photographs to locate intertidal fishing structures in the Prince of Wales archipelago, southeast

Alaska. Public Data File Document no. 86-9. Anchorage: Alaska Dept. of Natural Resources, Division of Geological and Geophysical Surveys.

Lentz, David, ed. 2000. *Imperfect balance: Landscape transformations in the Precolumbian Americas.* New York: Columbia University Press.

Maschner, Herbert. 1992. The origins of hunter and gatherer sedentism and political complexity: A case study from the northern Northwest Coast. Unpublished PhD diss., University of California, Santa Barbara.

———. 1997a. The evolution of Northwest Coast warfare. In *Troubled times: Violence and warfare in the past,* ed. D. Martin and D. Frayer, 267–302. War and Society Series, vol. 4. Langhorne PA: Gordon and Beach.

———. 1997b. Settlement and subsistence in the later prehistory of Tebenkof Bay, Kuiu Island. *Arctic Anthropology* 34 (2): 74–99.

Maschner, Herbert, Bruce Finney, and Amber Tews. 2004. Did the North Pacific/Bering Sea ecosystem collapse in AD 1150? Paper presented in the symposium "The Northern World AD 1100–1350." Society for American Archaeology Annual Meeting, Montreal.

Maschner, Herbert, and Katherine Reedy-Maschner. 1998. Raid, retreat, defend (repeat): The archaeology and ethnohistory of warfare on the North Pacific rim. *Journal of Anthropological Archaeology* 17:19–51.

McIntosh, Roderick, Joseph Tainter, and Susan Keech McIntosh. 2000. Climate, history, and human action. In *The way the wind blows,* ed. R. McIntosh, J. Tainter, and S. K. Tainter, 1–42. New York: Columbia University Press.

Moser, Jefferson. 1899. Salmon and salmon fisheries of Alaska. *United States Fish Commission, Bulletin* 18:1–178.

Moss, Madonna. 1989. Archaeology and cultural ecology of the prehistoric Angoon Tlingit. Unpublished PhD diss., Department of Anthropology, University of California, Santa Barbara.

———. 1998. Northern Northwest Coast regional overview. *Arctic Anthropology* 35 (1): 88–111.

Moss, Madonna, and Jon Erlandson. 1992. Forts, refuge rocks, and defensive sites: The antiquity of warfare along the North Pacific coast of North America. *American Antiquity* 54 (3): 534–43.

———. 1998. A comparative chronology of Northwest Coast fishing features. In *Hidden dimensions: The cultural significance of wetland archaeology,* ed. Kathryn Bernick, 180–98. Vancouver: University of British Columbia Press.

Moss, Madonna, Jon Erlandson, and Robert Stuckenrath. 1990. Wood stake weirs and salmon fishing on the Northwest Coast: Evidence from southern Alaska. *Canadian Journal of Archaeology* 14:143–58.

Olson, Ronald. 1934. Fieldnotes from Klawock, Alaska. Bancroft Library, University of California, Berkeley.

———. 1967. Social structure and social life of the Tlingit in Alaska. University of California Anthropological Records 26. Berkeley.

Peck, Cyrus. 1975. *The tides people.* Juneau: Juneau-Douglas School District.

Putnam, David, and T. W. Greiser. 1993. The inter-relationship of prehistoric wooden stake traps and estuarine sedimentological processes: An example from northern Prince of Wales Island. Paper presented at the 20th Annual Meeting of the Alaska Anthropological Association, Fairbanks.

Rabich Campbell, Chris. 1989. A study of matrilineal descent from the perspective of the Tlingit Nexa'di eagles. *Arctic* 42 (2): 119–27.

Ream, Bruce, and Becky Saleeby. 1987. *Archaeology of northern Prince of Wales Island: A survey of nineteen timber harvest units in the Tongass National Forest, southeast Alaska.* Report to the U.S.D.A. Forest Service, Alaska Region, Ketchikan Area Tongass National Forest.

Smith, Eric, and Mark Wishnie. 2000. Conservation and subsistence in small-scale societies. *Annual Review of Anthropology* 29:493–524.

Swanton, John. 1909. *Tlingit myths and texts.* Bureau of American Ethnology Bulletin 39. Washington DC: Government Printing Office.

Tainter, Joseph. 2000. Global change, history, and sustainability. In *The way the wind blows,* ed. R. McIntosh, J. Tainter, and S. K. Tainter, 331–56. New York: Columbia University Press.

van der Leeuw, Sander, and Charles Redman. 2002. Placing archaeology at the center of socio-natural studies. *American Antiquity* 67 (4): 597–605.

Whiteley, Peter. 2002. Archaeology and oral tradition: The scientific importance of dialogue. *American Antiquity* 67 (3): 405–15.

Zavaleta, Erika. 1999. The emergence of waterfowl conservation among Yup'ik hunters in the Yukon-Kuskokwim delta, Alaska. *Human Ecology* 27 (2): 231–66.

Contemporary Resource Management Issues

11. The Politics of Cultural Revitalization and Intertribal Resource Management

The Great Lakes Indian Fish and Wildlife Commission
and the States of Wisconsin, Michigan, and Minnesota

Larry Nesper and James H. Schlender

Introduction

In multiplying current examples of putatively anti-ecological practice among American Indian peoples in *The Ecological Indian: Myth and History*, Shepard Krech (1999, 216) included the Wisconsin Ojibwes, who "reportedly let thousands of fish spoil in warm weather," a cryptic reference to a legal, social, and political conflict between the bands of Lake Superior Ojibwe Indians in northern Wisconsin that spanned the last quarter of the twentieth century. Krech was making a general point: Indians have "a mixed relationship to the environment," and the practice of regarding them as conservationists strips real people "of all agency in their lives except when their actions fit the image of the Ecological Indian" (216). It is nonetheless unfortunate that he chose to make his point at the expense of the Wisconsin Ojibwes, partially owing to the nature of the evidence he drew upon (though admittedly signaled by the use of the qualifier "reportedly"), but also because they are deeply, effectively, and legally involved in the management of the natural resources of the northern third of Wisconsin, by virtue which they are critiquing the image of the ecological Indian in the region's shared collective consciousness.

In 1983, after nearly ten years of litigation, the bands of Lake Superior Ojibwes had their treaty-based off-reservation hunting, fishing, and gathering rights of use and self-regulation upheld by the Seventh Circuit Court of Appeals. The bands are regarded implicitly as sovereign entities in the U.S. Constitution (see the commerce clause, art. 1, §8, and the supremacy clause, art. 6, cl. 2), and these rights were inherent aspects of their internal sovereignty and had been explicitly reserved at the time the treaties were signed. Well before, at Greenville in 1795, the tribes had forgone their *external* sovereignty—that is, their unencumbered right and historic practice to treat with any other sovereign—in favor of the protection of the United States, thus giving rise to a political and moral relationship of trust fraught with honor and promise. With their usufructuary rights affirmed by the federal judiciary after a lapse of more than a century, the next eight years entailed a process of negotiating the exercise of these rights with the state of Wisconsin, orchestrated by a non-Indian protest movement and shaped by an Ojibwe cultural renaissance (Nesper 2002). A similar process would later take place in Minnesota.

In northern Wisconsin, as well as earlier in Washington State (Cohen, La France, et al. 1986) and in Michigan (Doherty 1990), when Indian people became viable political actors in a particular context—that is, when they have been able to establish their right to manage a resource that is not perceived by the dominant society as diminishing (Sider 1987, 16)—whatever ambient image of the ecological Indian might have been previously lurking in the consciousness of local non-Indians quickly gave way to the alternative of the rampaging savage. Given what little political power Indian and non-Indian people in the northern tier of Wisconsin counties really had in the early 1980s, threats to the perpetuation of a lucrative image of the North Woods that cannot be ignored or suppressed are genuinely frightening. The state's natural resource policy in the north for the last century has been to seek to reclaim "the cutover"—a wasteland left by the logging companies between 1880 and 1920 when they logged off more than sixty billion board feet of timber (Gough 1997)—and maintain it as a forest crop land for use as a source for timber and as a recreational playground for midwestern metropolitans. As a result, the reality of local political weakness had not worked to the locals' disadvantage. However, when the federal government recognized the right of the bands whose forebears signed the land cessions to not only hunt, fish, and gather on these lands but also to regulate themselves in so doing, northern Wisconsin generated some memorable reactionary images.

Within a week of the Seventh Circuit Court's decision, a local semiweekly, the *Lakeland Times* (published in Minocqua, a prominent North Woods tourist destination just outside the Lac du Flambeau reservation), headlined, "Ruling Allows Chippewa Off-Reservation Hunting Anytime." The article asked, "[Is] wholesale slaughter of fish and wild game . . . a reasonable exercise of treaty rights? . . . Tourism will be devastated if the ruling is not overturned before spring spawning runs of walleyes, musky, and other gamefish begins and Indians harvest thousands of vulnerable fish" (qtd. in Nesper 2002, 70). This is fear that the "savage" will rape and plunder. It is fear of political power, fear that the historical tables have been turned, fear of reprisal for bad treatment of Indians in the past.

To support the claim that the Indians allowed fish to spoil, Krech cites "Mississippi of the North: A First Hand Experience of Protests over Northern Wisconsin's Indian Treaty Rights," an article that appeared in the September/October 1989 issue of *The Humanist*. It is an account of the experiences of three Northland College students on May 6, 1989, the date the Lac du Flambeau band's treaty fishing season ended with a rally, feast, and massive demonstration at the boat landing at Butternut Lake, where, for the first time, Indian supporters outnumbered and displaced hundreds of non-Indians protesting their exercise of federally recognized usufructuary rights. The three students had visited the office of Stop Treaty Abuse–Wisconsin (STA-W), a virulently anti-treaty and anti-Indian organization that sought to end the exercise of treaty rights by very selectively drawing upon tactics used in the civil rights movement, but adding innovations such as harassing Indians fishing on the lakes they were spearing at night by creating large wakes in boats that STA-W folk referred to collectively as "the Cavalry," dragging their anchors through walleyed pike spawning beds, and marketing "Treaty Beer: True Brew of the Working Man" to raise funds to support the organization's activities (as well as pay their jail bonds).

The students were given a pamphlet that STA-W had produced titled "Wisconsin's Treaty Problems: What Are the Issues?" wherein a series of calumnies about Ojibwe people were recited. The section contrasting spearing fish historically and spearing them today concludes: "Instead of taking only what is needed for subsistence, *thousands of fish spoil because of warm weather* and the lack of ambition to clean them. Each year thousands of spoiled game fish are dumped in dumps and along roadsides because tribal members don't want to clean them" (emphasis added). No evidence for this claim was offered; indeed, the wide-ranging seven-page pamphlet cites no other literature at all. Of course, laws adopted by all of the bands in northern Wisconsin that have off-reservation hunting, fishing, and gathering rights interdict such waste. In the model code that all the tribes are required by the federal court to adopt, Section 3.03 states: "No member shall unreasonably waste, injure or destroy, or impair natural resources while engaging in the exercise of off-reservation treaty rights regulated by this code." Chapter 4 of the same code specifies that, if convicted, a tribal member might face the suspension of his or her off-reservation rights, forfeiture of any property used in the commission of the violation of the code, and a natural resource assessment not to exceed 75 percent of the amount of the civil remedial forfeiture (in this case $8.75 for each walleyed pike and $43.75 for each muskellunge).

Moreover, enforcement and tribal court statistics do not support STAW's claim. Between 1990 and 2002 there were nine convictions for wasting resources among the hundreds of fishermen from half a dozen reservation communities. Four of them were commercial, two for hook-and-line fishing, one for ice fishing, and two for spearing. In the same period, however, there were 117 violations for taking *more* than the bag limit. These are typically the result of mistakes made in counting the fish that are already in the boat. According to tribal court records, when the bag limits are exceeded, it is in the low single digits. And these violations often represent a decision to take a ticket instead of letting a fish go to waste by throwing it back.

Non-Indians living in close and tense proximity to the members of the bands of Lake Superior Ojibwes perennially allege that Indians leave fish to rot. This is not based in pure anti–ecological Indian fantasy. The *Lakeland*

Times, which from many tribal members' perspective is often happy to print bad news about the reservation, has gone so far as to publish a photo that might be taken by the uninitiated as evidence for the mostly *sotto voce* image of Indians as dependent and lazy wastrels. The photo we have in mind shows a pile of dozens of fish that have been cleaned for their fillets, which often resemble whole fish at first glance. We know of at least one place on one reservation where cleaned fish carcasses are left for eagles who nest nearby. The practice of filleting fish dates to the early twentieth century, an era when many Ojibwe men earned a living as fishing guides for affluent non-Indians and offered their metropolitan clients a shore lunch of walleye and fried potatoes. This might be thought of as a creative response to the de facto policy of assimilating Indians into the working class that began when the state of Wisconsin arrogated to itself the right to regulate Indian resource use, treaties signed with the federal government reserving this right to the tribes notwithstanding. Aggressive assimilation was effected by allotment that sought to break up the now-impoverished tribal estates into eighty-acre farmsteads. This was followed by mandatory manual education, the goal being to make Indian people into yeoman farmers. To this day, some people who do not fillet will point out the traditional practice of scaling the fish, cutting it up in chunks, and leaving the bones in place. But the practice is as uncommon as preparing fish head soup, the traditionality of which is currently being debated.

Filleting walleye and other fish is a subtle reminder of the emergence of class differences in the late nineteenth and early twentieth century that came with greater articulation with the regional economy. And with the greater affluence came refrigerators and freezers, which further encouraged both the practice of filleting and the current debate as to whether the new technologies were facilitating or preventing waste. Guiding, it might be added, should be counted as the reproduction of traditional ends by commercial means. Indian men could finally get paid for doing what they had always done, and thus they were able to purchase the tools that made at least a dimension of traditional life possible.

This extended introductory digression into the sociology of claims about Ojibwe resource use, contemporary tribal law, and the history of Ojibwe piscine culinary practice is not intended to exonerate the bands from anything but faultless ecological behavior. Its purpose is rather to provide a backdrop for the emergence of an institution that organizes the process of cooperative resource harvesting and management between the tribes. The Great Lakes Indian Fish and Wildlife Commission (GLIFWC) has emerged since the treaties signed in the mid-nineteenth century were upheld in federal appeals court in 1983, a date eight years after the passage of the Indian Education and Self-Determination Act, itself four years after the appearance of the crying Indian, the Iron Eyes Cody image deployed so effectively by the environmentalist movement in the 1970s and with which Krech begins his book.

The Emergence of GLIFWC

When the Seventh Circuit Court of Appeals in Chicago handed down the Voigt decision in January 1983, Gordon Thayer at the Lac Courte Oreilles reservation recognized that something significant had been won for more than just Lac Courte Oreilles, the tribe that initiated the suit. The six Wisconsin bands of Lake Superior Ojibwes (St. Croix, Lac Courte Oreilles, Red Cliff, Bad River, Lac du Flambeau, and Sokaogon), the Fond du Lac and Mille Lacs of Minnesota, and the Keweenaw Bay, Bay Mills, and Lac Vieux Desert in Michigan, each a separate "domestic dependent nation," in Chief Justice John Marshall's infamous and ambiguous words, now collectively held rights on the lands and waters ceded in the treaties of 1837 and 1842. Though intermarrying for more than a century since distinct bands had emerged as tribes because of the treaty of 1854, which ceded lands in Minnesota on the condition that reservations be established, these communities had rather distinct histories given the different natural resources in their vicinities and in their immediate hinterlands, their different legal statuses, as well as their differential engagement with the particular non-Indian communities that surrounded them. For example, the Bad River and Red Cliff reservations border on Lake Superior, have access to the commercial big lake fishery, and had formed the Great Lakes Indian Fisheries Commission in 1982. The Lac du Flambeau and Lac Courte Oreilles reservations are in regions dense with inland lakes and tourist industry installations. St. Croix and Mole Lake communities did not receive reservations in the 1854 treaty and were landless until the 1930s, when they were given reservations by executive order. The former was relatively dispersed into four communities in western Wisconsin, and the latter was concentrated in an area around wild rice lakes in the eastern part of the state.

In recognition of a complex polity in collective possession of property, Thayer motivated his community to invite all the other bands to a meeting in Telemark, Wisconsin. He wanted the leaders to understand that a tribal right had been recognized that would be exercised by individuals but, as such, be susceptible of tribal regulation. He sought to consolidate an understanding of these points and so not risk the consequence of individuals going off the reservation, being cited by state officials, and generating a series of legal opinions that would cover the waterfront and jeopardize tribal regulation, enforcement, and exercise of the rights. The solution to the problem of exclusive jurisdiction over their own tribal members in a common territory was to get each of the bands to delegate its enforcement power and model regulatory authority to one agency. That agency would be named the Voigt Intertribal Task Force. Within a year, the task force merged with the Great Lakes Indian Fisheries Commission and became the Great Lakes Indian Fish and Wildlife Commission (GLIFWC), an intertribal agency that exercises "delegated tribal sovereign authority in the areas of ceded territory/ off-reservation natural resource management, harvest regulation, and conservation law enforcement" (Zorn 2003, 2). This process of commission formation had taken place earlier, following important off-reservation treaty rights cases elsewhere. The Northwest Indian Fisheries Commission was established after *United States v. Washington* (384 F.Supp. 312) in 1974, the Columbia River Intertribal Fish Commission emerged out of *United States v. Oregon* (745 F.2d at 552) in 1978, and the Chippewa Ottawa Resource Authority followed *United States v. Michigan* (471 F.Supp. 192) in 1979.

Formalizing their relationship with each other in recognition of a profound and now legal bond that united them, the six Wisconsin tribes that joined in the Voigt case developed and signed the "Chippewa Intertribal Agreement Governing Resource Management and Regulation of Off-reservation Treaty Rights in the Ceded Territory." The commission's constitution reads:

> The Great Lakes Indian Fish and Wildlife Commission was begun in recognition of the traditional pursuits of the Native American people and the deep abiding respect for the circle of life in which our fellow creatures have played an essential life-giving role. As governments who have inherited the responsibilities for protection of our fish, wildlife, and plants we are burdened with the inability to effectively carry out tasks as protectors and managers. This is especially true now that the state and federal courts have recognized our traditional claims. We have never intended to abandon our responsibilities.

This attention to "traditional pursuits," "responsibilities," and "tasks" communicates a sense of the weight of the moral charge that the tribes feel they have taken on even in a complicated political context wherein they would have to share that, thus their "inability" to do that in a way that is unburdened by the interests of others.

Although it would take most of the 1990s for the commission to grow to its present size, being joined by five more bands from the Upper Peninsula of Michigan and Minnesota, of the six divisions, the Biological Services Division is the most prominent with Great Lakes, inland fisheries, wildlife, and environmental biologists and technicians. The Conservation Enforcement Division has wardens stationed on every reservation. The Division of Intergovernmental Affairs tends to the legal and policy analysis. The Public Information Division publishes a quarterly newspaper and a large array of materials, many of which are available on or via the commission's website at http://www.glifwc.org/. The Planning and Development Division brings in grant money that supplements the operating funds for which the commission, a "tribal organization" within the meaning of PL 93–638, contracts with the Department of the Interior, Bureau of Indian Affairs (Schlender 1992). With nearly sixty employees, the commission is big enough to have an Administration Division.

The appeals court remanded the case to the district court. The commission's task force "rolled up their sleeves and set to work" (Ashi-naanan 2002), chiefly on what would become forty interim agreements negotiated with the Wisconsin Department of Natural Resources (WDNR) over a period of seven years to determine how the treaty rights were going to be exercised species by species and season by season until a final court decision. The state's goal was to "mesh the exercise of Chippewa reserved hunting and fishing rights into the present system of state hunting and fishing regulation with a minimum impact on sports fishing and the tourism industry" (Silvern 1995, 260), to quote the WDNR's chief negotiator. Federal law permitted the state to regulate only within constraints defined by conservation, public health, and safety. Determining exactly what that encompassed entailed negotiations that were rough, especially when it came to walleyed pike and muskellunge, very important fish in a regional tourist industry valued in the hundreds of millions of dollars.

The task force sought to gain agreements with the WDNR that would permit Indian people to employ the hunting and fishing methods that had evolved on the reservations throughout the ceded territory since the last quarter of the nineteenth century, when the lands were surveyed. These included transporting loaded and uncased rifles in vehicles, shooting from vehicles on unpaved roads, and shining—using artificial light to hunt at night. The tribes succeeded in winning most elements except shining and were also able to negotiate a much longer hunting season. In the area of fishing they sought the right to spear spawning game fish at night using motorized boats. The WDNR recoiled at these demands and attempted to represent the practices as unsafe and anti-conservation. Here, the bands succeeded again, and were met by protestors at the boat landings who accused them of "raping the resources," a powerful and widely circulated metaphor that revealed a latent image of Indians residing in the collective imagina-

tion of non-Indians that evoked Hollywood-movie stereotypes where Indians savaged white women. It was however, non-Indians who denounced
treaty rights as unequal rights and orchestrated their political opinions with
the savagery of "bomb threats, . . . gun shots, and roofing nails scattered
at boatlandings" (Silvern 1995, 260), while Indian people tacitly embraced
the nonviolent political philosophy of Gandhi and Martin Luther King Jr.
though all the while representing themselves as warriors.

Of the approximately one million walleyed pike in the lakes of the ceded
territories, the bands took between twenty and thirty thousand per year, av-
eraging 15.6 inches in length in the first ten years of the harvest, with every
fish counted and 80 percent sexed and measured. Eighty-three percent of
these were male. It may be the most tightly regulated and monitored walleye fishery in the world. By contrast, the sports fishery took an estimated
624,000 in the 1980s and about half that in the 1990s when the WDNR instituted a fifteen-inch size limit.

Throughout the negotiation of the interim agreements with the state, the
tribes argued for the right to implement a harvest organized and timed in a
traditional manner. This meant, for example, taking deer at the time of the
fireflies, and musky when the popple leaves were as big as a squirrel's ear.
They construed this as a property right and demanded that the state cast
its arguments in biological rather than social and economic terms. Unable
to demonstrate that spearing had a significant impact on the walleye and
muskellunge populations, the state went on to attempt to win forbearance
agreements from the bands, surprising them at the first joint press conference in 1985 with the public position that "spearing will never be acceptable in the north." Subsequently, two tribal councils would negotiate forbearance agreements, but the efforts would fail at referendum.

The forbearance agreements—or "buy-outs," as some called them—came
after other avenues of curtailing Indian resource use had come to be seen as
unfruitful. Some tribal members represented the state's effort as reducing
traditional practice to property and therefore to a potential monetary value.
A discourse emerged wherein these practices were represented as not like
property in the American sense at all, but as something more. In the context

of a regional revitalization of indigenous culture, the meaning of fishing—and to a lesser extent hunting—began to be elaborated along traditionalist lines by some, and this approach circulated and gained currency as the state persisted. The rights began to be associated with the wisdom of their ancestors, with Mother Earth, with something they had to protect for their children and their children's children. They came to symbolize Ojibwe distinctiveness and were seen as both a sign of and a means of cultural preservation and survival. This came to be thought of as their "psychic value" and was understood as the value of the rights that could not be monetized.

The appearance in 1988 of Edward Benton-Banai's *The Mishomis Book: The Voice of the Ojibway* and the emergence the previous decade of the Three Fires Midewiwin Lodge, of which Benton-Banai continues as the grand chief, were important moments in the process of elaborating and giving form and meaning to a set of practices and beliefs that had lain dormant for many years in some cases and were practiced surreptitiously, even illegally, in others.

Benton-Banai was born in a traditionalist enclave on the Lac Courte Oreilles reservation during the depression. He co-founded the American Indian Movement in Minneapolis (Churchill and Vanderwall 1988) and played an instrumental role in the 1971 takeover of the Winter Dam at Lac Courte Oreilles (Rasmussen 1998), infusing these political actions with cultural significance. *The Mishomis Book* articulates a revived traditional Ojibwe cosmology, history, and prophecy. It appeared just as the conflict over the exercise of off-reservation hunting, fishing, and gathering rights was reaching its peak and played a part in shaping how that conflict was understood.

Unlike the Midewiwin lodges documented in the nineteenth and twentieth centuries (Hoffman 1891; Landes 1968; Vecsey 1983), the Three Fires Lodge is both international and to some extent intertribal. It is also more inclusive, as English translations are provided for the ceremonies conducted in Anishinaabemowin "so that no one is left behind," in the words of the grand chief. The lodge has members from all the Wisconsin Ojibwe reservations, and a few members are also employees of the commission.

In the judgment of most observers, the conflict between tribal members fishing off their reservations and non-Indians protesting that right reached its peak in 1989 (Schlender 1991; Silvern 1995; Nesper 2002). It was at this time that some Indian people began to articulate a nonviolent philosophy. Many Indians had found their *asemaa* (tobacco) and were using it in the traditional way, offering it as a sacrifice to the spirits. It seemed that Indian country in the north country was in the midst of a spiritual and cultural renaissance.

Big Drums and Little Boy waterdrums (used in the Midewiwin Lodge) were finding their voices sounded, some for the first time in decades. In 1989 the sacred pipe led a procession to the state capitol in Madison on the Walk for Justice, in which a dozen Indian walkers were joined by what the organizers estimated to be three thousand people, mostly non-Indians who refused to allow the protesters at the boat landings be their voice. In the summer of that same year, the first Peace and Solidarity Run was staged wherein runners from all the Ojibwe communities involved in the Voigt litigation formed a core group that relay-ran a staff between the reservations in a show of unity. The run was a physical manifestation of the consensus among the tribes to peacefully defend their treaty rights. It was also an embodied and dramatic repatriation of the ceded territory, another dimension of the spiritual and cultural renaissance that was taking place in the north country. The practice would develop into related contexts in the years to come.

Both the Sokaogon and Flambeau bands' tribal councils negotiated forbearance of the rights with the state of Wisconsin in 1989, only to have their memberships vote it down in referenda. Lac Courte Oreilles, led by their trial chair, Gaiashkibos, who had earlier adopted a translation of his Euro-American family name, took the position that the treaty rights were not for sale and refused to negotiate an out-of-court settlement. These were watershed events both on the reservations, where the votes were taken, and in the intertribal community, where the votes symbolized an affirmation and re-emergence of a traditional order of values.

In 1991 the bands followed up their rejection of a state forbearance of the rights with actions that had the effect of settling the social conflict on rather favorable terms. Members of the Lac du Flambeau band sued the protest leaders for violation of their civil rights, winning injunctions, costs, and attorney fees, thereby gutting the organized protests. A year-long study assessing the fishery undertaken by the six Wisconsin bands, the Bureau of Indian Affairs, the U.S. Fish and Wildlife Service, the Wisconsin Department of Natural Resources, and the Great Lakes Indian Fish and Wildlife Commission, and funded by a special congressional appropriation, was published and concluded that the walleye populations in the lakes were healthy and unaffected by the spearfishing. When the study was presented in Rhinelander, Wisconsin, Senator Daniel Inouye faced down the anti-treaty leader of the protest moment. The process of the study's production, however, was so fraught with difficulty—largely between the tribes and the WDNR—that when it came time to title the report, no agreement could be found. Seeking to mediate, embrace, and transcend differences, James Schlender suggested "Casting Light upon the Waters," bringing together both angling and harvesting by evoking the lightness of fly fishing, the light of the spearfishermen's fishing torches, and the light cast by the report that would illuminate the good health of the fishery. In May 1991 both the state and the tribes let the deadline pass to appeal the final judgment of the district court. In the memory of those on the commission through the "war years," the post-Voigt era had begun.

Tribal Ecological Practice

Reflecting the change in era, *Mazina'igan*, the GLIFWC's newsletter, which had been published monthly since 1984, became a quarterly in 1991, with a circulation of twelve thousand. Aggressive efforts in the Voigt era to educate the non-Indian public about the treaties and Ojibwe history shifted in the post-Voigt era to an effort to educate people both within the tribal communities and within the expanding organization. More articles describing and encouraging the traditional use of resources began to appear as well as biographical sketches of exemplary tribal members often featuring their commitment to traditional activities and the teaching thereof. Every issue now included language pages. Some articles were written in both languages. The Anishinaabemowin terms for particular species began to appear in articles about management. The conception of the reading public was changing, and the newsletter was becoming a way for members of the intertribal community of Anishinaabe in the upper Great Lakes region to reimagine themselves and the meaning of their presence on this landscape. There would be institutional shifts as well.

In February 1992 the commission rewrote its mission statement to add a cultural infusion function to its existing governmental functions:

> To provide assistance to member tribes in the conservation and management of fish, wildlife, and other natural resources throughout the Great Lakes region, thereby insuring access to traditional pursuits of the Chippewa people;
>
> To facilitate the development of institutions of tribal self-government so as to insure the continued sovereignty of its member tribes in the regulation and management of natural resources;
>
> To extend the mission to ecosystem protection recognizing that fish, wildlife, and wild plants cannot long survive in abundance in an environment that has been degraded;
>
> To infuse traditional Anishinaabe culture and values as all aspects of the mission are implemented. (Strategic Directions 1992, 3)

The cultural renaissance that had begun in conflict would now be carried forth by the commission in efforts to shape the management of the resources within the ceded territory, driven by the goal of sustaining and revitalizing Ojibwe society and reproducing those resources by ethically managing and harvesting them. A theory of human society in the natural world is embedded in this practice. Simply put, Ojibwe society is distinguished and viable as a society of hunters, fishers, and gatherers. Although most Ojibwe people are also active participants in the wage economy, everyone has close kin who assume this responsibility to carry on the traditions.

Harvesting nearly 50,000 pounds of walleye in Wisconsin and 54,000 pounds in Minnesota, more than 2,500 deer, and between 3.7 and 20 metric tons of wild rice each year are all indices of this commitment and value. The development of nine tribal fish hatcheries, seven of which have emerged since the Voigt decision, and which collectively contribute over one hundred million fish to both the inland and Great lakes, are also measures of this. The detailed studies of mercury contamination in walleye and the publication of a series of six maps—centered on each of the six Wisconsin reservations—showing the mercury levels and the size of edible fish indexed for human age and gender are not only icons of the way in which this landscape is being counter-mapped (and therefore counter-imagined) but also measures of the extent to which this community is committed to a hunting, fishing, and gathering mode of production. These maps are available on each reservation and also on the commission's website. Working with the U.S. Fish and Wildlife Service, the U.S. Forest Service, and WDNR from the very first years of its existence, the commission has undertaken a wild rice restoration project that has reseeded scores of waters with between 2.7 and 6.3 metric tons of seed each year. This is particularly significant in that the Ojibwes of the western Great Lakes believe they migrated to this region in response to the first prophet's exhortation to live "where food grows on water." The Circle of Flight program, a series of waterfowl and wetland enhancement projects that brings together both public and private agencies with the tribes, is changing the landscape of the ceded territory (Circle of Flight 2006).

In that human beings were the last to be created and are dependent upon the power of nonhuman persons in order to act effectively as social persons, generative engagement with those nonhuman persons comes in the form of hunting, fishing, and gathering. The "essential life-giving role" played by "our fellow creatures" requires that humans assume responsibility for a relationship of respect with them by engaging in the exchange of honor, often symbolized by gifts of tobacco in thankfulness for the sacrifice of their physical bodies that is part of the covenant between Anishinaabe and the animals and plants, and earth generally. Their physical bodies, now food, are then widely shared in feasts, honoring their spirits and sustaining human life. In the first years of court-sanctioned off-reservation spearfishing, spearers actually cleaned, cooked, and consumed some of the fish at the boat landings in their temporary fishing camps. Non-Indian spectators were invited to share in the lakes' bounty. This sharing was commonly refused by non-Indians in the memory of the spearers.

This complex of values is encompassed by the term *nikaaniiganaa*, "respect for all our relations." It undergirds the dispositions articulated in a statement titled "The Anishinaabe Way," which followed the commission's 1992 mission statement:

> In comparison to non-Indians who protect and enhance most natural resources for recreational purposes, the Anishinaabe people hold the basic philosophy that the Creator provides fish, game, and plant resources for subsistence purposes.
>
> The "Anishinaabe Way" underlies the unique approach to resource management which is brought by tribal people into the critical, modern day decisions regarding natural resources. Traditional thought directs management to be holistic and integrated, respectful of all creation. An understanding of the universal order and recognition of man's dependence on all other life forms, rather than his dominance, assures holistic management. Traditional thought also demands long-term vision, protecting the well-being, not just of the next generation or two, but of the "Seventh Generation," thus extending responsibility for the impact of management decisions far into the future. (Strategic Directions 1992, 2)

The Anishinaabe Way is grounded in hunting as a mode of production, relationship, and means of management. In 1995 James Schlender addressed the Governor's Symposium on the North American Hunting Heritage in Green Bay. "More important than sharing our game," he said, "we share the responsibility of effective management of these resources which we all prize so highly. . . . . [T]he tribes have been working hand in hand with state, federal and local organizations to enhance the knowledge of the resources we hold in common so that we can jointly preserve our hunting privileges. . . . Anishinabe nations bring diversity into resource management" (Schlender 1995).

The right to work "hand in hand" with the state derives from the stipulations and court orders in the series of court cases that make up the Voigt litigation as well as pretrial agreements. The tribes are represented on sixteen WDNR species advisory committees as a result. They are also on a few other committees dealing with specific aspects of management, such as setting quotas for deer harvests, deer population goals and management unit boundaries, and committees for the management of wild rice. A Technical Working Group has been established that meets twice a year and deals with the inland fishery. The committees are to make decisions by consensus (Silvern 1995, 289–90). Because the treaty rights in the Minnesota section of the 1837 treaty cession were upheld by the U.S. Supreme Court in 1999, the federal court has approved an analogous committee there.

As a result of this involvement, the GLIFWC has deployed monetary and technical resources to the study of many of these species. The commission does population assessments on a number of fish on the inland and Great Lakes as well as land mammals and wild plants throughout the ceded territory. It keeps harvest and survey data on all the fish species that are speared and netted as well as harvest data for deer, bear, fish, otter, bobcat, turkey, waterfowl, and wild rice. In 1999 the commission convened a two-day conference on wild rice that brought together more than two hundred people to hear twenty-five presentations on the place of wild rice in Ojibwe society, history, archaeology, ecology, genetics, and management. The commission went on to publish the proceedings (*Proceedings* 2000). Commission biologists have studied the concentrations of mercury and other heavy metals in walleye and wild rice. The commission has also done developmental and ecosystem studies. The effect has been a manifold increase in the quantity and variety of scientific knowledge about animals and plants in the ceded territories.

The GLIFWC has staked its work product and hence its reputation on the principle of sound science. In recent years this has been enhanced and complemented with traditional knowledge. Grants from the Administration for Native Americans support the development and dissemination of traditional knowledge about these species, including proper stewardship of ecosystems. The commission has published *Plants Used by the Great Lakes Ojibwa*, a 440-page compendium of hundreds of plants that identifies their location in the ceded territory, the name in Anishinaabemowin, and their use. In 2002 it produced *Onjiakiing: From the Earth!*, a CD on the nonmedicinal uses of plants that includes the transcripts of the meetings with the elders that generated the database.

Tribulations and Triumphs of Cooperative Management
The policy implications of cooperative management of treaty resources in the context of self-determination are divided into protection and enhancement. In the area of protection, the commission monitors state and federal policies that potentially threaten the integrity of the resources that make a contemporary hunting, fishing, and gathering society possible. It has been especially attentive to efforts on the part of mining corporations engaging in the legal process with both the Army Corps of Engineers and the Department of Natural Resources over permitting. In the mid-1980s it monitored and critiqued a Department of Energy initiative to build a crystalline repository for radioactive wastes in the ceded territory. It has commented on issues to the Environmental Protection Agency. It has been working with both state and federal agencies in efforts to eradicate lamprey in the Great Lakes as well as exotic plant species such as purple loosestrife and water milfoil inland. It supported tribal efforts to gain Treatment-as-State status under the Clean Water Act and the Clean Air Act. Via the commission the tribes have actively sought a more prominent position on the International Joint Commission, an entity created by the 1909 Boundary Waters Treaty between the United States and Canada that advises the governments of both nations regarding Great Lakes waterways. GLIFWC staff chair two and are members of four committees of the Great Lakes Fisheries Commission, a binational public organization representing the eight Great Lakes states, the provinces of Ontario and Quebec, and the Northeast-Midwest Institute, a group focusing on Great Lakes legislative issues. GLIFWC is a signatory of the Joint Strategic Great Lakes Fishery Management Plan.

In 2000 the commission won a Harvard University governance award for negotiating a Memorandum of Understanding with the U.S. Department of Agriculture–Forest Service that establishes protocols for the exercise of treaty-guaranteed hunting, fishing, and gathering rights in the U.S. national forests within the territories ceded in treaties of 1836, 1837, and 1842 and sets up a collaborative consultation process regarding management decisions on those forests. This was a wise and bold step forward by Robert Jacobs, regional forester of the Eastern Region, which has permitted the parties to avoid litigation over the exercise of the rights on these lands. Since that time, bands have established tribal sugarbushes and begun to harvest maple sap in two of the national forests. The tribes administer a permit system for gathering these resources. In recognition of the retention of general usufructuary rights, camping fees are suspended for tribal members in the national forests.

Realizing *nikaaniiganaa* as policy and practice vis-à-vis the authority of the WDNR, however, has been a challenge within the parameters established by the federal district court. In 1989, in the context of the walleye trial, Judge Barbara Crabb defined the relationship between the tribes and the state in regard to the resources of the ceded territory as follows:

> The fact that plaintiffs may be regulating their members' exercise of their treaty rights does not make them the manager of the fisheries. That responsibility and authority remains the defendants'. They have the fiduciary obligation of managing the natural resources within the ceded territory for the benefit of current and future users. . . . The tribes' regulation of their members does not relieve the department of this obligation or prevent it from carrying it out, although it narrows its management options to a significant degree, and imposes burdens on them beyond those it has carried out in the previous implementation of the Voigt decision. (Crabb 1989)

Those "narrows" and "burdens" echo the constraint the tribes felt when they described themselves in GLIFWC's constitution as "burdened with the inability to effectively carry out tasks as protectors and managers." For a short period of time after this decision, the state and the tribes explored co-management, looking at the ways in which the arrangement was working in Washington and Oregon. The tribes were enthusiastic, as this would entail their participating as equals in decision making. It was also attractive to some of the state administrators as a means of diffusing tensions. However, in a backhanded recognition of the tribes' legal status, the state abandoned the initiative as inviting an "independent and sovereign government" to share the state's public trust responsibility. The forces opposed to co-management were able to represent the model as leading to more tension (Silvern 1995, 383).

The state was more comfortable with what it calls "cooperative management." In this model the state and the tribes jointly develop projects and work together to protect and enhance resources. Although the state retains final authority as resource manager, that authority is circumscribed as to the extent to which the tribes' rights are realized. The tribes then are the managers of the resources they harvest. In the trenches, and in the area of fisheries, cooperative management has placed the burden of initiatives on the tribes: if they take the responsibility to remind the WDNR of the intent of the stipulations in the district court cases, and then coax the WDNR to take more serious recognition of their concerns as stakeholders in the ceded territories, the WDNR will usually acquiesce and listen to their issues. However, the expectation that the joint committees will operate by consensus is conservative, and therefore conflict often resolves to the status quo.

This is less true for wildlife management, but then again, it is the fisheries that have historically been the most contested issue in the ceded territory. In fact, when setting the quotas for the deer harvests became politicized for a short period of time in the early 1990s, GLIFWC's demands for state accountability resulted in a more transparent account of a process that had previously been understood very poorly. The wildlife section of the WDNR has publicly thanked the commission for initiating this policy. Both organizations recognize that the tribes can always go back to court as litigants in an adversarial mode or as supplicants seeking clarification of previous rulings.

The disinclination to co-manage has politically benefited the WDNR vis-à-vis the sports fishing tourist interests in the state, which have been accommodated in the district court order. In the 1989 walleye trial (Crabb 1989) the state won the right to use its walleye and muskellunge management plan in determining the levels at which the lakes could be harvested by tribal spearing and netting with the introduction of the "safe harvest" concept. Safe harvest reduces a biologically sustainable harvest rate of 35 percent of the total estimated adult fish population by another 30–35 percent as protection against potential worst-case scenarios using data gathered at Escanaba Lake, the WDNR's research lake in the region. The concept would permit the WDNR to index sports fishing bag limits to the level at which lakes were speared by the bands, thus reducing the traditional bag limit of five walleye per person per lake per day for anglers. The concept of safe harvest is not applied to lakes that are not speared in a particular year. These lakes are designated self-regulating. Rennard Strickland (1990) commented on the policy: "The only way to make sense of this inconsistent policy is to conclude that non-Indian anglers' bag limits are being manipulated by the WDNR in order to prompt those anglers to pressure the Chippewa into reducing their harvest. Non-Indians are thus used as pawns and the public deceived. Resulting public outrage, which should be focused on the WDNR policymakers, is diverted to the Chippewa."

The policy works as intended, with tribes pressured to scale back the percentage of safe harvest they declare each March 15 in order not to have an adverse impact on relations with the state in other areas. In fact, the Wisconsin Conservation Congress has publicly recommended that gaming compacts between the Ojibwes and the state be held hostage to lower declarations. After the spring harvests the tribes are further pressured to release the fish in the declarations that were not speared, thus raising the bag limits for anglers. In May 1998 the WDNR changed its regulations to allow higher angler bag limits on lakes that were speared below the level of tribal declarations. The decision was experienced as unilateralism and a violation of the spirit of cooperative management. From this point on, a tribe that decides to harvest in the summer and fall is doing so in the face of the likelihood of additional politics entering the picture if the WDNR lowers the bag limit in the following year as a response following its own rules. Adding to the complexity of the regional scene over this issue, the Lac du Flambeau band negotiated an agreement with the state that the band would declare harvests at a level leaving the lakes with a three-walleye bag limit for anglers in exchange for being able to sell state fishing, snowmobile, and ATV licenses and keep the revenue. Some of the other tribes looked askance on this.

Despite the potential political costs, the tribes are economically diverse enough that each has sectors that continue to push for bigger harvests. The effect has been some ongoing tension between the tribes and the state over the walleye harvest. After determining the sustainable harvest levels on a series of lakes, the tribes declared their intention to take a total of about fifty thousand walleye each spring. The distribution of this declaration over many scores of lakes reflects a great deal of cooperative work done by the commission and WDNR in assessing the fish populations, with the agencies sharing responsibility for assessing the fish populations by electroshocking most of the lakes that will be harvested. That cooperation was hard won. In one of the very early years, the WDNR threatened the tribes' Inland Fisheries biologist with arrest and confiscation of GLIFWC's electro-fishing boat on the Chippewa Flowage if he "rolled a fish," as they say referring to this technique of survey work. Before 1983 the WDNR undertook about twelve spring population estimates a year; between 1990 and 2001 it was doing more than forty a year and the commission was doing nearly twenty. In this domain, cooperative management has made a great deal of difference.

Even in the best of years, however, the tribes have been able to take only thirty thousand walleye, about 60 percent of their declared harvest level. Spearing may be very efficient compared to angling, though the anglers take the vast majority of the fish. There is also far more accountability for the spearers. Spearing, however, is not so efficient that the hundreds of tribal members who go out can reach either their personal or the tribes' collective goal. There are too many lakes to go to and not enough time or energy in a season that typically lasts for two weeks. The tribes have suggested that very restrictive netting regulations be amended, having learned a great deal at Mille Lacs in the Minnesota section of the 1837 ceded territory in recent years where the tribes are taking about fifty thousand pounds of walleye each spring, most of which are netted. But the WDNR will not agree to this and so there is a stalemate, though it could be because the tribes and the state agreed to a mechanism to change the stipulations in the final judgment by mutual consent.

The WDNR's circumscription of the concerns of the bands included management of the Great Lakes as well. In 1991 the handful of commercial treaty fishermen who take whitefish from Lake Superior were nearly devastated economically by a WDNR rule that required lake trout inadvertently netted to be tagged and kept. The number of gill nets they could set was also reduced. By virtue of the law, the tribes are in a position of having to regulate subsistence harvesting more carefully than the state regulates its recreational users of the same resources. Although this is often a point of conflict, it has some salutary effects. It foregrounds an opposition between the recreational and subsistence engagement with nonhuman life forms, a cultural distinction that has been elaborated since the Voigt decision. Freedom to use the resources recreationally is counterposed against the tribal responsibility to harvest. This is regarded as "a responsibility to feed ourselves, to the souls of our ancestors, to preserve the right for our children, and to the fish in gratitude for the gift of their offering to us," in the words of a tribal leader (Schlender 1995).

The political cost of monitoring is far greater for the state than for the tribes. But by having to monitor the harvests more carefully than the state is monitoring recreational use of the same resources, the tribes are in a stronger position to argue using scientific data and to reveal where the WDNR is sidelining science for political concerns. An example is WDNR resistance to considering netting. From the tribal perspective, their scientific arguments often fall on deaf ears when the WDNR perceives that there would be too great a political cost for exploring higher tribal harvests given the heterogeneity of the WDNR's constituency. Of course, the option to litigate these differences is available as both sides continually and carefully assess the strengths and weaknesses of the other's arguments, their political resources, and the general political climate.

Despite, or perhaps because of, these realities, memoranda of understanding have been negotiated in the areas of law enforcement, wildlife management, fisheries management, and cultural awareness, and the WDNR has established an office of Tribal Co-Operative Management (Silvern 1995, 390–91). There has been great progress in the restoration of wild rice in many of the lakes of northern Wisconsin due to the cooperation between the tribes, federal agencies, and WDNR, which agreed to create a Species Management Committee to be co-chaired by the tribes.

The tribes, via GLIFWC, and the state of Wisconsin, via its Department of Natural Resources, are equally committed to the protection and enhancement of natural resources. Both mission statements use these terms. People within the commission are sensitive to the suggestion that it is an "Indian DNR," as this critique is typically leveled when the commission is perceived by some as acting like the bureaucracy it sometimes has to be when it finds itself realizing the burdens of sovereignty among the sisterhood of nations and states on behalf of its constituent tribes. To overcome the mistrust and distrust of each as litigants, states are wise to assess and value the certainty and rectitude of co-management as a vehicle that is best powered by concepts of fairness and equality tempered by need.

Both the GLIFWC and the WDNR manage by responding to social, economic, and legal processes that emerge from within the sovereigns they serve. Both are equally committed to science, and both are equally sensitive to their respective political realities. The state manages to accommodate a variety of interests, including those of legal persons with far more power than others (e.g., corporations). The tribes, however, manage for purposes of subsistence and for the reproduction and revitalization of a society that continues to be organized by kinship, age, and gender—not class, as tribal members see it, like the dominant society.

The renewed engagement with the land, lakes, and animals in the ceded territory has revitalized an interest in tribal history. In 2000 the GLIFWC began a process of commemorating the failed and illegal attempt to remove the bands to Sandy Lake in Minnesota, which killed an estimated four hundred Anishinaabe people (Clifton 1987); this commemoration culminated in the placing of a marker near the site of the graves and a 150–mile relay run from Sandy Lake to Madeline Island, the Ojibwes' symbolic home, in December 2000 on the 150th anniversary. The undertaking represented an important moment in the emergence of an intertribal national consciousness among the eleven GLIFWC bands. It also represented an expansion of the commission's role as an indigenous national institution.

Conclusion

As a confederacy of culturally and ethnically similar indigenous nations, the Great Lakes Indian Fish and Wildlife Commission represents a legal and scientific means by which that confederacy imagines itself. The rhetoric of the ecological Indian is inappropriate here, and there is very little of it in the many hundreds of pages in the now-eighteen-year run of *Mazina'igan*, GLIFWC's most accessible public face. There is an understanding that protecting and enhancing opportunities to harvest the undomesticated resources of the ceded territories is at the heart of Ojibwe Indian ethnicity in the upper Great Lakes. Of course, the land, the waters, and the forms of life that inhabit them are the condition of the possibility of human society for all of us. But human societies engage with the nonhuman domain in different ways that are typically mediated by orders of value and theories of human and nonhuman personhood—that is, cultures—that yield societies which have certain forms and shapes. And, of course, the reverse.

These now-postmodern tribal societies, with their relations of production developed in the Paleolithic, and which reproduce themselves not only by means of a particular engagement with nature but also through particular engagements with other societies organized by historically more recent modes of production, may thrive depending on the particular character of that relationship. The Ojibwe tribes that are members of GLIFWC are such a group. Their capacity to appropriate biological science and law is both a sign of their vitality and the means by which they perdure. With this at stake, the ecological or the crying Indian should be regarded only or merely as an exploitive objectification of indigenous people for non-Indian purposes and mostly at Indian expense. The image trivializes the complicated relations between both Indian people and the nonhuman "persons" in the form of animals and plants that make their lives possible, as well as with the different kinds of groups in the dominant society. With this caveat in the foreground, we recognize that the crying Indian did and does make sense to Indian people. He really is crying over the despoliation of the earth, but he also cries for the despoliation of the soul, our collective soul. When the lessons of history are ignored or forgotten, a popular recollection informed only by the fiction of television, film, and dime-novel images robs all of us of our humanity and spirituality.

References

Ashi-naanan: GLIFWC's first fifteen years, 1984–1999. Typescript. Odanah WI: Great Lakes Indian Fish and Wildlife Commission.

Benton-Banai, E. 1988. The Mishomis book: The voice of the Ojibway. Saint Paul MN: Red School House.

Churchill, W. A., and J. Vanderwall. 1988. Agents of repression: The FBI's secret wars against the Black Panthers and the American Indian Movement. Boston: South End Press.

Circle of flight: Tribal wetland and waterfowl enhancement initiative. 2006. Odanah WI: Great Lakes Indian Fish and Wildlife Commission.

Clifton, J. 1987. Wisconsin death march: Explaining the extremes in Old Northwest Indian removal. Transactions of the Wisconsin Academy of Sciences, Arts and Letters 75:1–39.

Cohen, F. G., J. La France, et al. 1986. Treaties on trial: The continuing controversy over Northwest Indian fishing rights. Seattle: University of Washington Press.

Crabb, B. 1989. Lac Courte Oreilles et al. v. State of Wisconsin. Federal Supplement, United States District Court for the Western District of Wisconsin: 707.

Doherty, R. 1990. Disputed waters: Native Americans and the Great Lakes fishery. Lexington: University Press of Kentucky.

Gough, R. 1997. Farming the cutover: A social history of northern Wisconsin, 1900–1940. Lawrence: University of Kansas Press.

Hoffman, W. J. 1891. The Mid'wiwin or Grand Medicine Lodge Society of the Ojibwe. Washington DC, Bureau of American Ethnology Seventh Annual Report: 143–300.

Krech, S., III. 1999. The ecological Indian: Myth and history. New York: Norton.

Landes, R. 1968. Ojibwa religion and the Midéwiwin. Madison: University of Wisconsin Press.

Nesper, L. 2002. The walleye war: The struggle for Ojibwe spearfishing and treaty rights. Lincoln: University of Nebraska Press.

Proceedings of the Wild Rice Research and Management Conference, July 7–8, 1999, Carlton, Minnesota. Odanah WI: Great Lakes Indian Fish and Wildlife Commission.

Rasmussen, C. O. 1998. Where the river is wide: Pahquahwong and the Chippewa flowage. Odanah WI: Great Lakes Indian Fish and Wildlife Commission.

Schlender, J. 1991. Treaty rights in Wisconsin: A review. *Northeast Indian Quarterly* Spring:4–16.

———. 1992. *Affidavit of James H. Schlender*. Dane County WI: United States District Court for the Western District.

———. 1995. Address given at the 1995 Governor's Symposium on the North American Hunting Heritage, Green Bay WI. Manuscript in possession of the Schlender family.

Silvern, S. E. 1995. Nature, territory, and identity in the Wisconsin Ojibwe treaty rights conflict. PhD diss., University of Wisconsin, Madison.

Strategic directions for the Great Lakes Indian Fish and Wildlife Commission in off-reservation treaty resource management. 1992. Odanah WI: Great Lakes Indian Fish and Wildlife Commission.

Strickland, R. 1990. Keeping our word: Indian treaty rights and public responsibilities: A report on a recommended federal role following Wisconsin's request for federal assistance. Manuscript. Madison: University of Wisconsin, School of Law.

Vecsey, C. 1983. *Traditional Ojibwa religion and its historical changes*. Philadelphia: American Philosophical Society.

Zorn, J. E. 2003. Testimony of James E. Zorn, policy analyst of the Great Lakes Indian Fish and Wildlife Commission, before the Senate Committee on Indian Affairs, June 3, 2003.

12. Skull Valley Goshutes and the Politics of Nuclear Waste

Environment, Identity, and Sovereignty

David Rich Lewis

"Over my dead body!" thundered Utah governor Michael Leavitt (*Indian Country Today* 1993). Normally, every committed environmentalist in Utah and the Intermountain West would have lined up to accommodate the Republican governor's challenge. But this time, there was a resounding silence, even an endorsement of the governor's stand. At issue was an agreement between the Skull Valley Band of Goshute Indians and Private Fuel Storage LLC to store forty thousand metric tons of high-level radioactive waste for up to forty years on a concrete pad forty-five miles southwest of Salt Lake City. The eighteen-thousand-acre Skull Valley Goshute Reservation is already surrounded by military bombing ranges, federal nerve agent storage facilities, and private hazardous waste sites, and it affords the approximately 124 band members few if any options for economic development. The agreement would bring the Goshutes jobs and millions of dollars annually. For Skull Valley tribal chairman Leon Bear, the issue is about cultural survival and tribal sovereignty, the paternalism of the state, and the environmental racism of Goshute critics. For Governor Leavitt, the state legislature, and environmental opponents, it is about the lack of state control or fiscal benefit, the fear of having two million residents live downwind from a nuclear repository, the environmental racism of the nuclear industry, and the conflicting images of ecological Indians versus Indians as modern human beings (Verdoia 2001).

This chapter surveys the political and cultural landscape of the nuclear waste storage issue in Utah. It examines the historical background and present realities affecting Goshute decision making; the emerging coalitions and their rationales for opposing the Skull Valley facility; and the larger issues of economic development, environmentalism, tribal sovereignty, and Indian identity at the beginning of the twenty-first century. There are no easy answers here. My intent is to ask questions that will complicate discussion of an issue that on the surface seems morally, politically, and ecologically simple, and then to use that ambiguity in the modern context to reconsider larger arguments about culture and history, about Indians and the environment, and about arguments over the "ecological Indian."

But first, the question: Who in their right mind would store highly radioactive nuclear waste in their own backyard, and why? The story begins fifty years ago at the height of the cold war. In 1954 Congress passed the Atomic Energy Act, terminating the Atomic Energy Commission's monopoly over nuclear technology and encouraging the development of private nuclear energy. Congress promised to handle the disposal of radioactive wastes and to protect the fledgling nuclear power industry by limiting its financial liability in the event of an accident. The industry responded and spent fuel rods began to pile up at the nation's nuclear power plants, but governmental action on waste disposal lagged.

In 1982 Congress enacted the Nuclear Waste Policy Act, directing the Department of Energy (DOE) to study and locate a national nuclear waste repository. The act also established a nuclear waste disposal fund, financed by consumers through a tax of one tenth of one cent for every kilowatt-hour of energy billed by nuclear utilities. Amended in 1987 (and know locally as the "Screw Nevada Bill"), the Nuclear Waste Policy Act practically mandated Yucca Mountain, Nevada, as the DOE national repository study site. It also created the Office of the Nuclear Waste Negotiator to oversee creation of temporary monitored retrievable storage (MRS) facilities in states not slated for the permanent waste repository (Hanson 2001, 27; Johnny 1994, 16; Gross 2001; Carter 1987). The Yucca Mountain study site—land actively claimed by the Western Shoshones under the 1863 Ruby Valley Treaty (Kappler 1904, 2:851–53; Crum 1994) and slowly taken by the government over the following century without Shoshone consent—was riddled with political, geological, and construction problems from the beginning. It became clear to everyone, and particularly to power producers who were fast approaching their onsite storage capacity, that the repository was not going to come online anytime soon (Kuletz 1998; Nokkentved 1991; Hebert 1995; Jacob 1990).

Facing lawsuits from nuclear utilities, the DOE decided to pursue a short-term fix. Acting through the Nuclear Waste Negotiator, the DOE went shopping for an MRS site. By April 1992, eighteen local governmental agencies (county and tribal), representing underdeveloped communities across the country, had applied for the $100,000 "study grants." Among the applicants were the commissioners of San Juan County in southeastern Utah as well as the Skull Valley Band of Goshute Indians in Tooele County in northwestern Utah. Sensing they were sitting squarely in the cross hairs of this siting process, state officials mobilized opposition to the study grants. Utah governor Norman Bangerter (Republican), his successor Michael Leavitt (Republican), and Utah House speaker Craig Moody (Republican) all made it clear that bringing high-level nuclear waste to Utah—or even studying the possibility—was unacceptable, even grounds for calling out the Utah National Guard. San Juan County commissioners complained that they were simply being open-minded about finding real jobs and multimillion-dollar payrolls in a corner of Utah ignored by state government. "Everybody wants to help rural Utah economically," shot back commission chairman Ty Lewis, "but nobody wants to do anything" (qtd. in Bauman 1992; Woolf 1992, 1993; see also Bourke 1994; Church 2004).

In order to bypass the preemptive power state governments would have over interested county commissioners or private corporations, the DOE and the Nuclear Waste Negotiator increasingly tailored their pitch to American Indians (Anquoe 1993). The study grants, designed to help tribes explore the siting issue and to keep them interested, increased in stages from $100,000 to $200,000. Ultimately more than twenty tribes responded, including the Skull Valley Goshutes, Mescalero Apaches, Prairie Island Mdewakanton Sioux, Northern Arapahos, Fort McDermitt Paiute-Shoshones,

Lower Brulé Sioux, Chickasaws, Sac and Fox, Alabama-Quassarte, Poncas, Eastern Shawnees, Caddos, Yakimas, and several Alaska Native communities (Hanson 2001, 42–43; Gowda and Easterling, 1998; Erickson and Chapman 1993; Erickson, Chapman, and Johnny 1994).

Indian leaders and environmental activists across the country protested the program on environmental justice grounds. "It's genocide aimed at Indian people who will suffer the consequences of poisoning our rivers and our land with nuclear waste," warned Klickitat tribal chief Johnny Jackson of the Confederated Yakima Nation. "Even if tribes say they just want to study it, the government intends to hook tribal governments with the money. I know from experience that the government never gives you money for nothing" (qtd. in Taliman 1992). Anishinaabe activist Winona LaDuke spoke out against the government and nuclear power industry "for seeking a political solution to the deadly environmental problem of nuclear waste they created by targeting isolated Native communities. It's bad policy and it's wrong" (qtd. in Kamps 2001, 6; see also Churchill and LaDuke 1992). Some tribes debated the project and backed out of the process. A handful took the project seriously, using the grants to send delegations nationally and internationally to learn firsthand about nuclear power and MRS operations. Both the Mescalero Apaches and the Skull Valley Goshutes were ready for the final-stage $2.8 million study grant when Congress killed funding in 1994 (Lewis 1995, 435–36). At that point, U.S. nuclear power utilities took matters into their own hands.

The utilities had more than 32,000 tons of high-level radioactive waste with a half-life of 10,000 years, produced by the industry's 105 active and 12 decommissioned commercial nuclear reactors. They argued that 68 temporary onsite nuclear waste dumps in 31 states across the country posed a serious security and environmental risk (Project on Government Oversight 2002; Skibine 2001, 316; Fedarko 2000, 2). The industry had a federally managed nuclear waste fund but no way to ensure that the government would complete a permanent repository or locate a temporary MRS before power plants exceeded their onsite storage capacity and had to cease production. And their proposal to transport nuclear waste to a temporary MRS at the

Nevada nuclear weapons test site near Yucca Mountain (a bill dubbed "Mobile Chernobyl" by opponents) was stalled in Congress (Rasmussen 1998; Kamps 2001, 2–3).

On the plus side, the nuclear power industry had its own money and an audience already identified and prepped for them by the DOE study grants—Indian nations, entities beyond the preemptive regulation of state governments. In 1994, Mescalero Apache tribal chairman Wendall Chino and his council negotiated a deal with Northern States Power of Minnesota and a consortium of thirty nuclear power utilities to construct their own temporary MRS on Mescalero land. But over the next two years, and against the background noise of New Mexico state officials threatening legal action to prevent nuclear waste from entering the state, Mescalero tribal members voted the agreement up, then down. As intratribal factionalism and opposition to "Chernobyl Chino's" leadership grew, the agreement fell apart (Leonard 1997; Sachs 1996).

At the same time this deal was unraveling, Nuclear Waste Negotiator Richard Stallings (a former Republican congressman from Idaho) announced that Skull Valley Goshutes had agreed to streamline talks on a temporary waste repository. Stallings hailed the Goshute decision, telling the press, "I appreciate the fact the tribe is looking for economic development. Their land has little economic potential." The announcement stunned Utah governor Michael Leavitt, who lashed out that "to make an agreement without contacting the state is somewhere between impolite and arrogant." He promised to object "actively and strenuously." Goshute tribal attorney Danny Quintana pointedly reminded Utahns (and Leavitt) that "The issues of nuclear energy and nuclear power are environmental problems which involve all of us. . . . This requires decisions made on the basis of fact, not hysteria" (Herald Journal 1994; Gorrell 1994).

Despite state protests, Skull Valley leaders entered negotiations with Private Fuel Storage LLC (PFS), a Delaware-based limited-liability corporation made up of eight of the largest public utilities operating nineteen nuclear power plants in Minnesota, Wisconsin, Illinois, Ohio, New York, New Jersey, California, and Alabama. By the end of 1996 the Skull Valley band had reached a private agreement to lease 820 acres of reservation land for up to forty years to PFS to construct a privately owned and operated independent spent fuel storage installation (ISFSI) for consortium members. The parties sealed the deal in May and June 1997, submitting lease requests to the Bureau of Indian Affairs (BIA) and their application and draft environmental impact statement to the Nuclear Regulatory Commission (NRC). Both agencies subsequently approved the respective applications, and the NRC review process got under way (Woolf 1996; Porterfield 1997; Rasmussen 1998, 343–45; Verdoia 2001, script 5:2). The difference in outcome between the Mescalero and Goshute cases, in part, was that where the Mescalero Apaches had a relatively large and active reservation population and plenty of other resources and development options—a successful casino and ski resort, tourism, hunting, cattle, timber, and natural gas—the Skull Valley Goshutes did not (Satchell 1996). And that, in part, was a result of Goshute contact history.

Goshutes call themselves Kusiutta (literally ashes, dust, desert), "people of the dry earth." They are Shoshonean speakers of the Central Numic branch of the Uto-Aztecan language family (Defa 2000, 77; Thomas, Pendleton, and Cappanari 1986, 262). For hundreds of years before white intrusions into the Great Basin, they lived in one of the harshest environments in the West—the desert area immediately south and west of the Great Salt Lake, extending westward to the Egan Range and Steptoe Valley in eastern Nevada and southward to Utah's Sevier Lake desert. Their territory varies in altitude from arid valley floors of 4,200 to 6,000 feet above sea level to the numerous low, dry mountain ranges (6,000 to 8,000 feet) of the eastern Great Basin that support few if any permanent water sources. While the basin was a cooler and moister environment ten thousand years ago, in the historic period precipitation (five to ten inches annually) and temperature (below zero to over 110°F) vary widely, both seasonally and with altitude and exposure. Aside from a handful of fertile oasis environments in the Deep Creek, Skull, and Tooele valleys where adjoining mountain ranges (8,000 to 12,000 feet) capture and release more moisture, the thin alkali soils of the Great Salt Lake drainage basin support only the most scattered and tenacious vegetation—various seed grasses and cacti, salt, rabbit, and sage-brush, stunted cottonwoods along ephemeral watercourses, and scattered piñon-juniper forests in the higher elevations. In the Great Salt Lake Desert, which makes up the northwestern proportion of the Goshute territorial range, vegetation is nearly nonexistent. This environment supported only the most tenacious human populations as well, at an estimated density of one person to thirty or forty square miles (Steward 1938, 48–49, 132–34; Defa 2000, 73–77; Harper 1986).

In this spare environment, Goshutes built a life where others later would try and fail. Despite deprecatory comments by early Euro-American observers, Goshute cultural adaptations were complex, built around an accumulated generational knowledge of and experience with the basin ecosystem. They were ultimately flexible by necessity given the dispersion and variability of resources from season to season and year to year (Thomas, Pendleton, and Cappanari 1986; Fowler 1986; Chamberlin 1911; Malouf 1940, 1974; Defa 2000, 73–83; Steward 1938, 132–41). Foraging for plant foods was the economic mainstay of the Western Shoshones in general and Goshutes specifically. Extended families of twenty to thirty people foraged together during the summer and fall, making temporary camps and moving regularly to take advantage of localized sources of water and plants. Goshute families gathered resources broadly in the valleys and lower canyons, utilizing forty-seven different species of grass seed, roots from eight different species, and berries from twelve. Piñon pine nuts, gathered in the higher foothills, were an important but irregular foodstuff. Women also gathered and processed grasses and sage or willow bark for coiled and twined baskets and rudimentary summer clothing. During the winter months, multiple family groups would congregate in more stable villages of brush shelters, located in the lower and warmer south-facing foothills of the Deep Creek, Rush, Skull, and Tooele valleys, typically near reliable water sources and food caches of seeds or pine nuts. As stored foods ran low, Goshute winter camps dispersed so the people could collect from among a dozen recognized species of edible greens sprouting in the warmer valleys.

Hunting animals—not exclusively the province of men—provided fewer, but still important, calories and materials for clothing. Individuals stalked bighorn sheep and mule deer with bows made of mountain mahogany. More important were the communal summer pronghorn antelope and jackrabbit drives, the only time when more than two dozen families might congregate outside their winter camps. Goshute hunters demonstrated a ritual respect for large game through proper butchering and disposal, as well as some very limited food taboos. Women dried and stored extra meat for winter use and made leather shirts and rabbit-fur robes for winter wear. Goshute families also relied on more numerous burrowing rodents and other small mammals, birds, reptiles, insects, and insect larvae, and on occasion traveled significant distances to fish. Like other Numic peoples, Goshutes manipulated their environments with fire, and to a lesser extent with water, broadcast seed sowing, and pruning, to benefit themselves and their game animals.

Scarcity and mobility marked Goshute society. Despite accessing a wide variety of foodstuffs, families produced little if any surplus from year to year and had to keep moving in search of those thinly scattered resources. They recognized non-exclusive and overlapping family foraging areas but no sense of exclusive ownership. Movement helped them avoid neighboring Utes, who traded and intermarried with them but also raided Goshute camps for slaves. Goshute mobility limited their accumulation of material goods to the most functional and portable items—baskets, hardwood digging sticks, hunting equipment, flint knives, rabbit-skin robes, and other personal items.

Goshutes were highly individualistic and self-reliant. Given their mobile and flexible group structure, they marked descent bilaterally, practiced a patrilineal cross-cousin marriage as well as sororal polygny, and recognized major life-course events such as birth, puberty, marriage, and death with straightforward ceremonies. The summer Round Dance was a social event and time for courtship, but it also functioned to elicit supernatural assistance in assuring pine nut harvests and successful hunts. Winter camps were places to socialize with other families, to play games and gamble, and to share their oral traditions—stories to bring an early spring, stories not properly told in other seasons. Goshutes recognized no hereditary chiefs or elaborate political organization beyond informal family councils. Family and local groups chose leaders for specific events or purposes based on proven abilities. Goshutes did recognize *puhakanti*, or shamans, those endowed with dreams or a spirit helper that allowed them to use and interpret *puha*, the "power" that pervades all things. Shamans often possessed some particular ability to heal through their use of *puha* or their understanding of medicinal herbs. Warfare, beyond family feuds, was defensive in nature, and in death Goshutes burned or buried their kin, along with some of the dead person's belongings, in the desert valleys they called home.

As with other Numic peoples, Goshute stories connected them to myth-time animal beings who created the world and instructed humans in proper behavior. Chief among them were Coyote, the Goshute culture hero who created people, distributed then in nations, stole fire, fathered the stars, and generally oversaw both the good and bad that exists in the world; Wolf, who formed the world but also caused death; hawk, who created mountains and the basin-range landscape; mountain jay, who obtained pine nuts; cottontail, who stopped the sun from burning the world; and sparrow, who argued with Coyote to keep the length of each season to three months. Their stories were meant to amuse and to instruct, to connect them together and to their place. They were "the vocalizations of things hoped for and things realized" (Malouf and Smith 1947, 364 [quote]; A. M. Smith 1993, xxv–xxxi, 3–46).

While early ethnographers classified them among the simplest of human societies, Goshutes were highly adaptive foragers, with a strong sense of identity and place. Their place insulated them from excessive contact and conflict with other Indian groups and the earliest Spanish entradas into northern Utah. They felt the impact of the Spaniards and Mexicans indirectly, through trade with and slaving by Utes who participated in the Southwest horse-slave trade networks. After 1827, Euro-American "others" began crossing through Goshute territory to get somewhere else. Jedidiah Smith and two companions passed Skull Valley on their way from California to a trapper's rendezvous at Bear Lake (Utah) in 1827. Like others who staggered across the Great Salt Lake Desert after him, Smith thought little of the land or the people he saw living there.

Few other trappers followed Smith into that streamless region, but Ute and Shoshone raiding increased between 1830 and the 1850s, pushing Goshutes further north and west into Skull and Deep Creek valleys. Government explorer John C. Frémont followed Smith's passage across Goshute territory in reverse on his way to California in 1845, but it was Lansford Hasting's 1846 guidebook—showing a cutoff from the overland trail at Fort Bridger, south of the Great Salt Lake, then west to the Humboldt River— that opened the floodgate. Edwin Bryant followed that route in 1846 and described the Skull Valley Goshutes he saw as "miserable Digger Indians . . . naked, with the exception of a few filthy ragged skins, fastened about their loins" (Malouf 1974, 73–79; Defa 2000, 83–92; Bryant qtd. in Steward 1938, 134–35). Overland migrants and their livestock opened a contest with Goshutes for the limited forage and water of the region that Mormon settlers would finish.

Beginning in 1847, Mormons fleeing the pluralism of American society overran the few fertile, watered valleys of Utah. They displaced Utes, Shoshones, Paiutes, and Goshutes from their accustomed resources and lifestyles, initiating a cycle of starvation, raiding, and military reprisal (Bigler 1998; Cuch 2000). Mormons surrounded the Goshute homeland, moving into Tooele Valley in 1849, Skull Valley in 1851, Rush Valley in 1855, Cedar Valley in 1858, and Deep Creek Valley in 1859. They appropriated the springs and overgrazed the range with their livestock, plowed and irrigated fields until the alkali salts emerged, hunted out the antelope, cut piñon timber, and drove Goshutes into the desert hills. On top of that, tens of thousands of California gold rushers grazed their livestock along the trail, and by 1860 there were twenty-two overland mail stations on Goshute land (Defa 2000, 92–101).

Goshutes felt the subsistence impact of these events immediately and responded by raiding Mormon settlements, harassing overland trail parties and Pony Express riders, attacking stagecoaches and mail stations, and sticking livestock full of arrows or running them off for food. In 1851 they stole or destroyed an estimated five thousand dollars' worth of livestock near Tooele (Allen and Warner 1971, 163–64). In retaliation, Mormon militia captain William McBride and fifty-five men chased a group of Goshute raiders for four days. They found and burned a camp with signs of butchered cattle but never caught the Indians. In frustration McBride wrote his superiors: "We wish you without a moment's hesitation to send us about a pound of arsenic we want to give the Indians' well a flavour. A little strychnine would be of fine service, and serve instead of salt, to their too-fresh meat." "Don't forget the Arsenic!" wrote McBride in conclusion. "Don't forget the spade and arsenic! Don't forget the spade, strychnine and arsenic!" (McBride qtd. in Bagley 2002). Whether or not they actually carried out this particularly brutal deed, Mormon militiamen and settlers retaliated freely and violently against Indian peoples across Utah over the next fifteen years, even to the point of explicit localized exterminations (Christy 1991, 301–6). At the same time, they sent out missionaries and created farms to "civilize" the Indians—the "open hand" to the brutal "mailed fist" Indian policy of Mormon Church leader Brigham Young (Christy 1978). But Goshutes received little of that attention (Defa 2000, 96–100).

Reports of starving Indians continued as the Mormon population of Tooele surpassed estimates of the total Goshute population of eight hundred to a thousand. In 1858 Utah Indian superintendent Jacob Forney visited Skull Valley, noting that the Goshutes he found "have heretofore subsisted principally on snakes, lizards, roots, Etc." He distributed clothing and provisions and tried to establish a farm for them, but he failed to find adequate water. "They are, without exception," reported Forney, "the most miserable looking set of human beings I ever beheld" (qtd. in Allen and Warner 1971, 165; Steward 1938, 49). Two years later, as he traveled through Utah, Mark Twain summed up white America's lasting impression of the people and their land, calling Goshutes the "wretchedest type of mankind I have ever seen, . . . a silent, sneaking, treacherous-looking race, . . . indolent, . . . prideless beggars, . . . always hungry, and yet never refusing anything that a hog would eat, though often eating what a hog would decline; hunters, but having no higher ambition than to kill and eat jackass rabbits, crickets, and grasshoppers, and embezzle carrion from the buzzards and coyotes; . . . a thin, scattering race of almost naked black children . . . who produce nothing at all, and have no villages, . . . whose only shelter is a rag cast on a bush to keep off a portion of the snow, and yet who inhabit one of the most rocky, wintery, repulsive wastes that our country or any other can exhibit." "They deserve pity, poor creatures; and they can have mine—at this distance," concluded Twain. "Nearer by, they never get anybody's" (1962, 118, 120).

Between 1859 and 1861, efforts to concentrate scattered Goshute groups and to create viable farms at Deep Creek failed. Skull Valley Goshutes in particular refused to leave their valley, even as starvation motivated more violence against overland mail stations in 1862 and 1863. This "Goshute War" was only one expression of a larger regional struggle of Utah Indians against Mormon settlements and subsistence displacement (Malouf 1974, 83–107; Defa 2000, 101–5; Peterson 1998). To quiet the growing conflict, representatives of the federal government signed a series of treaties in 1863 with the Indians of Utah and Nevada. Goshutes agreed to end all hostilities, to allow whites to travel through their territory, and to accept the construction of military posts, railroads, telegraph lines, and mines, mills, farms, and ranches as required. The treaty stipulated annual payment of one thousand dollars (in goods and livestock) for twenty years to compensate Goshutes for their subsistence losses and suggested their removal to a reservation at some future date. Goshutes ceded no land in the Treaty of 1863, which confirmed a large part of western Utah as their territory (Kappler 1904, 2:859–60). Most importantly, the treaty recognized their inherent sovereignty within the evolving legal framework of federal Indian relations.

Every few years after 1863—even as they ignored Goshutes in general—federal officials proposed relocating Goshutes to the Fort Hall Shoshone or Uintah-Ouray Ute reservation, but each time their proposals met stiff resistance by Goshutes deeply attached to their homeland (Crum 1987). In 1871 Skull Valley Goshutes voiced their concerns through William Lee, longtime Grantsville resident who was helping them operate a small farm. "They have a decided objection to go to Uintah or any other place," wrote Lee. "They are willing to do anything on their own land, the land of their fathers which their Great Father at Washington may wish them to do, but they are not willing to go to the land of the strangers. The land of their fathers is sacred to them. On it they wish to live. And in it they wish their bodies laid when dead" (qtd. in Crum 1987, 256). The government relented, having no real use for Skull Valley anyway. But the Mormon Church did, settling a colony of Hawaiian converts at Iosepa in Skull Valley, where they scratched out an existence next to the Goshutes. In 1893 leprosy broke out and villagers were shunned. In 1916–17, Iosepa survivors gave up and fled back to the islands, leaving their dead buried alongside Goshute ancestors in a valley so far and so different from their Pacific homeland (Malouf 1974, 127–28).

Over time, Goshutes began to divide between those living and attempting to farm under the limited supervision of federal agents and Mormon missionary settlers in the Deep Creek Valley, and a much smaller group in Skull Valley who did some farming and wage work but refused to relocate. Populations dwindled to fewer than two hundred Goshutes, and according to one ethnographer, "The old men weep at the doom of extinction which they believe plainly to see ahead of their people" (Chamberlin 1913, 1). After years of neglect, the federal government codified those two Goshute communities, establishing the 34,000-acre Deep Creek Reservation by executive order in 1914 and the 18,000-acre Skull Valley Reservation in 1917 and 1918 (Malouf 1974, 108–31; Skull Valley Band of Goshute Indians n.d., Sovereignty). No one paid much attention to the Skull Valley Goshutes after that. By 1921 the BIA had closed its school and withdrawn its farm agent from Skull Valley. Proposals to consolidate band members at the Deep Creek Reservation or to legally terminate their tribal status continued into the 1950s, even as the Skull Valley population dwindled to about fifty enrolled members, few of whom lived on the reservation (Crum 1987, 260–67; Malouf 1974, 135).

That few lived in Skull Valley was, in part, a result of World War II, when the very isolation and barrenness of Utah's west desert made it perfect for the military. Air crews training at Wendover and Hill Air Force bases bombed the Utah Test and Training Range. The army opened Dugway Proving Grounds and Tooele Army Depot to develop and store weapons. During the ensuing cold war, Dugway, Tooele, and the Deseret Chemical depots evolved to develop, test, and store the nation's chemical and biological weapons. Dugway, surrounding Skull Valley on the west and south, was the worst and most secretive. Between 1951 and 1969 there were 1,635 open-air tests involving more than fifty-five thousand chemical rockets, artillery shells, bombs, and land mines, as well as low- and high-altitude aerial spraying tests in all sorts of weather conditions. Cameras rolled to record the deadly effects on animals caged in the test range. Weapons scientists released a half million pounds of nerve agent, equivalent to 3.5 trillion lethal doses. Spent and unexploded army ordinance was scattered over fourteen hundred square miles of public land in Utah, not all of it within the recognized test ranges. Accidents were common. Nerve agents released at altitude dispersed widely, and 10 to 30 percent target hits were not unusual. In 1962, only 4 percent of a test drop of twenty-eight hundred pounds of VX nerve agent reached the target grid. In 1968 a Phantom jet leaked twenty pounds of VX that drifted thirty miles into Skull Valley, sickening ranchers and killing wildlife and sixty-four hundred grazing sheep. The government denied responsibility but took the sheep for testing and then buried them back on the reservation, without tribal knowledge (Ward 1999, 98–105; Woolf 1997b).

Utah's Tooele County became home to the least-desirable cold war relics and private industries—a national sacrifice zone of deadly agents and waste. In the mid-1980s the government began to consolidate and incinerate its aging biological weapons stockpile at the Deseret Chemical Depot and the Tooele Chemical Demilitarization Facility. Tooele County officials created the one-hundred-square-mile West Desert Hazardous Industries area, upwind from Grantsville and Tooele. Tenants included Aptus hazardous waste incinerator, the Grassy Mountain Hazardous Waste Storage facility, and Envirocare, which runs a landfill for low-level radioactive waste. On the southwest end of the Great Salt Lake sits Magnesium Corporation of American, the worst air polluter in the country, spewing sixty million pounds of chlorine gas and six million pounds of hydrochloric acid into the air annually—85 percent of the point-source chlorine emitted nationally. Tooele County reaps the economic benefits of these facilities in terms of jobs, taxes, and "mitigation fees," as well as the health problems associated with having workers in those industries (Ward 1999, 62–90, 149–214; Davis 1998; Ishiyama 2003, 127–28; Selcraig 1996).

The Skull Valley Indian Reservation is surrounded by these live-fire zones and toxic sites. "And I think the federal government snuck one in on us also because surrounding our reservation we have all those things," observed Skull Valley band chairman Leon Bear. "And we were never consulted on those issues whether we liked it or not. They didn't tell us that these things were dangerous. They didn't come out and tell the Goshute band or the Council, 'How would you guys like to have a hazardous and toxic waste dump by you? Or how would you like to have a low level radioactive dump by you? Or how would you like to have the biological labs by you? Or the storage of nerve agents by you?'" (Bear 2001, 3). But in 1997 the tables were about to turn.

"When I saw the proposal and it was going out to the Indian community," recalled Danny Quintana, former attorney for the Skull Valley Goshute, "I suggested . . . that we get the proposal because my intent was to gather the data and put together a report and kill the proposal. Because I had thought initially what was occurring was the Department of Energy and the utility companies were in a conspiracy to dump high level nuclear waste on reservations." Longtime band chairman Richard Bear (Leon's father) agreed. But after using $300,000 in federal study grants to investigate temporary waste storage and thinking seriously about the long-term health of their territory and their people, Quintana said, "it became crystal clear [to the council] that this could be done safely" (Quintana 2001, 1).

Even though Congress canceled the National Waste Negotiator's budget for 1994, Richard Bear and the Skull Valley Goshutes continued educating band members about dry-cask storage by touring national and international nuclear facilities. "We also went to . . . Governor Leavitt, and we had told him that this was our plan," says Leon Bear, who was tribal secretary at the time, "and asked him if the state of Utah wanted to be involved we would appreciate it" (Bear 2001, 1). With Leavitt's "Over my dead body" response, the state of Utah drew a line in the sand and the Skull Valley Goshutes proceeded to step across it.

In 1996 tribal leaders hooked up with Private Fuel Storage LLC to discuss a private-sector development. On May 20, 1997, Chairman Leon Bear and the Skull Valley Band of Goshutes signed a lease with PFS to accept up to forty thousand metric tons of high-level radioactive waste and to store that waste above ground in an independent spent fuel storage installation for twenty years, renewable to forty years. Ten million spent nuclear fuel rods—3.5- to 4.5-meter-long zirconium alloy tubes packed with thousands of pencil-eraser-size uranium pellets and bundled into groups of two hundred—will be removed from their water-cooling tanks and dry packed into four-inch-thick steel casks, encased in two feet of concrete. Packaged casks from the PFS member utilities will be shipped via rail to the 820-acre Skull Valley ISFSI and placed inside stainless steel containers capable of holding ten metric tons of waste. Some four thousand containers, each eighteen feet tall, will sit spaced out for cooling on a one-hundred-acre pad of reinforced concrete, three feet thick, surrounded by a low wall. Surrounding the perimeter of the ISFSI will be two eight-foot-high chain-link fences (Rasmussen 1998, 344–46; Verdoia 2001, 8; Fedarko 2000, 4). Construction costs are estimated at $500 million, creating four hundred temporary and forty to sixty permanent jobs (Skull Valley Goshute Tribe Executive Office 1995, 65; Fedarko 2000, 4). Contract payments to the Skull Valley band are confidential, but rumors put the figure between $48 and $240 million, plus preferential hiring for band members (Kamps 2001, 3; Fedarko 2000, 7). PFS project manager Scott Northand estimated total operation costs at $3.1 billion over the forty-year life of the project (Verdoia 2001, 8).

So, back to the fundamental question: Who in their right mind would support storing highly radioactive waste in their own backyard, and why? Obviously, Leon Bear and the Skull Valley Band of Goshutes. They studied the issue intensively and voted two to one to support the project as a means of revitalizing the band, politically and socially. In the 1960s the band had only fifteen adult members. "People just gave up," recalled Bear. "They just got up and left. June grass moved in, houses fell apart. Skull Valley pretty much died off at that point." Bear said a few older people like his mother tried to maintain seasonal subsistence traditions of gathering pine nuts and chokecherries, while his father served as tribal chairman and worked at Deseret Chemical Depot. "So we did most of our gathering at Safeway," he joked (qtd. in Fedarko 2000, 6).

Today between 25 and 30 of 124 band members live on the reservation. Only four are fluent Goshute speakers. The rest live nearby in Grantsville, Stockton, and Tooele or in cities along Utah's Wasatch Front. Unemployment and poverty are three times the national average. Thirty percent cuts to federal Indian programs in the mid-1990s hurt the band, as did the loss of defense-industry jobs as the cold war collapsed into America's "peace dividend."

Opportunities for economic development have always been limited given Skull Valley's isolated location surrounded by toxic neighbors. Ninety percent of band income came from their Tekoi Rocket Test Facility, where Hercules Corporation and Alliant Techsystems once tested rocket motors, but that has ended. The band operated a convenience store ironically named the Pony Express Station, and they lease some land to local ranchers. In the last decade they were majority owners of Earth Environmental Services, selling dumpsters to government agencies and private industry, and they tried a landfill recycling company that failed. PepsiCo and a local water company both approached them about setting up bottling plants until they heard about Dugway. Other corporations have approached them about storing municipal wastes and mining by-products or operating hazardous waste incinerators (Defa 2000, 118–22; Ward 1999, 216–17; Fedarko 2000, 1, 3, 6; Zent 1997; Skull Valley Goshute Tribe Executive Office 1995, 66–67). There was talk of installing an elaborate irrigation system to rehabilitate marginal farmland and grow hothouse tomatoes, but it proved too costly for the return. Skull Valley Goshutes recognize the hand they have been dealt. "We can't do anything here that's green or environmental," Leon Bear told one journalist. "Would you buy a tomato from us if you knew what's out here? Of course not. In order to attract any kind of development, we have to be consistent with what surrounds us" (qtd. in Fedarko 2000, 4).

At the same time, avenues of economic development open to other Indian tribes remain closed to Skull Valley Goshutes. Since the state of Utah has no legalized gaming or lotteries, tribes cannot establish casinos, bingo parlors, or even racetracks with pari-mutuel betting. The state has rejected discussing gaming compacts and proposals from the Skull Valley band and has never made a serious effort to explore other significant development options for the reservation (Semerad 1992; Miller 1997). Leon Bear has called gaming "an equitable possibility," one they would consider, but one fraught with its own social and political consequences (Bear 2001, 4). In the long run, bringing nuclear waste into morally conservative Utah appears to be easier, politically and socially, than opening the door to any form of gambling.

With no other economic options, with hopelessness, alcoholism, migration, and language loss threatening their political and cultural existence, Skull Valley leaders view the ISFSI as a bottom-line tool for cultural survival. The project will create jobs, bringing people back to the reservation. It will help build houses, roads, utilities, businesses, a school, and a health clinic to keep them there. It will support education scholarships and health insurance and put money in people's pockets. "That's why they put me in office," says Chairman Bear, "so that we can make money and so that we can prosper and build infrastructure on our reservation. That's the whole purpose of this whole thing. And also, to keep our traditions and our cultural resources intact at the same time." Ultimately, he says, "it's up to the people themselves to determine how much culture or traditions they want to maintain" (Bear 2001, 3; Woolf 1997a).

Bear recognizes the potential dangers of an ISFSI but stresses the industry's safety record, the assurances of science and scientists, federal oversight and liability responsibility, and his personal commitment that this is a temporary storage facility, not a permanent waste dump. "[We] would never compromise . . . to harm any of our children, the tribe, the land or the territory around it" (Bear qtd. in C. Smith 1993). "We'll always be part of this land," says Bear. "We're not going anywhere. We're survivors" (qtd. in Christensen 1995, 26). Attorney Danny Quintana agrees: "They look at what is going to be the long term effect on their community and on the environment.

. . . So they're very, very protective of their territory and they know exactly who they are and exactly what they're doing" (Quintana 2001, 1).

Just off the reservation, Tooele County officials welcomed the facility, acknowledging that site construction and operation would generate jobs for their non-Indian citizens who are already surrounded by and working at such hazardous facilities. In May 2000 county commissioners signed an agreement with PFS that will net the county between $90 and $250 million over the forty-year life of the project (Verdoia 2001, 11; Fahys 2000). "Our interest was to make sure again that if something was going to happen that we had no control over, we protected our citizens to the best of our ability," said former county commissioner Gary Griffith (Griffith 2001, 2). And in the realm of what had been located in his county, Griffith found the proposed ISFSI innocuous: "I would submit to you that it probably would be the safest, cleanest business that we could bring into this county. Because, think about it, it produces not one thing that goes into the atmosphere, into the ground, into the water" (2001, 1). Others, like Tooele County commissioner Teryl Hunsaker, agree that they are protecting the interests of their citizens and serving the nation: "We've done more then our share in fighting the wars, and now we're doing more then our share in cleaning up our environment and when we get through . . . we will have a better world and we'll have a cleaner Mother Earth" (Hunsaker 2001, 3).

But fear and opposition to the project is strong across the state, in Tooele County, and within the small Skull Valley band itself. "This project is a no-brainer for a politician," said attorney Danny Quintana. "It involves high level radioactive waste. It involves a Native American community and it involves an opportunity to appear green even if they're not. So for a politician to oppose this is a slam dunk" (Quintana 2001, 1). Until he resigned in 2003 to head the Environmental Protection Agency in the George W. Bush administration, Governor Leavitt led the opposition, making it acceptable for Utah Republicans—particularly Utah's ultraconservative "Cowboy Caucus"—to embrace environmentalism and partner with environmental organizations as distasteful as Greenpeace, the Sierra Club, the Southern Utah Wilderness Alliance, and the Green Party. Long-term opponent of environmentalists Utah representative James Hansen (Republican) and his First District successor Rob Bishop (Republican) even appropriated the rhetoric of wilderness advocates in a disingenuous plan to create the Cedar Mountain Wilderness area, adjacent to Utah's Test and Training Range, thereby preventing road or rail construction in order to derail the Goshute project (Gehrke 2004; C. Smith 2004; Foy 2006). Likewise, Utah environmentalists, religious leaders, and citizen groups such as HEAL Utah, Utah Downwinders, and Citizens Against Nuclear Waste in Utah have swallowed their pride to partner with their environmental opponents against this Native American minority, endowed with mythological and ecological connections to Mother Earth and environmentalism.

Together, opponents of the Skull Valley ISFSI argue that the environmental impact assessments are flawed and the science is wrong; that transporting nuclear waste through the state is dangerous; that this will become a permanent nuclear waste dump by default; that accidents are inevitable; that in the event of an accident or abandonment, financial liability is not clear; and that the region is seismically unstable. After the events of September 11, 2001, they argue, the facility will be an easy target for similar terrorist attacks, or military jets from Hill Air Force Base might crash into the facility on their way to bomb the Utah Test and Training Range. All of these are legitimate concerns, especially in a state that remembers how the federal government used it as a cold war guinea pig for fallout from the Nevada Nuclear Test site (Department of Environmental Quality, State of Utah 2003; HEAL Utah n.d.; Truman 1997; J. Spangler 1998; Israelsen 2000a; Fedarko 2000, 2; Leavitt 2001; Hansen 2001; Nakahara 2001; McConkie 2001; Bauman 2005b).

But as the argument extends, elements of financial self-interest emerge. Leavitt has made it clear, "We don't produce it. We don't benefit from it, and we don't want to store it for those who do. . . . [H]aving lethally hot nuclear waste 40 miles from where I sit now and within a very close range of the major population center of this state is inconsistent with our vision of what we want this state to be" (Leavitt 2001, 1). Yet radioactive waste is a national phenomenon, from locally generated low-level medical and industrial waste to the national power grid that ties all of us to the 20 percent of electricity generated by nuclear fuels. Indirectly, one could argue, we all benefit and bear the costs. More problematically, Utah actively accepts and protects notorious corporate polluters, including radioactive waste companies that pay fees and taxes to the state. The state bends over backward wooing federal defense dollars for Dugway, Tooele, and Deseret, a trio capable of accidentally unleashing mass destruction against that same Utah population center. Leavitt even ticked off these facilities as an "important economic asset to the state" that would be threatened by the Skull Valley IS-FSI (Leavitt 2001, 1; Fahys 2001a, 2001d). As Mormon historian D. Michael Quinn observed, "When it suited the white majority of Utah to invite hazardous waste in, they did so . . . now they want to deny both the benefits and the risks to the Goshutes" (qtd. in Mims 2000).

The arguments also reveal the troubling paternalism and underlying thread of racism that permeates the history of Mormon-Indian relations in Utah (Holt 1992; Metcalf 2002; Ishiyama 2003, 124–25). Opponents of the Skull Valley ISFSI claim that PFS enticed the Goshutes with money and misinformation. Representative James Hansen voiced this brand of paternalism: "I guess our concerns is, and I don't mean to be unkind to anybody but it [PFS] put an awful lot of money on some of our Indian friends out there . . . the financial reward was maybe overwhelming to some folks who probably haven't seen much money in their lifetime, and we didn't think that was a proper thing to do" (Hansen 2001, 5). Other state officials adopted the language of environmental justice advocates—including prominent Indian activists—arguing that the project is ethically unjust and yet another example of corporations targeting Indians with the worst by-products of industrialization. But such arguments are double-edged, capable of perpetuating stereotypes that Indians are incapable victims, children, or dupes—stereotypes that can be used to undercut the sovereignty and wishes of those who might disagree on (in this case) an environmental issue (Ishiyama 2003, 130–34; Laws 2001). Skull Valley leaders responded that "charges of 'environmental racism' and the need to 'protect' and 'save' us smack of patronism [sic]. This attitude implies that we are not intelligent enough to make our own business and environmental decisions" (Skull Valley Goshute Tribe Executive Office 1995, 67). In Utah's social and political climate, such paternalistic attitudes and beliefs about Indians lie unfortunately close to the surface.

In April 1997 Governor Leavitt went on the offensive, forming an Office of High Level Waste Storage Opposition within the state's Department of Environmental Quality to mobilize opposition to the Skull Valley ISFSI proposal. That summer he met with Leon Bear and asked him to "step away" from the project or face active opposition. Bear refused, later suggesting to journalist Kevin Fedarko that "the governor's request might have carried a bit more weight if the people of Utah hadn't spent the better part of the past 170 years treating the Goshutes like pariahs" (Fedarko 2000, 5). Between 1997 and 2000 Leavitt secured a resolution from the Western Governor's Association supporting his opposition. He moved to have the state annex county roads leading to Skull Valley in order to stop transportation of high-level nuclear waste—creating a metaphorical "land moat" around the reservation. Leavitt and the state legislature petitioned the federal government to oppose the Skull Valley ISFSI, and they proposed or passed various measures to regulate companies handling or transporting nuclear waste. Leavitt's department heads and Utah's congressional delegation filed a continuous stream of petitions, motions, and lawsuits to derail the Nuclear Regulatory Commission licensing process (Clarke 2002, 52–55; Thomson 1998; Woolf 1997c; Maddox 1997; J. Spangler 1998; Israelsen 1998, 2000b; Groutage 1998).

In 2001, following NRC approval of the draft environmental impact statement, the gloves came off as the Utah Legislature passed three measures: the first levied steep taxes and security bonds on PFS to drive it away; the second authorized $1.1 million for a dream team of lawyers to tie PFS in legal knots; and the third offered the Skull Valley band $2 million for economic development if they would step away from their agreement with PFS. All three bills passed, but only the Goshute economic development bill carried no appropriation, no action (Fahys 2001c; D. K. Spangler 2001; Verdoia 2001, 10). "The federal government came to us, signed a treaty with us, broke those treaties with us and we're out today. The state of Utah is following that same mode," said Leon Bear. "On the one hand . . . they promised us $2 million for economic development. The bill passed but there's no appropriations in the bill. It's an empty shell of a bill. I mean, is that the message that the state of Utah wants to send to the Goshute people or to any Indian nation?" (Bear 2001, 3). Considering the estimated $5 million the state has spent through 2005 trying to defeat the project (unsuccessfully), Bear poses a legitimate question (Fahys 2003; Gehrke 2005b). Cynics say this is indicative of the strategy the state has always taken toward Indian peoples: white corporations would be engaged in serious negotiations with economic incentives, but Indians are treated to paternalism and legal assaults on their sovereignty (Quintana 2001, 3–4; Cuch 2001, 3; Ward 1999, 226–28).

The issue of storing high-level radioactive waste on the Skull Valley Reservation has become a fight between Indians and tribes, devolving at its worst moments into an acrimonious identity war. Deep Creek Goshutes, Northern Utes, Navajos, and tribes across the country have voiced their opposition to nuclear waste on tribal lands, yet they defer to the ultimate sovereignty of the Skull Valley band to decide their own future (Confederated Tribes of the Goshute Reservation 1997; Cesspooch 1998; Mims 2000, 2002; *Indian Country Today* 2001; Fedarko 2000, 2). Within the Skull Valley band, an opposition party led by Margene Bullcreek and Sammy Blackbear emerged to challenge the council's decision. They charge that their leaders were bribed and misled by PFS, that they in turn paid off tribal members and retaliated against plan opponents, and that they have failed to disclose the financial and legal terms of the PFS lease. Opponents claim that a majority of reservation residents oppose the ISFSI and that supporters are greedy off-reservation dwellers who have lost their cultural connections and do not care about the land. Divisions over the issue closely parallel the two major family groups within the Skull Valley band, but individuals have changed sides on the issue over time, making this situation even more complex and particularly personal (R. Egan 1997; Woolf 1999; J. Spangler and Spangler 2001; Fedarko 2000, 7).

In 1997, Margene Bullcreek organized Ohngo Gaudadeh Devia (OGD, meaning mountain- or ridge-top timber, timber-setting community), a grass-roots coalition of fifteen to twenty tribal members along with environmental supporters. As part of its "try everything" strategy, the state has covered more than $500,000 in legal bills for OGD to challenge the BIA lease approval and to file an environmental justice contention with the NRC against PFS, all without success (Kamps 2001; Clarke 2002, 57; U.S. Nuclear Regulatory Commission 2002; Johnson 2005). Undeterred, Bullcreek and Blackbear have waged a very public and acrimonious debate in the press and courts, even dividing themselves into separate camps with separate lawyers. In 2001, Goshute opponents of the ISFSI contested reservation election results and tried to install a rival slate of tribal officials. Eventually the BIA intervened in favor of Chairman Leon Bear, but the event precipitated a federal grand jury investigation of tribal finances. In 2003 that investigation resulted in the indictment and conviction of Bear for embezzlement and tax evasion and of the rival tribal officials for bank fraud (Israelsen 2001; Fahys 2002a, 2002b, 2002c, 2005b; D. K. Spangler 2002). Bear remains in control of a very divided band despite internal recall attempts and several canceled (or failed) tribal elections (Henetz 2004: Fahys 2005a; Roosevelt 2006).

Bullcreek and Blackbear frame their most potent arguments in cultural terms, as "traditionalists," where "seventh generation" decision making and environmental standards define Indian identity. "The land is not ours," says Sammy Blackbear. "We're caretakers of the land . . . for the next generation and I don't see us doing that putting a nuclear facility there" (Blackbear 2001, 1). Bullcreek calls the facility "an insult to American Indians and all people who believe in their ways and that the Earth is sacred" (qtd. in Porterfield 1997) and blames the young people of the tribe who are turning their backs on "tradition" (Melmer 2000). "The real issue is not the money," says Bullcreek. "The real issue is who we are as Native Americans and what we believe in. If we accept these wastes, we're going to lose our tradition." Bullcreek and Blackbear fear that the ISFSI will drive them away from the valley, away from the graves of their ancestors that anchor them culturally, and toward an urban melting pot that obliterates Indianness. "There is peace out here," Bullcreek says. "I felt I had to be outspoken or lose every-thing that has been passed down from generations. The stories that tell why we became the people we are and how we should consider our animal life, our air, things that are sacred to us. Leon Bear is trying to convince him-self that what he is doing is right, but this waste will destroy who we are" (qtd. in Kamps 2001, 4; Fedarko 2000, 7; Mims 2002).

Here Bullcreek and Blackbear are joined by others (Native and non-Na-tive) arguing that this is simply an environmental justice issue. Sincere ex-pressions like singer Bonnie Raitt's "Didn't we do enough [to American Indians] already?" oversimplify the conflict for an uninformed public, em-phasizing continued victimization while ignoring the realities of modern and studied self-rule (Griggs 2000; Fialka 1998; Taliman, 2002a). Others pursue the related argument that Goshute supporters of the ISFSI are act-ing very un-Indian-like, more like modern whites than ecological keepers of the Earth; that they have lost that "inextricable spiritual attachment to the land" that marks "traditional tribal members" (qtd. in Kamps 2001, 4; T. Egan 1998, 1; Ishiyama 2003, 130–32). In the public mind the battle gets cast as one between "traditionalists" defending Mother Earth and "progres-sives" who just want to get rich quick and are not "real" Indians anymore. Such rhetorical "ecological Indian" devices are applied simply and effec-tively through the media, using the fabricated Chief Seattle speech and the Iron Eyes Cody "crying Indian" image to define who is an Indian and who is not, who has a legitimate voice or position on the environment and who does not. It privileges the simplicity of myth and past and denies the com-plexity of modernity and conscious change (Lewis 1991; Lewis 1995, 438–40; Krech 1999, 211–29; see also Waller 1996).

The most profound claim Bullcreek, Blackbear, and other opponents of the Skull Valley ISFSI make is that the tribe is selling its sovereignty: that PFS is using the band's sovereignty against itself, thereby limiting the ability of the state or federal government to "protect" Goshutes from themselves. Blackbear has gone further, arguing that by signing on to this nuclear waste proposal their "tribal sovereignty has been waived," giving Goshute oppo-nents the right to team with the state in challenging the tribe's decisions

(Melmer 2000; May 2001; Clarke 2002, 57). Such arguments are inherently dangerous attacks on the legal tradition of tribal sovereignty vis-à-vis the preemptive power of states, highlighting the complex realities and contested status of true tribal self-rule. They also indicate the flip-side consequences of simply framed and mythopoeic images of and political arguments about Indians, sovereignty, and environmental justice (Ishiyama 2003).

Unfortunately, these are the very political and cultural arguments that state officials are encouraging—even funding—fueling a general assault on Indian sovereignty and identity in Utah (Clarke 2002). The easiest to dismiss are those that try to ignore the legal realities of sovereignty altogether. The more powerful are those that twist the essential meaning of tribal sovereignty from formal legal status to a mere formality capable of being ignored when convenient. Some equate sovereignty with private property rights, subject to transient judgments about the collective good. "Something is dead wrong when a small group of people can ignore the will of 90 percent of our state," complained Republican Utah congressman Merrill Cook (qtd. in T. Egan 1998, 22). Governor Leavitt, who had a crash course in sovereignty from the losing end of nearly every lawsuit and procedural challenge, continued to insist, "I recognize the sovereignty of this group but let's put it in perspective. This is 30 or 40 people who actually live there. We're talking about that by comparison to the public safety of two million people" (Leavitt 2001, 2; Fahys, 2002f, 2002d). Attorney Connie Nakahara, who directed the opposition from the Utah Department of Environmental Quality, cuts to the heart of the sovereignty assault: "I guess it's a little bit troubling that they have so much control over what happens to the state" (Nakahara 2001, 4). Few care to confront the question from the other side: the impact of more than 150 years of state and federal control on the land and people of Skull Valley.

In 2002, as the state's legal options waned, as the editorial page of Utah's leading newspaper lamented the expense of litigation and suggested a serious economic offer to dissuade the Goshutes from their ISFSI project (Salt Lake Tribune 2002), and as Utah voters put a "Radioactive Waste Restrictions Act" initiative on the November ballot to limit all waste dumping in Utah

(Fahys 2002e), a group of Utah lawmakers floated an end run they called "Plan B." Led by then-Utah Republican Party chairman Joe Cannon, the group discussed siting a MRS on remote state school–trust lands, thereby tapping into the Nuclear Waste Fund (estimated at $11 billion), establishing state oversight, and circumventing the Skull Valley–PFS project entirely. "It would be a great shame for Utah to be stuck with this [nuclear waste] and not get a benefit," said Cannon (Harrie 2002). That logic resonated with many, while others saw the hypocrisy. Leavitt was embarrassed and dismissed the plan as inconsistent with his personal philosophy and political strategy against PFS, but the plan did not die. Utah director of Indian Affairs Forrest Cuch stormed, "It is appalling to me and smacks of racism at its highest . . . an outrage and selfishness and an abuse of power" (Harrie and Fahys 2002).

Later that fall, Utah lawmakers suddenly voiced overwhelming opposition to the radioactive waste ballot initiative because (according to industry lobbyists distributing a million industry dollars) it would hurt existing corporations like Envirocare (which pumps $5 million into the Tooele County budget each year) and keep others from locating in Utah (Fahys and Fantin 2002; Fahys 2004c). In a telling turnaround, Utah voters followed lawmakers' advice and rejected the initiative. While opposition to the Skull Valley ISFSI continued and there was still no support for allowing Indian gaming as an alternative path for economic development, Utah politicians and voters continued to support the idea of more west desert commercial dumps accepting hotter radioactive waste (Walsh and Fahys 2003) and the possibility of a Plan B storage facility on state trust lands—both things that would be under state administrative and financial control (Fahys and Harrie 2003; Fahys 2004d; Church 2004). Utah's schizophrenic relationship with hazardous waste, free enterprise, morality, federal dollars, and American Indians is disturbingly clear.

In the final analysis, as state laws and lawsuits fail and with final NRC approval of PFS's commercial waste storage license in February 2006 (Fahys 2004a; Henetz 2005; Gehrke 2006b), some opponents of the Skull Valley ISFSI are still pinning their hopes on the completion and licensing of the federally designated Yucca Mountain facility. In 2002 Utah's senators cut a deal, trading their votes for Yucca Mountain as the national waste repository in return for a pledge from Department of Energy secretary Spencer Abraham to block funds for the Skull Valley ISFSI. Only recently has Utah's congressional delegation begun to reconsider this tactic, realizing that transported waste will still come through Utah and might get stuck there permanently given the scientific and political problems emerging at Yucca Mountain (Fahys 2002g, 2004e; Gehrke 2005a).

In supporting Yucca Mountain, Utahns have simply shifted the burden of nuclear waste onto Nevadans ("thrown us under the bus," says Marta Adams, a senior Nevada deputy attorney general [Bauman 2005a]), who have had their fill of atomic weapons and nuclear waste; onto a storage system riddled with geologic, scientific, and political faults; and onto the Western Shoshones, who have been fighting nuclear testing on lands they claim as tribal and sacred. Utah's "Not In My Back Yard" approach takes an opportunity from one tribe that wants it and forces it on another tribe against their sovereign will; it irretrievably buries waste in a dangerous space rather than leaving it isolated, monitored, and assessable should time provide better options like reprocessing (Gehrke 2006a). For both environmentalists and environmental justice advocates, Yucca Mountain is still an Indian loss, a loss for future generations. The politics driving Yucca Mountain against the science that questions it demonstrates how little we as a nation actually care about science, Indian peoples, sovereignty, and even the future (Sonner 2004; Kuletz 1998; Stoffle and Evans 1992; Christensen 2001; Fahys 2001b; Taliman 2002b; J. Spangler 2002; Bauman 2005c).

"The racism that surrounds it, well it's really amusing how the white environmental movement knows what's best for an Indian tribe," said attorney Danny Quintana. "They know exactly how Indians should behave, how they should live and what they should study. And when an Indian tribe studies a hard science issue . . . and does something that is counter revolutionary and what they perceive to be as anti-green, they get mad about it" (Quintana 2001, 4; see also Waller 1996). Quintana and Leon Bear point to the Treaty of 1863, which underlies Skull Valley's right to self-determination, and marvel at the "environmental racism" used to dismiss them—as "real" Indians, as capable, as modern, as sovereign. "No matter how stupid people think we are, we are still here," said Bear. "How do you think this country was built? . . . How do you think we survived? Not because of stupidity" (Bear 2001, 2). "They want to keep us the way they think of us: living in tepees and riding horses," said Bear. "That's not real. You can't feed your family on a stereotype" (qtd. in Kundson 2001). "My ancestors ate grasshoppers," he told another reporter. "I don't want to live like that" (qtd. in Fialka 1998).

Skull Valley Goshutes studied the issue of temporary nuclear waste storage deliberately and openly, even if details of the lease agreement are not open to tribal members. The science and safety record of the industry seems to support their case, as did two-thirds of Goshute voters then, and a narrow majority now. When the band asked the state for other options, they were rebuffed. "We're simply looking at this as economic development" said Leon Bear, a way for Skull Valley Goshutes to survive as a modern people, on a sovereign reservation, surrounded by others' toxic waste (Mims 2000). Bear acknowledges the dangers, "but it's just like the coming of the white man, that was dangerous to us, too" (qtd. in Kestenbaum 2005).

Bear bristles at suggestions that he is not acting like a traditional Indian, and he points out what Goshute traditions are—survival as mobile and adaptive desert dwellers in a harsh environment (Bear 2001, 4; Mims 2000, 2002). "Look, I'm not here to lay down and die like the buffalo. . . . This is a survival issue for us. But in order to bring my people back to the reservation, we're going to have to provide them with a livelihood. That means real jobs, real houses. As far as being traditional and protecting Mother Earth, I don't understand how we can do that. . . . There's no way we can go back to living off the land. Not with what they've done to it" (qtd. in Fedarko 2000, 8). "Yes, a long time ago, we were the stewards of the land," says Bear. "Now the stewards are you guys, and I don't think you guys are doing a very good job, to tell the truth" (qtd. in Kestenbaum 2005). "I consider myself to be a traditionalist, too, to some extent. I have reverence for the animals, plant life and the Earth. But I also have reverence for the people" (qtd. in Mims 2000). "I don't know about seven generations," Bear says.

"Without us, there won't be a seventh generation and that's what this is all about" (Bear 2001, 4).

Opposing a high-level radioactive waste storage facility in Utah seems like a simple issue: Who in their right mind would want one? In reality, no one does, not even Leon Bear. The contest in Utah is more complex than that. It marks a fundamental struggle over economic development options, environmental safety, identity, sovereignty, the past and the future. Underlying these debates are the persistent images of the ecological Indian, the childlike Indian, the disappearing Indian, and the modern Indian who does not act like a "traditional" Indian. Plan opponents walk the tightrope of paternalism and environmental racism; of dismissing Indians as "real" because they have changing environmental imperatives and desire the same material world others enjoy; of treating sovereignty as a political illusion, a matter of convenience and not conscience. At the same time, proponents of the plan put millions of people along transportation routes at risk, irretrievably alter their homeland, threaten the very community they intend to revitalize, and put tribal sovereignty up for public and political debate—a dangerous arena for all Indian nations given the conservative political atmosphere of the new century.

For 150 years we have (at best) ignored the Skull Valley Goshutes, and now that they have captured our attention we are angry that they have learned so well from our example. As Utah environmental activist Chip Ward puts it, Goshutes "are only guilty of being the last ones through the door with the straw that broke the camel's back" (Ward 1999, 228).

Generalizing about a generalized environmental or conservationist ethos of a generalized "Indian" population over a generalized past is like trying to nail Jell-O to the wall. Likewise, trying to universalize human motivation by reading examples of present-day ideals and actions into past behavior is problematic. Yet the ideal of the ecological Indian seems oddly exempt, even after mountains of scholarship suggesting a more complex reality. The stereotype haunts our political debates, our racialized ways of defining the "other," and our views of the past and present (Warren 2002). Instead of recognizing the coexistence of conflicting and inconsistent beliefs and behaviors in any individual, individual variability within any group, group variability within and across defined periods of time, and the ease of maintaining idealized behavior in times of plenty versus the survival necessity of adapting that behavior at other times, we cling to simple but untenable universals that revolve around such stereotypes. Even when we see more complex examples of the multiplicity of ways of thinking, acting, and being "Indian"—the Skull Valley Goshute case offered here for example—we try to essentialize them and explain them away as aberration and declension from some universal or "traditional" ideal.

Ultimately, the Goshute experience is a stark reminder that no stereotype is benign or without consequence—even a positive trope like the ecological Indian is a double-edged sword that can be used against indigenous peoples. No matter how beneficial, no matter how much political capital or moral authority it brings those who incorporate it as tradition, it can be turned around and used to restrict, dismiss, and deny that political standing and authority. More importantly, the stereotype can be used—and is being used—by Indians and non-Indians alike to deny the authenticity, identity, sovereignty, human agency, and modernity of Indian individuals, groups, and tribal governments. Here is where the political rubber meets the road, where the culture and identity wars rage, where the image of the ecological Indian does its real damage.

Even in its exceptionality, the Skull Valley case underlines some of Shepard Krech's (1999) basic arguments about Indians, the environment, and the stereotype of the ecological Indian. It points to the range of choices people might make when they perceive their very cultural or physical survival at stake. Facing certain political, environmental, or cultural constraints, unable to see the future or the long-term consequences of their choices, humans act on judgments about present needs, cultural tradition, and what they assume that unseen future might hold. They weigh the relative adaptability of their cultural and ecological structures and alter those relationships, pulling back from or building more elaborate traditions or technological fixes. That any one group over any extended period of time would act consistently seems to defy logic and the chaotic dynamism that roots history and biology as fields. That multiple beliefs and behaviors as disparate as an environmental ethic and actions that negatively affect one's environment can and do coexist should not surprise any of us who espouse a "green" lifestyle yet live the way we do in the modern United States. While the scale is certainly different, the fundamental choices that Skull Valley Goshutes are making are ones all groups have made at one time or another in human history: choices about subsistence, self-preservation, environment, identity, and sovereignty. In this case, the outcome of those choices has yet to be seen.

References

Allen, James B., and Ted J. Warner. 1971. The Gosiute Indians in pioneer Utah. *Utah Historical Quarterly* 39 (Spring): 162–77.

Anquoe, Bunty. 1993. New nuclear waste official pledges negotiations for tribes. *Indian Country Today* (Rapid City SD), December 15, A3.

Bagley, Will. 2002. Goshutes feared two savage enemies: Starvation, and the white man. *Salt Lake (UT) Tribune*, October 13, B1.

Bauman, Joseph. 1992. San Juan County, Goshutes bristle at Moody's N-blockade proposal. *Deseret News* (Salt Lake City UT), April 21, B1.

———. 2005a. Nevada seeks united front against Yucca. *Deseret News* (Salt Lake City UT), March 22. http://deseretnews.com/dn/view/1,1249,600120317,00.html (accessed March 22, 2005).

———. 2005b. Nuclear storage battle fires up. *Deseret News* (Salt Lake City UT), March 18. http://deseretnews.com/dn/view/1,1442,600119494,00.html (accessed March 18, 2005).

———. 2005c. Was Yucca data falsified? *Deseret News* (Salt Lake City UT), March 17. http://deseretnews.com/dn/view/0,1249,600119181,00.html (accessed March 17, 2005).

Bear, Leon. 2001. Interview. *Skull Valley: Radioactive waste and the American West*, directed by Ken Verdoia. Salt Lake City UT: KUED-TV. Transcript in four parts at http://www.kued.org/skullvalley/documentary/interviews/bear.html (accessed August 1, 2001).

Bigler, David L. 1998. *Forgotten kingdom: The Mormon theocracy in the American West, 1847–1896*. Logan: Utah State University Press.

Blackbear, Sammy. 2001. Interview. *Skull Valley: Radioactive waste and the American West*, directed by Ken Verdoia. Salt Lake City UT: KUED-TV. Transcript in two parts at http://www.kued.org/skullvalley/documentary/interviews/blackbear.html (accessed August 1, 2001).

Bourke, Lisa. 1994. Economic attitudes and responses to siting hazardous waste facilities in rural Utah. *Rural Sociology* 59 (3): 485–96.

Carter, Luther J. 1987. *Nuclear imperative and public trust: Dealing with radioactive waste*. Washington DC: Resources for the Future.

Cesspooch, Curtis R. 1998. Threat to tribal sovereignty. *Salt Lake (UT) Tribune*, June 7, A2.

Chamberlin, Ralph V. 1911. The ethnobotany of the Gosiute Indians. *Philadelphia Academy of Natural Science Proceedings* 53: 337–44.

————. 1913. Place and personal names of the Gosiute Indians of Utah. *Proceedings of the American Philosophical Society* 52 (208): 1–20.

Christensen, Jon. 1995. Surprises of sovereignty. *High Country News* (Paonia CO), April 3, 25–26.

————. 2001. Can Nevada bury Yucca Mountain? *High Country News* (Paonia CO), July 2, 1, 8–11.

Christy, Howard A. 1978. Open hand and mailed fist: Mormon-Indian relations in Utah, 1847–52. *Utah Historical Quarterly* 46 (Summer): 216–35.

————. 1991. "What virtue there is in stone" and other pungent talk on the early Utah frontier. *Utah Historical Quarterly* 59 (Summer): 300–319.

Church, Lisa. 2004. San Juan County Commission revives plan for nuclear waste site. *Salt Lake (UT) Tribune*, April 7, B1.

Churchill, Ward, and Winona LaDuke. 1992. Native North America: The political economy of radioactive colonialism. In *The state of Native America: Genocide, colonization, and resistance*, ed. M. Annette Jaimes, 241–66. Boston: South End Press.

Clarke, Tracylee. 2002. An ideographic analysis of Native American sovereignty in the state of Utah: Enabling denotative dissonance and constructing irreconcilable conflict. *Wicazo Sa Review* 17 (2): 43–63.

Confederated Tribes of the Goshute Reservation. 1997. Resolution no. 97–G-022 of the governing body of the Confederated Tribes of the Goshute Reservation. 2 June. http://www.eq.state.ut.us/no_high_level_waste_/opposition%20resolutions/or.htm (accessed February 23, 2004).

Crum, Steven J. 1987. The Skull Valley Band of the Goshute Tribe—Deeply attached to their native homeland. *Utah Historical Quarterly* 55 (Summer): 250–67.

————. 1994. *The road on which we came, Po'i Pentun Tammen Kimmappeh: A history of the Western Shoshone*. Salt Lake City: University of Utah Press.

Cuch, Forrest S., ed. 2000. *A history of Utah's American Indians*. Salt Lake City: Utah State Division of Indian Affairs and the Utah State Division of History.

————. 2001. Interview. *Skull Valley: Radioactive waste and the American West*, directed by Ken Verdoia. Salt Lake City UT: KUED-TV. Transcript in three parts at http://www.kued.org/skullvalley/documentary/interviews/cuch.html (accessed August 1, 2001).

Davis, Mike. 1998. Utah's toxic heaven. *Capitalism, Nature, Socialism: A Journal of Socialist Ecology* 9 (2): 35–39.

Defa, Dennis R. 2000. The Goshute Indians of Utah. In *A history of Utah's American Indians*, ed. Forrest S. Cuch, 73–122. Salt Lake City: Utah State Division of Indian Affairs and the Utah State Division of History.

Department of Environmental Quality, State of Utah. 2003. Opposition to high-level nuclear waste. http://www.eq.state.ut.us/no_high_level_waste/index.htm (accessed February 18, 2004).

Egan, Rick. 1997. Goshutes protest tribe's nuclear-waste proposal. *Salt Lake (UT) Tribune*, May 1, B1.

Egan, Timothy. 1998. New prosperity brings new conflict to Indian country. *New York Times* (NY, National Ed.), March 8, 1, 22.

Erickson, Jon D., and Duane Chapman. 1993. Sovereignty for sale: Nuclear waste in Indian country. *Akwe:kon: A Journal of Indigenous Studies* 10 (3): 3–10.

Erickson, Jon D., Duane Chapman, and Ronald E. Johnny. 1994. Monitored retrievable storage of spent nuclear fuel in Indian country: Liability, sovereignty, and socioeconomics. *American Indian Law Review* 19:73–103.

Fahys, Judy. 2000. Tooele signs deal for N-waste. *Salt Lake (UT) Tribune*, May 25, B1.

——. 2001a. Defections hit group opposing N-waste. *Salt Lake (UT) Tribune*, February 9, C2.

——. 2001b. Nevada N-waste battle closely tied to Utah's. *Salt Lake (UT) Tribune*, August 19, A1.

——. 2001c. N-waste battle heats up. *Salt Lake (UT) Tribune*, February 26, A1.

——. 2001d. N-waste: How hot is too hot? *Salt Lake (UT) Tribune*, March 18, A1.

——. 2002a. Feds demand Goshutes open financial books on N-waste deal. *Salt Lake (UT) Tribune*, March 14, A1.

——. 2002b. Feds recognize Bear as Goshute leader. *Salt Lake (UT) Tribune*, April 2, A1.

——. 2002c. Utah fears waste plan is shoo-in. *Salt Lake (UT) Tribune*, April 22, A1.

——. 2002d. Yucca vote unlikely to deter Skull Valley dump. *Salt Lake (UT) Tribune*, July 15, A1.

——. 2002e. Judge rebuffs state on N-waste. *Salt Lake (UT) Tribune*, July 31, A1.

——. 2002f. Family feud: Skull Valley Goshutes fight an internal battle over the lucrative nuclear waste storage proposal. *Salt Lake (UT) Tribune*, August 18, A1.

——. 2002g. Nuclear waste measure ordered onto Utah ballot. *Salt Lake (UT) Tribune*, August 27, A1.

——. 2003. Walker takes reins of fight against nuclear waste site. *Salt Lake (UT) Tribune*, December 1, A1.

——. 2004a. Court rules against Utah in nuke fight. *Salt Lake (UT) Tribune*, August 5, B1.

——. 2004b. More trouble ahead for Goshutes. *Salt Lake (UT) Tribune*, January 8, A1.

——. 2004c. New approach planned on N-waste. *Salt Lake (UT) Tribune*, April 13, B1.

——. 2004d. Plan to use trust lands for N-waste reappears. *Salt Lake (UT) Tribune*, May 7, B8.

——. 2004e. Yucca slips, Skull Valley stock rises. *Salt Lake (UT) Tribune*, August 16, B1.

——. 2005a. Nukes at root of Goshute dispute: Tribe divided; opponents of the Skull Valley dump say tribal leaders are quashing their voices. *Salt Lake (UT) Tribune*, November 14, B1.

——. 2005b. Would-be Goshute leader sentenced in theft case. *Salt Lake (UT) Tribune*, November 29, B1.

Fahys, Judy, and Linda Fantin. 2002. N-waste initiative critics deny bias: Envirocare contributions make backers suspicious. *Salt Lake (UT) Tribune*, November 2, A1.

Fahys, Judy, and Dan Harrie. 2003. "Plan B" aims to outbid Goshutes' N-waste site. *Salt Lake (UT) Tribune*, February 6, A1.

Fedarko, Kevin. 2000. In the valley of the shadow. *Outside* (May). See *Outside Online*, http://outside.away.com/magazine/200005/200005skullvalley1.html (accessed February 17, 2004).

Fialka, John J. 1998. Goshute Indians' plan to store nuclear waste for eight utilities is opposed by Utah governor. *Wall Street Journal*, August 26, 1.

Fowler, Catherine S. 1986. Subsistence. In *Handbook of North American Indians*, vol. 11, *Great Basin*, ed. Warren L. D'Azevedo, 64–97. Washington DC: Smithsonian Institution.

Foy, Paul. 2006. Utah's latest wild area not just about scenery: Move will keep nuclear waste out of Skull Valley. *Deseret News* (Salt Lake City UT, February 12, B1.

Gehrke, Robert. 2004. Bishop engages new strategy in attempt to derail N-waste storage. *Salt Lake (UT) Tribune*, October 18, B1.

————. 2005a. Hatch: Don't move N-waste. *Salt Lake (UT) Tribune*, April 5, B1.

————. 2005a. Utah's nuke case dumped by court. *Salt Lake (UT) Tribune*, December 6, A1.

————. 2006a. Nuclear experts push for waste re-use plan. *Salt Lake (UT) Tribune*, May 3, B1.

————. 2006b. PFS gets desert N-dump license. *Salt Lake (UT) Tribune*, February 14, A1.

Gorrell, Mike. 1994. Leavitt to tribe: Don't waste Utah. *Salt Lake (UT) Tribune*, November 12, A1.

Gowda, M. V. Rajeev, and Doug Easterling. 1998. Nuclear waste and Native America: The MRS siting exercise. *Risk: Health, Safety and Environment* 9:229–258.

Griffith, Gary. 2001. Interview. *Skull Valley: Radioactive waste and the American West*, directed by Ken Verdoia. Salt Lake City UT: KUED-TV. Transcript in three parts at http://www. kued.org/skullvalley/documentary/interviews/griffith.html (accessed August 1, 2001).

Griggs, Brandon. 2000. Raitt, Indigo Girls share music, politics at U. *Salt Lake (UT) Tribune*, October 8, B6.

Gross, John Karl. 2001. Note: Nuclear Native America: Nuclear waste and liability on the Skull Valley Goshute Reservation. *Boston University Journal of Science and Technology Law* 7 (Winter): 140–67.

Groutage, Hilary. 1998. Sign of the times: No N-waste here. *Salt Lake (UT) Tribune*, March 22, C1.

Hansen, James. Interview. *Skull Valley: Radioactive Waste and the American West*, directed by Ken Verdoia. Salt Lake City UT: KUED-TV. Transcript in six parts at http://www.kued. org/skullvalley/documentary/interviews/hansen.html (accessed August 1, 2001).

Hanson, Randel D. 2001. Half lives of Reagan's Indian policy: Marketing nuclear waste to American Indians. *American Indian Culture and Research Journal* 25 (1): 21–44.

Harper, Kimball T. 1986. Historical environments. In *Handbook of North American Indians*, vol. 11, *Great Basin*, ed. Warren L. D'Azevedo, 51–63. Washington DC: Smithsonian Institution.

Harrie, Dan. 2002. Officials covet N-waste profits: If Goshutes win approval, some quietly propose "Plan B" so Utah reaps windfall. *Salt Lake (UT) Tribune*, September 22, A1.

Harrie, Dan, and Judy Fahys. 2002. State leaders assail "Plan B" for nuclear waste storage. *Salt Lake (UT) Tribune*, September 25, A1.

HEAL Utah [Healthy Environment Alliance of Utah]. n.d. http://www.healutah.org (accessed February 17, 2004).

Hebert, H. Josef. 1995. Americans at impasse on site of N-dump. *Salt Lake (UT) Tribune*, June 25, A5.

Henetz, Patty. 2004. Bear maintains grip on power. *Salt Lake (UT) Tribune*, December 6, B1.

————. 2005. Utah loses key battle over N-waste. *Salt Lake (UT) Tribune*, February 25, A1.

Herald Journal (Logan UT). 1994. Goshutes sign agreement to streamline nuke talks. November 13, 4.

Holt, Ronald L. 1992. *Beneath these red cliffs: An ethnohistory of the Utah Paiutes*. Albuquerque: University of New Mexico Press.

Hunsaker, Teryl. 2001. Interview. *Skull Valley: Radioactive Waste and the American West*, directed by Ken Verdoia. Salt Lake City UT: KUED-TV. Transcript in three parts at http://www. kued.org/skullvalley/documentary/interviews/hunsaker.html (accessed August 1, 2001).

Indian Country Today (Rapid City SD). 1993. Amendment may doom Goshute plans for proposed nuclear waste dump. October 6, A6.

———. 2001. Editorial: When nuclear waste is last resort. January 17, A4.

Ishiyama, Noriko. 2003. Environmental justice and American Indian tribal sovereignty: Case study of a land-use conflict in Skull Valley, Utah. *Antipode* 35 (1): 119–39.

Israelsen, Brent. 1998. Utah sues feds for data on Goshute N-plan. *Salt Lake (UT) Tribune*, May 28, A1.

———. 2000a. Leavitt leads angry opposition to N-waste on Goshute reservation. *Salt Lake (UT) Tribune*, July 28, A1.

———. 2000b. Pols target N-waste at Skull Valley. *Salt Lake (UT) Tribune*, September 5, A1.

———. 2001. Scuffle threatens to push Goshutes deeper into divisive power struggle. *Salt Lake (UT) Tribune*, September 1, A1.

Jacob, Gerald. 1990. *Site unseen: The politics of siting a nuclear waste repository*. Pittsburgh: University of Pittsburgh Press.

Johnny, Ronald Eagleye. 1994. Showing respect for tribal law: Siting a nuclear waste MRS facility. *Akwe:kon Journal* 11 (Spring): 16–27.

Johnson, Kirk. 2005. A tribe nimble and determined, moves ahead with nuclear storage plan. *New York Times*, February 28, http://nytimes.com/2005/02/28/national/28tribe.html (accessed February 28, 2005).

Kamps, Kevin. 2001. Environmental racism, tribal sovereignty, and nuclear waste: High-level atomic waste dump targeted at Skull Valley Goshute Indian Reservation in Utah. Nuclear Information Resource Service, factsheet, February 15. http://www.nirs.org/factsheets/pfsejfactsheet.html (accessed November 7, 2002).

Kappler, Charles J. 1904. *Indian affairs: Laws and treaties*. 2 vols. Washington DC: Government Printing Office.

Kestenbaum, David. 2005. A tribe split by nuclear waste. National Public Radio, Morning Edition, aired October 21. http://www.npr.org/templates/story/story.php?storyID=4967885 (accessed October 21, 2005).

Krech, Shepard, III. 1999. *The ecological Indian: Myth and history*. New York: Norton.

Kuletz, Valerie L. 1998. *The tainted desert: Environmental and social ruin in the American West*. New York: Routledge.

Kundson, Tom. 2001. Environment, Inc.: Drilling debate jolts old image of Indians. *Sacramento Bee*, December 9.

Laws, Rufina Marie. 2001. Interview. *Skull Valley: Radioactive waste and the American West*, directed by Ken Verdoia. Salt Lake City UT: KUED-TV. Transcript in two parts at http://www.kued.org/skullvalley/documentary/interviews/laws.html (accessed August 1, 2001).

Leavitt, Michael. 2001. Interview. *Skull Valley: Radioactive waste and the American West*, directed by Ken Verdoia. Salt Lake City UT: KUED-TV. Transcript in 3 parts at http://www.kued.org/skullvalley/documentary/interviews/leavitt.html (accessed August 1, 2001).

Leonard, Louis G., II. 1997. Sovereignty, self-determination, and environmental justice in the Mescalero Apache's decision to store nuclear waste. *Boston College Environmental Affairs Law Review* 24 (3): 651–93.

Lewis, David Rich. 1991. Reservation leadership and the progressive-traditional dichotomy: William Wash and the Northern Utes, 1865–1928. *Ethnohistory* 38 (Spring): 124–48.

_____. 1995. Native Americans and the environment: A survey of twentieth-century issues. *American Indian Quarterly* 19 (Summer): 423–50.

Maddox, Laurie Sullivan. 1997. Leavitt, Cook battle Goshute waste storage. *Salt Lake (UT) Tribune*, June 27, A10.

Malouf, Carling. 1940. A study of the Gosiute Indians of Utah. Unpublished MS thesis, Sociology and Anthropology, Salt Lake City: University of Utah.

_____. 1974. The Goshute Indians. In *Shoshonean Indians* (American Indian Ethnohistory: California and Basin-Plateau Indians, comp. and ed. David Agee Horr), 25–172. New York: Garland.

Malouf, Carling I., and Elmer R. Smith. 1947. Some Gosiute mythological characters and concepts. *Utah Humanities Review* 1 (4): 369–78.

May, James. 2001. Skull Valley Goshutes sue state of Utah. *Indian Country Today* (Rapid City SD), May 2, A1.

McConkie, James. 2001. Interview. *Skull Valley: Radioactive waste and the American West*, directed by Ken Verdoia. Salt Lake City UT: KUED-TV. Transcript in four parts at http://www.kued.org/skullvalley/documentary/interviews/mcconkie.html (accessed August 1, 2001).

Melmer, David. 2000. Leon Bear re-elected Goshute chairman. *Indian Country Today* (Rapid City SD), December 6, D2.

Metcalf, R. Warren. 2002. *Termination's legacy: The discarded Indians of Utah*. Lincoln: University of Nebraska Press.

Miller, Phil. 1997. Tribe to try its hand at gambling? Seeking a revenue source, Utah Goshutes say "Bingo!" *Salt Lake (UT) Tribune*, October 11, A1.

Mims, Bob. 2000. Different views: For the Goshutes, a test of tradition. *Salt Lake (UT) Tribune* 17 July: D1.

_____. 2002. For Goshutes, the issue has always been simple: Survival. *Salt Lake (UT) Tribune*, September 1, A1.

Nakahara, Connie. 2001. Interview. *Skull Valley: Radioactive waste and the American West*, directed by Ken Verdoia. Salt Lake City UT: KUED-TV. Transcript in four parts at http://www.kued.org/skullvalley/documentary/interviews/nakahara.html (accessed August 1, 2001).

Nokkentved, N. S. 1991. Geological controversy haunts Nevada waste site. *High Country News* (Paonia CO), March 25, 13.

Peterson, John Alton. 1998. *Utah's Black Hawk War*. Salt Lake City: University of Utah Press.

Porterfield, K. Marie. 1997. Goshute activists fight nuclear waste dump. *Indian Country Today* (Rapid City SD), September 8–15, A1.

Project on Government Oversight. 2002. Nuclear power plant security: Voices from inside the fences. September 12. www.pogp.org/p/environment/eo-020901–nukepower.html#introduction (accessed August 18, 2003).

Quintana, Danny. 2001. Interview. *Skull Valley: Radioactive waste and the American West*, directed by Ken Verdoia. Salt Lake City UT: KUED-TV. Transcript in four parts at http://www.kued.org/skullvalley/documentary/interviews/quintana.html (accessed August 1, 2001).

Rasmussen, C. Michael. 1998. Note: Gaining access to billions of dollars and having a nuclear waste backyard. *Journal of Land, Resources, and Environmental Law* 18:335–67.

Roosevelt, Margot. 2006. Utah's toxic opportunity: Some Goshute Indians want to create a nu-
clear-fuel dump on their land. Controversial? Of course. *Time*, March 8. http://www.
time.com/time/insidebiz/printout/0,8816,1169904,00.html (accessed March 24,
2006).

Sachs, Noah. 1996. The Mescalero Apache Indians and monitored retrievable storage of
spent nuclear fuel: A study in environmental ethics. *Natural Resources Journal* 36 (4):
881–912.

Salt Lake (UT) Tribune. 2002. Editorial: Make Goshutes an offer. August 7, A2.

Satchell, Michael. 1996. Dances with nuclear waste. *U.S News and World Report*, January 8, 29–30.

Selcraig, Bruce. 1996. The filthy West: Toxics pour into our air, water, land. *High Country News*
(Paonia CO), September 16, 1, 6–10.

Semerad, Tony. 1992. Utah tribes want piece of gaming business: Goshutes study parimutual
track; Utes set sights on E. Utah casino. *Salt Lake (UT) Tribune*, June 30, B1.

Skibine, Alex Tallchief. 2001. High level nuclear waste on Indian reservations: Pushing the
tribal sovereignty envelope to the edge? *Journal of Land, Resources, and Environmental
Law* 21:287–316.

Skull Valley Band of Goshute Indians. n.d. http://www.skullvalleygoshutes.org (accessed February 20, 2004).

Skull Valley Goshute Tribe Executive Office. 1995. Native Americans have the right to make
their own land-use decisions. In *Environmental justice*, ed. Jonathan S. Petrikin, 65–
69. San Diego CA: Greenhaven Press.

Smith, Anne M. 1993. *Ute tales*. Salt Lake City: University of Utah Press.

Smith, Christopher. 1993. Tribes still considering storing radioactive fuel. *Salt Lake (UT) Tribune*, December 28, D3.

———. 2004. Will Reid's new job heat up N-waste fight? *Salt Lake (UT) Tribune*, November 17,
A1.

Sonner, Scott. 2004. Nuke expert says Yucca Mountain unsafe. *Washington (DC) Post*, February
19. http://www.washingtonpost.com/wp-dyn/articles/A54048–2004Feb19.html (accessed February 23, 2004).

Spangler, Donna Kemp. 2001. Leavitt gets the tools to fight N-waste storage by Goshutes. *Deseret News* (Salt Lake City UT), March 1, A1.

———. 2002. A tribe divided: Goshutes fight over N-waste and feel abandoned by state. *Deseret
News* (Salt Lake City UT), October 6, A1.

Spangler, Jerry. 1998. Series to explore fight over N-waste storage. *Deseret News* (Salt Lake City
UT), six-part series, January 24–29, A1.

———. 2002. In harm's way: Is Yucca Mountain a Utah fight? *Deseret News* (Salt Lake City UT),
April 28, A1.

Spangler, Jerry, and Donna Kemp Spangler. 2001. Toxic Utah: Goshutes divided over N-storage.
Deseret News (Salt Lake City UT), February 14, A1.

Steward, Julian H. 1938. *Basin-plateau aboriginal sociopolitical groups*. Smithsonian Institution,
Bureau of American Ethnology Bulletin 120. Washington DC: Government Printing
Office. Reprint, Salt Lake City: University of Utah Press, 1970.

Stoffle, Richard W., and Michael J. Evans. 1992. American Indians and nuclear waste storage:
The debate at Yucca Mountain, Nevada. In *Native Americans and public policy*, ed. Fre-

mont J. Lyden and Lyman H. Legters, 243–62. Pittsburgh: University of Pittsburgh Press.

Taliman, Valerie. 1992. Tribes denounce interest in nuclear wastes. *Lakota Times* (Rapid City SD), April 22, A6.

———. 2002a. Opponents call nuke deal environmental racism. *Indian Country Today* (Oneida NY), April 10, A2.

———. 2002b. Tribes, states will fight nuke waste dump. *Indian Country Today* (Oneida NY), March 6, A1.

Thomas, David Hurst, Lorann S. A. Pendleton, and Stephen C. Cappanari. 1986. Western Shoshone. In *Handbook of North American Indians*, vol. 11, *Great Basin*, ed. Warren L. D'Azevedo, 262–83. Washington DC: Smithsonian Institution.

Thomson, Michael F. 1998. Highlight: Placement of high level nuclear waste. *Utah Law Review* no. 3:729–36.

Truman, J. 1997. Utah could become high-level dump site! Downwinders Inc., http://www.downwinders.org/cstory5.html (accessed February 23, 2004).

Twain, Mark. 1962. *Roughing it.* 1872. Reprint, New York: New American Library, 1962.

U.S. Nuclear Regulatory Commission. 2002. Docket No. 72-22-ISFSI, CLI-02-20. http://www.nrc.gov/reading-rm/doc-colle.../commission/orders/2002/2002–20cli.html (accessed 15 November 2002).

Verdoia, Ken, director. 2001. *Skull Valley: Radioactive waste and the American West.* Salt Lake City UT: KUED-TV, aired July 11. Script in thirteen parts at http://www.kued.org/skull-valley/documentary/script.html (accessed August 1, 2001).

Waller, David. 1996. Friendly fire: When environmentalists dehumanize American Indians. *American Indian Culture and Research Journal* 20 (2): 107–26.

Walsh, Rebecca, and Judy Fahys. 2003. Waste issue: Disconnect stokes debates. *Salt Lake (UT) Tribune*, November 23, A1.

Ward, Chip. 1999. *Canaries on the rim: Living downwind in the West.* New York: Verso.

Warren, Louis S. 2002. The nature of conquest: Indians, Americans, and environmental history. In *A companion to American Indian history*, ed. Philip J. Deloria and Neal Salisbury, 287–306. Malden MA: Blackwell.

Woolf, Jim. 1992. Nuclear waste interests San Juan County. *Salt Lake (UT) Tribune*, April 11, B1.

———. 1993. Leavitt says San Juan out as nuclear-waste repository: "Not in state's best interest." *Salt Lake (UT) Tribune*, January 14, A1.

———. 1996. Utah's not aglow over Goshute deal to store N-waste. *Salt Lake (UT) Tribune*, December 25, A1.

———. 1997a. Nuclear $torage: Goshute defends band's right to riches; Goshutes want to profit from nuclear storage. *Salt Lake (UT) Tribune*, October 5, A1.

———. 1997b. Tribe digs into mystery of sheep that died near Dugway in 1968. *Salt Lake (UT) Tribune*, December 14, A1.

———. 1997c. Utah tribe won't dump plan for its N-facility: Goshutes press ahead with N-plans. *Salt Lake (UT) Tribune*, April 16, A1.

———. 1999. More than half of Goshutes sue tribe over waste plan. *Salt Lake (UT) Tribune*, March 13, D4.

Zent, Maureen. 1997. Last stand in Skull Valley. *Edging West* no. 12 (Summer): 28–29.

Afterword
Shepard Krech III

Before commenting on the insightful, constructive, and at times challenging essays in this volume, I wish to thank Michael Harkin and his colleagues at the University of Wyoming, in the departments of anthropology, history, and American Indian studies, and at the American Heritage Center, for having courageously invited me to be the George A. Rentschler Distinguished Visiting Lecturer at the American Heritage Center Symposium "Re-figuring the Ecological Indian." Courageous because at the time, as Harkin and David Lewis state in their introduction, there was a big flap and the promise of protest over the political implications of *The Ecological Indian*.

Aside from the keynote I delivered in that symposium, printed here essentially as spoken, I had little to do with this present work—the major exception being responding to an appeal for names of scholars working on topics related to the conference—and am therefore grateful to the editors for their request to write this afterword. I do not take this task on lightly, in part because, despite the nominal confinement of "criticism" to the section titled "Shepard Krech and His Critics," all contributors engage *The Ecological Indian*, positively or negatively, and are therefore critics in the full sense of the word. For this reason my remarks touch on all chapters in this volume.

Another motivation for engaging all essayists is to reciprocate their having taken on *The Ecological Indian*. I hope that none minds that my remarks are brief, for two reasons. First, many people of different persuasions have already weighed in on *The Ecological Indian*, and even though the collective criticism here is more sustained than in any other single work, much is anticipated and some is addressed in my keynote address printed in this volume (and readers wishing more detail might consult a recently published essay [Krech 2005]). Second, although it might be tempting (because the editors unexpectedly granted me the final word) to engage in a kind of "He said . . . I said" monologue, it would, I believe, be tedious rather than productive, for which reason I will largely forgo the temptation.

By the time this volume appears, some five years will have elapsed since the Laramie conference and eight years since the publication of *The Ecological Indian*. Thus it is of more than passing interest to provide a selective update (for more details, see Krech 2005) and address, among other matters, the extent to which the ideas explored in the book have been thrust into the shade by cultural difference, as the editors suggest. While museum displays continue to foreground human-environmental relations, as John Dorst shows in his unveiling of the Ecological Indian as icon, of even greater relevance on this particular point is an essay on the Nez Perces in which Hiroaki Kawamura (2004, 159) states that "the debate on the Indian-environment relationship is, for most Nez Perce, actually the issue of ethnic survival." If this is the case more generally in Indian country, then human-environment relationships, past and present, and their analysis remain as enduringly important today as they were a decade ago. I comment further on these issues in my keynote and below.

Of the ground covered in the various essays in this volume, the case that presented the greatest challenge for explanation when *The Ecological Indian* was researched more than a decade ago, the Pleistocene extinctions, remains intractable today. Robert Kelly and Mary Prasciunas argue (along the same lines as in *The Ecological Indian*) not only that one cannot rule out climate change as causal in the extinctions but that one cannot rule in, on the basis of current evidence, human predation as the exclusive or even major cause (providing ironic convergence with Deloria's [1995] complaint that the jury is still out on a human role even if his assumptions, evidence, and methodology are all different). Compared with the evidence a decade ago, the signatures of rapid and consequential climate change at the end of the Pleistocene are today slightly less opaque, while the evidence for human culpability is as hard as ever to come by. Nevertheless, these and other factors remain a topic of robust debate (e.g., Guthrie 2003; Grayson and Meltzer 2003, 2004; Fiedel and Haynes 2004; Shapiro et al. 2004). Yet neither Kelly, Prasciunas, nor I would be surprised if more persuasive evidence for a human role came to light.

As for other relatively inaccessible cases, although no one here takes up the disappearance of the Hohokam (but see Waters and Ravesloot 2001; Ensor, Ensor, and De Vries 2003; Waters and Ravesloot 2003) or similar examples discussed in The Ecological Indian, those who do reach into the deep past show the continuing difficulty of accurately deducing behavior from culture. A case in point is Steve Langdon's essay on the archaeological signatures of Tlingit behavior related to the well-known Salmon Boy story, which provides a charter for proper behavior toward salmon, the signatures of an ethic of "relational sustainability." The difficulty, as implied, is in the leap from ideology or artifactual remains to behavior engaged in expressly for conservationist ends. Largely elided are the implications for conservation of the idea, widespread among Northwest Coast people, that to guarantee the annual recurrence—the reincarnation—of salmon all one need do is burn their bones or return their carcasses to the water (Gottesfield 1994). As Michael Alvard (2003) suggests, a similar methodological problem plagues the equation of contemporary Huna Tlingit seagull egg procurement behavior to a conscious conservation strategy or its projection to the past (Hunn et al. 2003).

Langdon's is one of several essays on ideology and behavior in non-agricultural hunting or fishing societies; others are by Harvey Feit, Ernest Burch, and Dan Flores. Feit claims to reveal deep flaws in my argument yet does no such thing. To start with (succumbing partly to the temptation I had hoped to forgo), he quite conflates ecology and conservation, claiming that I argue that Indians lack ecological thought when, in fact, I am hard pressed to find firm or widespread evidence of what we think of today as conservation (behavior) until after a certain point in the history of commodification, the fur trade, and the decline of animal populations. Disquietingly, Feit omits statements that counter (or agree with) his, seemingly when it suits, and undermines putatively "damning" points with a narrow and selective reading of the book. Quite rightly, he makes no claims to being a historian—indeed, most of his quotations are of documents provided or researched or quoted by others—and although he cites important information relating to the era after the Hudson's Bay Company established monopoly conditions, he reports no significant new early historical evidence to countermand the analysis of the beaver pelt trade in The Ecological Indian. He hopes to dislodge the conclusions of the book but instead undermines his own cause through his assumptions and methodology (for which I refer readers to The Ecological Indian [Krech 1999, 199–209]) as well as by his misstatements.

Just one example of the latter is Feit's accusation that The Ecological Indian falls short in giving Indian people their due for their environmental knowledge. Rather, one can read in the one chapter that nearly exclusively occupies Feit's attention that there is no doubt that "Native people who spend their lives hunting, fishing, and trapping possess the ability to understand animal behavior and population dynamics." There is no dispute that "senior hunters have gained a detailed and sophisticated understanding (albeit cultural) of their surroundings and the animals they have pursued during their lives." Moreover, when "beaver hunters read population health and breeding success in minute signs like incisor marks on trees and uterine placental scars, their knowledge parallels if not exceeds that possessed by many wildlife biologists" (Krech 1999, 209). Thus Feit's complaint is clearly a canard. But it is also part of the unfortunate trend noted by Alvard (2003) to manufacture debate over traditional environmental knowledge when in fact there is none.

As unfortunate for his analysis is Feit's assumption that an ideology of respect for living things (justifiably conspicuous and widespread among American Indians) translates automatically into conservation. Others begin their inquiry with a far more open mind—or admit to the existence "in any society . . . [of] prudent and imprudent resource users" (Sherry and Myers 2002, 355) no matter the existence of an ideology of respect and avoiding waste. Compare Burch—another who writes on foraging people in this volume—for example, who not only is more open to alternatives to conservational behavior but concludes from historical and ethnographic research that the image of the primordial conservationist does not fit the northern Alaskan Iñupiat or central Arctic Caribou Inuit. In neither society does the image of the Ecological Indian mesh with behavior. Burch's opinion ranges from deep skepticism to outright denial (see also Burch 1994), and he concludes that Inuit and Native Americans generally "were no wiser than anyone else" (this volume).

Dan Flores also avoids the assumptions ensnaring Feit. Flores observes that Plains Indians were focused on jockeying and warring against each other in order to gain exclusive access to refuges for game, which unintentionally develop in the dangerous neutral zones between mutually antagonistic people, and that they were probably as myopic in their nineteenth-century hunt for buffalo as non-Indian people. And in a sophisticated contribution, Michael Harkin ends with the thought that there might well have been no "developed ethic of conservation" on the Northwest Coast, at least with regard to salmon, until after the arrival of people of European descent and the fundamental changes they wrought.

Harkin's is one of several essays that explore not just traditional environmental knowledge but culture—specifically, reanimation or reincarnation, the implications of which are at the heart of the argument in The Ecological Indian. For Harkin it is the reanimation specifically of salmon; Flores suggests that today's conservation biology is alien in the face of the belief that buffalo spent part of the annual cycle underground; and Burch explains that for the Iñupiat and Inuit, "animate resources existed in essentially unlimited supply." For all, the indigenous idea of reincarnation is antithetical to Western conservation. One strength in this volume (seldom encountered in the many reviews of The Ecological Indian) is the attempt to understand ethology and ecology as Native people themselves comprehended them.

Several contributors to this volume explore the contemporary environmental scene, to which I turn next. This had been the focus of the epilogue to The Ecological Indian, which attracted its share of venom (discussed in my essay), and today, as illustrated by the contributions of Sebastian Braun, Larry Nesper and James Schlender, and David Lewis, environmental and ecological issues in Indian country continue to defy generalization.

Braun speaks of "buffalo commons" projects under pressure to deliver profit, and Lewis of the attempt of the Goshutes of Skull Valley, Utah, over the opposition of the state and environmentalists, to store radioactive waste on their land (see also Johnson 2005). Nesper and Schlender usefully complicate my treatment of contemporary Wisconsin fishing rights and in the process provide a fine example of the in-depth analysis advocated (but not undertaken uniformly) in The Ecological Indian. Had their essay been available when I wrote the book, the one qualified sentence in the epilogue on Wisconsin fishing would have changed (and expanded) considerably.

Lewis's analysis deserves additional comment. The Goshutes are just one of several widely separated Native American people in recent years to advocate development projects–others involve oil drilling, natural gas pipelines, or liquefied natural gas terminals—with potential to affect more than the local environment (Krech 2005). None is uncontested on the local level, a sign of the continuing strength of the privileging of sacredness, place, "tradition," and respect for other living forms of life.

It is difficult to predict what will happen in these and other cases. In some instances there are only hard choices. Native people without access to other means of economic development, casinos especially, will no doubt continue to regard mega-projects as the means to needed or desired income. Yet the contemporary environmental movement in Indian country is important (Clark 2002; Krech 2005; Nesper and Schlender, this volume), and environmentalists can be seen in action practically on a monthly basis—this month (as I write) in the hope of the Onondagas that by bringing a land claim against New York State they will be able to force the cleanup of sacred Lake Onondaga, a severely polluted federal Superfund site (Semple 2005).

The final issue I must take up is the contemporary charge that environmental histories of American Indians are politically suspect and unremittingly biased. Clearly, The Ecological Indian was caught up in identity politics and charges of political incorrectness (Krech, this volume). A hurdle today for would-be environmental or anthropological historians is that their work, if perceived negatively, will be caught up in the same charges.

Darren Ranco's challenge in this volume can be read in this context. With a rhetorical strategy suitable to a student of environmental law, Ranco slashes with innuendo and burns with association, indicting The Ecological Indian for eliding its political implications and for hostility to Indians. He clearly wishes that the book had been different: focused on the present and on colonialism and neocolonialism (but others have done that, so why more of the same?); a work, in his terms, of "engagement, not judgment." He claims to be unable to find in the book any interest in the meanings that constitute people's lives, which can only result from limiting his case study largely to the introduction and epilogue and reading them selectively. The epilogue, which represents fully the range of debate and opinion (and, yes, contra Ranco, the constitution of culture in Indian country), in particular attracts his ire, as it did that of several other American Indians. Is this because, unlike others that survey the contemporary scene (see the discussion in Krech 2005, 82–84), the book does not judge negatively Indian people who opt for economic or development strategies with actual or potentially adverse environmental consequences? Ranco also reproaches the work for being wedded to objectivity, dispassionate analysis, and analytical interest in behavior and agency, not merely belief. I plead guilty on all counts, with the caveat that, philosophically, objectivity in inquiry like ours seems to me to be ultimately elusive.

However, I thank Ranco for bringing to light an infelicity that probably crept in during editing. I never meant to imply (but somehow did) that the image of the Ecological Indian stands outside of or distorts contemporary culture (Krech 1999, 27), only that it is a distortion of certain traditional cultural beliefs (explored increasingly in the heart of the book, which Ranco ignores). Mea culpa. I would have thought this obvious and hardly worth its new role as straw man.

As in the 1990s (see my essay in this volume), few in the larger arena throw down Ranco's gauntlet with greater force than Vine Deloria Jr., who urges Indian scholars to "[s]tart writing rebuttals" to assessments in environmental history (no doubt including The Ecological Indian) and to counteract those (presumably activists) who say, "We have to restrict Indian hunting and fishing because they killed off all the animals. They can't be trusted." Deloria concludes: "We need political writers to respond" (qtd. in Denetdale 2004, 140).

The implication is that to hypothesize or demonstrate the poor fit between the idea of the Ecological Indian and American Indian behavior at any time in history is both wrong and unjust, and that what is needed are political writers armed, presumably, with correct and just information, with Truth. If more confirmation is required, here again is sign that the issues explored in The Ecological Indian are very much alive today and will remain so for some time to come, for the simple reason that they are can be linked, and by many are linked, to sovereignty and identity. Yet perhaps someone needs to ask whether or not such an overtly political agenda as Deloria's is in the best long-term interest of those Indian people who demonstrate today, or try to, through their behavior that they deserve a role in the management of resources, including fish and game; or of those who advocate development projects with economic promise yet potentially adverse environmental consequences. However that question is answered, those who wade into the waters of North American environmental history should be aware of the reception that awaits them in some parts of Indian country. To judge from his remarks in this volume, Dan Flores is clearly concerned with the same issue. So are others.

In its introduction, I wrote that "The Ecological Indian does not pretend to be exhaustive" or the "last word" on a complex subject. Instead, the hope was expressed that it would "rekindle debate on the fit between one of the most durable images of the American Indian and American Indian behavior" as well as "spawn detailed analyses of the myriad relationships between indigenous people and their environments in North America" (1999, 28). This is happening, to judge from the increasing number of works addressing human-environmental relationships, past and present, that take The Ecological Indian as a work to cite or to agree with or debate on matters as disparate as ecological restoration, the greening of religion, human-environment relations, political ecology, demography, the imagery of indigenous people in the Western imagination, sustainability, traditional environmental knowledge, and political ecology (e.g., Alvard and Kuznar 2001; Callicott 2002; Dietz, Ostrom, and Stern 2003; Ehrlich 2002; Grayson 2001; Grewe-Volpp 2002; Hunn et al. 2003; Kawamura 2004; Kay and Simmons 2002; Murray 2003; Nelson and Schollmeyer 2003; Scarborough 2003; Smith and Wishnie 2000; Taylor 2004; Warrick 2003; Whiteman 2004; Wilson 2002). It is inevitable (and welcome) that when one attempts to paint with a broad brush, as I did in The Ecological Indian, the critique, positive and negative, will refine our understanding of, in this case, American Indians, ecology, and conservation. This present collection, which gratifyingly provides a full range of critique in which can be found much constructively critical support for the core of the thesis of The Ecological Indian, advances this work and underscores the importance of, and further need for, richly contextualized and, where possible, historically deep case studies.

References

Alvard, Michael S. 2003. Comment. Current Anthropology 44 (Supplement): S93–S94.

Alvard, Michael S., and Lawrence Kuznar. 2001. Deferred harvests: The transition from hunting to animal husbandry. American Anthropologist 103 (2): 295–311.

Burch, Ernest S., Jr. 1994. Rationality and resource use among hunters. In Circumpolar religion and ecology: An anthropology of the North, ed. Takashi Irimoto and Takako Yamada, 163–85. Tokyo: University of Tokyo Press.

Calicott, J. Baird. 2002. Choosing appropriate temporal and spatial scales for ecological restoration. Journal of Bioscience 27 (4), Supplement 2: 409–20.

Clark, Brett. 2002. The indigenous environmental movement in the United States. Organization and Environment 15 (4): 410–22.

Deloria, Vine, Jr. 1995. Red earth, white lies: Native Americans and the myth of scientific fact. New York: Scribner.

Denetdale, Jennifer. 2003. Planting seeds of ideas and raising doubts about what we believe: An interview with Vine Deloria, Jr. Journal of Social Archaeology 4 (2): 131–46.

Dietz, Thomas, Elinor Ostrom, and Paul C. Stern. 2003. The struggle to govern the commons. Science 302:1907–12.

Ehrlich, Paul R. 2002. Human natures, nature conservation, and environmental ethics. BioScience 52 (1): 31–43.

Ensor, Bradley E., Marisa O. Ensor, and Gregory W. De Vries. 2003. Hohokam political ecology and vulnerability: Comments on Waters and Ravesloot. American Antiquity 68:169–81.

Fiedel, Stuart, and Gary Haynes. 2004. A premature burial: Comments on Grayson and Meltzer's "Requiem for overkill." Journal of Archaeological Science 31:121–31.

Gottesfield, Leslie M. Johnson. 1994. Conservation, territory, and traditional beliefs: An analysis of Gitksan and Wet'suwet'en subsistence, northwest British Columbia, Canada. *Human Ecology* 22:443–65.

Grayson, Donald K. 2001. The archaeological record of human impacts on animal populations. *Journal of World Prehistory* 15 (1): 1–68.

Grayson, Donald K., and David J. Meltzer. 2003. A requiem for North American overkill. *Journal of Archaeological Science* 30:585–93.

———. 2004. North American overkill continued? *Journal of Archaeological Science* 31:133–36.

Grewe-Volpp, Christa. 2002. The ecological Indian vs. the spiritually corrupt white man: The function of ethnocentric notions in Linda Hogan's *Solar Storms*. *Amerikastudien/American Studies: A Quarterly* 47 (2): 269–83.

Guthrie, R. Dale. 2003. Rapid body size decline in Alaskan Pleistocene horses before extinction. *Nature* 426:169–72.

Hunn, Eugene S., Daryll R. Johnson, Priscilla N. Russell, and Thomas Thornton. 2003. Huna Tlingit traditional knowledge, conservation, and the management of a "wilderness" park. *Current Anthropology* 44 (Supplement): S79–S103.

Johnson, Kirk. 2005. A tribe, nimble and determined, moves ahead with nuclear storage plan. *New York Times*, February 28, A15.

Kawamura, Hiroaki. 2004. Symbolic and political ecology among contemporary Nez Perce Indians in Idaho, USA: Functions and meanings of hunting, fishing, and gathering practices. *Agriculture and Human Values* 21:157–69.

Kay, Charles E., and Randy T. Simmons, eds. 2002. *Wilderness and political ecology: Aboriginal influences and the original state of nature*. Salt Lake City: University of Utah Press.

Krech, Shepard, III. 1999. *The ecological Indian: Myth and history*. New York: Norton.

———. 2005. Reflections on conservation, sustainability, and environmentalism in indigenous North America. *American Anthropologist* 107:78–86.

Murray, Martyn. 2003. Overkill and sustainable use. *Science* 299:1851–53.

Nelson, Margaret C., and Karen Gust Schollmeyer. 2003. Game resources, social interaction, and the ecological footprint in southwest New Mexico. *Journal of Archaeological Method and Theory* 10 (2): 69–110.

Scarborough, Vernon. 2003. How to interpret an ancient landscape. *Proceedings of the National Academy of Sciences* 100 (8): 4366–68.

Semple, Kirk. 2005, Tribe seeks Syracuse, but a clean lake may do. *New York Times*, March 12, B3.

Shapiro, Beth, Alexei J. Drummond, Andrew Rambaut, Michael C. Wilson, Paul E. Matheus, Andrei V. Sher, Oliver G. Pybus, M. Thomas P. Gilbert, Ian Barnes, Jonas Binladen, Eske Willerslev, Anders J. Hansen, Gennady F. Baryshnikov, James A. Burns, Sergei Davydov, Jonathan C. Driver, Duane G. Froese, C. Richard Harington, Grant Keddie, Pavel Kosintsev, Michael L. Kunz, Larry D. Martin, Robert O. Stephenson, John Storer, Richard Tedford, Sergei Zimov, and Alan Cooper. 2004. Rise and fall of the Beringian steppe bison. *Science* 306:1561–65.

Sherry, Erin, and Heather Myers. 2002. Traditional environmental knowledge in practice. *Society and Natural Resources* 15:345–58.

Smith, Eric Alden, and Mark Wishnie. 2000. Conservation and subsistence in small-scale societies. *Annual Review of Anthropology* 29:493–524.

Taylor, Bron. 2004. A green future for religion? *Futures* 36:991–1008.

Warrick, Gary. 2003. European infectious disease and depopulation of the Wendat-Tionontate (Huron-Petun). *World Archaeology* 35:258–75.

Waters, Michael R., and John C. Ravesloot. 2001. Landscape change and the cultural evolution of the Hohokam among the Middle Gila River and other river valleys in south-central Arizona. *American Antiquity* 66:285–99.

———. 2003. Disaster or catastrophe: Human adaptation to high- and low-frequency landscape processes—A reply to Ensor, Ensor, and DeVries. *American Antiquity* 68:400–405.

Whiteman, Gail. 2004. Why are we talking inside? Reflecting on traditional ecological knowledge (TEK) and management research. *Journal of Management Inquiry* 13 (3): 261–77.

Wilson, Patrick Impero. 2002. Native peoples and the management of natural resources in the Pacific Northwest: A comparative assessment. *American Review of Canadian Studies* Autumn:397–414.

Contributors

Judith Antell is an enrolled member of the Minnesota Chippewa Tribe, White Earth Reservation. She is Director of the American Indian Studies Program at the University of Wyoming. Her teaching and research interests include American Indian women and contemporary Indian affairs. She received a PhD in Ethnic Studies from the University of California, Berkeley.

Sebastian F. Braun received a master's degree in Ethnology from the University of Basel, Switzerland, and a PhD in Cultural Anthropology from Indiana University. His dissertation focused on contemporary tribal bison ranching on the Great Plains. He is currently Assistant Professor with the Department of Indian Studies at the University of North Dakota.

Ernest S. Burch Jr. is a historical ethnographer specializing in the study of northern peoples. He received his BA in Sociology from Princeton University and his MA and PhD in Anthropology from the University of Chicago. Currently he is a research associate of the Arctic Studies Center, Smithsonian Institution.

John Dorst is a Professor of American Studies at the University of Wyoming. He received his MA in Folklore/Folklife from the University of California, Berkeley, and his PhD in Folklore/Folklife from the University of Pennsylvania. He is the author of *The Written Suburb* (1989) and *Looking West* (1999), both published by the University of Pennsylvania Press.

Harvey A. Feit is a Professor of Anthropology at McMaster University. His main research is on indigenous rights struggles and conservation by James Bay Crees. He coedited, with Mario Blaser and Glen McRae, *In the Way of Development: Indigenous Peoples, Life Projects and Globalization* (2004).

Dan Flores holds the A. B. Hammond Chair in Western History at the University of Montana, where he specializes in the environmental and cultural history of the West. He is the author of seven books, most recently *Horizontal Yellow: Nature and History in the Near Southwest* (1999), *The Natural West: Environmental History in the Great Plains and Rocky Mountains* (2001), and *Southern Counterpart to Lewis and Clark: The Freeman and Custis Accounts of the Red River Expedition of 1806* (2002).

Michael E. Harkin is a Professor of Anthropology at the University of Wyoming. He is the author of *The Heiltsuks: Dialogues of History and Culture on the Northwest Coast* (1997), and he edited *Reassessing Revitalization Movements: Perspectives from North America and The Pacific Islands* (2004) and *Coming to Shore: New Perspectives on Northwest Coast Ethnology* (with Marie Mauzé and Sergei Kan) (2004), all published by University of Nebraska Press.

Brian Hosmer is Director of the Newberry Library's D'Arcy McNickle Center for American Indian History and the Committee for Institutional Cooperation American Indian Studies Consortium. He is also an Associate Professor of History at the University of Illinois at Chicago. He previously taught at the University of Wyoming. He is the author of *American Indians in the Marketplace: Persistence and Innovation among the Menominees and Metlakatlans, 1870-1920* (1999) and coeditor (with Colleen O'Neill) of *Native Pathways: American Indian Culture and Economic Development in the Twentieth Century* (2004).

Robert L. Kelly is Head of the University of Wyoming's Anthropology Department. Specializing in hunter-gatherer archaeology, he has conducted archaeological research in the western U.S. and ethnographic research in Madagascar. He authored *The Foraging Spectrum: Diversity in Hunting and Gathering Societies* (1995), and, with David Hurst Thomas, *Archaeology* (4th ed., 2006) and *Archaeology: Down to Earth* (3rd ed., 2007).

Shepard Krech III is a Professor of Anthropology and Environmental Studies and Director of the Haffenreffer Museum of Anthropology at Brown University. A former fellow of the National Humanities Center and Woodrow Wilson International Center, his many publications include *The Ecological*

Indian: Myth and History (1999) and *Encyclopedia of World Environmental History*, 3 vols. (edited with J. R. McNeill and Carolyn Merchant; 2004).

Stephen J. Langdon is a Professor of Anthropology and Chair of the Department of Anthropology and Geography at the University of Alaska–Anchorage. He earned his doctorate in Anthropology from Stanford University (1977) and has conducted numerous research projects in southeast Alaska on Tlingit and Haida societies both pre- and postcontact. He is the author of *The Native People of Alaska* (4th ed., 2002) and the editor of *Contemporary Alaska Native Economies* (1986).

David Rich Lewis is a Professor of History at Utah State University and editor of the *Western Historical Quarterly*. He is the author of *Neither Wolf Nor Dog: American Indians, Environment, and Agrarian Change* (1994) and coeditor with Clyde A. Milner II and Anne M. Butler of *Major Problems in the History of the American West* (1997).

Larry Nesper is an Assistant Professor of Anthropology and American Indian Studies at the University of Wisconsin–Madison and the author of *The Walleye War: The Struggle for Ojibwe Spearfishing and Treaty Rights* (2002).

Mary M. Prasciunas is a doctoral candidate in Anthropology at the University of Wyoming. She specializes in Paleoindian archaeology of the western United States and lithic analysis. Her dissertation research focuses on testing the idea that Clovis was the initial colonizing population of North America.

Darren J. Ranco is an Assistant Professor of Native American Studies and Environmental Studies at Dartmouth College and a member of the Penobscot Indian Nation. His research focuses on the ways in which Indian nations build culturally relevant environmental management programs to protect tribal populations from environmental risk.

James H. Schlender held the position of Executive Administrator of the Great Lakes Indian Fish and Wildlife Commission from 1986 to August 2005, when he unexpectedly passed on. He received his undergraduate degree from the

University of Wisconsin–Milwaukee and his law degree from the University of Wisconsin Law School. He was a member of the State Bar of Wisconsin and acted as tribal attorney from 1978 until 1986 for his band, the Lac Courte Oreilles Ojibwe. Schlender was member of the Lynx clan, and his Anishinaabe name was Sauguhjiwe (Man Cresting the Hill). He was also a member of the Three Fires Midewiwin Lodge.

Index